Kipp's Bay

Turtle

R I V

E

A S T

Newtown Creek

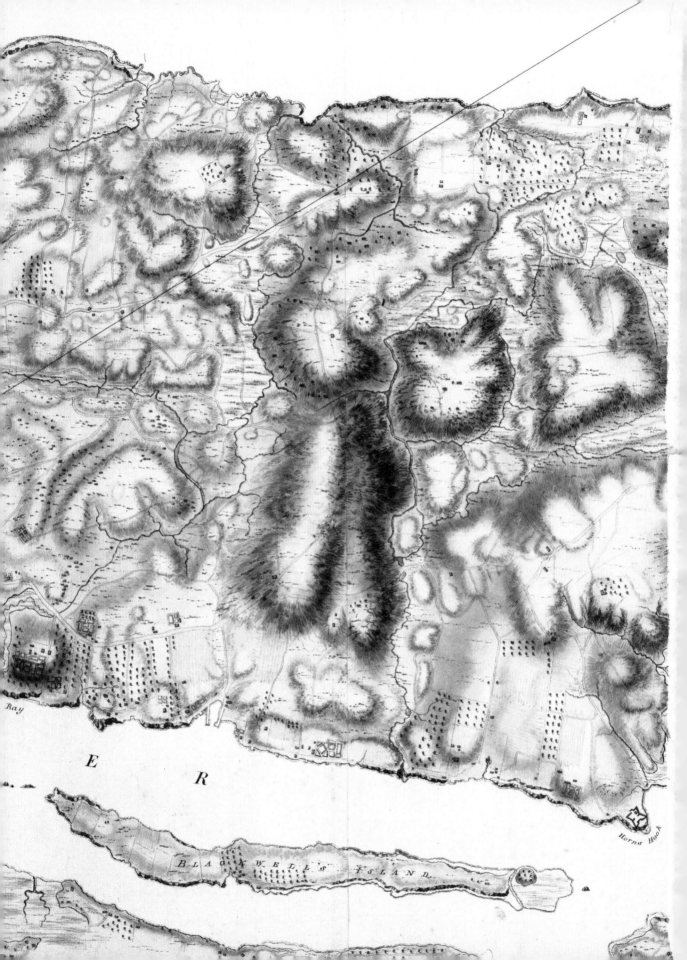

Bay

E

R

Horns Hoo.k

BLACKWELL'S ISLAND.

Mannahatta

Mannahatta: A Natural History of New York City

Eric W. Sanderson
Wildlife Conservation Society

Illustrations by Markley Boyer

Abrams, New York

Editor: Deborah Aaronson
Designer: Abbott Miller and Christine Moog / Pentagram Design Inc.
Production Manager: Anet Sirna-Bruder

Library of Congress Cataloging-in-Publication Data

Sanderson, Eric W.
Mannahatta : a natural history of New York City / by Eric W. Sanderson ;
illustrations by Markley Boyer.
    p. cm.
 ISBN 978-0-8109-9633-5 (Harry N. Abrams, Inc.)
 1. Natural history—New York (State)—New York. I. Title.

QH105.N7S26 2009
508.747'1—dc22
                        2008042042

Printed and bound in China
10 9 8 7 6 5 4 3 2 1

Abrams books are available at special discounts when purchased in quantity
for premiums and promotions as well as fundraising or educational use.
Special editions can also be created to specification. For details, contact
specialmarkets@hnabooks.com or the address below.

harry n. abrams, inc.
a subsidiary of La Martinière Groupe

115 West 18th Street
New York, NY 10011
www.hnabooks.com

Page 2: Manhattan, circa 1609 and 2009.

This book was supported by Furthermore: a program of the J. M. Kaplan Fund.

To Mom and Dad

I was asking for something specific and perfect for my city,
Whereupon lo! upsprang the aboriginal name.
Now I see what there is in a name, a word, liquid, sane, unruly,
      musical, self-sufficient,
I see that the word of my city is that word from old . . .

—Walt Whitman, "Mannahatta,"
  Leaves of Grass 1891–92

Chapter One

The Mannahatta Project

As the moon rose higher the inessential houses began to melt away until gradually I became aware of the old island here that flowered once for Dutch sailors' eyes—a fresh, green breast of the new world. Its vanished trees . . . had once pandered in whispers to the last and greatest of all human dreams; for a transitory enchanted moment man must have held his breath in the presence of this continent, compelled into an aesthetic contemplation he neither understood nor desired, face to face for the last time in history with something commensurate to his capacity for wonder.

— F. Scott Fitzgerald, *The Great Gatsby* 1925

Mannahatta, 1609.

On a hot, fair day, the twelfth of September, 1609, Henry Hudson and a small crew of Dutch and English sailors rode the flood tide up a great estuarine river, past a long, wooded island at latitude 40°48' north, on the edge of the North American continent. Locally the island was called Mannahatta, or "Island of Many Hills." One day the island would become as densely filled with people and avenues as it once was with trees and streams, but not that afternoon. That afternoon the island still hummed with green wonders. New York City, through an accident, was about to be born.

Hudson, an English captain in Dutch employ, wasn't looking to found a city; he was seeking a route to China. Instead of Oriental riches, what he found was Mannahatta's natural wealth—the old-growth forests, stately wetlands, glittering streams, teeming waters, rolling hills, abundant wildlife, and mysterious people, as foreign to him as he was to them. The landscape that Hudson discovered for Europe that day was prodigious in its abundance, resplendent in its diversity, a place richer than many people today imagine could exist anywhere. If Mannahatta existed today as it did then, it would be a national park—it would be the crowning glory of American national parks.

Mannahatta had more ecological communities per acre than Yellowstone, more native plant species per acre than Yosemite, and more birds than the Great Smoky Mountains National Park. Mannahatta housed wolves, black bears, mountain lions, beavers, mink, and river otters; whales, porpoises, seals, and the occasional sea turtle visited its harbor. Millions of birds of more than a hundred and fifty different species flew over the island annually on transcontinental migratory pathways; millions of fish—shad, herring, trout, sturgeon, and eel—swam past the island up the Hudson River and in its streams during annual rites of spring. Sphagnum moss from the North and magnolia from the South met in New York City, in forests with over seventy kinds of trees, and wetlands with over two hundred kinds of plants. Thirty varieties of orchids once grew on Mannahatta. Oysters, clams, and mussels in the billions filtered the local water; the river and the sea exchanged their tonics in tidal runs and freshets fueled by a generous climate; and the entire scheme was powered by the moon and the sun, in ecosystems that reused and retained water, soil, and energy, in cycles established over millions of years.

Living in this land were the Lenape—the "Ancient Ones"—of northeast Algonquin culture, a people for whom the local landscape had provided all that they and their ancestors required for more than four hundred generations before Hudson arrived. On Mannahatta these people lived a mobile and

opposite Manhattan, 2008

top Manhattan is the archetype of the twenty-first-century city, providing food, water, shelter, and meaning to millions of people, on a planet of billions. The human population is increasingly urbanized; by 2050, 70 percent of the world's population may live in cities. *bottom* Mannahatta is an archetype of nature—nature in all its diversity, abundance, and robust interconnections. In 1609 it also supported a human population three hundred to twelve hundred strong.

productive life, moving to hunt and fish and plant depending on the season; they had settlements in today's Chinatown, Upper East Side, and Inwood, and fishing camps along the cliffs of Washington Heights and the bays of the East River. They shaped the landscape with fire; grew mixed fields of corn, beans, and squash; gathered abundant wild foods from the productive waters and abundant woods; and conceived their relationship to the environment and each other in ways that emphasized respect, community, and balance. They lived entirely within their local means, gathering everything they needed from the immediate environment, participants in and benefactors of the rhythms of the nature that obviously connected them to their island home.

Many things have changed over the last four hundred years. Extraordinary cultural diversity has replaced extraordinary biodiversity on the island; today people from nearly every nation on earth can be found living in New York City. Abundance is now measured in economic currencies, not ecological ones, and our economic wealth is enormous —New York is one of the richest societies the world has ever known, and is growing richer each year. Millions of people fly in from all over the world to a narrow, twelve-block-wide island to gather in buildings a thousand feet high to see what's new and what's next. Thousands of tons of materials follow them into the city—foodstuffs from six continents and four oceans; concrete and steel and clothing from the other side of the globe; power from coal, oil, and atomic fission—all the resources necessary for the modern megacity, delivered as the natural systems once delivered, through elaborate networks, though now the networks are composed of people, products, money, and markets, as opposed to forests, streams, sunshine, and grass.

It is a conceit of New York City—the concrete city, the steel metropolis, Batman's Gotham—to think it is a place outside of nature, a place where humanity has completely triumphed over the forces of the natural world, where a person can do and be anything without limit or consequence. Yet this conceit is not unique to the city; it is shared by a globalized twenty-first-century human culture, which posits that through technology and economic development we can escape the shackles that bind us to our earthly selves, including our dependence on the earth's bounty and the confines of our native place. As such the story of Mannahatta's transformation to Manhattan isn't localized to one island; it is a coming-of-age story that literally embraces the entire world and is relevant to all of the 6.7 billion human beings who share it.

To many outsiders, Manhattan Island is a monument to self-grandeur and a potent symbol of the inevitable—but yet to be realized—collapse of our

top The black bear was abundant in the forests and meadows of Mannahatta in 1609. One was shot in the vicinity of Maiden Lane, in Lower Manhattan, in 1630. This painting by John James Audubon dates from the nineteenth century, but could easily have been from Mannahatta two hundred years before. *bottom* To ecologists, a landscape is the mosaic of different types of ecosystems that makes a particular place unique. The combination of different ecosystem types makes habitat for species, like these white-footed mice, or, in an urban context, for people.

The New World that Henry Hudson explored had long been inhabited by Native Americans; the Lenape and their ancestors had inhabited Mannahatta and its surrounding areas for perhaps ten thousand years prior to Hudson's arrival. This portrait by Gustavus Hesselius, from the 1730s, depicts the Lenape sachem Tischohan, from Pennsylvania. No images of the Lenape from Mannahatta exist today.

hubris. But inside of New York another way of thinking is emerging, a new set of ideas and beliefs that do not depend on disaster to correct our course and instead imagines a future where humanity embraces, rather than disdains, our connection to the natural world. Many New Yorkers celebrate the nature of their city and seek to understand the city's place in nature. They see their city as an ecosystem and recognize that, like any good ecosystem, the city has cycles, flows, interconnections, and mechanisms for self-correction. New Yorkers love their place with a ferocity that the Lenape would have recognized; active observers of and participants in their neighborhoods, where every change is a source of discussion and debate. We know, when we stop to think of it, that no place can exist outside of nature. As was true for the original Manahate people, our food needs to come from somewhere; our water, our material life, our sense of meaning are not disconnected from the world, but exactly and specifically part of it.

Moreover, we are coming to realize that cities are ecological places to live. The average New Yorker emits 7.1 tons of CO_2 into the atmosphere each year; the average American, 24.5 tons. A third of the public transit trips made in America each year are made in New York. New York is a leader in urban planning and green buildings. The city has seen some of its wildlife return, from the expanding fish runs to the restocked oyster beds to bird populations that give Central Park some of the best, most concentrated bird-watching in the country. New Yorkers recycle and compost; we use energy-efficient bulbs; we meter our water usage; we have a system of bike lanes and kayaking spots. I can see wild turkeys not five minutes from my front door, in a park with a wildlife sanctuary. This isn't to say New York has done everything necessary to be sustainable—we are still cursed with the automobile and an enormous appetite for resources—but we're moving in the right direction.

All of this was news to me when I moved to New York ten years ago, delivered from a comfortable life in suburban northern California, drawn to the city, like many newcomers, by a job, a new way to make a living. I boxed up my bicycle; bought a soot-colored trench coat and a black hat; packed my volumes of Ralph Waldo Emerson, Henry David Thoreau, and John Muir; said good-bye to the local food co-op; and clambered into my beat-up blue '77 Volvo station wagon to drive east. My friends thought I was crazy. Like Hudson, I came to New York looking for something, but once here found something else—something I wasn't expecting at all.

Coming to New York

In 1998, as a young, newly minted PhD scientist from the University of California, Davis, I arrived to take up employment with the Wildlife Conservation Society, based out of Bronx Zoo, in New York City. Most non-conservationists don't know what the Wildlife Conservation Society is, at least by that name, but it is a venerable institution, founded in 1895 as the New York Zoological Society, and one of the first wildlife conservation organizations in the world. I soon learned that telling people, even people I met in New York, that I worked for the Wildlife Conservation Society (WCS) was not a successful strategy. Usually I received a bemused but blank look—did I save baby seals from the slaughter? Did I harass whalers from a rubber raft? Was I a member of yet another conservation group whose name starts with a *W*? (Even my mom sometimes accidentally introduces me as working for the "*World* Conservation Society." That group, sadly, doesn't exist.)

I thought a better gambit was to tell new acquaintances that I worked at the Bronx Zoo, which everyone had heard of—but that introduction led to new misunderstandings. No, I didn't keep the elephants or get to play with the gorillas. I rarely got to go behind the exhibits. Rather, I mainly worked on the computer and helped incredibly dedicated and intelligent people do their utmost to save wild animals in large, natural landscapes in Africa, Asia, and the Americas—not through stunts, but through the hard work of science, consensus, and long-term engagement. It sounds like bragging, but it's true: you can't believe these people or the places they work. In the heart of a cultural institution that New Yorkers loved for sharing time with their families, there was an extended family of people trying to save the world. The WCS, though nearly unknown in New York, was known to people all over the world as one of the most practical and efficient scientific conservation organizations. I had taken a job where on a rotating basis I worked to help save tigers, the oceans, and the Eastern Steppe of Mongolia, among other things. Not bad.

The price was abandoning my easygoing existence in the Sacramento Valley for the big city, which even today I would not describe as easygoing, just a bit on the brash side. I struggled to find my place in New York and, as a coping mechanism, started visiting the city's wilder places and reading about its history. I found winter bewildering (is that really ice floating in the harbor?), spring late coming (how long can a forest exist as just sticks and no leaves?), and summer discomfiting (I thought this was the *temperate* zone), but I liked

The wolf persisted on Manhattan Island until the 1720s, when a determined hunt finally cleared the carnivorous mammals from the forests of Inwood. Nearly four hundred years later, exploiting the gap created by the loss of wolves, coyotes entered Manhattan for the first time in 2005. Dogs, domesticated from wolves, may have lived on Manhattan continuously for the last ten thousand years.

the fall, with clear, blue skies, warm weather, and sparkling waters. I learned New York City was built on an archipelago in an estuary. New Amsterdam, as it was first known, was originally settled by the Dutch—a remarkably diverse and tolerant seventeenth-century people, if a bit moneygrubbing—and, later, New York played a major role in the American Revolution. Battles were fought in 1776 along the same ground as the bike path where I rode to work; Revolutionary snipers once hid in a hundred-plus-foot white pine that stood beside the Bronx River. Teddy Roosevelt, who as president had protected so many of the landscapes out West that I loved, had himself fallen in love with nature sailing and hiking on Long Island (and helped found the WCS as a result). Strangely, though, for all the city's history and nature, most New Yorkers didn't seem to know about it, either not remembering their grade-school lessons or, like me, arriving from new places having never learned them.

It was in the midst of this period of adjustment that I saw a map that would change my life, though I didn't know it at the time. You will learn more about that map in the next chapter, and experience the consequences of that encounter in the chapters that follow, so perhaps it suffices here to say that, like any good hobby, I found this one a successful diversion from reality, but a diversion that ultimately enriched my reality as well. For my experience with the British Headquarters Map would eventually lead to a method of reconstructing what I found missing from the historical record of the city—namely, the answer to the question, what was Manhattan like before the skyscrapers and asphalt, that September afternoon when Hudson arrived?

Reading a New Landscape

Historians work from the written record, but there are only a few tantalizing accounts of what Hudson and his crew saw, which means that history as a discipline can only get us so far. Hudson's first mate, Robert Juet, kept a diary during the 1609 voyage. Here is what Juet wrote about the day they reached Mannahatta:

> *The twelfth [of September:]* Very faire and hot. In the after-noone at two of the clocke wee weighed, the winde being variable, betweene the North and the North-west. So we turned into the River two leagues and Anchored. This morning at our first rode in the River, there came eight and twentie Canoes full of men, women and children to betray us: but we saw their intent, and suffered none of them to come aboord us. At twelve of

preceding pages

left The Hudson River estuary shaped the sandy shore of Mannahatta. Smoke from fires indicate Lenape camps. *right* Today Battery Park City and the West Side Highway occupy the same territory.

the clocke they departed. They brought with them Oysters and Beanes, whereof wee bought some. They have great Tabacco pipes of yellow Copper, and Pots of Earth to dresse their meate in. It [the Hudson River] floweth South-east by South within.

Not much for the enterprising historian to work from, though many have tried. Even the geography is unclear. I read this day as starting near Staten Island and ending up somewhere off the West Fifties, but others have suggested that it starts near Greenwich Village and ends just north of the George Washington Bridge. Hudson's ship's log is lost, but thanks to a Dutch chronicler, Johann de Laet, we have a quote from it, which reads: "It [Manhattan] is as pleasant a land as one can tread upon, very abundant in all kinds of timber suitable for ship-building, and for making large casks. The people have copper tobacco pipes, from which I inferred that copper must exist there; and iron likewise according to the testimony of the natives, who, however, do not understand preparing it for use." De Laet also reported that Hudson had caught in the river "all kinds of fresh-water fish with seines, and young salmon and sturgeon." (He was probably right about the sturgeon and wrong about the salmon; those were more likely weakfish or sea-run trout.)

On the trip back down the river, after Hudson and his crew abandoned the search for China and found instead what would come to be lower Albany, Juet concluded his description with this passage, dating from early October:

> [W]e saw a very good piece of ground: and hard by it there was a Cliffe, that looked of the colour of white greene, as though it was Copper, or Silver myne; and I thinke it to be one of them, but the Trees that grow on it. For they be all burned, and the other places are greene as grasse, it is on that side of the River that is called *Manna-hata*. There we saw no people to trouble us: and rode quietly all night; but had much wind and raine.

Thus ends the complete documentary evidence from 1609.

One wants to know so much more! What of the Native Americans with their copper pipes and clay pots, who were Manhattan's first inhabitants? The "men, women and children to betray us"—what was their story? What of the plants and animals of the burned cliffs and pleasant land, as "greene as grasse"?

preceding pages

left As Hudson made his way upriver on the western side of Mannahatta, he would have seen salt marshes, red-maple swamps, and deep oak-hickory and tulip-tree forests. *right* The same view today emphasizes skyscrapers, buildings, and streets in Manhattan's Garment and Theater districts.

If New Netherland was really as incredible as Hudson suggests and as her Dutch promoters would later enthusiastically advertise, what made it so wonderful?

It turned out that to tell these aspects of the past, ecology, and not so much history, were required. Ecology is the science of life, and life is what characterized Mannahatta (and, later, in a different sense, Manhattan). Ecology focuses on the study of the abundance and distribution of living things, which includes people but also extends to birds, bees, whales, ants, lichens, and so on; name the species and an ecologist wants to know how it makes its living and how it fits into the fabric of nature. Ecology encompasses the wolves that Hudson didn't see, but might have heard, while anchored off Midtown; explains the patterns in the tall, dark forests of Washington Heights that lay near his small ship; and describes the reasons of small piping birds sporting with the tides along the Hudson River strand.

Hudson didn't know about ecology—the term would not be defined for another 250 years—and his focus was elsewhere in any case. And historians work from what is said and written down (and to a lesser extent what is drawn and mapped) in telling the story of the past. When one picks up Edwin G. Burroughs and Mike Wallace's preeminent historical account of the city, *Gotham*, whose nearly fourteen hundred pages recount the city's history from 1609 to 1898, one begins with "O this is Eden!" but within a few pages has already made the transition to the Dutch fur trade.

When I moved to the Bronx, I came to the WCS as an expert in the esoteric but increasingly useful discipline of landscape ecology. To landscape ecologists, a *landscape* is not just a considered view of the outdoors (as seen in a landscape painting), nor is it a manicured garden (as created by a landscape architect). A *landscape*, to scientists like me, is the particular pattern of ecosystems, their composition and arrangement, that forms habitat for plants and animals. That is, we study why a forest is where a forest is, why a stream is where a stream is, and why a stream and a forest together make a particularly salutary combination. By analogy (and of concern to a conservation organization), we also study what happens when people decide they don't want the forest or the stream anymore and build a parking lot across half of the one and divert the other—what are the consequences for the birds and the bees? Landscape ecology is relatively new, because it has grown out of new technological marvels, like satellite images, which reveal the patterns of landscapes from space, and the expanding power of computers, which allows us to simulate experiments across the landscape. (The direct experimental method is not encouraged in landscape ecology—we leave that to market forces.)

Pl. 95.

On September 12, 1609, Hudson could have found both the migratory black-throated blue warbler and the red columbine, shown in this painting by Audubon, on Mannahatta.

Fortunately, these same techniques are not confined to modern data sets. Using the tricks of the trade and some new ones we invented along the way, my colleagues and I have been able to assemble a natural history of Mannahatta as the island thrived on the afternoon of September 12, 1609. In the end, four steps were required to make this possible: First, we needed to set the stage by describing the fundamentals of the landscape in terms of soils, rocks, waters, and shore, the physical environment of Mannahatta. Second, we needed to understand how people influenced the landscape. People are "landscape species"; our habits of creative destruction both make and break the landscape for other species, so we needed to know who the Lenape were and how they were involved in the ecology of the island. Third, we needed to describe all the species that lived on Mannahatta and how they formed communities—the forests, streams, wetlands, and beaches; the neighborhoods that preceded TriBeCa, Chelsea, Midtown, and Harlem. Fourth, we needed to link these different ways of seeing the landscape together, to show how one long, narrow island could support the diverse lifestyles and habitat requirements of all these different species. An unintended result of this final step is a new way of seeing the dense networks of ecological relationships that characterize nature; we call these networks Muir webs, after John Muir, the famous naturalist.

Through this work, we now know that the forests that Hudson saw were comprised of oaks and hickories and American chestnut, white pines and hemlock and Atlantic cedar, old-growth trees sprawling over an open understory maintained by Lenape fire. We know that there were likely over 230 kinds of birds on the island that afternoon and nearly 80 kinds of fish in the rivers and streams. We can describe the relationship of the rocks to the soils, and the soils to the forests, and the forests to the people and plants and animals. It's not a stretch to say that red columbines grew in Harlem or that beavers were swimming in Times Square or that black bears browsed blueberries in Central Park when Hudson's ship sailed into the estuary.

Using these data, we can make virtual time travel possible, to see what Hudson could see, though didn't understand. Working with my colleague, Markley Boyer, we can literally reconstruct the view out of any office building or apartment in Manhattan as it appeared four hundred years ago. Using computer techniques borrowed from the moviemakers, we place trees and streams according to scientific probability distributions, true to the ecology and the landscape, and faithful to the geography of the city, block by block, street by street. These images show us nature in all her beauty, complexity, and loveliness at a time before streets and blocks and tall buildings, before the human footprint lay so heavily on Manhattan and the world.

top The Human Footprint map shows that people directly influenced 83 percent of the earth's land surface at the end of the twentieth century. The scores indicate levels of human influence: black and purple indicate high human influence; green indicates low influence. Wilderness areas have scores of less than 10; Manhattan's score ranges from 96 to 100. *bottom* In the northeastern United States, the pattern of the human footprint is shaped by cities, suburbs, and the highways and roads that interconnect them. The inset photographs show the same biome—mixed temperate deciduous forest—at three levels of human influence: in the Adirondacks, in the Hudson Valley, and in Manhattan.

The Human Footprint

The account of Mannahatta would be extraordinary on its own merits, but the story of Manhattan's original natural history is all the more fascinating because the island that Hudson visited has since become one of the most intensely developed places on the planet. In an earlier project for the WCS, I worked with a team of other scientists to systematically map how people have influenced and transformed the earth. Our approach was conceptually simple, though computationally demanding: We gathered global maps representing population density; land use; access from roads, rails, rivers, and the coast; and lights visible to a satellite at night; and then we laid them on top of one another, like layers of a cake, summing them together in the computer. We obtained the data at a resolution of one kilometer (less than half a square mile); this fine resolution means that we can scale our "Human Footprint map" from the perspective of a neighborhood to that of the entire planet. We can zoom into Manhattan or zoom out to see all of North America or the entire globe. Colors show the different levels of human influence—the less influenced, wilder places we mapped in dark green; the intermediate areas, in shades of yellow and orange and red; and the most influenced places, in purple and black. Wilderness areas are colored forest green. New York City, outside its parks, is black as night.

Analysis of the Human Footprint map indicates that 83 percent of the earth's land surface is influenced by people (and that without considering climate change or air pollution, which nevertheless touches the remaining 17 percent—areas we dubbed the "Last of the Wild"). Moreover, people influence 98 percent of the places where the International Food and Agriculture Organization (FAO) says it is possible to grow rice, wheat, or corn. Looking at the whole world, one sees that most human influence is concentrated along the coasts; centered in temperate regions; and mainly avoids deserts, boreal forests, polar ice caps, and the deepest portions of the Amazon forest—places generally inhospitable to people. Zooming in, for example to the northeastern United States around New York, one recognizes the pattern of human influence in the geography of our roads, towns, and cities. One can clearly see the New York State Thruway and the New Jersey Turnpike and the networks of smaller roads that feed the highways. One can see the major cities of the eastern metroplex and the suburbs that bind them together. Rural areas in the Hudson Valley are yellow and orange; the suburbs are red and purple. One can

preceding pages

left Northern Mannahatta was topographically and culturally the most interesting part of the island in 1609. A large Lenape settlement named Shorakapok nestled beneath the wooded heights of Inwood Hill, with easy access to the Hudson and Harlem rivers. *right* Unlike most of Manhattan today, this area still retains much of its original topography and even has a designated "Forever Wild" area in Inwood Hill Park.

also see the remaining wilder places—the Adirondack Mountains, the New Jersey Pine Barrens, and even the protected New York City watershed in the Catskill Mountains—places that are protected by policy and relative remoteness, and that are greener as a result.

The Human Footprint map shows that every place in the world is somewhere in between the intensely developed (like Manhattan) and the wild (like Mannahatta), which represent either end of a graduated continuum, what we call the gradient of human influence. People often think of nature as occuring in one of two states: either pristine and untouched or influenced and degraded by people. Consideration of the Human Footprint map suggests that these are both abstractions that extend beyond reality. Nature exists in even the most densely inhabited places, like Manhattan; even in the megacity one cannot vanquish nature entirely. In fact, as New York has found, through simple acts, some of nature's diversity can be encouraged to return. By the same token, human beings, a particularly abundant and influential biological species, touch even the wildest places.

Conservation biologists describe the gradient of human influence as the most important factor constraining the planetary ecology today. The Human Footprint can be used to estimate habitat destruction (increasing the level of human influence and thus transforming ecosystems), biological fragmentation (creating smaller, disconnected pieces of wild habitat), and the introduction of new species (seeding foreign organisms along roads and in human-disturbed areas). Even climate change is implicit in the human footprint, for, moving along those channels of red and orange and toward the concentrations of black and purple are cars and trucks propelled by fossil fuels, exacting expensive tolls, paid in temperature rise and natural disasters.

The Mannahatta Project shows us what the world was like when the human footprint was dramatically less intense, and the rest of the natural world was freer to express itself. It shows what nature, given a chance, can deliver. It's not that Mannahatta was unpeopled, but rather that its form of human civilization did not overwhelm the ecological systems on which the island depended. The Lenape did not have the capacity, nor, as far as we can tell, the desire to remove the green woods and glittering marshes, their idea of home. In contrast to Mannahatta, Manhattan has been transformed by a civilization with a global reach, unprecedented technology, and enormous appetite; to satisfy *our* idea of home, we have created the quintessential modern city, New York.

The problem with today's human footprint isn't that there are cities; rather, it is the vast, unrelenting extent of humanity's influence. Cities done well can be just what nature needs, which is a good thing because cities are how humanity in the main is now choosing to live. The most important land-use trend in the last hundred years has been urbanization, and that trend is expected to continue well into the twenty-first century; 2007 marked the first time in human history that more people lived in cities than in rural areas. The United Nations predicts that by 2050, 70 percent of people will live in cities, making the size of the world's urban population equal to the entire world population in 2004 (approximately 6.3 billion). It happens that Greater New York constituted the first megacity, a city of at least 10 million inhabitants, in the years before 1950. By 2025, there could be as many as twenty-seven such cities on the planet, mostly in what is now the developing world. Cities are an indelible part of the human footprint.

We need a new way to live, a lifestyle that allows us to thrive within our ecological means, a mode of existence not unlike what Mannahatta's residents once knew in terms of sustainability and respect. As you will see, Mannahatta supported enormous numbers of living beings with diverse appetites and remarkable requirements; it did so powered entirely by the sun and through efficient recycling of its resources. The people who lived on Mannahatta had a profound effect on the landscape, but not one that excluded other creatures or was beyond the power of the landscape to accommodate over time. Mannahatta succeeded because of the extraordinary diversity of life-forms and the concentration of interactions and dependencies among them, much like New York City succeeds because of the extraordinary diversity of talents and interests among its people, concentrated and energized by the urban landscape. Cities are ecosystems—ecosystems dedicated to people.

The goal of the Mannahatta Project has never been to return Manhattan to its primeval state. The goal of the project is to discover something new about a place we all know so well, whether we live in New York or see it on television, and, through that discovery, to alter our way of life. New York does not lack for dystopian visions of its future; King Kong, climate change, war, and disease have all had their cinematic moments tearing the Big Apple down. But what is the vision of the future that works? Might it lie in Mannahatta, the green heart of New York, and with a new start to history, a few hours before Hudson arrived that sunny afternoon four hundred years ago?

Chapter Two

A Map Found

Awful & grand; I might say, beautiful, but for the melancholy Seriousness which must attend every Circumstance, where the Lives of Men, even the basest Malefactors, are at Stake. The Hills, the Woods, the River, the Town, the Ships, Pillars of Smoke—so terrible and incessant a Roar of Guns, few even in the Army & Navy had ever heard before—all heightened by a most clear & delightful morning, furnished the finest Landscape that either art and nature combined could draw, or the Imagination conceive.

— Ambrose Serle, describing the British assault on Manhattan at Kip's Bay during the American Revolution, September 15, 1776

Detail from the British Headquarters Map, showing Lower Manhattan during the American Revolution, circa 1782–83.

The first time I walked through New York City I wondered what giant or god had created such a place. Buildings like cliffs, avenues like canyons, traffic flowing like rivers, parks brimming with forests and urban fields, a landscape populated by people seemingly from every nation and all parts of the continent, moving rapidly and with a deliberate attitude about their business, even if that business was none at all. I was intoxicated. I felt amazed at the ambition of the place and humbled by the power that had created it, for neither giants nor gods had built the "awful & grand" city; generations of New Yorkers, poor and wealthy, native and immigrant, had created the metropolis over a span of nearly four hundred years. Those people had each come for their own reasons, with their own peculiar visions, to this particular piece of land and shore and decided through some strange, collective logic, to raise a city on a scale beyond the power of the imagination to conceive.

A law professor once described to me lying beneath the pillars of the George Washington Bridge as a child, cupping his hands around his eyes, and peering up the river to imagine the view that Henry Hudson might have seen as he sailed in on his small wooden ship. Jacob Astor, the industrialist, imagined a city where the wealth of an entire continent could accumulate in the hands of just a few men (and preferably one). Robert Moses, the planner, had a vision for New York City that included the automobile and access to ball fields and swimming pools and, in the midst of the Great Depression, reconfigured the city for the future. Michael Bloomberg, the mayor and billionaire, envisioned a future where the economy always hummed, with less traffic congestion, no smoking, and better subways.

Hudson's vision, to the extent that he had one, was to get rich and then get out of town. Adrian van der Donck, the *Jonkheer* who gave his name to Yonkers, New York, came to New Netherland in 1641, stayed, and became wealthy. He wanted others to join him and populate his lands; he wrote a lengthy paean to his new home called the *Narrative of New Netherland* (1650), describing the land as "naturally fruitful and capable of supporting a large population, if it were judiciously allotted according to location. . . . [It] is adapted to the production of all kinds of winter and summer fruits, and with less trouble and tilling than in the Netherlands. . . . The air is pleasant here, and more temperate. . . ."

Many others agreed, describing not only the "sweetness of the air" (Daniel Denton, 1670), but also the "wonderful size of the trees" (Johann de Laet, 1633), "all sorts of fowls, such as cranes, bitterns, swans, geese, ducks,

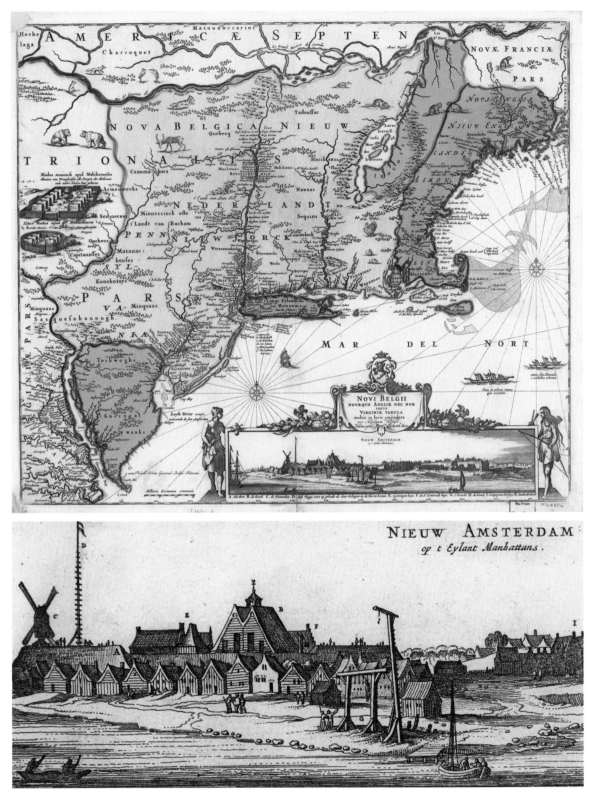

top The Visscher Map, circa 1651, shows northeastern North America as the Dutch understood it in the years following Henry Hudson's voyage. Manhattan is at the center of the map, at the mouth of the Hudson River, which in turn is the focus of the New Netherland colony. Europeans at the time knew the outlines of the continent, but were only beginning to explore its heart. *bottom* This detail of the inset image shows the small village of New Amsterdam as it appeared from just off the tip of Manhattan. Note the windmill, gallows, and rolling hills.

European explorers were astounded by the abundance of wildlife in the New World, including (a) beavers (note, though, that beavers are herbivores and do not eat fish as depicted), (b) white-tailed deer or elk, (c) turkey and cottontail rabbits, and (d) a red or gray fox and cranes, as shown in these details from the Visscher Map.

widgeons, wild geese, etc." (Nicholas van Wassenaer, 1630), and "great quantities of harts and hinds . . . ; foxes in abundance, multitudes of wolves, wild cats, squirrels—black as pitch, and gray, also flying squirrels—beavers in great numbers, minks, otters, polecats, bears, and many kinds of fur-bearing animals, which I cannot name or think of" (David Pietersz de Vries, 1633). Van Wassenaer complained, "[B]irds fill the woods so that men can scarcely go through them for the whistling, the noise and the chattering." Peter Kalm had a problem with the noisy frogs (writing in 1748). Walking out of town, he noted, "[T]ree frogs, Dr. Linnaeus's *Rana arborea*, are so loud it is difficult for a man to make himself heard."

Probably the most enthusiastic chronicler was Denton, who ends his account with the following extraordinary passage:

> Thus have I briefly given you a Relation of New-York, with the places thereunto adjoyning; In which, if I have err'd, it is principally in not giving it its due commendation; for besides those earthly blessings where it is store'd, Heaven hath not been wanting to open his Treasure, in sending down seasonable showers upon the Earth, blessing it with a sweet and pleasant Air, and a Continuation of such Influences as tend to the Health both of Man and Beast: and the Climate hath such an affinity with that of England, that it breeds ordinarily no alteration to those which remove thither; that the name of seasoning, which is common to some other Countreys hath never been known; That I may say, and say truly, that if there be any terrestrial happiness to be had by people of all ranks, especially of an inferior rank, it must certainly be here. . . . [I]f there be any terrestrial Canaan, 'tis surely here, where the Land floweth with milk and honey. The inhabitants are blest with Peace and plenty, blessed in their Countrey, blessed in their Fields, blessed in the Fruit of their bodies, in the fruit of their grounds, in the increase of their Cattel, Horses and Sheep, blessed in their Basket, and in their Store; In a word, blessed in whatsoever they take in hand, or go about, the Earth yielding plentiful increase to all their painful labors.

It can be a bit hard to credit descriptions like these for any place, but especially for a place like New York City, which has changed so radically over the intervening centuries. After all, these writers wrote from their own perspectives and understanding of the landscape, with specific ends in mind; many such descriptions were advertisements to entice others to leave their familiar lives in Europe and take a chance coming to the New World. Having arrived, they couldn't believe their eyes. These early accounts carry the enthusiasm of a real estate speculator or a tourist new to town.

But it is also appropriate to ask whether we find descriptions like this incredible because *we* have lost the ability to believe them. After all, few places on the planet today have the abundance of plant and animal life that was commonplace in the America these early settlers describe. The wildlife films produced by PBS or the BBC require carefully cropped shots and often months of filming in national parks to get the few minutes of "wild nature" we see on television. Psychologists explain that we form our impression of what nature "should be" from what we saw as children. The problem is, if the nature we knew as kids was impoverished before our time, we might never know what we are missing. We lack the proper baseline.

Fortunately, in the case of Manhattan, we have ways to confirm these fantastic descriptions of the New World from the scientific evidence that nature leaves us: pollen collected in layers at the bottom of still ponds, the width of tree rings hundreds of years old, the shape of rocks and the chemistry of water, and the profile of soil with depth. Ecologists, working backward from how ecosystems function today, make educated guesses about how they worked in the past, backcasting from general ecological principles to the specifics of what might have been. Archaeologists glean information from the leavings of former inhabitants—shell middens, fireplaces, potsherds, arrowheads, hammerstones, and bones. In most places, information like this is sufficient, in concert with historical descriptions, to assemble an idea of the ecological past, but it's not perfect; it is like attempting to view a painting when most of the canvas is torn and missing. The picture is tantalizing but incomplete.

The same would be true for Manhattan except that we have a canvas. What makes the quest to understand Manhattan's historical ecology different from that of other places is the existence of an extraordinary map. The British Headquarters Map is not from the time when Hudson first came to New York, in 1609; it is from over 170 years later, from 1782 or 1783 (we can't date it exactly), from the end of a bloody and costly war: the American Revolution. It is not a map of Manhattan primeval, but a map of a colonial eighteenth-century island girded for battle, with farms, fields, roads, and fortifications, and a small provincial town at its tip. But what the British Headquarters Map shows,

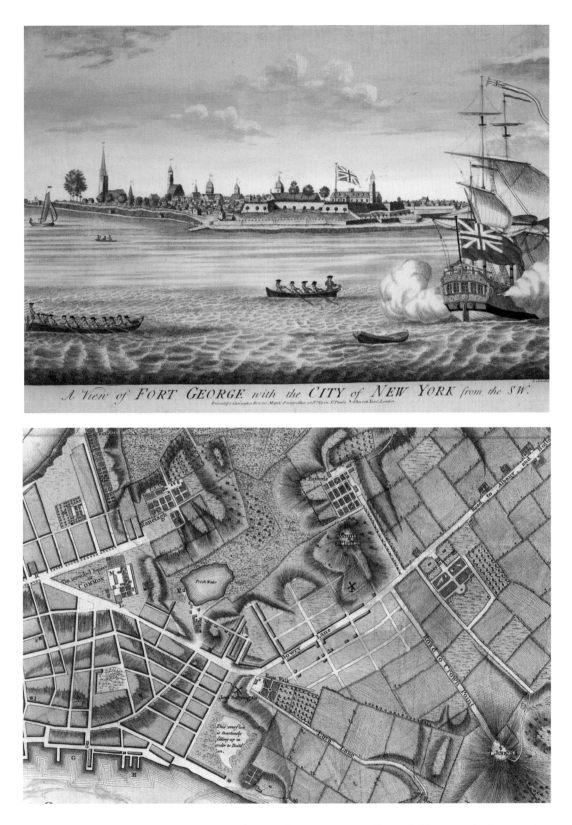

top This view of Fort George and Lower Manhattan emphasizes eighteenth-century British control of the New York colony. Note the beaches beginning just below the fort and extending north under the steeple of Trinity Church. *bottom* This detail from a 1766 plan of New York City before the Revolution, by British cartographer John Montresor, shows the outskirts of the city, where its blocks dissolved into farm fields (Uptown is toward the right). The note in the lower center reads, "This overflow is constantly filling up in order to Build on" and marks the former outlet stream of the Fresh Water into the East River.

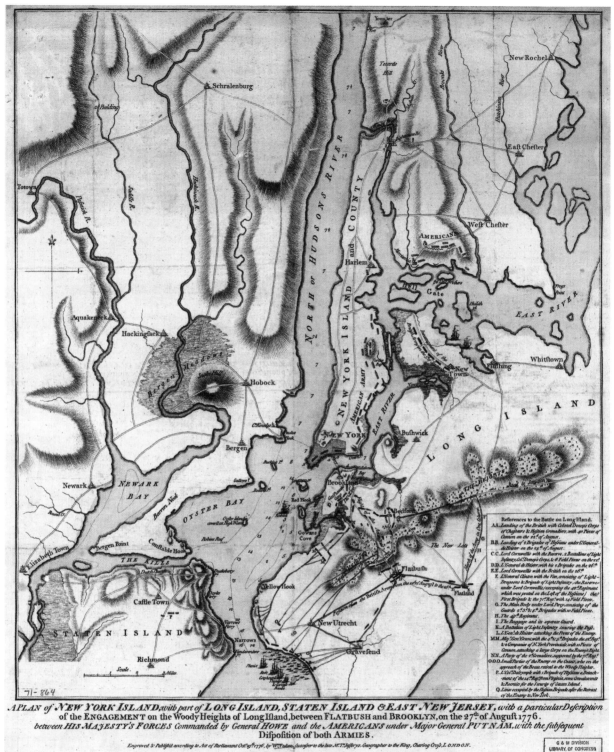

This campaign map, engraved by William Faden, shows the disposition of forces on August 27, 1776, following the Battle of Brooklyn. After landing in southern Brooklyn and making a flanking attack across the glacial moraine at Jamaica Pass, the British army (red lines) was arrayed below Brooklyn Heights; the American army (blue lines) was redeployed along the Heights and the eastern shore of Manhattan Island, having been soundly beaten, but not destroyed.

at a scale and with an accuracy remarkable in a map more than two hundred years old, is the natural landscape of the island—the topography, shoreline, streams, and wetlands—which makes it possible for us to understand and paint a portrait of "the finest Landscape that either art and nature combined could draw," a portrait of Mannahatta.

The Campaign of 1776

To understand the British Headquarters Map and why it is so accurate, we have to go back to New York in 1776, in the second year of the Revolution, years before the map had been conceived. While the Founding Fathers debated the Declaration of Independence over that long summer in Philadelphia, the actual war was being fought around New York; for most of the next eight years, New York City would be at the center of the action.

In 1776, New York was the second largest city in the American colonies, with more than thirty thousand inhabitants (including black slaves and freemen), lagging just behind Philadelphia, and larger than Boston. Nevertheless, the city proper occupied Manhattan Island to only just north of today's City Hall Park, with scattered buildings and farms in the Out Ward along the Bowery. Small settlements extended up the East Side to the small town of Harlem on the East River shore (located approximately where today's East 124th Street meets the FDR Drive, under the on-ramp to the Triborough Bridge). Colonists cultivated apple orchards and planted wheat, barley, and rye alongside cows, pigs, and chickens on productive smallholder farms. Greenwich Village was just an intersection of two dusty country roads in a rolling landscape of fields and broken woods.

Despite its provincial character, New York was a center of both radical patriotic fever and wealthy Loyalist sentiment. In January 1770, tensions came to a head in the Battle of Golden Hill, when a boisterous group of "Liberty Boys" had a series of run-ins with British soldiers stationed in New York. The elderly British governor Cadwallader Colden (a noted botanist) and the rich, conservative Delancey family had just agreed to support the newly enacted Mutiny Act with an appropriation of two thousand pounds for quartering British troops in the city. During a fight in a wheat field in the middle of town, a group of Redcoats, after being provoked by the Liberty Boys, "cut down a Tea-Water man driving his Cart, and [injured] a Fisherman's finger." Some later claimed the "Battle of Golden Hill," with its hurt heads and fingers, to be the first blood of the Revolution, predating the Boston Massacre by about six weeks. For its part, Golden Hill was named after the yellow celandine, an introduced flower, which bloomed between William and Fulton, John and Cliff streets in spring. The conflict would simmer in council chambers and flare up into mob demonstrations for another five years, until armed fighting broke out in 1775, with the shots fired on Lexington Green in Massachusetts.

What made New York essential to the armies vying for the colonies was the city's strategic position at the mouth of the Hudson. The North River, as it was called then, could carry warships 120 miles, nearly to Albany, and from there it was only a few overland portages and long rows up Lake George and Lake Champlain to British Canada. With control of the Hudson, King George's army could separate the fractious New England colonies from the rich agricultural lands of the mid-Atlantic. Control the Hudson, British military leaders in London reasoned as they regrouped in late 1775, and you control the rebellion. And to control the Hudson, you must first control New York.

This geography was not lost on the American Revolutionaries either. In March 1776, General George Washington moved his army south from New England to Manhattan, forcing the few British troops in possession onto naval vessels in the harbor and into fortifications on Governors Island. In late July the British landed a huge expeditionary army of British regulars and German mercenaries from Europe—over 22,000 men—on Staten Island; in August, they shifted these troops across the Lower Harbor on a hundred-plus British naval vessels, manned by 10,000 sailors—one of the largest amphibious operations of the age. The troops landed unopposed on the plains of Bushwick and Flatbush. The Battle of Brooklyn began three days later, in the early morning hours of August 26, when the British made a surprise flanking move over Jamaica Pass, turning Washington's left flank and driving his army, with heavy losses, back to Brooklyn Heights, from where it had been deployed across the rocky hills of the glacial moraine, in what is now Prospect Park and Greenwood Cemetery.

Three nights later, Washington evacuated his men across the East River, giving up the defense of Long Island and refortifying New York City. On September 15, the British continued the dangerous minuet, landing fifteen thousand troops five miles above the city proper on "York Island," near Kip's Bay—once again behind the American lines. A fifteen-year-old American private, Joseph Martin, described the massed red uniforms of the invading

These two views painted by Thomas Davies in November 1776 show the assaults that completed the British conquest of New York. *top* The assault on Fort Lee in New Jersey required a steep climb from the Hudson River to the top of the Palisades. Note the waterfall and sparse cover of eastern white pine on the rocky cliffs. *bottom* The simultaneous assaults on Fort George (middle foreground) and Fort Washington (background) were made through dense mixed deciduous forests fringed with fall color. The clear-cuts on the hills and the low-lying land around Sherman Creek provided positions for cannons.

force "like a clover field in full bloom"—and then the cannonade started from four British warships armed with eighty cannons tied not a hundred yards from shore, just south of the site of the United Nations building. While the thin American line scattered, the British troops formed on top of Murray Hill (Mrs. Murray apocryphally offered the British commanders tea in her farmhouse as a delaying tactic), and Washington rapidly recalled his troops from town along the Greenwich Road, then through the woods of Midtown Manhattan to the Bloomingdale (our Upper West Side). The British had taken the city.

Sharp skirmishes continued for several more days, particularly across Morningside Heights, around the present-day campuses of Columbia University and Barnard College, and near Point of Rocks in West Harlem. (Morningside Heights takes its name from the glow of the sun on the eastern slopes, as viewed from the Harlem Plains.) One clash took place in a buckwheat field near Broadway and 116th Street. In the dry woods and fields, Americans were giving as good as they got, but the overwhelming British land forces, supplemented by naval guns stationed in the Hudson River, eventually forced the Americans to retreat.

The desperate Rebels even tried a submarine attack, the first one in recorded history, to deter the British navy in New York Harbor. David Bushnell, a Connecticut inventor, had devised an oaken "Submarine Vessel [that] bore some resemblance to two upper tortoise shells, attached together." The *Turtle*, as it was called, was outfitted with thick glass plates that, in clear waters, allowed enough light to penetrate to read a book at three fathoms (eighteen feet deep). Hand winches propelled it forward and sideways, a rudder gave it direction, and a valve and set of pumps enabled it to ascend or descend. Bushnell also invented the first torpedo (which he named after *Torpedo nobiliana*, a fish capable of delivering an electric shock of up to 220 volts). Bushnell's torpedo contained 130 pounds of gunpowder, but during the inaugural engagement of the *Turtle*, a metal plate on the bottom of the target ship kept the bomb from attaching. Attempting to retreat, the volunteer submariner, Ezra Lee, lost his way. Surfacing to get his bearings, he was sighted by British soldiers on Governors Island; they pursued, ultimately causing Lee to let loose his torpedo bomb, which floated up into the East River, where it exploded harmlessly. On hearing the explosion in northern Manhattan, Washington's second-in-command, the indomitable General Israel Putnam, said, "God curse 'em, that'll do it for 'em." Lee and the *Turtle* were saved by a whaleboat, which pulled them ashore in the dark.

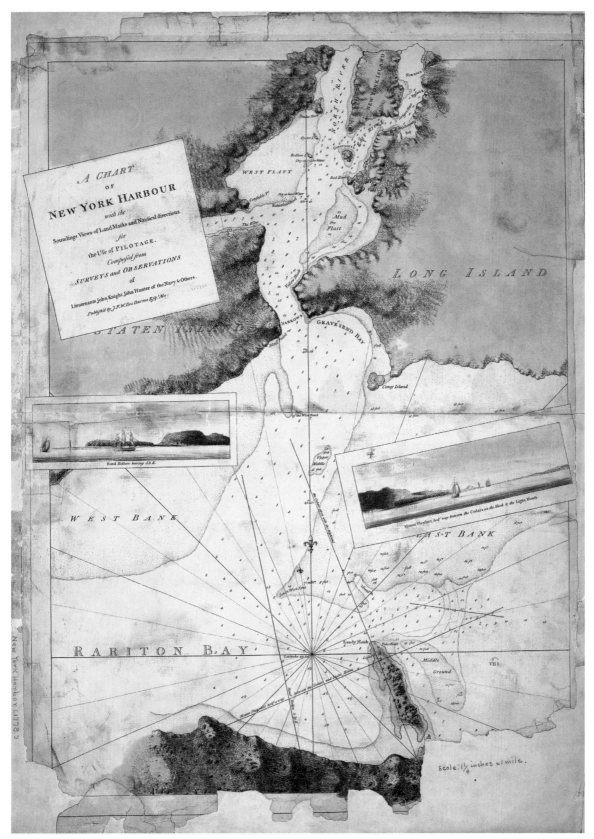

The British military created hundreds of maps of the New York City region during the American Revolution. J. F. W. DesBarres published this chart of New York Harbor in the *Atlantic Neptune* in 1779, with navigation views to help ships find their way through the sandbars that made entry into the harbor hazardous.

In October Washington decided that Manhattan Island could no longer be defended and retreated north, leaving a garrison of 2,300 men at Fort Washington, at the highest point on the island, in what we today call Washington Heights. British forces chased the American army through lower Westchester (our Bronx) and eventually to the White Plains, where yet another indecisive battle was fought. In November the garrison remaining on Manhattan surrendered to British forces after a fierce bombardment and assault, ending the armed resistance. The British renamed Fort Washington "Fort Kynphausen," as it is labeled on the British Headquarters Map, in honor of the German general who led the attack.

The British had won the campaign for New York. They had driven Washington's forces from Manhattan Island with casualties and hard lessons learned, but without the devastating loss that would have meant an early end to the war. The Rebel army, bloodied but largely intact, survived to fight another day. British forces would control New York City and Manhattan Island for the rest of the war, making occupied New York the headquarters of their operations and establishing a fortress for Loyalist Americans and British troops alike that swelled the city's population more than twofold. But no one, on either side, really believed that the battle for Manhattan Island was over.

The British Headquarters Map

The British immediately set about fortifying the city and making preparations for a large-scale attack, which, as it turned out, never came. Despite numerous skirmishes and midnight raids nearby in the Bronx and New Jersey, the Americans could never find a plausible way to launch an assault against the well-guarded island. Meanwhile, the British took control of City Hall on Wall Street (the site of today's Federal Hall) and made it their military headquarters; they established martial law and quartered troops with city residents. They redesigned and added on to the fortifications begun by the Americans. Small fortresses topped nearly every hill in Lower Manhattan: Bayard's Mount, Jones Hill, Richmond Hill, and Corlear's Hook all had their defenses; redoubts overlooked the Lispenard Meadows and the East River shore. (Several of these features can be seen on the detail of the British Headquarters Map that opens the chapter.) The British completed a wall that ran practically from one side of Manhattan to the other, along the line of modern-day Grand

Street, and defensive walls were constructed behind the beaches along the Hudson River shore up to West Thirty-third Street. They dammed Minetta Water to create a lake in what is now the West Village, and farther north fortified McGown's Pass; built a redoubt at Horn's Hook, overlooking Hellgate (where Gracie Mansion is today); constructed three walls across Washington Heights; and garrisoned Fort Kynphausen, Fort Tryon, Marble Hill, and Cox's Hill (our Inwood Hill). And, importantly for us, they found time to make maps. Maps, then as today, were essential data for prosecuting a war.

Maps served a variety of military purposes, especially for invading forces unfamiliar with the terrain. They provide leaders a means of rapidly coming to understand strategic factors—the dispositions of troops, the distances between places, the difficulty of travel, and the geographic relationships between different political units. Maps are also useful tactically—to plan surprise attacks, to place defenses, and to maneuver against the enemy (to draw him out, to box her in). Maps have been used in war since antiquity and were instrumental to the conduct of battle in the eighteenth century; they are even more crucial today. Modern militaries have generated many technologies that have revolutionized mapping: satellite imagery; the global positioning system (GPS); and the geographic information system (GIS), a means of analyzing maps using computers. Fortunately, these same technologies have found other uses—one can map trees as easily as bombs.

Before the Revolution began, from the time of the French and Indian War in the 1750s and 1760s through the opening of hostilities in 1775, a number of detailed surveys of North America had been undertaken by British cartographers. James Cook, who later charted Hawaii and much of the tropical Pacific, cut his teeth in surveys of the cold Saint Lawrence River. J. F. W. DesBarres mapped much of the colonial coastline in 257 plates of the *Atlantic Neptune* series, which were used for navigation well into the nineteenth century. Numerous surveys were conducted and maps drawn to delimit the boundaries of colonies in dispute, each colony viewing its territorial integrity as paramount, and the English authorities eager to consolidate their North American lands against the French and the Spanish.

These officers drew maps based on geodetic control, meaning that they located places according not only to local references, but also to where they were on the planet, with longitude and latitude fixed by astronomical observations. They mapped at carefully selected scales and used defined map projections, so that navigators could derive distances between any two objects

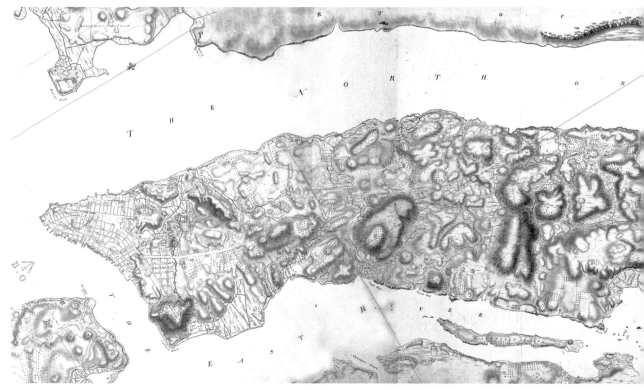

The British Headquarters Map, circa 1782–83, once described as a "topographical and historical encyclopedia" of Manhattan before modern development, shows the original hills, streams, shoreline, and wetlands of the island.

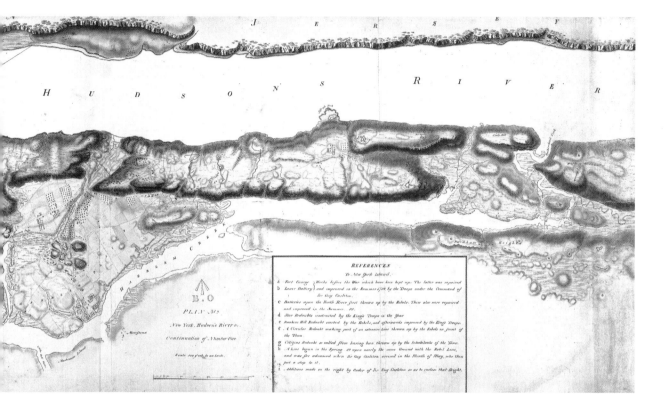

J E R S E Y

H U D S O N S   R I V E R

↑
B. O

PLAN N.º

New York, Hudson's River &c.

Continuation of Number One.

Scale two feet to an Inch.

from the map with a compass and ruler. They agreed on a set of standardized symbols, to show, for example, forests, coastlines, beaches, and wetlands, so that different maps had comparable conventions. To achieve these ends, most of these surveyors were trained at military academies, including the one in Greenwich, England, considered one of the best of its kind at the time. Their maps were not only accurate but beautiful, frequently supplemented by painted perspective views illustrating the appearance of the landscape for navigation. Unfortunately, the outbreak of wartime hostilities brought these ambitious, broad-scale surveys to an abrupt end.

However, wartime gave cartographers another motivation to produce exceptionally accurate maps. On Manhattan the British generals had a corps of well-trained, experienced cartographers attached to the engineers, the "Pioneer Guides," and teams of professional surveyors at their disposal. And these mapmakers had time—seven years in total, from November 1776 to November 1783—to draft, redraft, and perfect their understanding of the landscape. For Manhattan and the surrounding area (mainly Staten Island, western Brooklyn, western Queens, and the western Bronx), the British army prepared hundreds of maps. Many of these are now housed in archives in the United States and the United Kingdom.

Created toward the end of the war, the British Headquarters Map was the culmination of their efforts. One expert has described it as "a topographical and historical encyclopedia of the area during the Revolution." Drawn at a large scale, one inch to eight hundred feet, the map shows all of Manhattan Island and parts of Brooklyn in a detailed, colored manuscript covering two irregularly shaped sheets of paper, together over ten feet long and three feet wide. Features were sketched with pen and ink, then hand colored with blue, pink, brown, and green watercolor. Combinations of colors and hatching demarcate different features, including land use and infrastructure and natural features like hills, wetlands, and streams.

The British Headquarters Map documents the geography of significance to military planners: the fortifications and defensive works, the extent of the city proper, a small suburbia with treelined streets and backyards in today's Chinatown, a road network extending from the city toward small settlements in Greenwich Village and Harlem, important crossroads, fields and orchards, individual buildings, estates, and even formal gardens and alleys of trees.

When I first saw the British Headquarters Map, I was attracted, like almost everyone else who examines it, to the topography. One can make out

Murray Hill, the rocky slopes of Central Park, and the heights of northern Manhattan—Morningside Heights, Harlem Heights, Washington Heights, and Laurel and Inwood hills. But the British Headquarters Map also shows topography where today there is none—in Midtown, in the East Village, down through the Bowery, even under Downtown. There was once a hill just south of Wall Street, near the bronze *Charging Bull* at Bowling Green, not far from a stream along Beaver Street. What had happened to that hill?

But more than hills and dales, the British Headquarters Map also shows what to those hard-nosed military mapmakers were annoying tactical impediments, the same features which we would celebrate today as ecosystems: marshes, forests, beaches, rivers, ponds, streams, cliffs, coves, and bays. When I looked at the British Headquarters Map, I saw in the markings for "salt grass fields" the great green swards of salt marshes on the Lower East Side; in wavy blue hachures I saw red maple swamps in Times Square and precious bogs in Central Park; in dots I saw outlined sandy beaches on the Hudson River shore; and over the rest of the map, nearly everywhere across the upland, I saw the potential for forests—deep, old, massive forests. Even the human features told a story, for in the distribution of farms and orchards, the paths of the dirt roads were suggestions of the underlying soils and geology. I realized that the map provided important insight into the ecological foundations of the Manhattan landscape, the canvas of a natural landscape past, not just as it appeared in 1782, but as it existed long before, back in the time of Hudson, back when it was Mannahatta. The essential first hurdle to gaining that insight, though, was to lay the British Headquarters Map over a modern map of Manhattan and judge its fit. Could the geography of 1782 be matched to the geography of 2000?

A Remarkably Accurate Map

In 1997, Robert Augustyn and Paul Cohen, private map dealers in New York, published *Manhattan in Maps* (Rizzoli, 1997), a book of maps of the city that they felt were not well known or sufficiently appreciated, especially maps that were in private collections or in European archives. Prior to their book, the only version of the British Headquarters Map that was available in America was a tracing done by the American antiquarian Benjamin Franklin Stevens, who published a set of lithographic copies in 1902. (Facsimiles can be found at the New York Public Library, the Brooklyn Historical Society, and City University Graduate Center in New York.) Isaac Newton Phelps Stokes, the great early twentieth-century compiler of images of Manhattan, had published a small version of Stevens's tracing in his epic *Iconography of Manhattan Island* (R.H. Dodd, 1917–29), but with uncharacteristically little comment. Even Stevens's memoir gives the map only a single sentence.

In my work at the WCS as a landscape ecologist, I deal with a lot of maps from a lot of different places. In order to make these maps work together—whether the goal is saving tigers or understanding the history of New York—it is essential to get them into a common geography, so that maps of different kinds can be laid over one another, like layers in a cake. If I could "georeference" the British Headquarters Map to a known coordinate system, I could relate its depiction of the old hills and valleys to their modern street addresses and thus find that phantom hill near Bowling Green.

Critical to landscape ecology is the set of computer hardware, software, and spatial data called, collectively, a geographic information system. In a GIS, a map is really composed of two kinds of information: the spatial features (what we normally think of as the map) and an attribute database of numbers or words linked to features on the map. In the database each dot or squiggle on the map can have different kinds of associated information. For example, a stream might have its length, its width, and its flow rate associated as data; a hill might have measurements of its elevation, slope, and facing direction (called the aspect) tied to its representation. The GIS allows people to make distance and area measurements, to sort and query the databases, to analyze layers against one another, and to run ecological or other kinds of models. The police use GIS to analyze patterns of crime. McDonald's uses GIS to figure out where to put restaurants. Internet surfers use a kind of GIS when they log on to Google Maps or MapQuest.

With these possibilities in mind and my curiosity piqued, one Sunday afternoon, after much internal debate, I took the initiative and sliced open my beautiful, well-loved, not to mention expensive, copy of *Manhattan in Maps,* then carefully extracted the pages of the British Headquarters Map. To get a clean scan, I had to lay the map flat against the scanner plate. Next, I downloaded a modern-roads layer of the city from the U.S. Census Bureau. Then I reassembled the pieces of the British Headquarters Map in the computer and began the laborious process of picking out "control points," matching features on the British Headquarters Map to features in the city today.

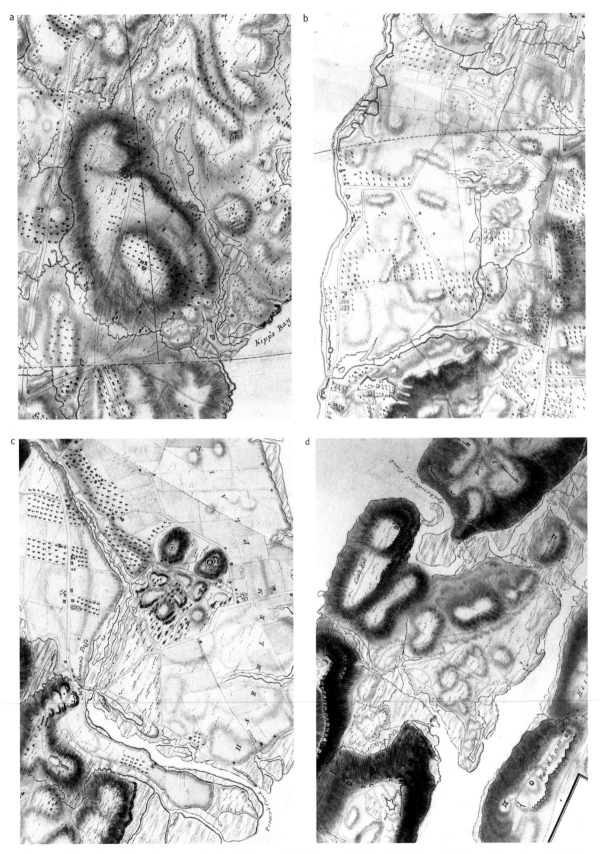

These details from the British Headquarters Map show (a) Murray Hill, (b) Greenwich Village, (c) Harlem, and (d) Inwood, in northern Manhattan.

After a few hours of work, I had my first results: I had matched the British Headquarters Map view of Manhattan to the modern-road network of the city with a spatial error of about 250 meters (820 feet, or roughly two and a half football fields). Not bad, but not great either. I felt disappointed—it wasn't clear that sacrificing my book had been worth it—but also intrigued; it was closer than I would have guessed. Strangely, most of the error came from the lower section of the city, which, rather than extending straight, in line with the rest of the island, pointed like the bottom of the letter *J* toward New Jersey. Manhattan looked vaguely like Italy. The problem was, of course, that Manhattan doesn't have a toe like Italy—Manhattan is long and narrow and reasonably straight, as islands go.

A couple of nights later, I was again examining my reproduction of the British Headquarters Map when I noticed a faint dotted line that extended across the map about a third of the way up the island. Recall that the original British Headquarters Map was drawn on two large sheets. To assemble the full map, these sheets need to be overlapped. I thought, what if the mapmakers meant for them to be aligned along this dotted line rather than assembled straight across, as displayed in *Manhattan in Maps*? Using the computer again, I reoriented the upper sheet to match the diagonal line, then reassembled the map and applied my control points. The georeferencing this time was much better—only 100 meters (320 feet) off, and better still, New York no longer leaned toward New Jersey. It also solved another problem that I hadn't noticed before. Although not immediately apparent on casual examination, the label for the East River was misaligned in the photograph that Cohen and Augustyn had published. The *E* in the label for the East River appears offset from the remaining letters *ast River* by several inches. Realigning the sheets properly fixed this label and restored the geometry of Manhattan, and resulted in a more precise match between Manhattan today and Manhattan circa 1782.

Emboldened by these results, I planned a visit to The National Archives of the United Kingdom, where the original British Headquarters Map is kept. Once there I found, to my amazement, that *Manhattan in Maps* wasn't the source of the problem—the original map was! Someone had glued the two pieces of the British Headquarters Map together, but not in the right place. Nevertheless, I obtained a one-to-one photograph of the map from the archivists, had it professionally scanned, reassembled the high-fidelity version, gained access to a much more accurate digital road map of the city—and embarked on an eighteen-month-long period of research into place-names and accounts of Manhattan's historical geography (see Appendix A). In spots

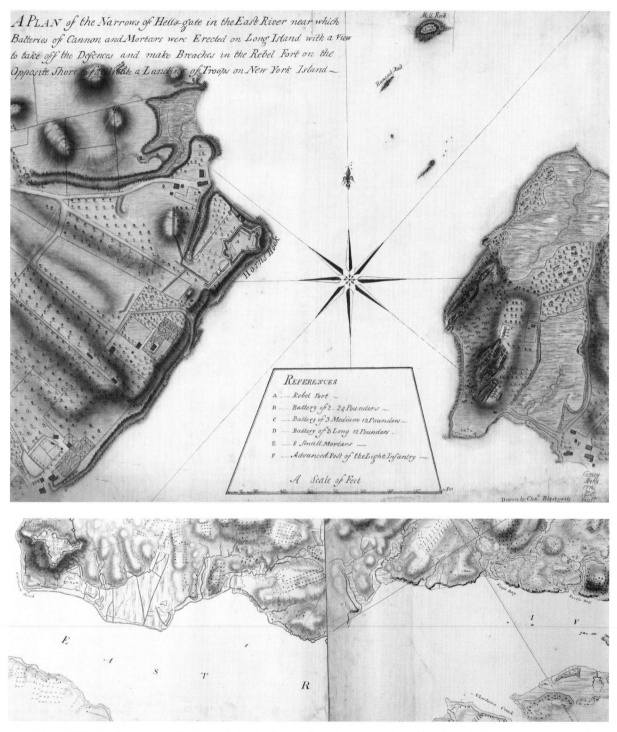

top This beautiful hand-colored 1776 map by Charles Blaskowitz shows Hellgate, between Horn's Hook (Manhattan), where Gracie Mansion is today, and Hallett's Point (Queens). Note the salt marshes on both sides, depicted with wavy, uneven hachures. This same area is depicted in the reconstructed view on page 88. *bottom* The misaligned label for the East River on the British Headquarters Map was the final clue about how to assemble it correctly.

above "Georeferencing" the British Headquarters Map in a geographic information system (GIS) allowed us to overlay the modern-road grid. Note the match between the colonial and modern streets. *opposite* Adding another layer to the GIS shows the modern building footprints against the eighteenth-century geography of the city.

where I knew both what the feature was on the British Headquarters Map and where it should lie in the modern geography of the city, I was able to place over two hundred control points.

The final georeferencing of the British Headquarters Map places its features within 40 meters (130 feet, or equivalent to about half a north-south block in Midtown Manhattan) of Manhattan's modern streets. Moreover, many of the features shown on the British Headquarters Map have historical documentation in other sources, often with descriptions dating from the seventeenth to nineteenth centuries. There are hills with names like Verlettenberg, Golden Hill, Mount Pitt, Mallesmitsberg, Richmond Hill, and the Kalck Hoek; valleys called Bloemmarts Vly, Smits Fly, Konaande Kongh, and Manhattanville Pass; streams like the Maagde Paetje, Lispenard's Creek, Minetta Water, Saw Kill, and Old Arch Brook. These titles reflect the layers of Native American, Dutch, British, and American naming that enlivens the history of New York City. Moreover, the georeferenced map means that not only are the named features available to us, but all the unnamed features are as well—the details of the slopes, wiggles, and bends of an entire island are unveiled for study. The British Headquarters Map opened up a past natural landscape, Mannahatta, at a scale unique in the study of historical ecology. Everything that follows, everything this book is about, suddenly became possible.

But there was still one more question that needed to be answered, a question a friend once asked me: *Why* was the map so accurate?

Why So Accurate?

Actually georeferencing the British Headquarters Map with this precision begs the question, how could these eighteenth-century cartographers have made a map with so much detail and spatial accuracy? Most attempts to reference historical maps like the British Headquarters Map to modern coordinate systems yield poorer results, so much so that it is out of fashion in historical studies to even try. Today maps are "texts" to be read for what they tell us about the perspectives and prejudices of times past—not necessarily as accurate records of actual geography. Such high levels of spatial fidelity from eighteenth-century maps are only known from a few English county maps georeferenced in the 1970s. It was clear that in controlled, domestic environments—the English countryside, for example—eighteenth-century surveyors could do a high-quality job. But what about during a war on a faraway continent?

The answer is not so clear, but I have a hypothesis. I believe that the British Headquarters Map is an accurate depiction of the landscape because of the fortunate confluence of three factors: one part strategy, one part affection, and one part ambition—as it turns out, not an uncommon recipe in the history of great New York creations.

First and most importantly, New York City was strategically significant throughout the war, a Loyalist center, the location of the British headquarters in the Americas, and a vital port for embarking troops and necessary materials from Europe. As the center of the British war effort, the headquarters was attended by the best the army had to offer, including cartographers. Although we don't know who exactly drew the British Headquarters Map, we do know that many famous British cartographers worked in New York around the time it was drawn. Among these was Captain John Montresor, who had offered his tent to the American Patriot Nathan Hale the afternoon before his hanging in September 1776; for a time Montresor owned Ward's Island, or Montresor's Island as it was called until Rebels burnt his house in 1777. Another was Charles Blaskowitz, who drew several fine manuscript maps, now in the Library of Congress and other archives. Two mapmakers from Scotland, Andrew Skinner and George Taylor, produced a striking watercolor map of the river valleys of the Bronx, showing the numerous streams and tidal wetlands of its fecund shores. These men and others produced maps of beauty and surprising accuracy.

Second, there is the personality and personal history of Sir Henry Clinton, the general in charge for the longest period of any British general during the war. Clinton had personal reasons for a particular affection for the Manhattan geography. His father had been governor of the New York colony in the 1740s and '50s; he spent his main teenage years (1743–46) growing up nearby, on Long Island. Clinton's first military posting was on Manhattan as a lieutenant of fusiliers in 1745. He later served in Germany during the Seven Years' War, where maps were central to the conduct of war. Frederick the Great once wrote, "Above all, a general must never move his army without being instructed about the place where he leads it and without knowing how he will safely get it to the ground where he wants to execute his plans." Clinton took this advice to heart.

Moreover, Clinton was by inclination a man of maps. Professor William Wilcox wrote in his 1945 biography of the general that Clinton was at his best as a planner, and "his plans were based, above all, upon sound geographical premises. He had a strategist's instinct for a map. . . . He was continually advising his friends to look at one, and assuming that they would see in it what he did, an outline of future operations." It was Clinton who suggested the flanking move around Washington's position in 1776 through Jamaica Pass and who criticized his fellow commanders, particularly his superior, Lord William Howe, for their lack of geographic sense. Clinton had urged before the assault at Kip's Bay that Howe land north of Washington at King's Bridge and cut off all of the Rebel army before it could escape Manhattan, as it eventually did. The suggestion was overruled, much to Clinton's vocal annoyance (subtlety and discretion were not Clinton's strong suits).

Unfortunately, if it was Clinton who ordered the creation of the British Headquarters Map (we don't know for certain, but it seems likely), he was not able to stay on in America to see the final benefit of his mapmaking diligence. Like his predecessor Howe, who was sacked after General John Burgoyne's failure in 1777, Clinton was recalled to London after General Charles Lord Cornwallis exceeded *his* orders and marched north when he should have stayed in the South, becoming trapped at Yorktown and thus losing his army and effectively ending the war for the British in 1781. Clinton took the fall for Cornwallis even though he was two hundred miles away in New York and had told Cornwallis previously to stay out of Virginia. Regardless, it was Clinton who returned to England a failure.

Clinton's name is nowhere mentioned on the British Headquarters Map, suggesting it was not complete at the time of his dismissal, but interestingly, his successor's name is everywhere. The British Headquarters Map may be so accurate because of Clinton's predilections and his mapmaking team, but the credit for the map, with its beautiful depiction of a landscape prepared for war, may have belonged to Clinton's replacement, the last British commander in chief, Sir Guy Carleton.

Carleton Takes Over

The third factor behind the British Headquarters Map's accuracy may have been Carleton's ambition. Carleton was technically Clinton's senior, having been made general four months before Clinton in 1763; he had served honorably in Canada, first under General Wolfe during the French and Indian War and then in defense of Quebec in 1775, but a bitter personal dispute with Lord George Germain, the American secretary, kept Carleton in Quebec and out of

top This detail from a 1778 map of King's Bridge, in northern Manhattan, shows the devastation brought to bear on Manhattan's forests during the Revolution, lamented by George Washington in 1781. Note also the indication of a spring and the names of the woods. *bottom* In the years after the war, liberated New York City rebuilt. This view of Wall Street from 1789 shows the Old City Hall, now Federal Hall, the former British headquarters during the hostilities and later the place where George Washington was sworn in as the first U.S. president.

the top British post in North America. In the darkening days of an unpopular war, however, Germain was sacked, thus giving Carleton an opening through which he could finally rise to the coveted post, though too late to have any real military impact.

The British Headquarters Map may have contributed to Carleton's and Clinton's relative places in history. Six reference notes on the map document Carleton all over the island preparing the city for an attack, which after 1781 was highly unlikely. "Sir Guy Carleton stops work on defenses"; "Sir Guy Carleton orders defenses extended to the right"; and so on, keyed with neat letters to locations on the map. Indeed, from a certain perspective, the map presents a testament to the energetic efforts of Carleton to defend a city and countryside flourishing even as it's being girded for war. A series of strategically placed, well-connected forts, bastions, and walls encircle the city; orchards stand in stately lines; mansions appear with formal gardens; fields are planted across the Harlem Plains—all seems well.

The problem was, all was *not* well with the city or the countryside. The city had burned twice during the war, once in 1776 and again in 1778, fires that left nearly half of New York City in charred ruins. Trinity Church would not be rebuilt until 1790. Similarly, the countryside was in bad shape. The winters of 1779/80 and 1781/82 were particularly harsh and frigid; the cold was so severe that New York Harbor froze solid enough for the British to drag their cannons from Staten Island back over the ice to the Battery in Manhattan. In the cold, the price of firewood skyrocketed, creating enormous pressure on the forests and standing wood of any kind. Orchards, fences, buildings, ships, and, of course, the remaining forest itself were consumed for firewood, desolating the landscape. George Washington personally reconnoitered the northern part of the island from the adjoining Fordham Heights in 1781, observing the scrubby wasteland where thick woodlands had once stood. He wrote in a letter, "[T]he Island is totally stripped of Trees, & wood of every kind; but low bushes . . . appear in places which were covered with wood in the year 1776."

The British Headquarters Map, accurate in so many aspects of the natural landscape, seems to have some significant omissions when it comes to the human landscape. To what end? It seems that in its final incarnation, the British Headquarters Map, begun as a mapping tour de force for Clinton, became a propaganda piece for Carleton's successful administration back in England. In a time before photographs, it was compelling visual testimony to his work. The map returned to England with Carleton's papers and passed from there eventually through the War Office into the British National Archives. (Clinton's papers, in contrast, eventually found their way into the archives at the Clements Library at the University of Michigan.) After the war, Carleton remained in favor, and was created First Lord Dorchester and reappointed governor of Quebec. Today he is remembered in the names of grammar schools across Canada and by Carleton University in Ottawa. Clinton was ignominiously forgotten, spending the last twenty years of his life writing a long, defensive account of his actions in America, resentful of his friends and colleagues. He is a footnote to history. We have no further record of the British Headquarters Map until Stevens gave it that name in 1900.

Whatever its origins and purposes, the British Headquarters Map is a remarkable record of Manhattan Island's landscape; the backbone of its ecology; and the canvas on which the nature of Mannahatta could be drawn, with specificity and precision. By placing the map in the modern geography and stripping away the eighteenth-century farms, fields, and towns, we have the opportunity to travel back in time toward the 1609 landscape, to envision what Hudson and his small crew had found. The British Headquarters Map means that we can frame the fundamentals of nature in the right places and in the right configurations, and thus take the first step toward discovering a new way of seeing what came just before New York City.

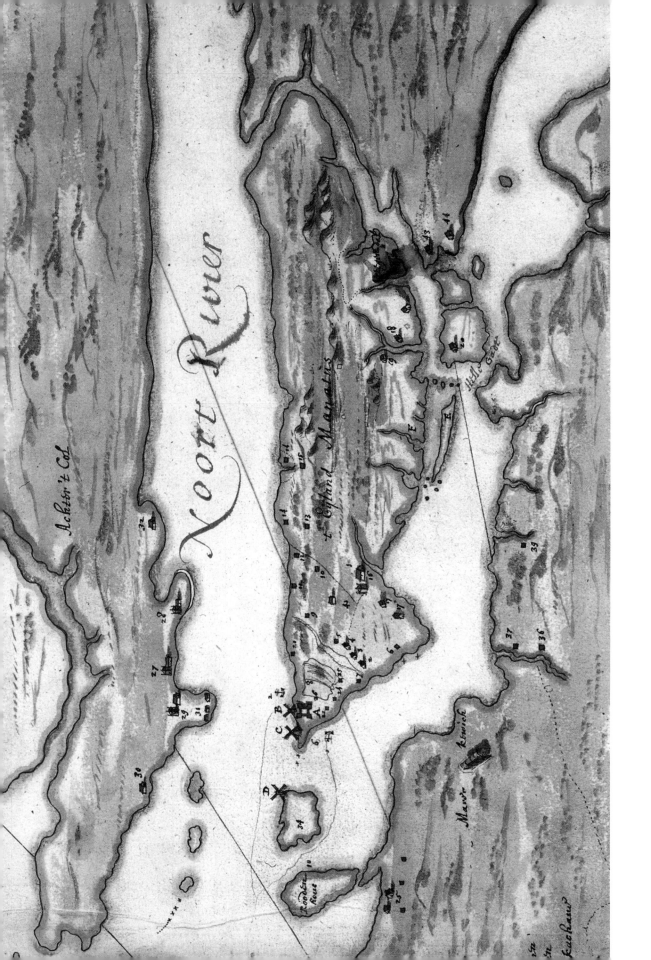

Chapter Three

The Fundamentals of Mannahatta

Along the seacoast the land is generally sandy or gravelly, not very high, but tolerably fertile, so that for the most part it is covered over with beautiful trees. The country is rolling in many places, with some high mountains, and very fine flats and maize lands, together with large meadows, salt and fresh, all making very fine hay land. It is overgrown with all kinds of trees, standing without order, as in other wildernesses, except that the maize lands, plains and meadows have few or no trees, and these with little pains might be made into good arable land....

— Adrian van der Donck,
   The Representation of New Netherland 1650

The Manatus Map, from 1639, is the first depiction of Manhattan as an island. Note in this transposed detail the prominent windmills, the tidal inlets, the Lenape settlement in Brooklyn, and the indications of Manhattan's hilly terrain.

On Wall Street, insiders often speak of the "fundamentals" of the market. Interest rates, the liquidity of capital, inflation, productivity, and consumer confidence are the bedrock of the economy. If the fundamentals are right, so it is said, we need not worry about the day-to-day ups and downs of the stock market or the success or failure of any one firm, for "the market is sound."

A similar argument holds for nature, although the fundamentals are of an altogether different kind. The fundamentals of nature are land and water, rock and wind, and their infinite combinations: hills and vales, ponds and brooks, ebb and flood tides, thunderstorms, snow showers and icy rivers, sunny days and gentle nights. They do not conveniently reduce to a balance sheet or a stock index, but they do integrate into a whole greater than its parts. Like economic fundamentals, if these basics of nature are functioning free from market manipulations, life will thrive.

Scientists, like most people, reveal their predispositions in the words they use. Ecologists call these fundamental characteristics of the landscape the *abiota*—literally "not-life," an unmelodious term at best. Geologists for their part refer to all the green stuff that ecologists study, the plants and animals and even the soils, as the *overburden*—the things that get in the way of seeing what is really interesting, the rocks beneath. But to see Mannahatta as it was, we need to look past these biases, to see the landscape as a whole, from the hidden bedrock to the tallest trees tossed in the wind and washed in the rain. We need to take the long view, and invest, as nature has done, in the fundamentals.

Thus, before we could delineate the life of Manhattan Island, we had to rough out the not-life—to know the geology and the topography (plus its underwater equivalent, the bathymetry), to reconstruct the climate and remap watercourses and their watersheds, and from these in combination, to derive the soils, the wind exposure, the tides, and the places where fires, floods, and other catastrophes might occur and where they might not, all to the scale of a city block. In each of these endeavors, the British Headquarters Map, with its full-island view of the hills, streams, and shoreline, was our essential guide. To this we added other maps and accounts, from Dutch times to the modern era, and used a bit of computer wizardry too, to realize the fundamentals of Mannahatta.

top This landscape painting by Victor Gifford Audubon shows the beach at Manhattanville, looking north along Washington Heights to Jeffrey's Hook, where the George Washington Bridge now crosses the Hudson River. The fishermen are bringing in American shad and striped bass. The man seated on the rock is the artist's father, John James Audubon, the famous wildlife painter, who lived on Washington Heights.
bottom This strange landscape, painted from life by Thomas Howdell, shows Greenwich Village looking south toward the city proper, in 1768. Notice the exaggerated topography, a representation of the now long-removed Sand Hills. The palm tree is ecologically inaccurate and was probably added later by an engraver in England.

The Many Lives of Manhattan

Manhattan Island is the result of titanic forces played out in slow motion. Whereas Wall Street tracks the market minute by minute, we, in order to understand the monumental forces that have shaped the fundamental geology of Manhattan, have to recalibrate our sense of time, to slow down to "rock time." What we experience as centuries amounts to just seconds on the cosmic clock of stone. Once we adjust our imaginations to rock time, then we can begin to understand the many lives of Manhattan. I won't dwell in the distant geologic past, but let's take a scamper through the millennia.

Ten thousand years ago, Manhattan was a hill beside a great fjord, the Hudson River canyon. Before that, Manhattan was a doormat to ice—at least twice in the last two hundred thousand years glaciers have bloodied Manhattan's nose and scraped off her skin. Manhattan has also been part of the seabed, and lain for hundreds of millennia in the crust of the earth, deformed by extreme heat and pressure. Manhattan has also been part of a mountain range, probably many mountain ranges, which over millions of years eroded away into rubble. Manhattan has had pimply volcanoes, spent a dissolute youth in the tropics, known Europe and Africa on intimate terms, and crashed like a hot rod (geologically speaking) into North America. Earthquakes, floods, drownings, and rebirths: Manhattan has known them all. Some of the rocks on the island today are over a billion years old.

The result of this history is laid down in the rock on which Manhattan is built. Most of Manhattan Island is underlain with schist, a rock derived from sediments in the seabed, then metamorphosed by heat and pressure. Strong, sturdy, and reliable, inky schist supports the pilings of most of Manhattan's skyscrapers. Closely related is Fordham gneiss, a slightly more twisted and consequently more lovely rock, noted for its curvy bands of lighter and darker minerals—originally sediments laid down over the seafloor. Gneiss is part of what makes Roosevelt Island so nice. Small areas of granitic pegmatite and granodiorite and the basic dikes found in northern Manhattan are all testament to volcanic activity, the result of molten rock cooled underground. Inwood marble is nearly pure white, and rarely seen above the surface because it is softer than other types and erodes so easily. Shaped from it are the humbler parts of the Manhattan landscape: the Harlem Plains, the lowlands around Sherman Creek, and the Lower East Side salt marshes—all formed where marble was the foundation.

Most of the city's bedrock lives unseen in the city's sub-basement, though outcrops were once exposed all over the island and can still be found scattered around town, especially in Central Park and other parklands. We can't see the bulk of the rock, however, because of the untidy habits of ancient rivers and, in more recent times, glaciers. The same glaciers that scraped the subsurface clean and gouged out the marble left in their wake dregs of scrambled, unconsolidated rubble, flotsam and jetsam gathered from all over New England and upstate New York and discarded when the ice melted away. Rocks, sands, and silts deposited by the flowing ice are called glacial till; they fall out in a huge, disorganized mess. Outwash deposits are what came out of the meltwaters of the retreating glaciers; huge ice blue rivers laid down horizontal beds of better sorted sediments. The last of the glaciers melted away into a lake 150 miles long and once extending from the Battery to Albany—glacial Lake Hudson, before it finally burst and blew out the Verrazano Narrows. The result of all this deposition is that the bedrock is more than 100 feet below the surface under most of Lower Manhattan; in some places it is more than 250 feet below. The foundation had been laid for the "overburden" to follow.

How High Were the Hills?

The Lenape called it the "Island of Many Hills," and the British Headquarters Map shows that, indeed, Manhattan was once a hilly place. But how high were those hills? The problem with the topography as drawn on the British Headquarters Map is that we have no idea how tall they were. Were they anthills or mountain ranges? The map was created before contour maps had been invented; instead, hills are depicted with shading, indicating vaguely their steepness and height. To turn the map's shaded relief into a computerized "digital elevation model" suitable for computer techniques, we needed to know exactly how high the hills were. Computers do not tolerate imprecision.

This problem stumped us for some time. In fact, it threatened to derail the project—and then I had a couple of lucky breaks. The first came while taking a geology walk in Central Park with the amiable Sidney Horenstein of the American Museum of Natural History, during the summer

top This engraving shows the northern side of Bayard's Mount, the highest elevation in Lower Manhattan, and a view of the Collect Pond and the city beyond, in 1798. *bottom* Eliza Greatorex drew this sketch of Arch Brook (also known as Saw Kill) on the eastern side of Manhattan in 1869, approximately where Seventy-fifth Street meets the FDR Highway today.

of 2004. Horenstein is a longtime observer of Manhattan's geology and other natural parts, and on this particular occasion, he was talking to a group of us on Umpire Rock, in southern Central Park, exhorting us to observe the glacial scratches on the outcrop, proof positive that where we stood had once been under ice. As I listened, I reasoned that if Umpire Rock had scratches made by glaciers fourteen thousand years ago, and if the same rock still had glacial scratches now, it must have had scratches in between, including in 1782, the year the British Headquarters Map was made. So, if I measured the elevation and position of this rock, I could compare it to the map and thereby begin the process of creating the digital elevation model.

Thus began my career as a stander-on-rocks. Along with a number of students, I have spent many a fine afternoon standing on Manhattan's large, glacially scratched outcrops, wherever we could find them, measuring their elevation with a barometric altimeter and their position with a GPS device. Central Park, Morningside Park, High Bridge Park, Marcus Garvey Park, and Inwood Park have all known us. Later we expanded our surveys to include eighteenth-century cemeteries, reasoning that, like the outcrops, ancient cemeteries have seen no drastic change in their elevations since first being constructed, and that they could thus provide us with useful elevation values for the southern part of town.

The second break came from *Manhattan in Maps*. A well-known source of early topographic information about the city is the set of Randel Farm Maps in the Manhattan Topographical Bureau. These maps were created by John Randel, Jr., a contentious and conscientious surveyor, whose work led to the adoption of the rectilinear streets that we know today as the New York street grid, a plan that would "provide space for a greater population than is collected on this side of China," according to its makers. Randel began his work in 1808 for the state-appointed commissioners, Simeon De Witt, John Rutherford, and Governeur Morris, preparing a proper survey of the island that would allow the commissioners to plan the future expansion of the city. In 1811, they published their "comprehensive and permanent" Commissioner's Plan, which defined the grid, and then contracted Randel to actually make it happen, placing markers to indicate where the streets would eventually go. Randel and his crews fanned out across the island of farms, woodlots, and small villages, relentlessly mapping avenues a hundred feet wide, interlaced with 155 streets sixty feet across. In places they found the woods "impassable without the aid of an ax"; they were chased by dogs, sometimes arrested, and once attacked by a furious woman throwing vegetables. As Randel described it, "I superintended

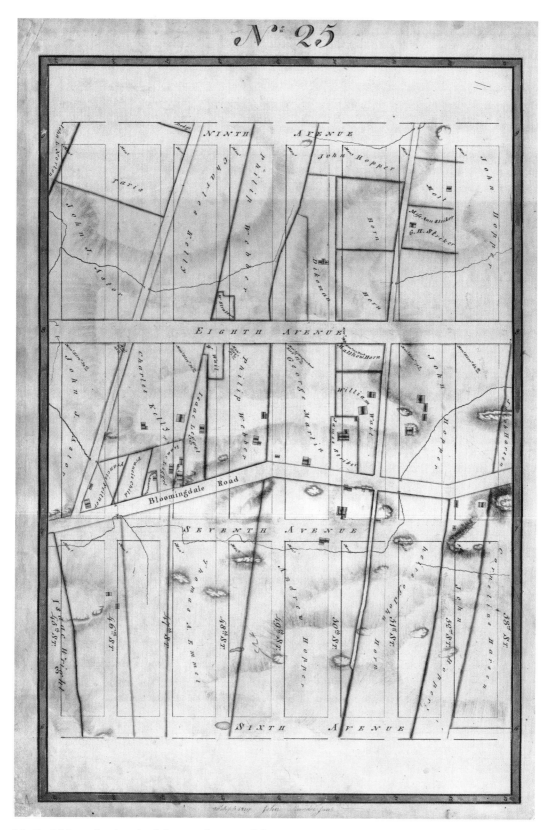

John Randel, Jr., produced a series of ninety-two "Farm Maps" showing property lines and owners in the early 1820s; natural features like streams, ponds, hills, and rocks; and the future street grid of Manhattan. Farm Map number 25 shows the area just north of today's Times Square.

the surveys with a view to ascertain the most eligible grounds for the intended streets and avenues, with reference to sites least obstructed by rocks, precipices, steep grades and other obstacles."

When they came to a rock outcrop that stood in the way of a future street, they placed a steel bolt to mark it for destruction; 98 outcrops were so marked. They also placed 1,549 marble markers at the northeast corners of street-and-avenue intersections, to indicate where the future streets should run over the hills and valleys. When they were finished, Randel drew the Farm Maps on 92 numbered folio sheets, showing simple outlines of the rocks, streams, and coastline, as well as the property lines in force at that time (the "farms") and the future streets of Manhattan. He also noted the elevations at selected corners. One map, of Midtown, depicts a stream, a property marked as belonging to "J. Astor," and the future path of Seventh Avenue. If assembled together, the Farm Maps create a single map eleven feet wide and fifty feet long.

One day when reading *Manhattan in Maps,* I noticed an aside about Randel's field notes being found in the collections of the New-York Historical Society. I planned a trip to Seventy-seventh Street and Central Park West, and applied to enter the grand library under the glass atrium. With great enthusiasm, I received forty-two red leather-bound field notebooks, delicate with age, enclosing hundreds of pages of neat columns of numbers. The notebooks immediately presented difficulties. Randel had developed his own surveying methods using his own specially designed equipment; moreover, he had managed several teams of surveyors over a decadelong period (from 1811 to 1821), many of whom were somewhat less systematic than Randel himself in following the survey methods. (One notebook, for example, includes documentation of an assistant surveyor being fired on the spot.) Some notebooks presented long calculations to multiple decimal places; some surveys were obviously resurveys over the same streets. For a long time neither my colleagues nor I could figure out why Randel had also measured temperatures when measuring the angles. We later learned he measured temperature so he could adjust for small differences in the length of the survey equipment as it expanded in the sun. But the biggest problem was that all of the measurements were only relative— that is, they provided only the angle from one survey location to the next, but were not, as far as we could tell, clearly referenced back to a common datum, or starting point.

Delightfully, Tim Bean, a Columbia University student working with me on his senior thesis, unscrambled Randel's trigonometry enough to translate the oddly transcribed angles into vertical measurements, and through

preceding pages

left The Collect Pond was the most important natural feature of Lower Manhattan. Probably a kettle pond formed when a retreating glacier left a large piece of ice in the soil, the Collect, or Fresh Water, was fed by underground springs, and supplied streams that drained into both the Hudson and East rivers. *right* Today this same area is the center of city government. Canal Street, which runs through Chinatown, was built over a canal dug to drain the Collect.

the efforts of Bean and others over the course of years, we eventually transcribed the lot. The result was over five thousand elevation measurements that we were able to both locate on the street grid and relate to known elevations on the Farm Maps. Apparently the notebook collection at the New-York Historical Society is incomplete, because the resulting survey lines are incomplete; nevertheless, many of the observations are placed within fifty feet of the next, providing a previously unknown level of topographic detail about the early nineteenth-century landscape.

After years of work, we finally had all the information we needed to produce the digital elevation model of Mannahatta. We took the GPS/altimeter survey data we'd gathered from the city's rocks and cemeteries, elevations from Randel's Farm Map and the associated notebook data, additional surveys from northern Manhattan, and a collection of anecdotal observations from written accounts, and, using the GIS, laid them down across the georeferenced British Headquarters Map. We contoured the entire island, hill by hill, valley by valley, drawing lines at ten-foot intervals, adjudicating on the fly between the various data sources. We also drew on landscape ecology, noting that the heights of salt marshes indicate the limits of the tides, that marshes and other wetlands are generally flat, and that, of course, streams must run downhill.

Now we knew not only that Mannahatta was a hilly place—573 hills in total—but also how high the hills were. The maximum height on Manhattan is and was in Bennett Park, in Washington Heights, where Fort Washington had once been located, at 268 feet. In Lower Manhattan, where the Dutch first settled, the hills were low, hardly more than thirty feet tall, but high enough to exercise the burghers' legs and to provide a venue for streams. Verlettenberg, the hill near the bronze bull at Bowling Green that had caught my attention on the British Headquarters Map, was, as it turned out, twenty feet high. It had once provided children with enough of a slope that merchants in the 1640s had to pass an ordinance against reckless sledding. City Hall Park sits atop a small rise, and behind City Hall, an amphitheater of hills cradled the Collect Pond: the Kalck Hoek to the west was named for the plentiful oyster shells that once decorated its slopes; Bayard's Mount to the north was the highest hill in Lower Manhattan, at nearly 110 feet; and the gentle slopes that still rise to the east, led to Corlear's Hook, a prominent nose of land jutting out into the East River. Extending from TriBeCa along the edge of Greenwich Village and up to today's Astor Place was a string of hills known to the Dutch as the Zandtberge (the Sand Hills); the Sand Hills originally separated

TOPOGRAPHY AND BATHYMETRY

This map illustrates the topography and bathymetry of Mannahatta, as represented by a digital elevation model, in the Geographic Information System. Assembling this map required five years of research to fix historical elevations to exact locations. Elevations of selected features are listed to the nearest 10 feet relative to mean sea level. See Appendix A for more details.

LOCATION	ELEVATION (FEET)
Inwood Hill	230
Mount Washington	270
Jeffrey's Hook	60
Jeffrey's Hook Hole	-160
Laurel Hill	220
Washington Heights	130–270
Manhattanville Valley	20
Harlem Plains	20–30
Morningside Heights	100–150
Mount Morris (Snake Hill)	110
Little Hill	80
Great Hill	120
Hellgate	0–-60
The Ramble	110
The Dove	70
Dutch Hill	70
Murray Hill	80–100
Rose Hill	50
Sand Hills	100
Richmond Hill	50
Bayard's Mount	110
Kalck Hoek	40
Corlear's Hook	80
Verlettenberg	20
Buttermilk Channel	-40
Governors Island	30

ELEVATION IN FEET

-160
0
+270

0   0.5   1
MILES

These two lithographed views by George Hayward show the evolving topography of Manhattan in the 1850s. *top* This view in June 1858, looking south from the Arsenal Building at Sixty-third Street and Fifth Avenue, shows how the streets have been built up to a common grade. *bottom* The equipment available for altering the landscape of Manhattan in the past was mainly pick, shovel, and mule, as shown in this scene from the construction of Central Park, circa 1859.

FILL AND EXCAVATION, 1609–2009

This map of fill and excavation on Manhattan was created by subtracting the historical topography, circa 1609, from the modern. Patterns of fill are shown in gray and excavation in red. Only elevation changes of more or less than 10 feet were detectable; some changes may also be due to slight misalignments between the two digital elevation models.

Politically still part of Manhattan, Marble Hill has been topographically part of the Bronx since the construction of the Harlem Ship Canal in the 1890s and the subsequent filling of land in the surrounding valleys.

Although Washington Heights is still the hilliest portion of the island, a comparison of the modern topographic map with our reconstruction of Mannahatta's highlands reveals extensive changes.

The Great Lawn in Central Park occupies the former site of the old Croton receiving reservoir, sometimes called "Lake Manahatta" on old plans. A hill was taken away to build the rectangular lake, which is why the ball fields in that part of the park are flat and uninterrupted by rock outcrops.

Murray Hill's slopes can still be detected on roller skates or a bicycle when cruising along Fifth Avenue, near the entrance to the New York Public Library at Forty-second Street. The hill's once precipitous slopes have been softened by both landfill and land removal.

The filling of land around the once narrow tip of Lower Manhattan began during colonial times with the sale of water lots. Wharf entrepreneurs could purchase water adjacent to land from the City. (The City owned "the land" between low and high tides.) After filling the lot with garbage and earth, owners could build wharves into the East River.

Governors Island is three times its original size today because of landfill. Most of the fill came from the construction of the Lexington Avenue subway line.

ELEVATION CHANGE IN FEET

■ -174–-80	
■ -80–-60	
■ -60–-40	EXCAVATION
■ -40–-20	
■ -20–-10	
□ -10–+10	
■ +10–+20	
■ +20–+40	FILL
■ +40–+60	
■ +60–+80	

0   0.5   1
MILES

the rolling forests of the Village from the wetlands and stream courses of the southern end of the island. Farther north was Murray Hill, a large two-tiered structure, from which springs flowed north, south, east, and west. Dutch Hill was just north of Murray Hill, and a hill called the Dove sat north of that, in the East Fifties.

Central Park was built over a rocky, broken land, with numerous hills, some of which still exist today, including the Ramble, Vista Rock, and the Great Hill, in the northern part of the park. Standing at Central Park West and about 103rd Street, one can see where the Great Hill once extended into the Upper West Side and where the hill was reduced—as indicated by the remains of drill holes where the explosive charges had been placed. Interestingly, prior to the great competition for the design of Central Park in 1857, Egbert Viele, the city engineer, had put forward a plan that called for retaining much of the natural topography of the place. In defense of his plan, he wrote:

> The hills, the valleys and the streams are nature's penciling
> on the surface of the earth, rivaling, in their pictured grace,
> the most beautiful conceptions of the finite mind; to alter
> them, would be desecration; to erase them, folly! Upon a
> proper understanding of these features, and a proper appre-
> ciation of their beauty, depends the unity of the design.

Risking desecration and folly, the judges instead chose the plan of Viele's subordinate, Frederick Law Olmsted, and Olmsted's partner, Calvert Vaux, which prized an open, "natural" look along English pastoral lines over the craggy nature that actually existed on the site. This is not to say Central Park was entirely remade by the nineteenth-century landscapers; rather, what changes they made, they made with pick and shovel, mule and TNT. They could take a hill away or dam a stream, but they couldn't lift up a hill and move it thirty yards to the right. The sizable hills found in Central Park today indicate areas sourced in the original topography. The opposite is also true: The areas featuring the least topography today, around the Great Lawn or the Reservoir, for example, indicate the places of greatest topographic reduction.

But the highest heights of Mannahatta were reserved for the northern part of the island, as reflected in the names: Morningside Heights, Washington Heights, Harlem Heights, Laurel Hill, and Inwood Hill. Small promontories, in the greater scheme of things, but New York, after all, is a coastal place, and coasts tend to be low-lying. The highest elevation on the

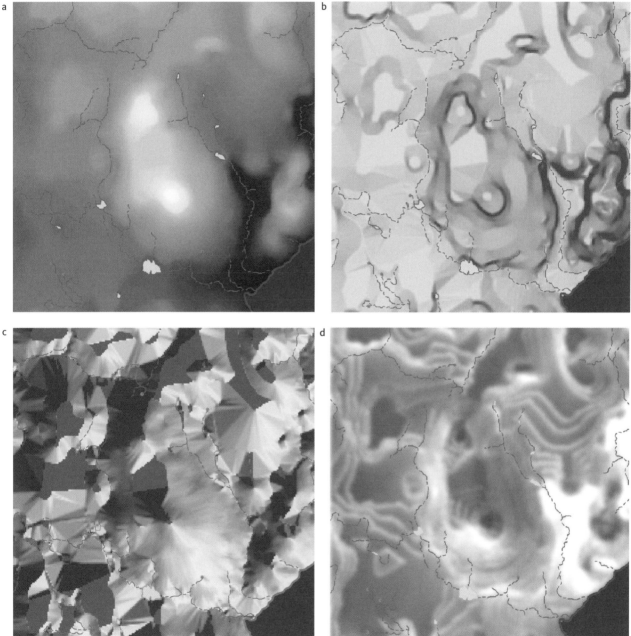

Digital elevation models, like the topography they represent, are fundamental to understanding the landscape. They can be analyzed to show (a) elevation, (b) slope, (c) aspect, or which direction the slope faces, and (d) wind exposure, in this case lighter areas are protected from northerly winter winds.

entire Atlantic Coastal Plain, from Florida to Cape Cod, is on Staten Island (Todt Hill, at 409 feet). That Mannahatta can't compare in height to the Rocky Mountains does not diminish its wonder, especially given that these are hills descending into the deep blue sea.

How Deep Were the Waters?

Rocks and hills are fundamental to a landscape, but they are nothing without water to enliven them. When it came to islands, the land that rises above the water, Mannahatta was far from the only island on the scene. Staten, Governors, Liberty, Ellis, Roosevelt, Ward, and Randall islands, and the western edge of Long Island form the archipelago on which New York City is built. (The Bronx is the only part of the city on the mainland, hence all the bridges, and all the traffic on the bridges during morning rush hour.) This archipelago is located in an estuary—that is, the place where freshwater meets saltwater; in this case, the massive freshwater Hudson River meets the tides of New York Harbor surrounding the island. The estuary has a three-dimensional seascape all its own, a set of hills and valleys and places where the currents prefer to run, an underwater landscape that defines the natural fundamentals beneath the surface.

Above water, the surface of the land is described by its topography, but below, that same surface is known as bathymetry and is measured in depths below average sea level. Fortunately, bathymetry is of intense interest to mariners, especially when its focus is the shallow waters that can catch a sailor unaware on the low tide; these shallow surfaces, where the water is thin enough for light to reach bottom, are also important ecologically. Sailors have left us charts of the bathymetry stretching back to the mid-eighteenth century, with intensive surveys beginning with the U.S. Coastal Surveys in the early nineteenth century. As with the British Headquarters Map and Randel's observations, we used this historical information to chart the bathymetry in the computer.

The deepest portion of Manhattan's waters is just off the highest part of the island, where a 145-foot hole exists in the Hudson River beneath the George Washington Bridge, just south of a point of land known as Jeffrey's Hook (home to the Little Red Lighthouse). During the Revolution, American patriots tried to hold back British warships by placing wooden obstacles in the water near the Hook; unfortunately, the spot they chose was at the narrowest—and deepest—part of the Hudson off Manhattan. Their defensive chevaux-de-frise sank more than a hundred feet below the bottom of the ships.

Lower Manhattan is blessed with deep waters just offshore; that depth, and the protected location, made the mouth of the East River a perfect harbor. New York Harbor was once over forty feet deep in the channel between Manhattan and Governors Island, according to our historical calculations, and nearly twenty feet deep just off Pearl Street, the former island's edge. Depths have changed subsequently because of landfill and dredging and altered currents caused by reconfiguration of the bounding land, conditions which are continually negotiated by the Hudson River's cleansing current, the action of the tides and the Army Corps of Engineers.

Also of interest to chart makers are the places where the water doesn't plunge so deep: sandbars, small islands, and drowned rocks. Up the East River from the harbor was trouble, especially just north of Roosevelt Island, where the pinching lands, fast tides, and obstructing rocks made "Hellgate" very hazardous indeed. The rocks themselves accrued names over time: Bald-headed Billy, Hen and Chickens, the Pot and the Frying Pan, Bread and Cheese, and the Hog's Back. Once, there was even a tidal mill sitting atop Mill Rock, just offshore of Ninety-sixth Street, which captured power from the churning water. (Other local tidal mills were found scattered through the wetlands of Red Hook in Brooklyn and Hackensack Meadows, nearby in New Jersey.)

The nineteenth-century technology that flattened the land of Manhattan also extended its good work into the sea. On October 10, 1885, the nine-acre Flood Rock met its maker in the largest human-caused explosion until the twentieth century's nuclear blasts. Over three hundred thousand pounds of explosives were used, resulting in tremors felt nearly fifty miles away, in Princeton, New Jersey. *The New York Times* wrote the next day that the event was yet "another triumph of human skill over the resistance of nature."

Complicating matters significantly is the fact that the rivers surrounding Manhattan are not exactly rivers as such; the East and Hudson rivers are more like extensions of the sea, rising and falling with the tides. By the same token, they are not exactly the sea either, surrounded as they are by the land that threatens to sunder them from the great oceanic expanse. Waters coming up the East River from the harbor meet waters coming through Long Island Sound, which have traveled separately three hundred miles around Long Island. Though arising from the same source, having traveled such distinct roads, they are out of sync by the time they meet again.

top Hellgate, shown in this nineteenth-century view from a garden where Gracie Mansion is today, was famous for its fierce currents, submerged rocks, and tidal fall. Differences in tidal level once created temporary waterfalls and whirlpools in the East River. *bottom* This idyllic scene from an 1852 Currier & Ives lithograph shows the Harlem River with the Macombs Dam Bridge connecting Harlem to the Bronx. Note in the distance the High Bridge, part of the Croton Aqueduct, carrying freshwater onto Manhattan, and the wooded shores of both Manhattan (left) and the Bronx (right) .

As a consequence, there are some very odd tides around Manhattan. The northern connection between the Harlem and Hudson rivers once experienced four tides per day (two high and two low)—one possible source of the name Spuyten Duyvil, Dutch for "Spitting Devil." Some early colonist may have reasoned that only the devil would sponsor four tides a day. In the East River, on certain tides, a tidal fall used to form where high-tide waters met low-tide waters, creating a standing waterfall over six feet high; whirlpools created by violent tides have also been reported off Manhattan. Prominent tidal rips—pockets of standing waves created by fast-moving currents abruptly changing direction—are still commonly seen in the East River. These rips mix bottom sediment into the water column, creating cover for species to hide, a nutrient-rich stew for plankton, and habitats for fish in the sea.

On the Hudson River side, the tidal dynamics are themselves complicated and enriched by the seasonal influx of freshwater. The Hudson River's watershed covers 13,000 square miles in New York, New Jersey, Connecticut, Massachusetts, and Vermont; some of its water has already flowed 460 miles before it reaches the Battery. In the spring the river discharges over 400,000 gallons of water per second to the sea, enough to create an ocean current of its own that extends along the Jersey Shore for 150 miles. Along the way, the freshwaters of the upland mix with the old, salty waters coming up the tidal river from the sea. The location of the "salt front" varies with the time of year, but it is generally north of Manhattan; Manhattan is always bathed in undrinkable brine. The majestic Hudson River transports not only water but also sediment into the estuary—between 400,000 and 1.4 million metric tons of it per year; in turn, the sea brings back between 139,000 and 734,000 metric tons of sediment into the harbor annually. By comparison, when the World Trade Center was constructed, engineers removed 1.5 million metric tons of sediment—approximately the same amount as the Hudson River carries in one year.

These sediments are mainly soil (in the form of mud) and sand. Sands are what previously formed and maintained the beaches on Manhattan's western shore. The British Headquarters Map shows sandy beaches extending from the Battery to Thirty-fourth Street and then forming pockets up the Hudson River side. The East River side had barrier beaches, junior cousins to those on Long Island's South Shore, which protected tidal wetlands on the Lower East Side and continued in pockets up to Harlem. Sandy beaches encircled 20 percent of Mannahatta's fifty-six-mile perimeter; the rest was broken into tide pools, teeming with life, and rocky strands.

Rich in Dirt

Soil is dramatically underappreciated in our civilization—to our detriment. Witness the connotations of words like *dirt*, *muck*, and *mire*; yet, without soil, an agricultural economy would be impossible, and without an agricultural economy, cities like New York would be impossible. Wendell Berry, the farmer-essayist, describes soil as "miraculous"; he writes: "A healthy soil is made by the life dying into it and by the life living within it, and to its double ability to drain and retain water we are complexly indebted, for it not only gives us good crops but erosion control as well as *both* flood control and a constant water supply." Think of that—a natural material that both absorbs the water it is not wanted and releases it when it is. No wonder the New York poet, Walt Whitman, wrote, a century before, that soil "gives such divine materials to men."

Mannahatta, as seems fitting given its diversity and abundance, was rich in dirt. The New York City Soil Reconnaissance Survey has identified eighty-seven different kinds of soil within the modern city, at a mapping scale of 1:62,500. Many of these modern urban soils have been modified by human activity, as is conveyed by their names: "Laguardia-Ebbets-Pavement & buildings, wet substratum complex"; "Bigapple-Fortress complex"; "Freshkills, geotextile liner substratum-Kleinekill sandy loams, 3 to 25 percent slopes." Soil descriptions of the modern city commonly include references to "coarse, anthropogenic materials"—that is to say, garbage.

Soils of the past, however, were made of different things. Soils are formed at the transition between ecology and geology, the boundary between ecosystems and earth. They are part rock, part decomposed leaves and roots, and part air spaces alive with millions of soil organisms—from bacteria and fungi to insects, worms, and moles—eating through the leavings of the lucky creatures in the sun, transforming our refuse into the foundation of plant and animal life. Soil scientists like to call soils "the living skin of the Earth." Plants like them so much that most bury over half their bodies in them (i.e., their roots), and in doing so, many have formed powerful cooperatives, called symbioses, with the fungi in the soil.

Hans Jenny, the famous American soil scientist, said that any soil could be completely described through reference to just five "soil-forming" factors: time, climate, topography, vegetation, and parent material (the rock beneath). We used these same principles to map Mannahatta's soils. Time over the breadth of the island is constant—approximately eighteen thousand years since the last glaciation. Climate, though changing through that time, has not

preceding pages

left The geomorphology of the eastern shore of Mannahatta was shaped by a combination of geological forces, the actions of the glaciers, and rising sea level. Historically these factors contributed to turbulent waters. *right* The Upper East Side landscape is shaped today by townhouses and business. The mayor's official residence sits in a park above the FDR Drive on the East River.

top Soil profiles show how soils vary with depth, depending on vegetation type, topography, climate, geological source, and time. These three soils were typical of Mannahatta's soils. The names are based on Natural Resources Conservation Service (NRCS) standard classifications: (a) Deerfield, (b) Charlton-Sutton, and (c) Pawcatuck. *bottom* This 1864 bird's-eye view of the newly created park in the center of Manhattan shows the transforming fundamentals of the landscape: new lakes and reservoirs, rerouted and buried streams, and altered hills and valleys. At the time, Central Park appeared more developed than the surrounding landscapes on the East and West sides, with their scattered buildings and emerging road networks, the latter serving carriages and horse-drawn streetcars.

changed from one part of the island to another, so it too can be considered a constant spatial factor. Topography we have from the digital elevation model. Vegetation we interpreted from ecosystems on the British Headquarters Map and historical accounts. Parent material, the name soil scientists give to the rocks from which the soil arises, we have from the surficial geology maps of what the glaciers, rivers, and oceans have left behind.

Combining these factors, we estimated that Mannahatta once had seventeen different soil types. We mapped those soil types according to standard classifications provided by the Natural Resources Conservation Service (NRCS), so we could take advantage of their extensive soil-properties database. Soils are described by their texture (referring to the particle size), organic material, acidity, moisture, fertility, and depth. They are composed of clays, silts, and sands, and intermixed with rocks sized as pebbles, cobbles, and boulders. Soils are essential to the habitats of plants and a variety of animals and we all depend on them, at least indirectly.

As it turns out, Mannahatta's soils were not particularly deep, having had only eighteen thousand years to form—it takes about forty years to form one centimeter of soil in our climate. Erosion, the churn of animals through the soil surface, the action of the glaciers, and the occasional fire seemed to have limited the soil depth as well. Many of the original Dutch farmers were disappointed with what they found on Manhattan; one wrote that the island was somewhat less fertile than other spots and gave more trouble on account of "the multitude of roots of shrubs and trees." Another felt that "most of the land was in need of manure; it was partly worn out by weeds." Their fundamental trouble, though, seemed to be having an inadequate number of horses and pigs from the old country to turn the leaves of the wild-growing plants into the manure requisite for European crops at the rate they desired. For their part, the multitudinous native forests seemed quite content.

The Brooks Above and Below

One thing the Dutch burghers were pleased with was the water. Mannahatta was copiously well-watered, with over twenty ponds, sixty-six miles of streams, and, it has been estimated, three hundred springs (we were able to locate only eighty-nine of these). These freshwater sources were essential to the colonization of the island; after all, Manhattan is an island in a saltwater

ORIGINAL SOILS

Soils are crucial to all plants and all organisms that depend on plants. Mannahatta's soils reflect the geological history of the island. This reconstructed soil map is based on analysis of geology, topography, and vegetation type and shows seventeen different soil series or types on Mannahatta in 1609. The names match soils mapped by the National Resource Conservation Service (except for rock outcrops and beach) and link to modern databases of soil properties.

SOIL TYPE	AREA (%)
Soils formed on glacial till	
Chatfield	38%
Charlton-Sutton	18%
Leicester	1%
Wotalf	<1%
Soils formed on glacial outwash	
Windsor	12%
Deerfield	10%
Pompton	5%
Plymouth	2%
Wareham	1%
Riverhead	1%
Cheshire	<1%
Soils formed in wetlands	
Ipswich	9%
Pawcatuck	5%
Pond muck	<1%
Rock outcrops and beach	
Rock outcrops	5%–15%
Beach	1%–3%
River rock	1%

Percentages do not sum to 100 percent because of rounding and because rock outcrop distributions were estimated separately from soil distributions.

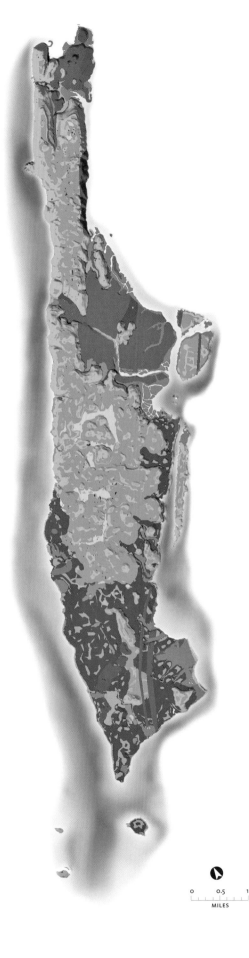

0   0.5   1
MILES

estuary, and most forms of life require freshwater. Mannahatta was blessed with so many ponds, streams, and springs because of a fortunate confluence of factors: a generously aquatic climate, an extensive green mantle that clothed it and slowed the floods, and a glacial history that left thick beds of sand and silt in its subsurface—a reservoir to hold the rain in aquifers for another day.

Streams are the conduits for water flowing aboveground; springs form where the underground water flow breaks the surface. Both are fed by rainwater and snowmelt. The rain falls, running down the leaves, stems, and trunks of trees and plants (known respectively as leaf flow, stem flow, and trunk flow; trees can hold up to nearly a quarter inch of rainfall, which is why they are a convenient place to hide when it begins to rain, but not later). As the rain penetrates the soil, the soil pores fill with water, holding a certain amount and letting more escape into the rocky subsurface; when the pores fill, the water runs off overland, following gravity into the lower places. These lower places connect according to the topography—small streams joining small streams to join larger ones, which eventually take the flow en masse through alternating patterns of pools, riffles, and runs, sometimes ponds and lakes, and finally to the sea. As we have seen with the Hudson River, the combined effect of thousands of small streams can be a deluge of water carrying large amounts of sediment; those metric tons of sediment begin as millions of individual small erosion events (the soil's gift to the rain) in the headwaters of the smallest streams. Streams marked on the British Headquarters Map or described in other historical accounts generally flowed year-round, supplied between storms with the aqueous reservoirs held underground. Other streams ran only ephemerally, after a rainstorm, for example, in some cases leaving small pools and ponds in the forest that dried over the summer. These so-called vernal pools were (and still are) habitats for frogs and salamanders, which enjoy a fish-free wet respite.

Mannahatta's streams have left their mark on the organization of the city streets, especially in Lower Manhattan. Broad Street, as is often written about, owes its breadth to the Dutch canal that once occupied the space, but before that, in its place was a small stream that wound through low marshy ground, fed by another branch that flowed along the line of Beaver Street (named for the beavers who called it home). Maiden Lane follows the former path of a small spring-fed stream that drained between two hills to the East River. Canal Street reminds us of the canal dug along the line of the outlet stream to drain the Collect Pond and salt meadows that ran to the Hudson

River shore. A bridge over the stream at Broadway and Canal Street was the original "Kissing Bridge" of Manhattan. Minetta Street in Greenwich Village was first a winding path alongside a stream called Minetta Water; Minetta Lane was named for the footbridge that crossed the stream.

Uptown streams drained through Times Square, along Sixth Avenue, and around either side of Murray Hill. In the high grounds of Bloomingdale (on the Upper West Side) and Central Park, numerous streams made a start on their mainly southeastward journey, reflecting the trend of the glacier that crossed the island in the same direction. The largest watershed belonged to the Saw Kill, which began within four blocks of the Hudson River, on the West Side, but eventually gave its water to the sea at East Seventy-fourth Street. The largest stream by volume was the partially fresh, partially tidal Harlem Creek. It too started nearly on the West Side, in the rough-and-tumble topography of the Narrow Way (also formerly known as Manhattanville, now known as West Harlem or the 125th Street canyon, where the No. 1 train emerges from the rocks of Morningside Heights, crosses a bridge, then enters a tunnel into Washington Heights). Once emerging from the hills, Harlem Creek shot straight as an arrow across the plain (just as 125th Street trundles across Harlem) to a deep tidal inlet near today's Harlem Meer, in Central Park. Numerous small streams drained off either side of Morningside and Washington Heights, in short, steep runs—some marked by waterfalls— before reaching home in the Hudson and Harlem rivers. Farther north in the Inwood section, Sherman Creek and its attendant marshes captured the water flowing down Inwood Hill, Laurel Hill, and Mount Washington before delivering it to the Harlem River and sinuous Spuyten Duyvil Creek, both themselves extensions to the sea beyond.

Natural reservoirs of water aboveground, lakes and ponds are the places where water collects to a regular depth. Although Manhattan did not have lakes as such, it did have several ponds, most important of which was the Collect Pond, in Lower Manhattan. The Collect Pond—also known as the Collect Water, the Fresh Water, or the Kalck—was the main freshwater source for New York City for its first two hundred years, from the first Dutch days until after the American Revolution; prior to that, a Lenape site existed on the pond's southwestern edge. The Collect seems to have been a kettle pond, formed when a large block of ice broke off and was abandoned by the retreating glacier; the block of ice creates a space in the subsequent glacial outwash before eventually melting away, leaving a large gap in the sediment perfect to form a pond. Seventy feet deep and fed by underground springs sufficiently abundant to keep the water "fresh," even though the pond surface was only about ten feet above sea level, the Collect Pond's embellishments included rumors of a Loch Ness–type sea monster that reputedly seized a Hessian soldier during the Revolution. Fishing was such a passion for early New Yorkers that in 1734 the City Council was forced to enact fishing regulations; from then on, only rods and reels, and not nets, were allowed when fishing in the Collect. Other ponds on the island included the Little Collect, beside the big Collect; Sun-fish Pond and Rose Hill Duck-Pond, south and north of Murray Hill, respectively; and the Stuyvesant Skating Pond, in the East Village.

The waters that flowed into these ponds often came from springs. The greatest commentator on the "active" and "bubbling, wholesome springs on Manhattan Island" was James Reuel Smith, who, after a successful career as a merchant on Front Street, found a second career peddling his bicycle around Manhattan Island and the newly formed borough of the Bronx to measure, photograph, and document the condition of springs and wells as he found them between 1898 and 1901. Apparently he took to his chosen task with relish, as revealed in the following passage from the introduction to his book on the subject:

> Greatly satisfying indeed is the draught from a spring where none is said to exist, and which has been come upon after patiently and inductively following a trail marked only by a moistened stone here, a willow farther on, and then a piece of watercress. . . . Springs are attractive not only to the thirsty traveler, but also to the artist, the photographer, and the lover of pretty nooks and rustic scenery. In general the Spring seems to delight in picturesque surroundings, and its moisture freshens and encourages neighboring vegetation, and offers attractions that allure the denizens of the pasture whose presence redeems the solitude from loneliness without disturbing the restful stillness that soothes the admiring wayfarer. A city spring frequently possesses all the beautiful surroundings of a rural one, and besides exciting that pathetic interest aroused by something pleasurable which will shortly cease to exist, it is, for the meditative, a link which connects the thoughts with the past.

STREAMS, PONDS, AND SPRINGS

Mannahatta's waterways consisted of sixty-six miles of streams, over three hundred springs, and twenty-one ponds and salt pannes, of which a selection are shown here. See Appendix A for more details.

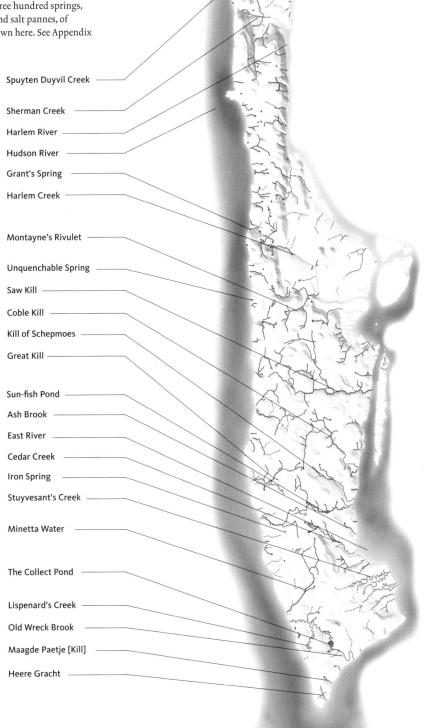

Spuyten Duyvil Creek

Sherman Creek

Harlem River

Hudson River

Grant's Spring

Harlem Creek

Montayne's Rivulet

Unquenchable Spring

Saw Kill

Coble Kill

Kill of Schepmoes

Great Kill

Sun-fish Pond

Ash Brook

East River

Cedar Creek

Iron Spring

Stuyvesant's Creek

Minetta Water

The Collect Pond

Lispenard's Creek

Old Wreck Brook

Maagde Paetje [Kill]

Heere Gracht

WATERWAYS

------ Intermittent streams

——— Permanent streams and creeks

● Springs

▇ Ponds

0   0.5   1
MILES

Though now less common than in Smith's day, springs can still be found in parklands around the city. Tanner's Spring, for example, still bubbles in Central Park near West Eighty-second Street, and Cold Spring provides a bathing pool to birds in Inwood Hill Park. Others no doubt surge under buildings and among the subway tunnels—though it can be difficult to differentiate a spring fed by the rain from a spring fed by a leaky water main.

The Changing Climate

Land and water are two of the great currencies on earth; the third great currency is the air. The interaction of these currencies is what creates the climate, and climate is what connects them (and, as we have recently learned, us) in a virtuous circle. *The weather* describes the daily goings-on of the atmosphere as reported every night on the evening news: the high and low temperature of a day, whether it snowed or rained and how much, whither the wind blew and how lustily. *The climate* describes the pattern behind the day-to-day transactions of the weather: the long-term trends in the weather of a given place, when the temperature will rise and fall that give meaning to the seasons and set the basic parameters for life.

Consider this: How much it snows or rains determines what is available for plants and animals to drink and if springs and streams flood or evaporate. Whether the temperature was above or below the freezing point determines whether the water in all things will be liquid or solid. Liquid water flows into cracks and down slopes; solid water (ice) expands with a force that can crush rock or the cells of frozen organisms. The strength and direction of the winds determines which birds will come, which trees will stand, the number of clouds, and the height of the waves crashing on the beach. If land is the stage and water the enlivening force, then climate is what describes what play is on and who can act.

The air is always in motion, driven by the planet's rotation on its axis and the amount of sunlight (and therefore heat) that different parts of the planet receive depending on latitude and season. Variability in movements of the air is what creates the weather. In New York the day-to-day weather is highly changeable, depending on the interactions of air masses arriving mainly from the west, the north, and the south. The jet stream drives westerly air across the country, so that the same storm can bring rain to Sacramento,

Kansas City, and then New York. Arctic air masses cooled at the North Pole descend when the jet stream shifts south, opening the door for Canadian cooling and lower humidity; by the same token, when the jet stream shifts north, warm, humid air from the southeast comes north, bringing tropical days and sultry nights.

Over winter, when Arctic pressure dominates and the sun declines toward the southern horizon, the frozen land drives the cycle of migration or adaptation. Living things that can, leave; those that can't, adapt; and those organisms for which neither path is an option, freeze and die—including the organisms that cause disease to others. A harsh cold snap, like a long winter's sleep, restores the health of the land.

Disturbances in the weather, also known as storms, can arrive on any of these tracks; when two disturbances arrive simultaneously, Manhattan receives what is prosaically called "a major weather event." These take many forms. Thunderstorms commonly crash over the summer, when charged air from the South meets a cool disturbance from the North. Famous nor'easters actually originate in southern climes, with low-pressure systems formed off the coasts of the Carolinas that are whipped up by Arctic winds and energy to lash the mid-Atlantic and New England states. Once in motion these storms track up the Atlantic seaboard, delivering heavy snows and ice, typically in winter and early spring, but sometimes in fall. Caribbean hurricanes can also reach New York and are important to the long-term disturbance dynamics of forests in the region. Hurricanes begin as tropical storms off the west coast of Africa and track across the Atlantic Ocean north of the equator before tilting north. Some track through the Caribbean toward Central America, some through the Gulf of Mexico to Texas and the Gulf States, and some track to the North. Generally by the time these storms reach New York they have lost some of their youthful power and arrive merely as tropical storms—with winds of thirty-nine to seventy-three miles per hour and sustained rains. Fortunately, recessed as Manhattan is in its harbor, and protected by western Long Island on one side and coastal New Jersey on the other, the probability of the island taking a direct hit is relatively remote, though not zero.

Given the variability of the weather in New York from one day to the next, the consistency of the climate from month to month is remarkable. Though it is hard to predict which days will see rain, on average from 1859 to the present, New York has received about four inches of precipitation per month, slightly more in summer and winter, and slightly less in spring and

top Manhattan is still an island, shaped by the land and the sea, as much as its edges have been hardened with concrete and asphalt. Climate change ensures that further changes to the Manhattan landscape are still to come. *bottom* This photograph from the hurricane of 1938 shows the storm surge at Battery Park, on the southern tip of Manhattan.

fall. Such equanimity of moisture is a godsend to plants and the animals that depend on them, and to the fish that need regularly flowing streams to live in. Like an investment that yields a consistent return month after month, New York's climate has long paid dividends to the local environment.

Which leads one to wonder what happens when the fundamentals shift. The climate, as we know, has changed on a worldwide basis as a result of human activity; in New York alone, the twentieth century saw a 2°F increase in average temperature. New York is a city built on a series of ocean-wrapped islands, and the sea is coming closer, rising around us by an average of 0.1 inches per decade over the last century. Predictions vary, but all models indicate a continuing rise in temperature over the next century; the only question is how much. The current range is estimated at +2.2°F to +10.2°F by the 2080s in the New York City region, with precipitation changes between -15 percent and +30 percent. With that will come rising sea levels and increased threats from higher storm surges—the sea may yet be coming to our doorstep, reconfiguring once again the shape of the island. The fundamentals of rock and sediment, tide and water, soil and wind are not done with Manhattan yet.

Chapter Four

The Lenape

In liberality they excel, nothing is too good for their friend; give them a fine Gun, Coat, or other thing, it may pass twenty hands, before it sticks; light of Heart, strong Affections, but soon spent; the most merry Creatures that live, Feast and Dance almost perpetually; they never have much, nor want much: Wealth circulateth like the Blood, all parts partake; and though none shall want what another hath, yet exact Observers of Property.

— *William Penn's Own Account of the Lenni Lenape*
   or Delaware Indians 1643

This photograph from Kansas, circa 1900, shows a Lenape dancer dressed as the Mesingholikan, an incarnation of the spirit who negotiated between people and the spirits of animals they killed.

One of the wonders of New York, perhaps the main wonder, is her people. Opinionated, quick with a word, insistent on getting ahead, generous in a pinch, New Yorkers are, nearly to the last individual, a tremendously alive bunch. It seems impossible to live in New York and be boring, or be bored—there is always something or someone to irritate, titillate, or stimulate you into action. Love it or hate it (arguments can be fairly made on either side), New York culture is a mind-altering experience. It can be a bit much, but when it works, it works like nothing else to please the human animal.

That New York culture is so vibrant today sometimes obliterates the fact that there are other ways to please. Before the whole party got started in 1609, there was another way, equally distinctive, for people to live on Manhattan. The first New Yorkers (to label them with a term they would not recognize) were the Lenape, also known as the Lenni Lenape, or Munsee, and later as the Delaware. In their language, Lenape meant the "the Real People"; to their peers in the region, they were honored as the "Ancient Ones," respected as the oldest of the northeastern Algonquin cultures.

Much of what we can say about the Lenape on Mannahatta comes from a composite of archaeological evidence, historical anecdotes, folk etymologies, interviews with modern Lenape, and inference from other places. Which is to say, what we know for certain is really very little. Knowing so little has not been an impediment to saying a lot on the subject, however; the historiography of Mannahatta's original people is a minefield of introduced terms, extrapolations, and poorly documented conclusions. One archaeologist of the region warned me in stern terms, "We know nothing about 1609. We *can* know nothing."

Having to rely on inference, though, is the archaeologist's stock-in-trade; indeed, it is a distinguishing aspect of any mature science. Debate over what can be safely inferred, what is possible but needs further study, and what is reaching too far is part of what makes science so much fun, as long as we don't take ourselves too seriously, and we maintain a willingness to be surprised. Many of the ecological particulars of Mannahatta, as you will have already concluded, are based on inference—extrapolating from general principles to specific conditions. We don't know for sure. But extrapolating soil distributions does not carry the same feeling as extrapolating conditions for people—with people we really want to get it right and feel guilty if we don't.

So what can be generally, and therefore safely, said about the seventeenth-century Lenape? We know that when Hudson arrived they lived in a traditional homeland that stretched from the edge of modern-day

Lapawinso, shown in this painting from the 1730s, was a Lenape sachem from eastern Pennsylvania. Note the tattoos on his forehead, cheek, and neck.

Connecticut to Delaware, including nearly all of New Jersey and most of southeastern New York—an area that has since been labeled Lenapehoking. Across this area, the people lived in small bands, moving from place to place with the seasons, following the available food supply. They were hunters and gatherers, hunting with bow and arrow and spear, and undoubtedly intimately familiar with the fruits, berries, leaves, and nuts of the region. They were also great fisherfolk, especially during the spring runs of alewife, eel, and shad returning from the sea, and relied heavily on the abundant shellfish resources (especially oysters, clams, and freshwater mussels) of the region, with the result that shell middens, large piles of discarded shells, are found wherever the Lenape were once found. However, the Lenape of New York also knew horticulture based on Mesoamerican crops: corn, beans, and squash, traded up from Mexico. Just how much they depended on these crops, though, as we will see, is a matter of debate.

The Lenape also had an elaborate belief system that passed from community to community through itinerant storytellers. It is to the Lenape and other Algonquin peoples that we owe the legend of North America as Turtle Island. They did not have money or property in the sense that we know it; they did not have a written language. They did not always get along. Yet they had lives founded in community and family and place that allowed them to persist for longer than New York City has persisted on the shores of Mannahatta.

The Manahate, Rechgawawank, and Wiechquaeseck

Naming people, any people, is confusing, because we all carry so many different affiliations. So too with the Lenape. Modern New Yorkers have political affiliations (e.g., Democrat, Republican, Libertarian, Green), geographic affiliations (e.g., Lower East Side, Upper West Side), cultural affiliations (e.g., Puerto Rican, Eastern European), religious affiliations (e.g., Catholic, Jewish), and linguistic affiliations (e.g., Spanish-speaking, Arabic-speaking, Cantonese), not to mention family genealogies, social networks, and workplaces. We have so many different ways to identify ourselves that sometimes we lose our individual identities, so, in the postmodern way, we declare them virtually on social-networking websites.

The Lenape also had their affiliations, but their means of identifying themselves were fundamentally different than ours. For example, they did not

LENAPE SITES AND TRAILS

It is difficult to know with much certainty where on Mannahatta the Lenape lived or how many people there were; this map represents one hypothesis compiled from the available evidence and inference. All numbers are speculative and based on estimated maximum population sizes in summer. Lenape names from the seventeenth century are shown where known; sites for which the Lenape name is unknown are supplied with names in square brackets. Native American names of later date are shown in quotation marks and may be of questionable authenticity. See Appendix B for additional details.

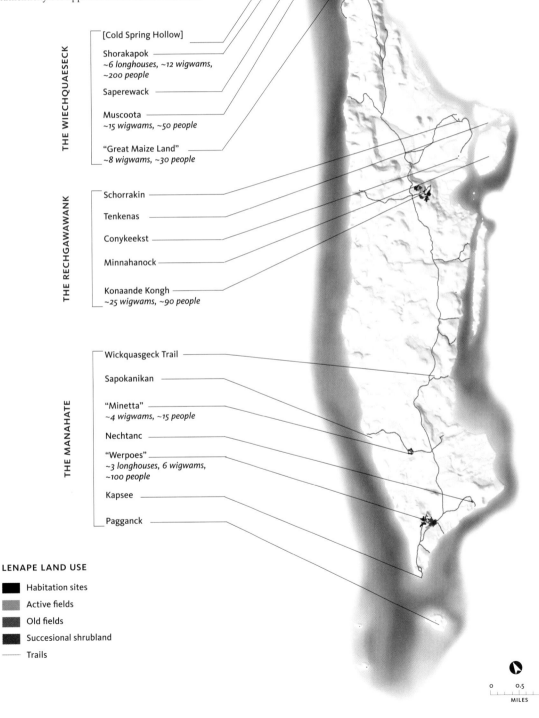

THE WIECHQUAESECK

[Cold Spring Hollow]

Shorakapok
~6 longhouses, ~12 wigwams, ~200 people

Saperewack

Muscoota
~15 wigwams, ~50 people

"Great Maize Land"
~8 wigwams, ~30 people

THE RECHGAWAWANK

Schorrakin

Tenkenas

Conykeekst

Minnahanock

Konaande Kongh
~25 wigwams, ~90 people

THE MANAHATE

Wickquasgeck Trail

Sapokanikan

"Minetta"
~4 wigwams, ~15 people

Nechtanc

"Werpoes"
~3 longhouses, 6 wigwams, ~100 people

Kapsee

Pagganck

LENAPE LAND USE

- ■ Habitation sites
- ■ Active fields
- ■ Old fields
- ■ Succesional shrubland
- —— Trails

0   0.5   1
MILES

Table I.

Selected animals and plants likely used by Lenape living on Mannahatta

COMMON NAME	SCIENTIFIC NAME	USE [ANIMALS]
American shad and other herring	*Alosa sapidissima, Alosa aestivalis, Clupea harengus,* etc.	American shad and other spring-run herring, a great relief after the hardships of winter, were caught in great numbers, dried or smoked, and consumed throughout the year.
American eels	*Anguilla rostrata*	Eels were caught in fall (when adults return to the sea), using weirs mounted at the mouths of streams. They were skinned, and excess eel meat dried for winter.
Oysters	*Crassostrea virginica*	Oysters were consumed in large numbers. Shells were used to decorate clothing; sharp-edged ones as cutting tools.
Clams	*Mercenaria mercenaria, Mya arenaria,* etc.	Lenape gathered and ate clams and used the shells as spoons, ladles, and other tools. Sharpened shells were used for scraping and cutting. The Lenape and other Native American groups on Long Island created wampum, necklaces of beads carved from the inner whorl of the quahog (*Mercenaria mercenaria*), which were used as a currency of respect throughout the Northeast.
Blue mussels, lobsters, crabs, and other shellfish	*Mytilus edulis, Homerus americanus, Pecten irradians,* etc.	Mussels and other shellfish provided a year-round food source. Lobsters, though scarcely referenced in the archaeological records, are mentioned in ethnohistorical accounts of the region. Shells were discarded on-site, creating shell middens, which collected in some places to over fifteen feet deep.
White-tailed deer	*Odocoileus virginianus*	Deer and related ungulates (elk, moose, and possibly bison) were prized for their meat, hides, and antlers.
Black bears	*Ursus americanus*	Black bears were hunted for their fur, meat, and claws, but most of all for their grease, which was used for cooking and as an ointment.
Ducks, geese, and other birds	Various kinds	Ducks, geese, and other medium- to large-sized birds were hunted and their eggs collected for food. Feathers of raptors, cranes, and herons were used to decorate robes and other items.
Fishes	Various kinds	Both salt- and freshwater fish were caught in season, including cod, weakfish, bluefish, striped bass, sturgeon, flounder, hake, mackerel, brook trout, pickerel, and perch. Large sturgeons were likely speared or harpooned, being too strong and armored for nets.
Frogs	Various kinds	Frogs, both fresh and dried, were consumed.
Snakes	Various kinds	Snakes, both fresh and dried, were consumed.
Turtles	Various kinds	Turtles were eaten, and their shells sometimes used for rattles and other instruments.

COMMON NAME	SCIENTIFIC NAME	USE [PLANTS]
Bluestem grass	*Andropogon gerardi*	Bluestem grass was valued for its mold-resistant properties; it was used to line beds and storage pits dug in the soil.
Indian Hemp	*Apocynum cannabinum*	Indian hemp fibers were twisted inot cordage and used for nets.
Jack-in-the-pulpits	*Arisaema triphyllum*	The roots of jack-in-the-pulpits were dug up and eaten.
Milkweeds	*Asclepias* spp.	Milkweed fibers were used for nets.
Hickories	*Carya* spp.	Hickory nuts were collected in fall, especially after large "mast" events occured, when trees would drop all their nuts nearly simultaneously.
Chestnuts	*Castanea dentata*	Chestnuts were gathered and eaten in fall; their bark and saplings were used to construct wigwams, and their trunks hollowed out to form large dugout canoes.
Goosefoots	*Chenopodium* spp.	Goosefoot seeds were collected to make flour.
Common persimmons	*Diospyros virginiana*	The fruit from common persimmons was consumed.
Wild strawberries, huckleberries, blackberries, blueberries, and cranberries	*Fragaria virginiana*, *Gaylussacia* spp., *Rubus* spp., and *Vaccinium* spp.	These berries were gathered and eaten.
Bedstraws	*Galium* spp.	The fragrant leaves and stems of bedstraws were used in bedding.
Jerusalem artichokes	*Helianthus tuberosa*	Tubers of these sunflowers were dug, dried, and pounded into flour.
Red cedars	*Juniperus virginana*	The berries of red cedars were eaten and also used in sweat baths, along with sage and mint leaves and goldenrod flowers.
Tulip trees	*Liriodendron tulipifera*	The trunks of tulip trees were carved to form dugout canoes.
Indian tobacco	*Nicotina rustica*	Tobacco was cultivated and ceremoniously smoked.
Pokeberries	*Phytolacca americana*	The red pigment of pokeberries was used for body decoration.
Wild cherries and plums	*Prunus* spp.	Wild cherries and plums were gathered and eaten.
Oak trees	*Quercus* spp.	Acorns, also a mast species, were mashed and boiled to remove tannins (sometimes by cooking with wood ash), then made into flour.
Currants	*Ribes* spp.	The fruits of currants were gathered and eaten.
Common elderberries	*Sambucus nigra*	Elderberries were gathered and eaten, and elderberry juice and tea from elderberry flowers were fed to babies for strength.
Skunk cabbages	*Symplocarpus foetidus*	Cabbages were eaten in spring, while succulent.
American basswood	*Tilia americana*	The fibrous inner bark of American basswood was used for cordage.
Cattails	*Typha* spp.	The roots of cattails were consumed, the light tufts of the seed heads used as baby diapers, and the fibers from the leaves used for cordage.
Elms	*Ulmus* spp.	Elm saplings and bark were used in the construction of wigwams.
Wild grapes	*Vitis* spp.	Wild grapes were gathered and eaten.

have political entities like we do; there was no chief of Lenapehoking like our president of the United States or mayor of New York City. It was only much later in their history that one could speak of a politically unified group of Lenape at all; in the seventeenth century, the small bands the Lenape lived in chose their own leaders, with no band owing allegiance to another except what was felt through ties of respect, kinship, and culture.

The Lenape recognized a different kind of lineage than most Americans do: They had phatries, or clan designations. A *phatary* is a belief in a shared lineage between people of the same clan, often to a remote, sometimes mythical, ancestor. Every Lenape person recognized membership in one of three dominant clans—the wolf, the turtle, or the turkey—which passed (along with everything else) through the mother's line. Marriage within the same clan was not allowed; a wolf could not marry another wolf but could marry a turtle or turkey. In every Lenape community there were people from all three clans, and there is evidence that each clan had ten to twelve subgenres, with names like "Yellow Tree," "Pulling up Stream," "Dog Standing by Fireside," "Green Leaves," "Old Shin," and (my favorite) the "Grand Scratcher."

The Lenape also identified themselves by where they lived and who they lived with. Although the exact relationships between the groups are not clear, it seems that there were at least three communities of Lenape on Mannahatta, which we call, for convenience (though not for ease of tongue) the Wiechquaeseck, the Rechgawawank, and the Manahate. The Wiechquaeseck were the most numerous of the groups and lived in northern Manhattan, the western Bronx, and northward into Westchester County, with a major center around Spuyten Duyvil Creek called Shorakapok; the Rechgawawank, named after a seventeenth-century leader, lived in Harlem and the Upper East Side and appear to have retreated to the central parts of the Bronx in winter, perhaps to villages along the Bronx River; the Manahate lived in Lower Manhattan and the harbor islands, with a small settlement near the Collect Pond. The Manahate were possibly connected to the Carnarsee living in nearby Paumanack (as Walt Whitman was fond of calling Brooklyn). All these groups must have had regular contact with one another, and with neighboring groups, including the Siwanoy of the eastern Bronx and Connecticut, the Hackensack across the river in New Jersey, and the Tappan and Sinsink of the Hudson Valley. In a wider arc were the Chappaqua of northern Westchester, the Massapequa of west-central Long Island, the Rockaway of south Brooklyn, the Raritan of Staten Island, and the hated Sankhikan of central New Jersey.

HABITAT SUITABILITY FOR PEOPLE

This map shows an extrapolation of habitat suitability for people on Mannahatta. It is based on known archaeological sites, listed in Appendix B, and habitat preferences as described below, using a maximum entropy algorithm. This map indicates that only two percent of the island was highly suitable and twelve percent of the island was moderately suitable for human habitation in the early seventeenth century, before modern economic relationships and technologies came to Mannahatta. See notes for additional details.

The Lenape preferred places protected from the winter winds, like the area around Sherman Creek in northern Manhattan, hidden behind Inwood Hill.

They also needed to be close to freshwater streams and lakes for drinking and washing water.

Although not ideal for long-term habitation, the Lenape almost assuredly hunted and gathered all over the island. They may have had favorite camping locations along streams and beside ponds, especially near places where important plants or animals were found.

The Lenape use the estuary waters for getting around on dugout canoes and for fishing, especially during spring's massive runs of fish returning to the Hudson River from the sea.

Mannahatta's original people preferred to live in flat areas with the best soils to grow their crops, like along the Collect Pond in Lower Manhattan.

HABITAT SUITABILITY

More suitable

Less suitable

0   0.5   1
MILES

All of these communities of people, though, were Lenape, sharing a common culture and most likely speaking a dialect of Lenape called Munsee.

We don't know for certain how many people lived in the communities on Mannahatta; estimates vary from three hundred to twelve hundred individuals, about the sidewalk population of one block on a busy afternoon in Midtown. Part of what complicates the estimation is that Mannahatta was probably not a year-round residence for most Lenape; rather, it was more of a three-season "resort." The Lenape moved to Manhattan for fishing in spring; stayed over to plant some crops, hunt, gather, and fish in the summer; then pulled together their things in a furious fit of activity in fall, bringing in the crops and smoking and drying the meat before the retreat to winter quarters. With New York's cold climate, winters were best spent with friends and family in large multifamily longhouses, telling stories, threading wampum, repairing nets and baskets, and staying out of the weather. A long, exposed island in the middle of the estuary was probably less desirable in winter than protected sites inland in the Bronx or Queens.

One consequence of this mobile lifestyle is that the Lenape owned only as much as they could carry. Although they were exact observers of individual property, there was no purpose in owning more than one needed; why bother having twenty deerskin cloaks when you could only use one at a time and would have to abandon the rest at the end of the season? The idea that one could collect wealth and store it, in an instrument like money, was foreign to them. Rather, what one could accumulate and carry was reputation and respect. Did a person share his meat with the community? Did a person listen to her neighbor and offer wise advice? Did a person remember the old ways and respect the elders? Even wampum, shell beads laboriously bored from clamshells collected on the shore, was a gift to mark respect on important occasions, not a currency of exchange, a practice later suggested by the Dutch. Such a social system worked well for a people with an abundant supply but geographically limited scope of resources, who lived in small communities where everyone knew one another, and for whom working together was essential for survival.

Following the archaeology and the history of place-names on Mannahatta, my colleagues and I reconstructed an approximation of the distribution of these communities as they might have appeared in September 1609. We created a computer model of Mannahatta's suitability for human habitation, using the locations of known Lenape artifacts to seed the model, and developing statistical predictors based on distance from freshwater, distance from the shore, and protection from the winter winds. We assumed a larger summer (six hundred) than winter (two hundred) population for the island, and apportioned the population to reflect the relative importance of Shorakapok and sites near Spuyten Duyvil Creek, in northern Manhattan, over sites on the eastern shore and near the Collect Pond—for the Lenape, Uptown was more important than Downtown. We estimated the number of wigwams and longhouses at each location, and, from these calculations, generated the approximate area of each site, matching to the archaeological and historical evidence where it existed. These sites we connected with a trail system that follows the scant evidence and fits the topography. And from these inferences we began to piece together Lenape life on the island of Mannahatta.

A Visit to Shorakapok

Walking down the center of Shorakapok on a fall day would have provided a lively sight. By all accounts, the Lenape were a handsome people. Van der Donck, the Dutch settler, wrote, "The natives are generally well set in their limbs, slender round the waist, broad across the shoulders, and have black hair and dark eyes. . . . The men generally have no beard, or very little, which some even pull out." Isaack de Rasieres, another settler, wrote, "[T]he women are fine looking, of middle stature, well proportioned and with finely cut features . . . with black eyes set off with fine eyebrows." William Penn agreed: "For their Person, they are generally tall, straight, well-built, and of singular Proportion; they tread strong and clever and mostly walk with a lofty Chin."

Not so different from many twenty-first-century Manhattanites, the Lenape liked to decorate their bodies. Tattoos were scratched onto arms, legs, chests, and faces with sharp flints and fish teeth, in designs representing animals, birds, serpents, or geometric figures. Body paint was important for festivals, ceremonies, mourning, and during war—faces, chests, and thighs were painted red with bloodroot or yellow and black with ocher and charcoal. The Lenape would sometimes paint one half of their face red and the other black, or their whole head red with black dots. During less auspicious times, they would grease their bodies with oil, like the ancient Romans. The English pastor, Charles Wooley, who visited the region from 1678 to 1680, described the practice: "They preserve their Skins smooth by anointing them with the Oyl of

The Lenape built wigwams, like this modern reconstruction in the New York Botanical Garden, from local materials. The interior arches were composed of bent saplings; the bark was stripped from old-growth trees in large sections.

Fishes, the fat of Eagles, and the grease of Rackoons, which they hold in the Summer the best Antidote to keep their skins from blistering by the scorching Sun, the best Armour against the Musketto's . . . and stopper of the Pores of their Bodies against the Winter's cold." They also rubbed clarified bear fat into their hair to make it shiny and silky smooth.

The Lenape lived mostly out of doors, but for protection from inclement weather and to rest during the night, they built wigwams and longhouse shelters. Wigwams were small conical buildings about fifteen feet in diameter, meant for a single family. Longhouses were larger structures, fifteen to twenty feet wide and sixty feet long; they might house seven or eight families. To build both, the Lenape buried tree saplings upright along the perimeter, then bent the saplings over to create an arched roof. They then lashed sapling crossbeams onto the structure horizontally to the ground, and covered the whole structure with overlapping sheets of tree bark, stripped from large old-growth trees, particularly American chestnut, but also elm and basswood. In some cases these bark sheets were six feet long and four feet tall, peeled carefully from trees in June, when the sap was running with full force. An outer frame of saplings might be built, especially for the larger structures, to hold the bark on tight during storms. Although sturdy, these structures were not meant to last forever; a well-maintained wigwam might last ten years before termites and wood-boring beetles would have their way with it.

Inside, wigwams and longhouses were dark and smoky, and space was limited. Sunlight entered only through the doors and through openings in the roof that served as chimneys; reed mats could be pulled over the holes in case of rain and snow. Pots of porridge or stews bubbled continuously over low fires, one for each family, to be sampled throughout the day. Longhouses were partitioned into sections, so that each family had its own space, with a center corridor connecting all. Small platforms, sometimes several levels high, were built into the side for sleeping and storage. Food was stored in pits dug into the ground, lined with bluestem and other grasses, and covered with stones, or hung from the sapling rafters. A family of four might have fifty square feet of space in the longhouse. With the neighboring family so close, privacy as we enjoy it today was probably unknown—yet another reason to spend time outside.

Outside there would be another fire burning, another pot stewing, large log mortars hollowed out for pounding corn or nuts with wooden pestles, huge piles of shells and other refuse, sweat lodges near the water, kids and dogs running all about, a few men lounging, and knots of very busy women.

top Coastal New York was an important center for the production of wampum, or shell beads, which were carved from the quahog clam and traded throughout the Northeast. *bottom* Hunting and gathering was essential to the Lenape way of life. This decoy of a large heron was found on Long Island.

Women labored near constantly, for they prepared the food, tanned the hides, cleaned the fish, sewed the clothes, made the pottery, planted the fields, and gathered the water, firewood, plant foods, and medicines. Men were responsible for hunting and, largely, fishing (though women also helped), and for building houses, making dugout canoes, crafting tools, growing tobacco, and felling trees. Both men and women worked in groups, for company and efficiency, often with the children. Children stayed close to their mothers when small, but as they grew older would begin imitating their parents at work. In the meanwhile, kids had lots of time to play. All the Lenape enjoyed sweating in small, sexually segregated wigwams designed for the purpose. They heated rocks over fires, then dropped them in baskets of water; when the heat became too much, they would dash to the nearest stream for a swim. The men smoked Indian tobacco and sometimes burned herbs and bark over fires to release a fragrant incense. Like people all over the world since the beginning of time, the Lenape also kept dogs, who provided constant companionship, spirit guardianship, and perhaps, when the occasion required, food. Special Lenape dog burials have been found in Inwood.

In these Lenape settlements on Mannahatta, everyone knew everyone else and everyone else's business; but of the larger world, especially the world outside the Northeast, they knew nothing beyond their stories. In that sense, their lives were intensely parochial and conservative. Hunting-and-gathering societies tend toward conservatism, because making a mistake—building a wigwam from the wrong saplings, eating a misidentified mushroom, being late for the fish run—can literally mean life or death. Best, in light of small margins of safety, to go with what has worked before. Yet the importance of tradition, the ignorance of the outside world, and the dangers of failure were the same factors that drove Lenape communities together, creating a cohesion and a sense of community life that must have been truly profound. With the benefits of working together so high, a mistake in human relations risked ostracism, even death. Best, when living in a small world, to go with your neighbors.

People as Landscape Species

Though Lenape communities were small, they exerted a dramatic influence on the Mannahatta landscape. Conservationists generally speak of plants and animals that create habitats for others, like beavers or corals or redwood trees,

top Amateur archaeologists, like William Calver, depicted here, excavated several sites in northern Manhattan between 1890 and 1930. This Iroquois pot indicates trading between the Lenape of Manhattan and people to the north. *bottom* Shell mounds, or middens, marked former habitation sites of Native Americans on Manhattan. This shell mound was discovered in Inwood around the beginning of the twentieth century. Shell mounds would have been a common feature of the Mannahatta landscape.

as landscape species; in this sense, people are probably the greatest landscape species that has ever lived. We build shelters, we farm the land, we construct dams, we pave parking lots, we erect skyscrapers; these structures destroy habitats for some species (e.g., wolves, mountain lions, wood ducks) and create habitats for others (e.g., rats, coyotes, pigeons). Most species adapt themselves to the environment by taking advantage of the aspects of the environment to which they are best fit. Human beings, because of our large brains and dexterous hands, do the opposite: We fit the environment to what is best for us.

The Lenape created the Mannahatta they desired through horticulture and fire. In older scholarship it is generally assumed that maize horticulture was the main food source for northeast Native Americans in the Contact Period, based on evidence of extensive fields found inland. Many of the early European explorers, including Hudson, wrote about trading for "Turkish wheat," their term for maize. However, in the 1970s a persuasive local archaeologist, Lynn Ceci, challenged this orthodoxy. She argued that for the people living in *coastal* New York, the environment was so abundant with resources that horticulture was an adjunct to the diet, not the primary source of calories. She argued along several lines of evidence. First, she noted that "flotation tests"—in which prehistoric fire pits or shell middens are flooded with water—floated relatively few seeds and corn kernels to the surface in coastal sites compared to inland sites. Second, she argued that the soils in coastal regions, generally sandy and rocky, are not particularly productive and would require a lot of work to till (an observation also noted by the Dutch). Third, she argued from ecological evidence that it really wasn't necessary for coastal people to adopt an agricultural way of life, given the year-round abundance of shellfish, fish, mammals, nuts, and berries. Other archaeologists corroborated these views by testing Lenape bones from local archaeological sites and showing that the Lenape primarily ate local plants, not maize, and a lot of seafood, and were generally healthy. (Adopting agriculture often leads to a reduction in the health of a population.)

Our research adds a couple of twists to Ceci's hypothesis. A Columbia University student, Daniel Sarna-Wojcicki, used a modern crop model to simulate maize horticulture on Manhattan, using representative soil types, climate, and maize varieties. He found that when maize was grown by itself, productivity was uneven, and there was a modest but significant probability of total crop failure each year. Soil nitrogen levels appeared to be the limiting factor. But the Lenape did not plant maize in monoculture, rather they practiced team planting (also known as multicropping); that is, they grew maize in combination with beans and squash—the traditional "three sisters" garden.

Beginning in late April, Lenape men cleared a plot of land by felling the large trees and burning the vegetation. Burning fertilized the soil with ash, which promoted plant growth by changing the soil chemistry from acidic to alkaline, releasing more nutrients. In early May the women created mounds and planted maize kernels saved from the year before. A few weeks later, they planted beans along the sides of the mounds and squash between. Over the course of the summer, the beans climbed up the maize stalks, using the six-foot stems as a ladder to reach the sun; in the meantime, the beans, which have nitrogen-fixing nodules on their roots, transformed nitrogen from the atmosphere into a natural fertilizer, which fed the maize and the beans. The squash, growing its large green leaves between the mounds, kept the weeds down and held in soil moisture between rain showers (the Lenape didn't practice irrigation). Crops were harvested from late summer until first frost, usually in October.

Modern crop models are generally not written to include team planting, because they assume monocultures—but they will accept inputs of fertilizer. We simulated nitrogen inputs from bean plants at three different levels and showed that even modest nitrogen support increased maize productivity, and, more importantly, enhanced the consistency of the crop. In our model simulations, maize rarely failed when grown with beans. Productivity, though, was still generally low, at about 700–2,300 kilograms per hectare.

How many people that level of productivity would feed depends, of course, on how large the fields were. As mentioned, gardening was a woman's responsibility, but women had many other tasks that would limit their time in the garden. The Lenape were not immune to the human-wildlife conflicts that bedevil suburban gardeners today—deer, squirrels, raccoons, and assorted other wildlife were pests in the fields. Keeping the animals out required diligence throughout the growing season; an older child, for example, might be tasked with sleeping near the fields to chase away the animals. We estimate, based on some observations made by the explorer Samuel Champlain on Cape Cod in 1613 (the nearest contemporaneous observation we could find to coastal New York) that when working together, women could maintain approximately 325 square meters (3,500 square feet) of garden per person. At this rate, and assuming that adult woman were approximately 25 percent of the population, Lenape gardens could have satisfied only between 3 and 20 percent of the annual calorie requirement on Mannahatta, just as Ceci had suggested. The

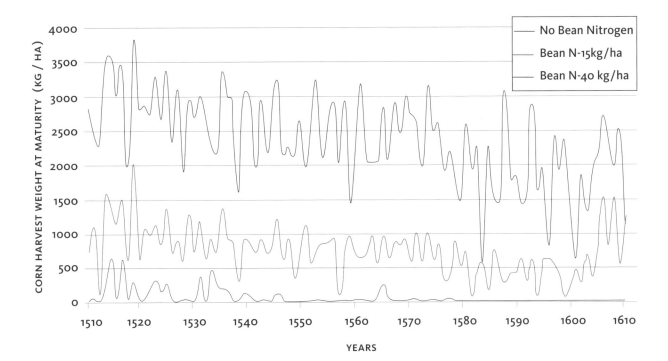

top Modern crop models were adapted to examine Lenape horticulture. These model results show the effects of different levels of bean-facilitated nitrogen on corn production over time. Grown with beans, corn is not only more productive but also fails less often. *bottom* The Lenape grew mixed gardens of maize (corn), beans, and squash—the traditional "three sisters" garden. Team planting these crops allows them to help one another (beans fertilize corn; corn provides structure for climbing beans; squash shades out weeds) and reduces pest populations.

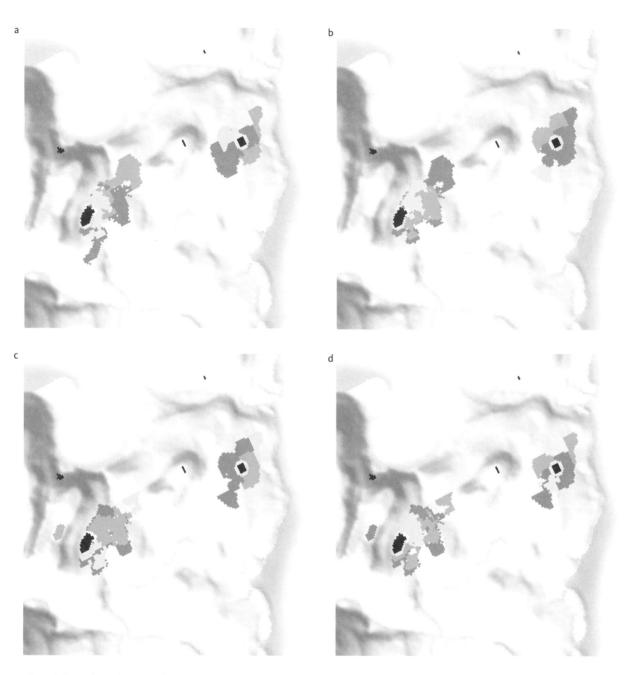

a

b

c

d

Through horticulture the Lenape shaped the landscape. They practiced a form of shifting cultivation whereby fields were cleared and then abandoned when the soil was depleted. The old fields became grasslands, then shrublands, before returning to forest. Dark gray areas indicate Lenape village sites, yellow areas are active fields, light green are abandoned old field grasslands, and dark green are successional shrublands. These details of Shorakapok and Muscoota in northern Manhattan show the distributions of these different ecological community types from model runs for (a) 1441, (b) 1483, (c) 1567, and (d) 1609.

remaining calories must have come from the abundant wild foods of the island and estuary.

To estimate how much of the land area was impacted by gardens, we constructed a geographic computer model of Lenape horticulture through time. Using the figures above, and assuming that horticulture occurred in the six locations on the island for which there is supporting evidence (see Appendix B), we modeled the process of garden initiation, abandonment, and ecosystem restoration. The Lenape could plant in one place for only about twenty years before the soil was depleted and a new field was needed. As will be described in the next chapter, when disturbed, ecological communities have the capacity to restore themselves over time through the process of "succession." Succession in this case involves the orderly transition from an active field to an old, abandoned field, then to a shrubland, and finally back to forest. We estimate from models that simulated the two hundred years prior to 1609 that Lenape gardens impacted 7 to 10 percent of the island by converting one ecosystem type into another, creating small, clustered mosaics of shrubland, grassland, and fields around habitation sites. Simply by gaining their daily bread, the people shaped the landscape around them and created habitat for species that prefer grasses and shrubs.

But horticulture was just the beginning. To create a field, the Lenape used the raven's gift of fire. One Lenape legend holds that the formerly rainbow-colored raven was charred black by bringing fire from the sun to melt the snow of a deep winter and save the other animals. But fire brought much more. It is through the raven's gift that the Lenape most profoundly managed and shaped the landscape.

The Lenape as Ecosystem Managers

Although at times scholars have contested the origin and extent of native-set fires across the landscape, that question seems mainly settled now; most students of the past believe that anthropogenic fire was a critical factor in the ecology of pre-European North America. Roger Williams, the early New England cleric, observed that Native Americans in 1643 "burnt up all the underwoods in the Countrey, once or twice a yeare and therefore as Noble men in England possessed great Parkes, and [as] the King, great Forrests in England onely for their game." John Heckewelder, a missionary who wrote extensively about

nineteenth-century Lenape in Pennsylvania, observed that they would burn "immense tracts of land" to make the country "more open to hunt in" and to produce a "greater abundance of grass for the deer to feed on." Many rural people around the world continue to burn the landscape for similar reasons.

To model the Lenape use of fire, Tim Bean (of Randel notebook fame), Kim Fisher (an analyst working for the WCS), and I took advantage of the U.S. Forest Service Fire Area Simulator (FARSITE) model. FARSITE simulates wildfire spread and intensity as an aid to firefighting in the western United States. Firefighters use FARSITE to predict where a fire will go given prevailing winds and terrain and to gauge where helicopters should drop water or crews should cut fire breaks; we used it to burn down Manhattan (virtually, of course). As with the horticultural model, we created map inputs representing the vegetation, climate, and topography of the East, then let the computer simulation run for a two-hundred-year period prior to 1609.

To students of Mannahatta, Harlem presents a particular conundrum. On the one hand, the historical record fairly clearly documents that in the colonial era, Harlem was an open landscape. De Rasieres, the Dutch colonist, made a reconnaissance by boat up the East River in 1624 and described "a large level field, of from 70 to 80 morgens [140 to 160 acres] of land, through which runs a very fine fresh stream; so that the land can be ploughed without much clearing." Subsequently, historians wrote movingly of the grassy "plains of Harlem" and by the time of the British Headquarters Map, most of Harlem had been planted in grain. On the other hand, ecologically, Harlem should have been clothed in a deep, lush forest, given its soil type and climate. Although there were extensive grasslands in the New York region during the colonial era (most notably the Hempstead Plains grassland on Long Island), most of those grasslands were the result of sandy, rapidly draining soils that are too dry to support woody plants. Harlem, in contrast, had some of the best soils on Manhattan, deep, loamy earth, developed on nutrient-rich calcareous bedrock (i.e., Inwood marble).

The reason for Harlem's grasslands appears to be fire. Bean showed through simulations with FARSITE that burning as little as once every ten years would be sufficient to turn Harlem's ecosystems into an open oak savanna, the perfect environment for deer to graze and for people to hunt, with abundant grass and small stands of trees for hiding. We hypothesize that fires may have once been lit along the base of Morningside Heights, driving animals across the open plains toward the East River, into the bows and spears of waiting hunters.

preceding pages

left As this reconstructed image shows, the Lenape managed the Mannahatta landscape with fire, sometimes disturbing flocks of grassland birds. They set fires to clear land for horticulture, to make trails passable, and to create hunting grounds, like the meadows of Harlem. They also cleared land near settlement sites for horticulture. *right* What was once Lenape hunting-and-gathering territory is now the Upper East Side and Harlem.

NATIVE AMERICAN FIRES

Computer simulations of Native American fire on Mannahatta show that 80 to 90 percent of the island was likely burned during the two hundred years prior to 1609. The spatial pattern of fire and frequency of burning influenced the composition of the forests and understory vegetation, and opened grasslands, particularly in what was later known as Harlem.

The Lenape used fire to clear land for horticulture, to keep trails open, and to create habitats for large, huntable animals like white-tailed deer. Most of the fires would have been low-level ground fires, not affecting the forest canopy. Simulations suggest that these fires touched most of Mannahatta during the two hundred years prior to 1609.

More intense burning on the Harlem Plains reflects the use of this area for hunting.

A combination of wetlands and stream valleys may have protected a portion of the West Side from fire.

Salt marshes, flooded regularly by the tide, did not burn, creating the white patches seen on the map in several places. It is not clear to what extent, if at all, the islands near Mannahatta burned.

It is also unclear what measures the Lenape took to keep their habitation sites from burning—for example, near the Collect Pond. It may have been that the compressed soils and reduced vegetation from regular use buffered their living areas.

NUMBER OF FIRES
BETWEEN 1409–1609

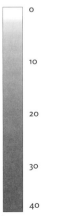

0

10

20

30

40

0   0.5   1
MILES

As we have seen, the Lenape also lit fires for other reasons. They burned the forests in spring to create a plot of land for horticulture; these fires might have escaped on occasion. They probably also lit fires to make it easier to move along their trails. Anyone who has visited an old-growth forest that doesn't burn (like in the damp Pacific Northwest) knows how difficult it can be to maneuver among the down logs and heavy understory vegetation. Finally, the Lenape may have set the landscape ablaze for fun—people all over the world seem to light fires for reasons that defy logical explanation. Fisher and I adapted Bean's model to assign ignition points near the horticultural fields to represent fires that accidentally escaped the planned bounds, along trails to represent fires lit when the vegetation became too thick, and in Harlem to represent active management for hunting grounds.

To our surprise, we found that fires have historically run amok on Manhattan—nearly all of the island may have burned on a patchwork, but regular, basis. Simulations over two hundred years show that, depending on small changes in the initial parameters, between 80 and 100 percent of the island would have cumulatively burnt over a two-hundred-year period. For the most part these were not large forest-clearing burns, like what Yellowstone National Park experienced in 1988; rather, they were mainly low-level fires that would char the trees but kill only the young saplings and most fire-sensitive species (as described by Roger Williams for Massachusetts). Shrubs and herbs on the forest floor were the primary victims. Only repetitive burning, like what Harlem may have experienced, would transform the land-scape into a more or less permanent grassland savanna. The exception to the widespread burning rule may have been the West Side of Manhattan, which, lying apart from Lenape trails, far from regular habitation sites, and protected by the cool wetlands of the center part of the island, burned only rarely. According to some of our simulation runs, a patch of land from West Thirtieth Street to West Seventy-seventh Street, with a fairly even edge along Eighth Avenue, is where the most untouched forests would have been found.

The Lenape burned the landscape for their own reasons, but the consequences would have been far-reaching, affecting many of the island's inhabitants. Not only would fires have made fire-sensitive species (e.g., hemlock, beech, and sugar maple) rarer, and fire-tolerant species (oak, hickory, and red maple) more common, but they would have allowed whole new ecosystems to occur. Pitch-pine barrens, like those found on Long Island or in southern New Jersey, depend on regular fire; after a hot blaze, they open their waxy cones and release their seeds, having learned through evolution to plant the next generation only when direct sunlight can reach soil enriched with ash. The grasslands of Harlem, which were critical to many grass-dependent species, would have depended entirely on the Lenape's fires. Fire also created uneven borders between ecosystems—edge habitats perfect for the deer and quail that the people liked to hunt—and promoted dense berry thickets (especially of blueberry and huckleberry) on which the people could feast. Fire, in proportion, is a good thing indeed.

"Spirits no less important..."

One aspect of Lenape life that neither computers nor latter-day archaeology can adequately reconstruct is the immense spirituality that the Lenape brought to their understanding of home. The scholar of the Lenape, Herbert Kraft, wrote that, like many people who live close to the land, they "saw themselves as an integral part of a natural world filled with an almost infinite variety of plants, animals, insects, clouds and stones, each of which possessed spirits no less important than those of human beings." This spiritual and moral relationship to the land was probably more important to their lives than all that we have yet explored, but it is also the hardest thing to know at this far remove.

What we do have are some stories, passed down through the generations and no doubt modified over time, but that perhaps give the best glimpse of the Lenape's relationship to the land and to each other. From the immediate New York region, we have only four brief tales handed down from the seventeenth century, as summarized by the folklorist, John Bierhorst. In abstract, here they are:

> **Turtle Island with humans created from fire.** At first there was only water; the tortoise raised its back, water ran off, and the "earth became dry." A tree grew up in the middle of the earth; the first man sprouted from the tree's root, the first woman from the tip of the tree as it bent over and touched the earth.
>
> **Visitor from sky world.** They have a Tradition... that about five hundred years agoe, a man call'd (*Wach que ow*) came down from above, upon a Barrel's-head, let down by a Rope, and lived amongst them sixty years, who told them he

The Lenape had a rich spiritual life that included ceremonial dances and storytelling. This mask, part of the American Museum of Natural History's collection, is from Lenape living in Ontario, Canada and might have been similar to objects used on Mannahatta.

came from an happy place, where there were many of their Nations, and so he left them.

Man near death visits the dead land. And they have another Tradition of one Meco Nish, who had lain as dead sixteen days ... in which interval he told them he had been in a fine place where he saw all that had been dead.

Crow brings corn. They have a tradition that their Corn was at first dropt out of the mouth of a Crow from the Skies.

These stoies told to Wooley from the 1670s are all that we have from near Mannahatta. However, there are other stories told by the Lenape, from over the generations and across their diaspora, that enrich our understanding. We learn, for example, that the Lenape believed in a Great Spirit, Kishelemukong, "Our Creator," or "He who creates us by his thoughts." From his imagination, Kishelemukong generated the Keepers of Creation—Rock, Fire, Wind, and Water—also known as the Grandfathers of the Four Directions. With their help he created the Father Sun, and the Grandmother Moon, and Kukna, Mother Earth; then together they made the plants and animals, with special powers and abilities, and placed them where they could be useful. Troublesome spirits were also created, like Matantu, the evil spirit, who placed poisonous plants among the edible ones, endowed blackberries with thorns, and created tormenting insects like mosquitoes and flies.

People were the last beings created, and they had to be made twice. In the first creation, Grandmother Moon and Grandfather Thunder conceived two children, who were born on Mother Earth, a man and a woman. Grandmother Moon gave them the power to dream and nurtured them until they were grown, then returned to the spirit world, promising never to forget and to always watch over them from above.

The second creation occurred after a great flood covered the earth. Nanapush, a powerful spirit, concluded many adventures with spirits and beasts to reclaim a small patch of soil from the bottom of the ocean, which he mounded on the back of a giant turtle (Turtle Island). The modern Lenape storyteller, Hìtakonanu'lax, finishes the story:

Then the Earth was dry, and good to look upon. Indeed, it was very beautiful, and there grew a pale and lovely tree from the Mother Earth, and the root of this new tree sent forth a sprout beside it. After a time there grew upon it a man, the first on the new Earth. This man was there alone, and may have remained there forever, but the shimmering tree bent over its top to kiss the Mother Earth. Where the tree had touched the Earth, there appeared another sprout, and there grew the first woman of the new Earth. The wise ones tell us that from those two beings, that man and woman, came our Lenape'wak, Lenape people, owing our origin and faithfulness to the shimmering tree and the good Mother Earth.

The Lenape'wak of Mannahatta would have heard stories like these around the campfire at night, during long winter days passed in the longhouse, and during special ceremonies and dances, sometimes led by professional storytellers who moved from place to place. These North American troubadours carried stones or seeds as mnemonic devices and drew pictures on the ground to aid in the storytelling. Ceremonies might be held to celebrate the harvest or a successful hunt, or to placate unsettled spirit beings or animal spirits. Particularly important was the spirit Mesingw ("Living Solid Face" or "Keeper of the Game"), who was responsible for the welfare of animals in the forest, and who patrolled the forests from the back of large buck. It was Mesingw's job to reconcile the human need to hunt animals with the animals' fear of being killed and butchered. To make amends, hunters understood that they were not to kill more than they needed and were to release the spirits of dead animals so that they might be reborn and replenish the population.

In ceremonies Mesingw was represented by a special dancer, the Mesingholikan, who took on the appearance, voice, and powers of Mesingw. The dancer would wear a large wooden mask, whose face was painted half red and half black, and don a coat of black bear skin. He would indicate his desires with a snapping-turtle-shell rattle and by calling out in an inhuman voice (described by one anthropologist as sounding like a horse's whinny). Although usually benevolent, Mesingw could also become angry and resentful if improperly treated, threatening to put disobedient children into a sack filled with snakes, or "breaking a hunter's speech," causing him to stammer, or scaring him to death. Fortunately, offerings of tobacco made to effigies of Mesingw would help appease him.

The Lenape told stories to explain their world and as reminders of successful ways of living. A common motif is of people who lose their way and must be rescued with the help of spiritual agents who remind them of the old ways. These agents reinforced the importance of connections people make to one another, to their world, and to the spirits that enliven it. One story, the Tale of Corn Woman, recounts how the Lenape lost and then regained their corn sister, that is, maize. Imagine a story like this being told in the longhouses at Shorakapok or near the Collect Pond in Lower Manhattan on a cold winter night, as fierce winds howl through the leafless trees. Imagine, the entire community—everyone you know, living in the only place you've ever known —gathered round you beside a roaring campfire to listen to an old man from over the water....

The Tale of Corn Woman

In a time now past, Corn Woman (the spirit who gave corn to the Lenape) became angry when a young man claimed that she did not exist and, more-over, that the people could never lose their corn. In retaliation, all the corn seed grew tiny wings and flew away like bugs, except for the case of one man, who had the foresight to keep some of his wife's seed in a tightly closed deer-skin bag. After everyone else had lost their seed, his wife badgered him into checking if her seed was still there, but when he opened the bag, her seed flew away too.

As winter came on, the people were hungry. They began to quarrel and treat each other badly. A heavy snow was followed by a visit from an old man from the south who gave the people an oyster. He instructed them to place the oyster at the end of a pipe and then strike the ice that had frozen the bay with the pipe. Each time the people did this, another oyster would appear on the end of the pipe. In a short time they had collected enough oysters to supply the entire village. Eventually, though, the people tired of oysters and regretted the young man's words about the corn.

The old man from the south said he had come from the Spirit World to assist and instruct the people. He took a young boy out on the ice to find Corn Woman. They chipped a hole into the ice and the boy looked down expecting to see fish in the sea, but instead he saw fields of corn. The old man and the boy went down to the fields near the house of Corn Woman. The old man lit a fire and they roasted oysters until the shells opened up.

Corn Woman came to the fire and asked for something to eat. The old man asked, "Are you the Corn Woman who is called Kahesana Xaskwim,

By the end of the seventeenth century, the Lenape had largely been forced from Manhattan Island. Eventually their diaspora led to settlements in Oklahoma, Wisconsin, and Ontario. Nora Thompson Dean, pictured here in 1972, helped record the Lenape's way of life, stories, and language.

Mother Corn, in the world above?" "Yes, I am Mother Corn, old man. Why do you ask?" she said. The old man replied, "I have come to ask you for seed corn, to bring it back to Earth, because the people are hungry and suffering." Then the old man offered tobacco to the Creator in name of the food they had eaten, and he sang and the boy danced, which lifted the sorrow from Corn Woman's heart. The old man made earrings from the shells of the oysters and gave them as a gift to Corn Woman.

Still, Corn Woman wanted to know why she should give corn to those who were not thankful and took her gifts for granted. The boy replied, "The people of my village would be very thankful if you gave us seed corn again. Many of the people on Earth are starving, many of them little children like myself." The boy's words touched her heart and she began to cry, but her tears were not water from the sea, but tear-shaped kernels of corn! The boy cupped his hands to catch Corn Woman's tears, and she gave the seed to the boy and the old man and taught them special dances of thanksgiving to be done when they returned to the world above.

On returning to Earth the old man told the people that the hard times they had experienced were a punishment for the wrongs they had done one another and for their lack of faith and thankfulness. From this experience he hoped that they would learn to be humble and to recognize the dependence they had on all things for their existence. The people listened intently. "It is not wise to take the corn and such gifts for granted," he said.

Chapter Five

Ecological Neighborhoods

My observations and conclusions thus far sum up to this: In our American cities, we need all kinds of diversity, intricately mingled in mutual support. We need this so city life can work decently and constructively, and so the people of cities can sustain (and further develop) their society and civilization.... Cities have the capability of providing something for everybody, only because, and only when, they are created by everybody.

— Jane Jacobs, *The Death and Life of Great American Cities* 1961

Ecological communities are akin to neighborhoods in the city. Fortunately, many of the communities that enlivened the Mannahatta landscape can still be found in New York City and its environs. Here salt marshes and oak woodlands grace the shores of Pelham Bay Park, in the Bronx.

New York is a city of neighborhoods. Ask New Yorkers where they live, and most will give their neighborhood first: TriBeCa, Lower East Side, Greenwich Village, Upper West Side, Harlem, Washington Heights, Inwood. Although all are found on the same island in the same city, these neighborhoods are distinctive; people in them may speak different languages, hold different beliefs, exercise different interests, and hail from different places, yet somehow they find a way to live and work together. The tapestry of human diversity that is New York did not arise spontaneously in its modern form, but required generations to develop, nurtured by waves of immigration and assimilation, fraught with conflicts and competitions, and marked by periods of both destruction and collapse, creativity and renewal.

When I came to New York, I didn't know what to make of the place—so many people going in so many different directions—and so I started pulling in my own direction, back toward nature, back toward the landscape. As the Mannahatta Project developed I wondered what ecological neighborhoods had been in place before the human neighborhoods I was exploring, and what relationships those ecological communities had to the communities that existed today. My friends began to tease me that I gave directions in two time zones ("Go down the Bronx River Parkway, catch the Bruckner Expressway east where it used to be a salt marsh, cross the Whitestone Bridge—not forgetting the old beaches on the right—continue past Shea Stadium, then left past an old Atlantic cedar swamp, and there you are at LaGuardia").

Mannahatta was characterized by a diversity different from that of Manhattan today, a diversity of all life, a celebration of frogs, fishes, and fowl. Plants and animals, and the ways that they interact and live with one another, collectively compose what we term *biological diversity,* or, for short, *biodiversity.* The biodiversity then, like the cultural diversity today, was found in marvelous neighborhoods, each the result of chance meetings, historical legacies, and an ever-changing—yet familiar—landscape of opportunity and disappointment.

Fifty-five different kinds of neighborhoods, or ecological communities, were once found on Mannahatta. This is a remarkable number for a landscape as small as Manhattan (only twenty square miles). Fifty-five distinct assemblages of life is more than is found on the average coral reef or in most rain forests of similar size. Like a neighborhood, an ecological community is defined by the combination of plants and animals (including people) that live there; those plants and animals, together with the energy, soil, water, and air

ECOLOGICAL COMMUNITIES

This map shows most of the ecological communities (i.e., neighborhoods) of Mannahatta. Fifty-five different ecological community types were once found on Mannahatta or within three-quarters of a mile (1,000 meters) of its shores. Different colors represent different forest, wetland, and grassland types. Communities not shown on the map include brackish intertidal shores, coastal plain pond shores, vernal pools, shoreline outcrops, calcareous shoreline outcrops, terrestrial caves, talus caves, cliffs, calcareous cliffs, and Lenape buildings (wigwams and longhouses).

ECOLOGICAL COMMUNITY NAME	AREA (ACRES)	LENGTH (MILES)
MARINE COMMUNITIES		
Marine deepwater community	3,651	
Marine eelgrass meadow	421	
Marine intertidal mudflat community	124	
Marine gravel-sand beach community	116	
Marine rocky intertidal community	56	
ESTUARINE COMMUNITIES		
Tidal river community	11,660	
Tidal creek community		18.3
Brackish subtidal aquatic bed community		2.1
Low salt marsh	349	
High salt marsh	576	
Salt panne community	<1	
Coastal salt pond community	1	
Brackish tidal marsh	78	
Brackish intertidal mudflat community	5	
Salt shrub community	169	
RIVER AND STREAM COMMUNITIES		
Rocky headwater stream community		34.9
Marsh headwater stream community		14.2
Midreach stream community		7.1
Intermittent stream community		12.5
Coastal plain stream community		0.5
LAKE AND POND COMMUNITIES		
Coastal plain pond community	6	
Eutrophic pond community	6	
WETLAND COMMUNITIES		
Deep emergent marsh	8	
Shallow emergent marsh	118	
Shrub swamp	57	
Highbush blueberry bog thicket	76	
Floodplain forest	72	
Red maple-hardwood swamp	121	
Coastal plain Atlantic white cedar swamp	13	
TERRESTRIAL COMMUNITIES		
Maritime beach community	70	
Maritime dunes community	6	
Maritime shrubland	8	
Hempstead Plains grassland	761	
Serpentine barrens	33	
Pitch pine-scrub oak barrens	86	
Chestnut oak forest	177	
Coastal oak-beech forest	58	
Coastal oak-hickory forest	2,864	
Oak-tulip tree forest	4,187	
Coastal Appalachian oak-pine forest	2,923	
Hemlock-northern hardwood forest	102	
Successional old field	24	
Successional shrubland	37	
Lenape horticultural field	14	
Lenape habitation site	6	

0   0.5   1
MILES

The spatial patterns of ecological communities form natural landscapes, whether those landscapes are (a) Lower Manhattan, 1609; (b) Lower Manhattan, 2008; (c) Times Square, 1609; or (d) Times Square, 2008.

of the place, form an ecosystem, a system of living and nonliving things. Ecosystems vary, like neighborhoods, each coming up with new sets of solutions to the same problems of finding food, shelter, and livelihood.

The ecosystems taken together, distributed over the land and into the water, form the ecological landscape. Landscape ecologists sometimes think of these distributions as a mosaic, like in an ancient Roman bath, where the small, individual pieces of tile are equivalent to the ecosystems, and the overall picture those tiles form is equivalent to the landscape. Landscape ecology is the study of how this mosaic of life comes to be, how it changes through time and varies over space, and how it forms habitats for species, which, in their entirety, represent biodiversity. Through an extraordinary combination of factors, not the least of which was the presence of the Lenape, Mannahatta in 1609 had come to possess a remarkably varied set of ecological neighborhoods. But then Manhattan was destined for wealth from the very beginning.

Destined for Wealth

The wealth of Mannahatta's ecosystems arose first from the city's history and then from its geography. As we have seen, Manhattan lies at the very southern extreme of the last glaciation. As a result, a great moraine (the technical name for a pile of rocks left after a glacier melts away) bisects Long Island, runs just off the southern tip of Manhattan, and cuts across Staten Island. North of this line, only fourteen thousand years ago, great depths of ice and snow buried the land, and nothing could live; south of this line, mastodons roamed along shorelines two hundred feet lower than today, browsing the tundra and pockets of boreal forest. Manhattan wasn't an island then, just a set of hills rising between two valleys, one with a sparkling, glacier-fed river, the great-great-great-grandfather of the Hudson River, which ran out yet another hundred miles to the sea.

As the glaciers retreated they left behind layers of sand and silt and scattered huge boulders like what we see today falling out of the retreating glaciers in Alaska and Antarctica; in other places, they left huge chunks of ice, which eventually melted away, leaving holes that filled with water to create ponds and lakes. The glaciers not only left rock, but carved it away too, digging deeper into the soft Inwood marble that underlies Harlem, leaving an even plain; where the resistant Manhattan schist, a tough, metamorphic rock, was found, knobby hills were left behind. Massive sand piles, the Sand Hills, were dumped in Lower Manhattan. All of these were laying the foundation for the ecological communities that followed.

As the ice let go its grip on the land, life returned, recolonizing the glacial till, building the soil, taking back the hills in successive waves of shrublands, coniferous forests, and eventually stately deciduous forests. The oceans rose, flooding the lower lands and filling out New York Harbor, making Staten Island an island, and flooding into the valley of the Hudson, transforming a river into an inland sea. It was a long time coming—thousands of years of adjustment, accommodation, setbacks, and sudden victories. Then, about ten thousand years ago, people arrived on the scene, the ancestors of the Lenape, to hunt the mastodons and other great beasts.

It was about four thousand years ago that the climate stabilized into a pattern similar to today's, and the ecological communities settled into a long period of assimilation and consolidation—in other words, the ecological neighborhoods started to figure out who they were. The long biological history of immigration and emigration resulted in modern New York's flora existing at a crossroads between the northern flora of boreal Canada and the southern flora of Virginia and the Carolinas. It's as if New York's plant life draws from those two great traditions—the South's and the North's—and as a result, there are many more plants here than there are in many cities of similar latitude and position; both peat moss and magnolias once marked time in New York City. As plants are the primary producers in the ecological economy of Manhattan Island, their great diversity is a source of strength for all its communities.

This fact was not lost on the birds. On the edge of a continent, marked with a great east-west signpost called Long Island, Mannahatta was a central stopping place along the migration routes that follow the eastern shore of North America. Migrating birds need places to rest as they track the seasons north and south, and Mannahatta, with its fringing marshes, thick forests, and abundant seeds, berries, and foliage, was like a gourmet grocery store. Hawks, warblers, shorebirds, and even hummingbirds, more than 260 species in all, still commute through Manhattan each year. The great bird-watching in Central Park, and the importance of New York's parks for the annual migration, are both due to Manhattan's place in America's geography.

Blessed with a climate that is tropical in the summer and frigid in the winter, Mannahatta had both fair-weather friends and tough, but adaptable residents. Summers with warm temperatures, high humidity, and frequent thunderstorms, though sometimes hard for people to bear, are like a spa for plants; plenty of sun, plenty of water, a bit of action—what more could our green friends desire? Frigid conditions require adaptation; deciduousness (dropping delicate leaves), hibernation (sleeping away the cold days), and/or an ability to endure (as in the tough, green, needlelike leaves of pines, or the warm pelage of wolves) are necessary traits for those species that stay on. Wood frogs actually freeze solid, only reviving when spring returns. The animals that could, mainly birds and insects but also fishes, went to Florida and the Caribbean (and sometimes South America) for the season.

History, geography, and climate all set Mannahatta up to be a biological success, but what makes Mannahatta wealthy beyond imagination is its crowning position atop an estuary. An estuary is to biodiversity what a mint is to money. By definition, estuaries are the places where the land and sea come together, and the result is like currency, both productive and variable. Freshwater rivers, like the Hudson and the numerous streams that are her sources and tributaries, discharge nutrients to fertilize the water, and cut the saltwater with fresh flow. As the seasons turn, the amount of freshwater swells and diminishes, and as the days and nights pass, the tide rises and falls. The competing traffic of freshwater and saltwater and the washing of water over land creates a small sea in the glacially excavated harbor, with layers of warm ocean water lying on top of the cold, fresh stuff. Sea-grass beds take root where the water is shallow enough for light to reach the bottom, beaches and dunes form along the windward shore, and salt marshes thrive in protected corners. The estuary is the motor, the connector, the driver, the great winding way, the central place that gathers all the old neighborhoods together and makes the rest possible.

The Neighborhoods of the Sea

Human neighborhoods divide for reasons, whether cultural, historical, or political, and though nature does not have culture, history, or politics, living things have their own ways of finding where they fit best, especially when it comes to soil, water, and a bit of fresh air. Scientists have found that these natural dividers are nearly always gradients; nature dislikes discontinuities and prefers gradual change. Elevation is a kind of gradient, starting from the bottom of the sea and reaching the tops of the hills. Water salinity is a different

above Intertidal mudflats, like this one at Rye Marshlands Conservancy, in Westchester County, are primary foraging habitats for a variety of shorebirds, like this egret. Similar mudflats were found in protected places along Mannahatta's shore. *opposite top* Sandy beaches studded with rocky outcrops, like this one on the South Shore of Long Island, once graced Mannahatta's shores. *opposite bottom* Eelgrass meadows are created in the ocean where the water is shallow and clear enough for marine eelgrass to grow. These meadows, seen here graced by black-necked stilts, are in California, but similar meadows once fringed the protected bays on the eastern side of Mannahatta.

kind of gradient; soil fertility another; air temperature yet another. Proceeding up the streams from the estuaries, over the hills from the streams, across the landscape of Mannahatta, different communities cluster where the mix of salt- and freshwater is just right, where the depth of the water makes the most sense, and where the basement of rocks and soil and slope of land meets their needs.

Take mudflats. Not the most glorious of ecosystems, but to the right creature, there is everything to love and nothing to disdain about a broad, wet, silky smooth flat of mud, humbly descending from the land into the sea. To connoisseurs like the American oystercatcher, the lowly mudflat provides delicacies on the half shell. And to the delicacies—mud snails, soft-shell clams, and blue mussels—mudflats are the perfect habitat, the equivalent, to New Yorkers, of a rent-stabilized two-bedroom, two-bath apartment with a view.

The cousin of the mudflat is the rocky tide pool. Manhattan once had tide pools wherever the hardscrabble shore met the edge of the sea, each pool a universe in miniature for predators and prey. Just offshore, where its roots could reach bottom (about six feet below the lowest tide), eelgrass once flourished in meadows. We don't think of grasses growing in the sea, because most don't, but eelgrass, *Zostera marina* (also known as widgeon-grass, for its popularity with the ducks) is an exception. Wispy green ribbons of grass form habitats for many small species of fish (especially sea horses), algae, and occasionally sea turtles, the latter of which enjoy grazing on a lazy summer afternoon. Sea grasses are the temperate ocean equivalent of a coral reef or a redwood forest, providing the structure that other species seek. Although most of the eelgrass in the New York region was wiped out in a mysterious disease outbreak in the 1930s, in areas with very clean water out at the end of Long Island, sea turtles still lounge in the grass.

Farther offshore are marine deep-water communities, which came to exist within a half mile of Mannahatta's edge. Marine-water habitats are characterized by their currents, fast or slow, and by their bottoms: hard bottom, soft bottom, shelly bottom, and unconsolidated bottom—all were found near the Battery. Organisms that live on the seafloor are called benthos; these include oysters—which famously once formed extensive beds in the harbor, including near Liberty, Ellis, Governors, and Staten islands—as well as lobsters, clams, and bottom dwellers like flounder and toadfish. Above the benthos, the water column itself is a three-dimensional fish-eat-fish world. The lowest rung on the food chain is occupied by small photosynthetic

top Extensive salt marshes, like these in Westchester County, once made Mannahatta a fertile nursery for fish and an important contributor to the region's ecological economy. Salt marshes formerly on the Lower East Side and Harlem were as productive as modern agricultural fields are today. *bottom* Salt pannes are small depressions that form within salt marshes, sometimes as a result of storm disturbances. Several are shown on the British Headquarters Map near today's Delancey Street. The pictured salt pannes adorn the South Shore of Long Island.

organisms (phytoplankton), which are eaten by microanimals called zooplankton, which are eaten by fish, which are eaten by other fish, which might get eaten by a porpoise or a seal or, rarely, a whale near Manhattan's shore.

Whales and porpoises were once a regular sight in New York Harbor. The 1705 charter for Trinity Church from Queen Anne included the right to claim any whales that beached on the sands nearby. Whale Creek in Brooklyn used to be a winding tributary to Newtown Creek (which divides Queens and Brooklyn), though whether its name comes from whales or whaling is not clear. Today, whales are still sometimes struck by ships in the harbor. In 2007 a juvenile minke whale, nicknamed Sludgy by local residents, found its way into Gowanus Creek in Brooklyn, then died the next day on a jetty belonging to an oil company. Seals do better—harbor seals are still regularly seen in winter in spots where they can haul themselves out and enjoy the sun.

Going back toward land, up the tidal profile from mudflats, we find salt marshes, those engines of biological productivity, which stand in stately yellow-green swards. Salt marshes produce as much vegetable mass as fertilized, chemically treated soybean fields in Iowa—over ten tons per acre per year—but these ecosystems are not feeding cows on the way to slaughter, but the estuary and embracing ocean and its food chain. Salt marshes are also the nurseries of the sea. The narrow corridors between the marsh's grassy stalks are like millions of tiny cribs, where no large predator can intrude; more than three-fourths of all the shellfish and seafood harvested today on the East Coast spent some portion of its life in a salt marsh.

Even before the days of bulldozers and landfill, it wasn't easy being a salt marsh. Inundated twice daily by saltwater, these wetlands suffer alternately from drowning and desiccation. Soil salinities in the higher parts of the marsh, washed only on the highest spring tides, can double the salinity of ocean water. Some birds have nasal glands to allow them to "blow brine"; salt-marsh turtles like the diamondback terrapin literally cry out the salt. In the fall, the humble pickleweed, after storing salt in its tissues all summer long, turns a brilliant crimson orange, in time with the oaks and maples onshore, and then senesces to wait for the next spring.

Salt marshes grow where they are protected from the energy of the waves, but beaches lie in the thick of the salt spray and the constant lapping of the seawaters. Manhattan once boasted many a beach; from just north of the Battery to Forty-second Street on the Hudson River shore, there was at one time a nearly continuous sandy beach. Victor Audubon painted his famous father (John James Audubon) on the Manhattanville beach in 1843, near where the Fairway market is today, at 125th Street and the Henry Hudson Parkway (see page 69). Although we associate beaches with swimming, they are actually very dry places, exposed to the sun and wind, and with unforgiving soil that holds little life-giving rainwater. But grasses hold the dunes down, and in the swales between, small pockets of life take root and grow.

The Neighborhoods of Freshwater

Uphill from salty marshes and sandy beaches, slightly salty brackish marshes give way to freshwater streams that drain down hills, collecting the waters of land and giving them back to the ocean mother. Where the waters slow and pool, wetlands form and species diversity flourishes. Streams and wetlands are the busy malls and downtown districts of the natural landscape. Three feet away, on the dry terrestrial land, there might be twenty plant species per square yard, but in the adjacent wetland, there might be three times that number.

Why? Plants live by turning sunlight into sugar, making sunshine into food. To let the air into the leaves, however, they need to open small doors, called stomata, on the underside. As the air comes in, the water goes out. In order to make the most sugar possible, plants need a regular, ready supply of water to keep them solvent, and that is what wetlands provide in abundance.

Plants and animals do have their preferences. Swamps exist where trees can stand to have their feet wet; soft, herbaceous marshes grow where they can't. How much water and how long the floodwaters last makes all the difference. If the water stands more than six inches deep, it's a deep marsh with cattails and wild rice; less than six inches, it's a shallow marsh, grassy and open, home to sedges and rushes. Bogs exist where the water can't escape except back into the air. The plants that grow there, sphagnum moss and the carnivorous plants (sundews, pitcher plants, flytraps), literally stew in their own nutrient-poor juices. Carnivorous plants eat insects not for energy, but for the nutrients. A bog receives mostly rainwater; the slightly wealthier fen gets some water through the ground, and a modicum of nutrients along with it. The Atlantic white cedar swamp that once filled a third of the Hackensack Meadows and had an outpost in Central Park, was a forested coniferous bog, with ferny, peaty hummocks and a rare butterfly, the Hessel's hairstreak, whose caterpillars like to feed, as do deer in winter, on cedar leaves.

top Freshwater wetlands form complex mosaics that vary according to how often and how deeply they flood. Sunny and wet, they are strongholds of biodiversity. These shallow emergent marshes in Sterling Forest State Park, in Orange County, New York, are similar to those that were found on Mannahatta. *bottom* Deep emergent marshes, like these recreated at the New York Botanical Garden, form in deeper standing waters.

top Swamps are forested wetlands. Times Square was once at least in part a red-maple swamp, like this one in Sterling Forest State Park.
bottom Highbush blueberry bogs were once a favorite of black bears in Central Park. A similar community occurred where Belvedere Lake is today.

The British Headquarters Map shows a small conifer wetland in what is now Central Park; it was likely a coastal Atlantic white-cedar swamp, like this one in Blydenburgh County Park, in Suffolk County.

Streams are the delight of any landscape, and Mannahatta enjoyed a sparkling necklace of streams, brooks, and small rivers—more than sixty-six miles of laughing waterways. Streams can be steep and rocky; they can be slow and meandering; they are liable to flood; and they can absorb the sudden shock of water after a summer thunderstorm. Another twenty-two miles of waterways were mere ephemera, here and then gone again. The waters disappeared because of Mannahatta's glacially shaped landscape, which left sand and silt in horizontal beds as natural, underground conduits for water—storm drains before they had been invented. Water came and went on Mannahatta, as rivers and streams ducked their heads into the ground and emerged later as springs, much to the delight of frogs and salamanders. Many of these streams and springs collected their waters in small ponds and lakes scattered across the landscape by geological accident or by the intention of beavers building dams. In colonial times, these places took names like Sun-fish Pond, Stuyvesant Skating Pond, Buttermilk Pond, and our friend the Collect Pond. The Collect's value to the local plants and animals lay in its being a coastal plain pond, similar to cousins in Brooklyn and the south side of Staten Island, that expanded and contracted on a regular schedule, creating halos of species along its shore.

Spring-fed in a deep hole, the Collect supplied two streams, one, Lispenard Creek, which meandered through marshes to the Hudson River shore, and another that took the more direct and steeper route down to the East River, the Old Wreck Brook. Legend has it that on the high tide, the Lenape could paddle canoes along the East River, across the Collect, and down to the Hudson shore. And a nineteenth-century account describes boys ice-skating from the Collect Pond, through the Lispenard salt meadows, out to the frozen Hudson, then up Minetta Water into Greenwich Village.

The other freshwater ponds were smaller and shallower. In winter some might have frozen solid, and in summer they would have turned green and murky with algae and abundant aquatic vegetation lining the edge—cattails, pondweeds, and bladderworts—and floating in the middle—duckweed and water lilies. Ponds had their own characteristic zooplankton, insect communities, and warmwater fish, like pumpkinseed and redfin pickerel —which can still be caught in the Harlem Meer—and they shared some species with the streams, like the American eel and the brook trout. The life journey of eels is opposite that of anadromous fishes like sea-run trout or shad, which are born in freshwater streams and rivers, grow large at sea, then return to freshwater to produce the next generation. Female eels spend most of their lifetimes in freshwater (males prefer slightly salty, brackish waters), then migrate to the sea to reproduce. The eels that once lived on Manhattan would have swum over a thousand miles to the Sargasso Sea in the mid-Atlantic (between the West Indies and the Azores). Once the elvers (as immature eels are known) grew to a certain size at sea, they returned to Manhattan and the surrounding waters in the millions to spin the wheel of life again.

In this way eels depended on beavers, as did brook trout, wood ducks, red maple, smartweed, and many other species. It is easy to underestimate the importance of beavers at our current ecological distance, but many problems can be solved through the diligence of beavers. Beavers are what ecologists call "ecosystem architects," because, through their daily business—cutting brush, hauling wood, and building dams—they create the ecosystems, in particular ponds and the fringing wetlands, that are so important to other species in the near term and to all of us in the long term. Every stream in eastern North America, including all the streams on Mannahatta, once had beaver denizens, generations of them, each literally "busy as a beaver." Beaver dams do more than back up water; they also back up soil, collecting the rich silt that the rain and snow are slowly weathering down off the hills. That silt builds up behind the dam and eventually drowns the pond in dirt. The pond dies, the beavers move on, and gradually the beavers' home morphs into a marsh, which eventually dries up and morphs again, to become a meadow. That meadow eventually becomes a forest, or, if a lucky person stops by and burns away the overgrowth, an extraordinarily rich parcel of cropland. The Lenape loved to grow their ceremonial tobacco in the rich soils beavers had left along Minetta Water, about where Washington Square Park is today; the Dutch, and then the British, followed on, leading to the founding of Greenwich Village. Today, farmers in Iowa and Illinois still make a living on soils created through the work of beavers ages ago.

The Neighborhoods of the Land

Above the sparkling waters and beaver ponds, forests grew—the likes of which are practically unknown today. These were *old-growth forests* before that term was necessary, places where individual trees, like monarchs, ruled for hundreds of years, lording their shade over the smaller, bowed understory trees, each waiting its turn, hoping for its chance in the sun. The king of kings in Mannahatta's forest was the American chestnut; it is estimated that more

top Most of Mannahatta's streams were rocky, like this one in the Ward Pound Ridge Reservation, in Westchester County. Others wound through grassy wetlands or through forested swamps. *bottom* The Collect Pond in Lower Manhattan may have looked something like this pond in Westchester County, blessed with aquatic plants like the water lily, and also fringed with trees and wetlands.

top The most common forest type on Mannahatta was the oak-tulip tree forest, which grew on deep, well-watered soils. Unlike this contemporary forest in central Long Island, Mannahatta's forests were dominated by large, American chestnuts. *bottom* The ridges and dry slopes of Mannahatta were clothed in Appalachian oak-pine forests, like these in Caleb Smith State Park Preserve, in Suffolk County.

top This oak-hickory forest at the Sterling Forest State Park has been thinned by disturbance processes (i.e., clear-cutting), creating a younger and more even-aged forest than was typical of Mannahatta. Otherwise, the rolling, rocky terrain is similar. *bottom* The sandy hills of Lower Manhattan may have been covered in pitch pine-scrub oak barrens, an ecological community type maintained by regular fire and still found today in eastern Long Island and southern New Jersey. This photograph is from the David Allen Sarnoff Pine Barrens Preserve, in Suffolk County.

than half the wood of the forest was chestnut, and that individual trees might have been as much as 4 feet wide and 120 feet tall. But the dukes and counts and princes of the forest were many: tulip trees, oaks of several colors, hickories, maples, birches, white pines, eastern hemlocks, sweet gum, and beech.

These trees stood together, but their relative sway over territory depended on differences of soil, water, slope, and fire. Soils vary with depth depending on the slope of the hills, with the thinnest soils over the crown of the hill, the mid-depth soils on the midslope, and the deepest soils at the base. Soil type depends on the rocks beneath. Soils won from nutrient-saturated rocks, like Inwood marble, are richer, but more fiercely fought over; metamorphic schists are stingier with the nutrition they provide. Sandy soils hold water less well than the rich, loamy, black soils created by centuries of leaf fall and the slow, gentle release of summer days back into the earth. Silty soils like to hold onto the water from which they were created. Soils on south-facing slopes receive more sun, are drier in summer and warmer in winter, and have their own forest type—though some woods prefer the cool, dark side of hills, saluting the north. Over the centuries these root factors defined the battlefields over which trees fought quiet, determined wars.

The hilltops of Mannahatta were the domain of the oak—chestnut, white, black, and scarlet. Where the soils were sandy and fire frequent, pitch pines grew instead, small outposts from the vast pine barrens of southern New Jersey and Long Island. The midslopes were dominated by chestnut, attended by red maples, hickories, and birches, and retainers from up- and downslope. The bases between the hills were the red oaks' realm, with the tulip tree, the white ash, the tupelo, and the hornbeam standing tall where the ground was not too wet. Majestic white pines grew where the glaciers left sandy lenses in flat places and on rocky slopes; evergreen hemlocks swayed on cooler north-facing slopes and in shadowy ravines; nearby, the hemlock's associate, the magnificent beech, sometimes eight feet in diameter, sought out the forest coves where it could protect its fragile skin from fire. These arrangements of trees—mosaics of forest, flavors of shade—were not exclusive arrangements; nor were they planned. Individual trees of different species came and went, stuck where they could find a chance, and mixed in combinations that were constantly reinvented, but that, over time, consistently reoccurred, to evolve into the communities of forest we recognize today.

Beneath the trees, shrubs and wildflowers, lichens and mosses, plant-eaters and meat-eaters inhabited the world the trees created. White-tailed

The Harlem grasslands were maintained by fire and may have had characteristics like the Hempstead Plains–type grassland, which once filled a large portion of south-central Long Island. Only a small patch is left today, near Nassau Coliseum. Grasslands can be maintained by other kinds of disturbance; these meadows at Ward Pound Ridge Reservation in Westchester County are maintained by mowing, not fire.

deer and elk foraged in the woods; beaver sought out the wetlands; hundreds of thousands of squirrels, mice, and birds foraged on the abundant supplies of nuts. A short list of nuts available on a fall afternoon would include chestnuts, acorns (at least eleven varieties), hickory nuts (five varieties), walnuts (two varieties), hornbeam nuts, and beechnuts. Also in abundance at various times throughout the year were numerous berries and fruits: blackberries, blueberries, raspberries, gooseberries (and currants), inkberries, huckleberries, snowberries, winterberries, chokeberries, elderberries, nannyberries, mulberries, partridgeberries, teaberries, cranberries, bayberries, strawberries, serviceberries, black cherries, thorn apples, and wild grapes. It was good to be a bird or a bear —or a berry-loving Lenape—on Mannahatta.

For all their virtues, forests can render a landscape monotonous if not relieved by an opening now and again. The open exceptions to Mannahatta's forests were the ponds, the marshes, the bogs, the beaches, and, surprisingly, the grasslands. Grassy meadows are not what ecologists commonly associate with the eastern shores of North America of the time, with their vast forests, but on Mannahatta, in the flat, wholesome plains of Harlem, and a little to the north, in the Round Valley of Inwood's Sherman Creek, grass ruled—small sections of the tallgrass prairie migrated east. These grassy communities had their own birds—heath hens, bobolinks, and Savannah sparrows—and their own way of doing business. Grasses, if given a chance, can form a thick sod that will keep other plants from digging in, but in places like Mannahatta, they lasted only as long as cleansing fires swept through at the right frequency. Grasses survive fires because most of the plant lives underground—their visible leaves are just an extension of their important parts, which are kept in the root cellar—but weakling baby trees mostly aboveground and without thick bark for protection burn up. As described earlier, the Lenape provided just that necessary fire, part of the creative destruction that enlivens the landscape, making sure that no one gets too comfortable for too long.

Disaster! Calamity! And . . . Renewal!

Ecological neighborhoods, like their human analogues, are not fixed and immovable, though scientists once talked of them in the same way old-timers sitting out on their stoops might describe their neighborhoods, as if they had never changed and never will. Neighborhoods do change, though, whether we like it or not, and, like them, ecosystems change and adapt to new conditions.

top Like the Lenape of four hundred years ago, land managers today use fire to maintain natural disturbance cycles. Changes in fire disturbance regimes have altered landscapes across North America and led to billions of dollars spent to protect life and property from unnaturally large and devastating fires. *bottom* Although floods can be locally catastrophic, they are an important and natural part of how rivers influence the landscape. They add sediment to floodplains and create new habitats for plants and animals.

Ecosystems are visited, colonized, and reinvented through time, and, like human neighborhoods, sometimes ecosystems suffer senseless, horrible catastrophes—only to rise up again in another cycle of renewal and regeneration. In fact, some ecosystems depend on these catastrophes for their existence; without them, they disappear through the very dynamics that have come to define them, like the beaver pond gradually filling in to create a meadow.

First the good news: Disasters don't happen everywhere and all at the same time. There are brief bouts of horror, and then what survives settles in, to live and grow again. Moreover, there is an ancient tradition in ecological communities called succession—the orderly advance of ecosystems from one state to another, succeeding much like generations of kids advancing through the grades, on to college, into adulthood, and eventually into retirement. Like generations of people, generations of plants and animals will leave things to their descendants. For example, alders and other "nitrogen-fixing" plants take the nitrogen gas from the atmosphere and transform it into nutritious forms that are a legacy to plant life. Temperate forest soils build up a store of carbon that supports the longevity and depth of the woodlands. Of course, not everyone makes it; there are many opportunities over a lifetime to fall down—sometimes it's your fault, sometimes it just happens—but there are always some folks—some plants and animals, that is—who do get through to prepare the way for the next generation.

Now for that bad news: There are lots of different ways for something to go wrong, many kinds of disasters. People have a powerful way of transforming landscapes to suit their ends, whether through fire, horticulture, or hunting and gathering, and often those transformations are locally disastrous (to the tree, for example, that becomes a canoe, or to the bear that becomes a bearskin and hair ointment). But that's just the beginning. There are lots of calamities not directly brought on by people, calamities such as blowdowns, floods, landslides, droughts, heat waves, hard frosts, lightning bolts, tornadoes, ice storms, and salt spray. And then there are all the things your neighbors can do to you: stabbing, clawing, grabbing, poisoning, infecting, smothering, interfering, stealing, grubbing, and the never-ending nibbling of so many small teeth, literally eating you alive until you are dead and then some. Competition is not limited to the price of jeans and automobiles. Predators are many and hungry, and there's always someone waiting in the wings to take your lunch.

Yet it is exactly these processes of destruction that keep nature refreshed and alive. Take the death of one of those huge old-growth American

preceding pages

Mannahatta seen from above Brooklyn, looking to the north. Note the subtle variations in forest type, the networks of ponds and streams, and the extensive salt marshes on the eastern side of the island. Together these different ecological communities formed Mannahatta's ecological landscape.

chestnuts on Mannahatta, perhaps already 350 years old the night that a big wind knocks it down. The next morning, the gap in the forest canopy floods the ground with sunlight, and all those younger trees that have struggled in the shade through the decades are let loose to grow as fast as they can toward the light. In the course of the twenty years it will take the trees to fill the place of that mighty chestnut, the sun-drenched meadow will accommodate ephemeral flowers and insects that wait for just this chance to reproduce. The meadow is drenched with birdsong from nests that dot its fringes; white-tailed deer graze the lush secondary growth, where wolves then come to hunt. Even the dead body of the chestnut, laid to rest in the undergrowth, becomes a habitat for mushrooms and insects, the perfect burrowing place for chipmunks and ground squirrels—until a weasel comes to ferret them out. At night a great horned owl silently falls on the timid deer mouse, and the frost descends beneath the starry sky to eclipse delicate flower buds where once the mighty chestnut grew.

Disturbing the Peace

These disturbances are as instrumental as the gradients of topography, soil, water, and air in determining how, why, and where Mannahatta's ecological communities developed as they did. To describe the ecological landscape for the Mannahatta Project, we needed to describe these disturbances to the peaceable development of communities, but how? How do you describe phenomena that literally vary with the way the wind blows? The options were either to pretend that these dynamics didn't exist, that is, to assume a "climax" community that never changes (not exactly an exciting proposition, and ecologically inaccurate), to pretend they were constant (also uninspiring, and entirely unfair to those that seek refuge in the aftermath of disturbance), or to try to simulate them, accepting some uncertainty in the final result in exchange for a more interesting and potentially more realistic payoff. Change is the rule, and in existing ecosystems these changes leave lingering signs, but the signs left on Mannahatta have, in Manhattan, long been erased by pavement and buildings. How could we guess where blowdowns circa 1609 might have been?

The answer involved turning to modern ecological science and its models. Computer models are scientists' versions of toys—like five-year-olds

top Landscapes by their nature change through time, as is apparent in this image of the landscape of Lower Manhattan in 1894. *bottom* Lower Manhattan in 1609 featured extensive salt marshes and forests, whose dynamics were dictated by the weather and tides.

building with Legos, we build them and test them until they fall apart. When they do, we study the cracks to know where we need to do more work to build them again. Fortunately, for many of the kinds of disturbances that once occurred on Mannahatta, computer models already exist: A model of fire (like the previously mentioned FARSITE) takes into account the fuel loading in the wood, the recent pattern of rainfall, and the wind direction. A model of horticulture runs off population size and time to soil depletion. A model of blowdowns tracks the frequency of severe storms, the age of trees, and the strength with which roots grip the earth.

Moreover, computers work tirelessly, so that we can run our models over and over again, all day and all night, and thus simulate what the average conditions of the disturbance, or other phenomena, might have been. We play these games to figure out, for dynamic processes like floods, fires, and blowdowns, what the probabilities are and what the consequences might be. Taken over a large number of games, the results allow us to figure out the odds that a given tree is going down, or that a given patch of forest will burn, and deduce where Mannahatta's meadows or flooded woods might have been.

The Old Collect

The result of this work is a consensus guess at the map of ecological neighborhoods on Mannahatta in 1609. As is true of Manhattan's human neighborhoods, the layout of Mannahatta's ecological neighborhoods had no singular logical cause; it arose as an emergent property of the entire landscape, as much by accident as by design. Some neighborhoods are expansive, like an oak-tulip tree forest; others are narrowly restricted to specific locales, like maritime tidal dunes. But in all cases, there is no one reason why a community is where it is or how it is composed. Ecology teaches us to think of the many different reasons why something happens, and to understand these reasons in context with the history and geography of a place.

City neighborhoods form and change similarly, despite the best-laid plans of city planners—as an example, consider the fate of the Collect Pond in lower Manhattan. In the early days of the nineteenth century, city leaders allowed a tannery to set up shop on the edge of the Collect. Tanneries preserve the skins of animals by soaking their hides in plant chemicals (tannins—the same compounds that give a young red wine its bite) extracted from local trees, especially hemlock and oak, which, when disposed of as waste in the convenient nearby pond, rapidly poisoned the water, spoiling what had been the city's best and most accessible drinking water. Remember that New York City was built on an island in a tidal (i.e., salty) estuary, with no possibility of drinking from the Hudson and East rivers. The spoilage of the Collect led to plans to bring in water from uptown, orders to dig wells to extract the groundwater downtown, and eventually construction of the Croton water system, which would bring water from Westchester, thirty miles away. (It also led to a bank—Aaron Burr formed the "Manhattan Water Company" in 1808 to bring water from streams uptown, but then used the assets to form a bank, later known as the Chase Manhattan Bank, and now a part of JP Morgan Chase) In the meantime, city leaders voted to fill in the verdant Collect, by leveling the adjacent hills into the stagnant waters and declining marshes.

The city advanced rapidly over the site with the construction of tenements, churches, and businesses around the short-lived and quickly forgotten "Paradise Square." Within a decade the land began to subside, having been incompletely filled; the formerly luxuriant vegetation of the shrub-swamp and coastal-plain-pond shore, now trapped in the soil, began to decompose and release unpleasant vapors. In other words, the landscape, disturbed by the pond being filled, began to adjust, by stinking and collapsing. Those people who could left for more salubrious uptown addresses, while those who couldn't, mainly immigrant Irish and freed blacks, stayed on in increasingly dangerous and crowded tenements that sank slowly into the mire. The neighborhood became known as Five Points, for the five streets that once met over the northern edge of the Collect Pond; some of its particular charms are recalled in Martin Scorsese's movie *Gangs of New York* (2002). Charles Dickens visited, and in his *American Notes* (1842) deplored the slum neighborhood, with its unpaved alleys filled with knee-deep mud, free-roaming pigs, rotting and sinking houses, and children sleeping on the steps. Gangs established their own competitive balance; the Plug Uglies, Dead Rabbits, and Roach Guards marked out territory as the woodcock and osprey had once done. It wasn't until Jacob Riis, the journalist and reformer, began documenting the conditions in the 1880s with a new invention, the camera, that things began to change. The city bought up and condemned most of the tenements and replaced them with large civic buildings, including the reconstructed Tombs, the city prison, and the New York Courthouse. Now, when accused criminals are arraigned in the gray stone buildings of Foley Square, they face the judge on the shores of the old Collect Pond.

This anecdote is just one of the hundreds of forgotten stories of how New York came to be and how Mannahatta, in subtle ways, continues to shape the city. If New York City is a mosaic, then the tiles of the mosaic are its neighborhoods. At one time those tiles were blue and green and represented ecological communities, neighborhood habitats for thousands of species. Now the mosaic is made of diverse human neighborhoods, and the mortar that binds the tiles is the social and cultural ties, the economic relationships and personal friendships of a thriving city. In the next chapter we turn to the ties that bound Mannahatta's diverse populations together, and come to understand that by simply defining different ideas of home, we can see how nature, and cities, are strengthened and renewed even as they change through time.

Chapter Six
Muir Webs: Connecting the Parts

Deer in the forest caring for their young; the strong, well-clad, well-fed bears; the lively throng of squirrels; the blessed birds, great and small, stirring and sweetening the groves; and the clouds of happy insects filling the sky with [a] joyous hum as part and parcel of the down-pouring sunshine . . . the plant people, and the glad streams singing their way to the sea. . . . When we try to pick out anything by itself we find that it is bound fast by a thousand invisible cords that cannot be broken, to everything in the universe.

— John Muir, Notebook, July 27, 1869

John Muir, the California naturalist, in the High Sierras in 1902. Muir was a prominent conservationist and ecological thinker.

Many people come to New York City as an act of independence. For young singles out of college, New York may provide a first job; for musicians, a first gig; for actors, a first show. New York is a place where people come to make it, to declare they can stand on their own two feet and escape the entangling bounds of their origins. Behind the desire for independence, however, stands the fact of interdependence, as the city's sanitation workers, police officers, and firefighters all know well. The Yankees don't play unless the men and women of Con Edison keep the power shunting down the transmission lines. The power workers don't throw the right switches unless the water company and grocery suppliers deliver on time, and no one gets to work without the bridge workers, street cleaners, and road crews completing their daily rounds.

Cities are platforms for independence precisely because vast systems are in place to support the basic necessities of millions of people. So too with Mannahatta, though as we shall see, fewer hard hats were required. Mannahatta afforded home and prosperity to millions of plants and animals of at least a thousand different species, each individual independently striving to find food, water, shelter, and a way to raise the kids—all in the context of interdependence. Like in New York today, there were many paths to success, but no guarantees. Just as in New York today, sometimes the failure of one was the key to success for another. Yet somehow, despite the competition, the predation, the disturbance, the tumult that marks any life, the system itself had a stability and presence that attracted newcomers from far and wide.

Naturalists in New York

After the work of the glaciers, the first newcomers to repopulate the rocky landscape were plants and animals. Over the years, these populations have changed and shifted, adjusting to different conditions, until they formed the communities described in the previous chapter. Knowing the species composition of these communities, however, posed new problems when it came to historical reconstruction, not the least of which is that four hundred years is a long time in a landscape as modified as Manhattan's.

Fortunately I had some help. New York City has long attracted not only artists, merchants, and financiers, but also scholars, scientists, and naturalists. Cadwallader Colden, the British governor of New York Colony who stirred up the Liberty Boys in 1770, was a better botanist than politician by all accounts; he corresponded regularly with Carolus Linnaeus about North American flora and taught his daughter Jane the Linnaean system of taxonomy, which she used to great effect to study the plants of the Hudson Valley. John Torrey, a prominent early American natural scientist, was born and bred on Manhattan and wrote his "Catalogue of the Plants growing spontaneously within 30 miles of the City of New York" (1818) after years of fieldwork; he was later a trustee of Columbia College, where he founded the first American periodical on botany, the *Journal of the Torrey Botanical Club*. John James Audubon, the painter and naturalist, lived on "Minniesland," his estate on the Hudson River at 155th Street, from the 1840s on. He and his sons worked on his last book there, the *Viviparous Quadrupeds of North America*, with its paintings of mammals—some not unlike those they had observed on Washington Heights—poised in American landscapes. Frank Chapman, Nathaniel Lord Britton and Elizabeth Britton, William Beebe, Roger Tory Peterson, and many others wrote about nature in the city.

In the nineteenth century, as New York grew in power and prestige, scientific institutions were established for the study, explanation, and conservation of the natural world. In 1801, Elgin Gardens, the first public botanical gardens in the United States, was established, on twenty acres of land, where Rockefeller Center is today. On the grounds of the garden, the Lyceum of Natural History brought scholars together for debate and study; today this institution, first founded in 1817, is the New York Academy of Sciences. The American Museum of Natural History (founded in 1868), the New York Botanical Garden (1891), the New York Zoological Society (1895, now the Wildlife Conservation Society), and the Brooklyn Botanic Gardens (1910) have all brought prominent natural historians like Frank Chapman, Henry Gleason, William Hornaday, and William Beebe to New York. Great scientific expeditions have been launched from New York City to Congo, Mongolia, Borneo, and countless other places. Yet many of the same scientists who traveled abroad to study the natural world also wrote about the nature they saw on the way home from the office.

Fortunately, that tradition continues today. The Mannahatta Project would not have been possible without the current resurgence of interest in the natural history of New York. Dedicated groups of amateurs and professionals gather regularly to observe the birds, butterflies, dragonflies, fish and shellfish, plants and mushrooms, and even the ferns of Manhattan and the surrounding areas. I owe a great debt to the many people who have volunteered their expertise and time to show me the ropes. Today, with the parklands, books, and social networks available, everyone can participate in the nature around us.

My colleagues and I leaned on these sources when we came to the task of putting together a "little black book" of the plants and animals of Mannahatta. To develop these lists of species, we compiled surveys from within seventy-five miles of Columbus Circle of the region's plants and vertebrate animals (i.e., fish, amphibians, reptiles, birds, and mammals) and selected invertebrate *taxa* (the plural form of *taxon*, a group of related organisms, as in a species, genus, or family). For the marine species, we included the waters within a thousand yards of the modern shoreline. For the invertebrates, we selected only a few of the most charismatic taxa (butterflies, dragonflies, oysters, and clams) but also others (tiger beetles and freshwater mussels), when we could find an expert to help with them. We concentrated on studies from Greater New York (not just Manhattan, but also the larger, wilder areas in the Bronx, Brooklyn, Queens, and Staten Island), and drew on studies done in Long Island, New Jersey, and the Hudson Valley, in habitat types similar to those originally found on Manhattan. For the plants, we compiled thirty-five references, including eight book-length treatments; for the birds, twenty-two references; for the mammals, twenty. To make the names consistent over time, we verified scientific names against current taxonomic references.

Our starting assumption was that a species of plant or animal that had been observed *since 1609* might have occurred on Manhattan *in 1609* if it could pass three tests: First, a species must not have been introduced from some other part of the world or other part of North America. Second, a species must not have expanded its range into the New York City region within the last four hundred years as far as we could ascertain. And third, a species must have had a habitat relationship with one or more of the ecological communities on Mannahatta or within the surrounding waters (as described in the last chapter). If a species could pass these three tests, it made it onto the "possible" list—we concluded that it was possible that the species might have occurred on Manhattan in September 1609.

We refined our list of Mannahatta possibles by considering where a species had been observed (on Manhattan or not, and if not, how close) and how frequently over time. Species that we could document as having occurred on Manhattan at some time in the past, and for which reliable observations were available, were designated as "likely." Species that we could document as having occurred within Greater New York, but not necessarily on Manhattan

Reconstructing the historical species list for Mannahatta required adding back in species that had gone extinct, like the heath hen—a former denizen of the Harlem Plains—shown in this print by Mark Catesby. The last heath hen died in 1929 on Nantucket Island.

top Some species were extirpated from Manhattan and have subsequently been reintroduced, like the bald eagle. A successful reintroduction effort by the Department of Parks and Recreation returned eagles to Inwood Hill Park, on Manhattan, in 2001. *bottom* One species that will never return is the passenger pigeon—pictured here with the acorns they loved so much—whose massive flocks once darkened Mannahatta's skies.

Island or neighboring waters, were designated as "probable." The remaining species were labeled as "possible," unless other evidence indicated that they were only infrequent visitors or additional evidence cast further doubt, but not enough to rule out a species' presence in September 1609. These last species were designated as "remote possibilities." The long list of Mannahatta's flora and fauna is provided in Appendix C of the book.

The Plants and Animals of Mannahatta

Different taxa present different problems when it comes to sifting through the information about which plants and animals originally lived on Mannahatta. Some species are very well known, like many of the birds or wild flowers, with thousands of regular observers and decent chronological records from at least the nineteenth century on. Other species are poorly known with only a small, devoted cadre of advocates. When A. J. Grout came to publish his "The Moss Flora of New York City and Vicinity" in 1916, he had to publish it himself, to what was likely a restricted audience. And new species are still being discovered. In 2002, a centipede found in the leaf litter of Central Park was previously unknown to science—no one had ever described it before and there it was in the leaf litter.

Reconstructing the species list also required us to deal with the species traveling through Manhattan only irregularly. Such species, described as vagrants, have only been observed a few times in recorded history. For example, some tropical fish like blennies or flyingfish, carried on the Gulf Stream from warmer climes, may end up in New York waters—though this is very rare. Another example: a manatee arrived in New York Harbor in 2006, far from its native waters in Florida. Storms can blow pelagic bird species, like jaegers and shearwaters, on shore, but this too is a rare event. These species are the kind that were "remote possibilities" for the afternoon of September 12, 1609—improbable, but not impossible.

For some taxa, we needed to add back species that have gone extinct between 1609 and now. Passenger pigeons were likely a component of the historical fauna, as were, possibly, the heath hen, and more dubiously, the Labrador duck and Carolina parakeet. For the mammals, no species that occurred on Mannahatta in 1609 is globally extinct that we know of, but many of the larger mammals are regionally extirpated—including wolves, lynx,

T. 98.

Nux juglans virginiana alba &c.
The Hiccory Tree.

The Pig-nut.

Coccothraustes ruber.
The red Bird.

Some species common around New York City today were unknown historically, like the northern cardinal. The cardinal shifted its range north during the twentieth century and is now observed regularly in parks and suburban yards in the Northeast. The pignut hickory, though, was common on Mannahatta.

eastern cougars, and elk. The best information sources for the mammals are actually the early Dutch and British records, from when the fauna was still intact and hunting was avidly pursued. Those records present their own problems, however, in matching the seventeenth-century names to the twenty-first-century ones; the colonial observers didn't really know what they were looking at, so neither do we.

Introductions also complicate the story. New York City has long been a port of entry not only for people and goods, but for many new species introduced to North America, a kind of Ellis Island for biological homogenization. The botanist Norman Taylor's 1915 study of plants from within a hundred miles of New York listed for each plant family an appendix of "ballast plants"—plants that (for the moment) could only be found in the harbor where ships off-loaded the ballast rocks used during transatlantic voyages. As a result of introductions, the plant diversity of New York City today may be twice today what it was in 1609. Animal introductions include such local favorites as the Norway rat, European starling, English sparrow, rock dove (i.e., pigeon), wooly adelgid (a small mitelike creature that sucks the life from hemlocks), and the chestnut blight (a fungus that has virtually wiped out the American chestnut)—all crimes to nature as far as local farmers, fishermen, foresters, and partisans of the native flora and fauna are concerned. The most famous New York introduction was that of starlings to Central Park in 1890, by an admirer who thought the park would be enhanced by having free-living examples of all the birds mentioned in Shakespeare's plays. The starling had been introduced previously in Pennsylvania, Ohio, and Oregon without success; after two tries in Central Park, though, it took—the hundred birds released in 1890 have now increased to an estimated at 150–200 million, one of the most abundant birds in the world.

On top of all this, many plants and animals don't stay put—they move, and the result is range shifts. Geographic ranges of species are not constant through time; rather, species adjust their ranges according to changes in the underlying habitat factors, including ecosystem type and climate. Many of the birds that we commonly see in New York in the twenty-first century are relative newcomers. The cardinal and northern mockingbird are the most often cited examples, but many of our waterbirds are also new arrivals, including the mallard, the snowy egret, and the yellow-crowned night heron, which were originally southern or western species, and which colonized the Northeast in the late nineteenth or early twentieth century. The cattle egret is also commonly

It is unlikely that the bison was ever found on Manhattan, but it is not impossible. A bison was shot in the Delaware Water Gap in the eighteenth century, and a similar habitat once extended across New Jersey to the Hudson River. Such species are identified as remote possibilities on the Mannahatta species list in Appendix C.

seen today, but was unknown historically, having colonized North America on its own in the 1940s, from Africa. One of the early Dutch settlers, David Pietersz de Vries, described the geese of Manhattan: "There are great numbers of two kinds of geese, which stay here through the winter. One kind is the gray geese, which weigh fifteen or sixteen pounds each; the other they call white-heads, weighing six or seven pounds, very numerous, flying by thousands, and of good flavor." He was probably referring to the greater white-fronted goose and snow goose, respectively, but he doesn't mention the black-headed Canada goose, which only made our list as a "possible," despite its prevalence today (Canada geese were originally more common in the interior of the continent). The coyote is a recent example of range shifts in mammals. Coyotes originally lived on the Great Plains—excluded by wolves from the eastern forests. However, over the course of the twentieth century, coyotes have made an expansion eastward. In 2005 one even made it into Central Park!

The Central Park coyote, Hal, provides an interesting case study in connectivity. If species are to move as changes in habitat or climate occur, then they need to have avenues for those movements—conservation biologists term these bits of connector habitat *corridors*. Like a clear path between the bedroom and the bathroom, corridors are essential for accommodating life's many emergencies. For Hal, the corridor onto Manhattan was probably a bridge (possibly the Henry Hudson Bridge from Riverdale, in the Bronx), but historically a major corridor onto the island of Mannahatta was the marshy, winding, shallow Spuyten Duyvil Creek, which separated the northern part of Manhattan from the heights of the Bronx. Many species could have walked or swum across the creek at low tide; people later crossed via the King's Bridge in the same place.

Of course, walking or swimming won't work for all species; different taxa need different kinds of connectivity. Most birds can fly where they please, though to some the Hudson River can be a barrier. Roger Tory Peterson, of field-guide fame, maintained that the tufted titmouse and the cardinal, for example, did not reach Manhattan until after the construction of the George Washington Bridge—apparently the watery trough of the Hudson River was too much for them to surmount on wings alone. Freshwater fishes and amphibians have an even tougher problem, because most can't cross saltwater. Some of the freshwater fish in Mannahatta's streams were probably remnant populations from the time when the glacial lake Hudson covered all the area; as it drained away, small populations were stranded, disconnected from others of their kind. For less mobile species, another strategy for connectivity is for the kids to leave home; fish eggs may sometimes "accidentally" hitch a ride on a more mobile species, like on the legs of a duck. Plants have evolved this strategy to an exquisite degree, regularly conniving with the birds, bees, and squirrels, among others, offering fruits and nuts to transport their seeds; not bad for lowly plants rooted in the soil. Those allergies in the spring? That's tree pollen taking advantage of the wind to get around.

All together, these factors make understanding the original biodiversity of Mannahatta a complicated exercise, but a satisfying one, especially as Mannahatta was remarkably diverse. We believe the plants (trees, shrubs, vines, and herbs, including ferns) that *likely* existed on or near Mannahatta on September 12, 1609, totaled at least 627 species, and *possibly* as many as 1,195 species. The animal wildlife (mammals, birds, fish, reptiles, and amphibians), not counting the insects or other invertebrates, totaled 658 possible species, of which 57 percent (374) were likely, including many of the favorites of nature films: wolves, black bears, mountain lions, white-tailed deer, bobcats, beavers, harbor porpoises and many others that made Mannahatta home.

Connecting the Parts

If the previous conundrum was which species populated Mannahatta in 1609, then the next is how did they make out. If there were this many species on one island, how did they manage to all succeed in such a narrow space?

To answer this, we need to remember what the game of life is about. The ecological game of life, for all living things, from viruses to chestnuts to people, is to reach maturity and reproduce, so that the next generation has a chance to outlive the current one. To reach maturity, organisms need food, water, shelter, and some time. To reproduce, they need to find a mate and then find the right resources to woo the mate and, after, raise the kids. The search for the necessities of life, which all organisms undertake, the remarkable strategies those organisms employ for gaining those resources while in competition with others, and the long-term consequences of who wins and who loses arc what shapes the game of life and the evolution of living things. They are also what make ecology fun.

Ecologists think constantly about *habitat*, a word that conveys many of these essential relationships. In fact, the word *ecology* derives from the Greek word *oikos*, meaning "house" or "home"; ecology is essentially the study of home. Field guides often include habitat descriptions with the specific purpose of helping people find plants and animals in the wild. Natural-history

Table II.

Summary of the species diversity of the flora and fauna of Mannahatta in September 1609

	PROBABILITY OF PRESENCE				
Biological Species	Likely	Probable	Possible	Remote Possibility	Total
Plants	627	24	544	—	1,195
Fish	85	17	28	25	155
Reptiles and Amphibians	32	10	6	7	55
Birds	233	74	11	35	353
Mammals	24	42	15	14	95
Total	1,001	167	604	81	1,853

accounts provide more detail and context, elaborating on interesting or unique behaviors and ecological interactions between species. For well-studied regions, like the northeastern United States, field guides and natural histories provide rich veins of information about habitat relationships, information we needed to infer where different species lived on Mannahatta.

Because organisms depend on other organisms, which depend on yet other organisms, it has long been recognized that habitat relationships can be combined into webs, or networks, of relationships. The best studied among these relationships are food webs, which lend themselves to quantification and analysis through studies of diet. Wildlife biologists love to follow animals around and examine their poop to find out what they ate; the scientific literature is loaded with thousands of pages of scatological analysis. In recent years, network analysis—which has been applied to the structure of the Internet and the AIDS epidemic—has also been used to study food webs, resulting in a proliferation of scientific output, with mathematicians, computer scientists, and graphic designers all pitching in.

Food is only one part of the habitat, however. Landscape ecologists attempting to predict the geographic distribution of a species (i.e., where an organism might be found) are more likely to use factors like soil type, topography, distance from water, and ecological-community type than what the species had for breakfast. One consequence of the focus on food webs is that ecological-network analysis has focused mainly on interactions between one organism and another ("biotic" interactions), but in ecosystems, organisms also interact with nonliving elements (e.g., soil, water, wind, and disturbance processes like fire—"abiotic" interactions). As we have seen, these abiotic interactions are just as important. Another consequence is that even in the "species-rich" food webs that have been studied so far, the number of elements is relatively small (typically less than three hundred), whereas in real ecosystems, composed of elements of many different taxa, processes, and nonliving entities, the number of potentially interacting elements can be much greater. For example, on Mannahatta, there could have been nearly 1,200 different species (and that with only a selection of the invertebrates), assembled in 55 different communities, living in a landscape composed of over 500 hills, 88 miles of streams, 21 ponds, 300 springs, and 17 soil types.

To express these relationships and create the maps of where the species might have been on Mannahatta, we needed a new way to speak about all the species and parts of the landscape. We needed a language that would connect the parts, a grammar of habitat.

A Grammar of Habitat

In the study of linguistics, grammar is the set of rules that describe how a language works. Baseball wouldn't make any sense if we didn't know that the hitter only gets three strikes and the pitcher four balls. The same principle holds true for a language—words strung together don't make sense unless we also know the rules that govern how the words taken together make meaning; those rules are what English teachers call the grammar. Grammar defines what kinds of words are allowed in what contexts and how they are connected together to form meaning. By analogy, a new grammar of habitat would express what "habitat words" are allowed and the kinds of relationships those elements of habitat could have to one another.

An example: In a 2003 study of the beaver, Dieter Müller-Schwarze and Lixing Sun describe what beavers need: "A slowly meandering stream

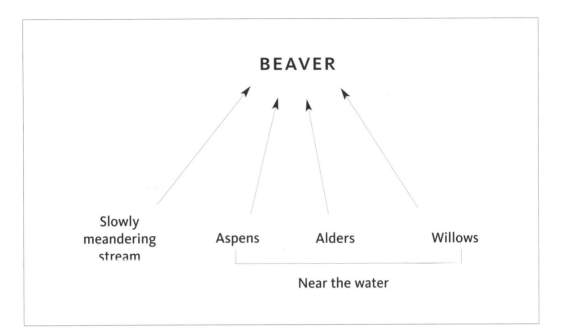

BEAVER

Slowly meandering stream

Aspens   Alders   Willows

Near the water

top Beavers' habitat requirements can be expressed as a web of relationships, like a network. As illustrated in this simplified example, beavers depend on different trees species and the presence of slowly meandering streams. *bottom* Beavers were abundant on Mannahatta and are still found on the city seal. Their habitat requirements and behavior structure the landscape for many other species.

with aspen trees and alder and willow thickets near the water comprises the ideal beaver habitat." If we were to attempt to construct a "habitat sentence" based on this description, we could begin by listing the elements that would be required to support a species: "a slowly meandering stream," "aspen trees" (*Populus tremuloides*), "alder shrubs" (*Alnus* spp.), "willow thickets" (shrubby *Salix* spp.), and "[areas] near the water."

We will call each of these things that we need to support a species a "habitat element." Habitat elements can be biota (the trees and shrubs) or abiota (the slowly meandering stream). They can exist alone (*Populus tremuloides*) or in groups (*Alnus* spp.—there were two different species of alder likely found on Mannahatta). Combinations of habitat elements are also possible—a "stream with aspens and alders near" (to paraphrase now) is actually the combination of the element "distance to stream" (which helps us define "near") and the elements "aspens" and "alders." Other elements are direct derivates of another element (e.g., beavers beget beaver cubs); yet others are creations (e.g., beaver dams are created by beavers). These habitat elements can be thought of as like the nouns in a sentence.

Habitat elements can be spatially identical to the habitat (the beaver is found where the stream is found) or can specify neighboring relationships ("near the water"). Some elements are explicitly stated in the habitat description, but many others are implicit, and as good naturalists we are assumed to know them. For example, we know that beavers need air to breathe, even though professors Müller-Schwarze and Sun omit that fact. We know that aspen trees need sunlight for photosynthesis. We assume that the climate is appropriate for both beavers and aspens—neither too hot nor too cold—even though that's not stated. The unstated habitat elements are "implicit."

In this unconventional grammar, every habitat sentence must have at least three parts: a subject, a predicate, and one or more objects. The subject is the element whose habitat we want to define (in this case, the beaver). It is usually, but not always, as we shall see, a biological species. The objects are the parts of the environment on which the subject depends (i.e., the stream, the aspens, and the alders). The predicate links them; it defines the type of dependency: Does the element supply something, like food, water, shelter, or a reproductive requirement (like materials for a bird's nest, or a winter den for a black bear)? In the beaver's case, the stream supplies water and shelter; the trees supply shelter and food. For reproduction, the beaver needs another beaver, a stream to dam, and sticks and mud to build the lodge. Once they have such a home, the beaver couple has every thing they need to succeed.

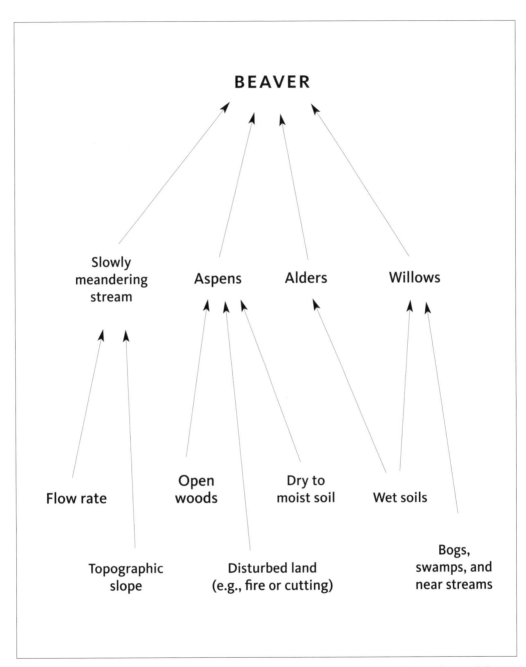

The habitat elements that beavers depend on also have habitat requirements. The web of relationships can be extended another level by including the requirements of aspens, alders, and willows. Streams also have conditions that create them, though these are not habitat dependencies per se, they can be included in the network of ecological relationships.

Habitat descriptions from field guides and natural history accounts often include modifiers, like "especially" or "often," that indicates the strength of the relationship ("Southern leopard frogs are found in wetlands, especially wet meadows"). Other phrasing indicates a negative or oppositional relationship ("Ravens are highly sensitive to human persecution"). By noting them, we can attribute strength and direction to the connections.

A profound quality of these habitat sentences is that elements can be subjects in one instance and objects in another. For example, we now know that beavers need aspens. But what do *aspens* need? Reaching for a field guide to trees, we read that *Populus tremuloides* prefers "open woods with dry or moist soil, especially in cut-over (i.e., disturbed) land." Thus we can write another habitat sentence for aspens—now as a subject, not an object—showing their dependence on "open woods" and "dry or moist soil" and "disturbance." Of course this sentence leads one to ask, what is the habitat for "open woods" or for "dry or moist soil" or for "disturbance"?

Interestingly, most ecologists would not describe "open woods," an ecological community type, as having "habitat" in the same way that plants or animals do; "habitat" is usually restricted to a species and defined in terms of food, water, shelter and so on. Nevertheless, if we expand our thinking slightly, it is possible to describe where open woodland types are found based on topography, soil type, and microclimate; in fact as a mapping exercise, that's what we regularly do to predict where different community types are found. Similarly, although streams or dry soil do not have food or water requirements per se, they do have conditions under which they form, which are the study respectively of hydrologists and soil scientists. Disturbance processes are the domain of landscape ecologists, who explore the causes and consequences of fire, flood and so on. As described in the last chapter, to model a disturbance we need to insert inputs into the computer model; those inputs are the factors that underlie the disturbance processes. In the context of a fire, those same factors—ignition source, wind speed, vegetation type—are elements in a habitat sentence. We can continue to write habitat sentences for all of these different habitat elements if we are willing to cross disciplinary boundaries to find the information we need.

Like a child who won't stop asking "why?" my colleagues and I began exploring outward through the web of relationships, documenting in each instance what we found. The search led us through fishing guides and accounts of wildlife hunts; through textbooks on pedology (the study of soils), hydrology, and meteorology; into descriptions of copepods, cephalopods, and

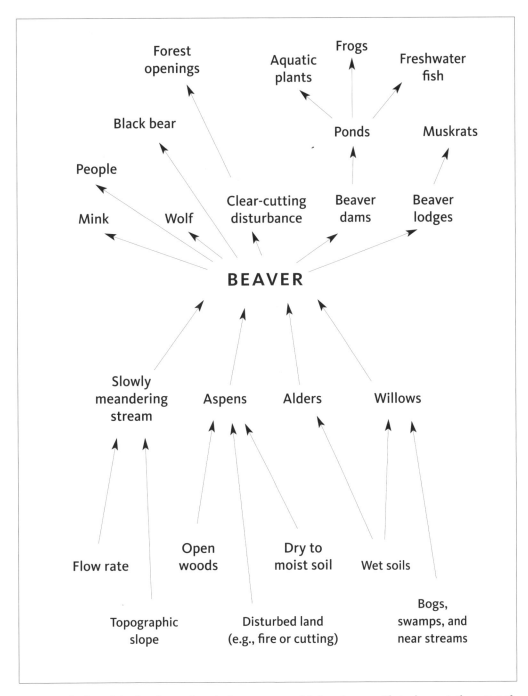

Beavers are also depended on by other species and other components of their environment. Placing beavers in the context of both their dependencies and their requirements illustrates their importance to the ecosystem as a whole.

decapods; and deeper than originally planned into annals of insects, for which we had to create a new category: the unresolved group. There are too many insects—and most of them are too little known—to say with much confidence exactly which species of flies or mosquitoes there were on Mannahatta.

Like the parent of that child who won't stop asking "why?" we eventually had to define "stops"—questions we would not answer; otherwise, the search would be infinite and the Mannahatta Project never-ending. Stops are elements that we could not or would not define the habitat sentence for; they include time, space, geology, climate, and the strange and surprising turns of human culture. I'm not a sociologist; I wouldn't try to explain why the Lenape told stories of how the earth formed on a turtle's back. I simply accept it as a given that they did.

Seeing the Invisible

One summer afternoon in the High Sierras, John Muir, the California naturalist, wrote in his notebook the epigraph that opened this chapter, an intuition that has been a cornerstone of conservation thinking ever since: "When we try to pick out anything by itself we find that it is bound fast by a thousand invisible cords that cannot be broken, to everything in the universe." Muir realized that each part of nature was dependent on other parts, and that those parts were connected to yet other parts, in a network that, if taken to its logical conclusion, would encompass the whole.

Interestingly the same idea seems also to apply to cities. Each citizen is dependent on other citizens, like the species in nature, and those citizens and their interdependencies taken together make the city itself. A city without its millions of connections, formed of the informal one-on-one relationships conducted in the course of daily life, begins to decay. John Donne, the seventeenth-century English poet, had the same idea, though in a different context when he wrote: "No man is an island, entire of itself, every man is a piece of the continent, a part of the main."

Without meaning to, in the search to reconstruct Mannahatta, we had found a way to make Muir's "invisible cords" visible, to name them and to count them. We were able to do this because the habitat sentences can be formulated as a network. Each node in the network is a habitat element, whether a species, a community, an abiotic element, or a group of these; sometimes these elements function as a subject, other times as an object. Each connection is a relationship based on food, shelter, water, or reproduction, or in the case of

T. 72.

Rana maxima   *Helleborena*

What is the connection between a bullfrog and a lady's slipper orchid? According to the Muir web, wetlands, wet woods and thickets, and boggy soils.

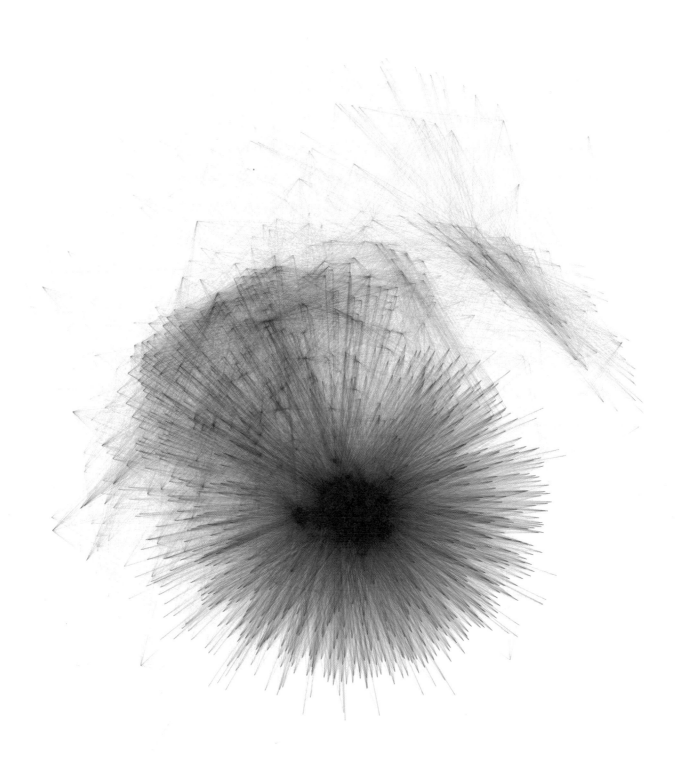

The Mannahatta Muir web. Computer algorithms map the structure based on the numbers of relationships between elements, putting related elements close together. The true Muir web structure is multi-dimensional.

abiotic elements, on physical process dependencies like soil formation or how topography defines slope and slope determines water flow. In honor of Muir and his insight, I called these new networks "Muir webs."

In its initial iteration, the Muir web built on the list of likely species contained a total of 1,623 elements, comprised of 80 percent species or groups of species, 10 percent abiotic elements or groups of elements, 5 percent ecological communities or groups of communities, and 5 percent "combinations," composed of living and nonliving elements. In other words, species dominated the network, but the abiotic environment (the "fundamentals" of Mannahatta) was also strongly present, and various combinations of elements—whether of ecological communities or of life and not-life (the aspens near the stream)—were critically important.

Between those 1,623 elements, we wrote 8,245 explicit habitat sentences based on descriptions available in field guides and natural histories of the food, water, shelter, and, where applicable, reproductive requirements, of the plants and animals of Mannahatta. Many species are just passing through in September; they aren't staying to reproduce (which is largely a spring- and summertime activity in the temperate northern latitudes), so their reproductive requirements are not included in the Mannahatta Muir web. Of the relationships in the 8,245 habitat sentences, 55 percent were central or primary relationships with other elements—the bread and butter of habitat relationships; 37 percent were relationships identifying membership within groups; and 6 percent were enhancing relationships—that is, relationships that were positive but not required parts of the habitat. The remaining relationships involved a small number of elements of lesser strength; very few were negative relationships that attenuated or excluded another species. These kinds of negative relationships were probably more important than this initial analysis would suggest, as we didn't include the not-so-nice sides of nature—competition, parasitism, and disease. They represent the next frontier in developing Muir webs. In addition, our Muir web is biased toward the species big enough to be easily seen and studied; the insects and other microflora and fauna get a short shrift, mostly because we know comparatively little about them.

The structure of the Muir web is difficult to illustrate in a book, because it exists simultaneously in many more dimensions than can be shown on a page. Viewing the web from any one direction necessarily obscures relationships visible from another perspective. Like the Wall Street businesswoman who sees the city only in terms of economics or the policeman who sees it only in

As this detail of the Mannahatta Muir web shows, each point represents a habitat element, which could be a plant, an animal, or a nonliving component of the environment (like a type of soil or a type of stream). The lines represent the interconnections between habitat elements.

terms of law and order, the perspective of any one "species" is partial and limited. Yet the lives of all species, just like the lives of all people, are connected together. In the big city we sometimes forget those connections, and worse, sometimes we deliberately ignore them—that's usually when the yelling starts—but the connections are there, just the same, making the city, and ecosystems, possible.

The Resiliency of Groups

In studying Mannahatta's Muir web, I became curious about the large number of habitat elements participating in groups. Groups are collections of elements—oak trees, marsh-dwelling birds, woodlands, and so forth—that form habitats for other elements in the Muir web. They appear very commonly in habitat descriptions. I found that 65 percent of the species in the Muir web *depend on* one or more group for their habitats, and 83 percent *belong to* one or more group. All told there were more than 231 groups participating in the Mannahatta Muir web—oaks, alders, turtles, snakes, young ungulates, and so on.

For example, in the description "eastern gray squirrels eat nuts," "nuts" is a group composed of acorns, hickory nuts, chestnuts, beechnuts—all the nuts. Squirrels might prefer one kind of nut to another, but in a pinch any nut will do. Nuts come from trees, and so the group "nuts" is equivalent in some sense to the list of all the trees that produce nuts: red oak, white oak, chestnut, beech, pignut hickory, shagbark hickory, mockernut hickory, and so on. The habitat sentence, then, for the gray squirrel is "squirrel (eats) nuts," where "nuts" are a group whose membership includes all the trees that make nuts.

Memberships are not limited to only trees—people also form organizations and institutions that we rely on—the police force, the power company, the sanitation department—without depending exactly on any one individual. For example, we need the police department when a crime is committed. However, if an individual officer decides to leave the force, we are not bereft of protection. The group, and the group's function, continues even if an individual member leaves. By the same token, neighborhoods persist even after certain of our neighbors move on—though ineffably the neighborhood is different as a result. The result of these group dependencies is resilience against loss. Like the squirrel that will survive even if one species of tree (the chestnut, for example) declines, the city will survive even as its individuals move on. Being connected to groups is a smart strategy for a species that wants to survive.

And yet individuals are important too. If you talk to New Yorkers about what makes the city special, they'll tell you about the individual people they know, and how they like living in the interesting and dynamic city because it draws such interesting and dynamic people. It's a self-reinforcing cycle that continues to add new and, just as importantly, diverse, connections — connections different from those we had before, connections that provide new ways to survive—which in turn lead to more connections, new ways to survive in a changing world.

Back in Mannahatta, I suspected the same was true of functioning ecosystems. After all, there are at least three possible ways to represent "squirrel (eats) nuts" in a Muir web: There could be one connection between "squirrel" and "nuts," there could be a connection between "squirrel" and the explicitly defined set of "nuts," or there could be connections between "squirrel" and each of the trees that have membership in the group "nuts." Obviously, the structure of the network would be vastly different depending on how these connections were drawn.

To test this idea, I wrote a computer program to "expand" the habitat relationships within groups. Rather than connecting "squirrel" to "nuts," the expanded relationships connect the gray squirrel to all of the nut-producing trees. In expanded form, each node in the Muir web network represents only a species, an ecological community, or an abiota, and groups and combinations of elements are removed. The result is a dramatic increase in the number of connections, with only a modest decline in the number of habitat elements; the Muir web connectivity expanded from 8,345 connections to 65,739, a nearly 700 percent increase! Simultaneously, the number of elements dropped from 1,623 to 1,261, (a 28 percent decrease) as now each connection in the Muir web represented an individual entity, equivalents if you like, that were no longer resolvable into finer units.

In human society those individual entities would be individual people, and, as described earlier, people, like the plants and animals of the Muir web, have affiliations in groups. For the Lenape, the affiliations were to language and culture, tribe and clan, and place. For modern New Yorkers, affiliations are to jobs and friends and interests. And, like in the Muir web, we both *depend on* and *are depended on* through our affiliations in groups. We are connected simultaneously through our participation in larger institutions and by the connections we make to other individuals. In some sense our uniqueness as actors in society derives in part from the composition and strength of our connections; certainly much of our satisfaction lies in our rela-

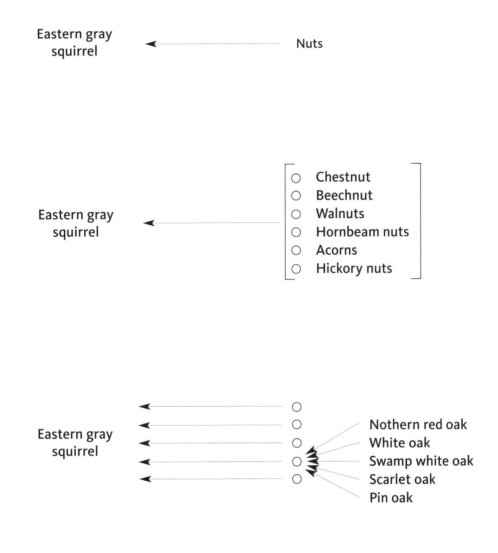

Groups of species are a prominent feature of Muir webs. They can be represented as a single link from a subject, like "squirrel" to a group element such as "nuts"; as a link between the subject and the explicitly defined group of "nuts"; or as individual links from the subject to all the elements within the group, for example, from "squirrel" to all the trees that produce "nuts."

Table III.

Summary of the twenty most important elements in the Muir web, in terms of number of other elements dependent on them ("group" elements are not expanded)

ELEMENT	NUMBER OF DIRECT DEPENDENCIES
Forests or woods	189
Swamps	128
Open woods	77
Insects	69
Woods and thickets	61
Fields	60
Freshwater marshes	59
Wet meadows	54
Meadows	53
Thickets	48
Streams	48
Ponds	46
Aquatic insects	43
Wet woods	38
Dry woods	37
Peatlands (bogs)	35
Salt marsh communities	34
Surface freshwater	33
Fruits	31
Small marine fishes	31

Table IV.
Summary of the twenty most important elements in the Muir web, in terms of number of other elements dependent on them ("group" elements are expanded to their constituent elements)

ELEMENT	NUMBER OF DIRECT DEPENDENCIES
Soil moisture	528
Floodplain forest	484
Coastal oak-beech forest	480
Coastal oak-hickory forest	479
Coastal Appalachian oak-pine forest	478
Chestnut oak forest	478
Oak-tulip forest	478
Hemlock-northern hardwood forest	477
Freshwater stream	289
Topographic position	202
Eutrophic pond	185
Large pond	183
Ravine	183
Coastal plain Atlantic white cedar swamp	178
Successional old field community	159
Time since disturbance	157
Red maple-hardwood swamp	156
Beaver (*Castor canadensis*)	146
Shrub swamp	145
Successional shrubland	134

tionships with others. Change our connections and at some fundamental level we change who we are.

What's different about nature is that the roles that different species play are not so flexible as human social connections. People can and do change groups and institutions—one is not trapped into being a police officer or schoolteacher or even a scientist, especially in America, where education is available and freedom of choice is cherished. One can choose different friends or an alternative lifestyle. For species in the Muir web, it is not so simple. Although species' roles do sometimes change, those changes happen over evolutionary time, over many generations, sometimes over millions of years. For any given type of plant or frog or bird, success or failure is largely determined by their genes and their environment—it might be said, by the luck of the draw and the consistency of the environment from one generation to the next. If someone cuts down their forest habitat or diverts the stream they need into a pipe, they can't just retrain and get a new job; loss of home is loss of life, with no unemployment benefits. By the same token, restore a patch of forest or bring a stream back to life and suddenly a new world of connections becomes possible.

The Mannahatta Time Machine

Muir webs were devised as a way of mapping the plants and animals in the Mannahatta landscape, and then became a way of mapping the relationships that bind nature together. But lurking behind this was always the question: Can we travel back in time to see Mannahatta as it was? And will that view change how we see our world today?

The reconstructed landscape views in this book are our attempt to realize the luxurious natural world of Mannahatta. These images were created by my friend and colleague Markley Boyer, using the kind of movie magic that Pixar or Disney is famous for, minus the fairy-tale forests, evil witches, and cute trash compactors. Recall what has gone into these pictures: georeferencing of the British Headquarters Map, construction of the digital-elevation model, modeling of the Lenape landscape, and careful mapping of the ecological communities along gradients. To finish the job, all that was left was to convert the Muir webs into maps of the individual species.

To translate the Muir webs into maps required some further programming. As I sat on my bed one evening typing away, my seven-year-old son bounced in and asked me what I was doing.

"Working," I said.

He peered around the laptop screen. "Working on what?"

"I'm writing a computer program, Everett."

"What for?"

"It's complicated." I continued typing, trying to concentrate, hoping he would find another way to distract himself.

Undeterred, he asked, "Can you give me a summary?" His second-grade class had been learning to write summaries of the books they'd been reading. They had to say in one sentence what the main idea was and then give concrete examples.

I looked up from my computer code. He looked back at me with that open-faced, completely casual confidence that children possess at a certain age—his age. I took my hands from the keyboard. Now I really had to concentrate.

I cleared my throat. "OK. I'm writing a computer program . . . that writes other computer programs . . . that tell the computer how to make maps of where all the species once were on Manhattan. If I can finish it, it will tell me where the beavers and other animals were four hundred years ago."

He sat back and smiled. "That was a really good summary, Daddy!" he said emphatically. Then he bounced away.

And that was the trick. The Muir web was so complicated that only an iterative computer program could work through all the relationships, find the right layers in the GIS (out of the nearly two hundred georeferenced layers that we had prepared from the British Headquarters Map and other sources), and not make a mistake along the way. Moreover, because the maps built on one another, automating the process meant that if we made a change on one of the input maps, all we needed to do to alter the maps for all the species was to press the button and the process could start again. So much easier than parenting!

The beautiful part of all this dry data processing and calculation, finally, was the maps themselves. Although it was a lot of work, the soft layering of the resulting maps reminds me of watercolor paintings. Each layer of information, like an intermediate wash of color, is in itself relatively simple. The lines of streams, the patches of forest, and the burned areas all have distinct forms, but as they combine together to make maps of species, and as those maps of species combine together to make habitat maps of other species, the landscape takes on a deeper tone, a more subtle aspect, gradients on gradients, creating extraordinary, intricate patterns. Artists and mathematicians have long known the value of combining simple shapes to create new and exciting forms. As the computer worked through the different habitat elements, we could see

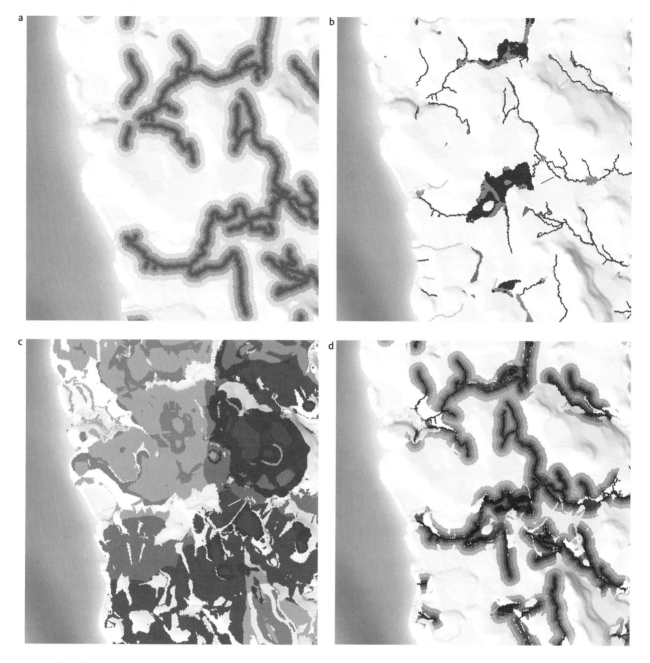

Muir webs can be used to compose habitat maps of species. Maps of (a) distance from water, (b) distribution of alders, and (c) distribution of aspens are required to create (d) Mannahatta's distribution of beavers in the vicinity of today's Times Square.

PROBABILITY DISTRIBUTION FOR BEAVERS

This map shows where beavers might have been found four hundred years ago, based on analysis of the landscape and the Mannahatta Muir web. It suggests that approximately two percent of Mannahatta was highly suitable for beavers. Analogous maps were created for all the 1,001 likely species of Mannahatta (shown in Appendix C). Because all the layers are georeferenced in a geographic information system, they can be overlaid with maps of Manhattan's landscape today.

Not surprisingly, the distribution of beavers four hundred years ago closely follows the former distribution of freshwater streams and ponds. It's likely that all the major stream networks on Mannahatta had at least one resident beaver family when Hudson arrived in 1609.

The rocky hills of the Upper West Side and Central Park were once particularly good beaver habitat. Young adult beavers disperse around age two, following stream corridors and crossing divides where necessary. They may begin by exploring the territory in the surrounding one and a half miles; eventually their sallies extend to lengths of two to six miles (e.g., Columbia University to the Upper East Side), and, rarely, up to twenty miles (e.g., Inwood to Downtown and back).

By comparing the beaver's distribution to today's street grid, we can see the correspondence between modern addresses and former beaver neighborhoods. By analyzing thousands of distributions like this one through the Muir web, we can estimate the historic biodiversity of every block on Manhattan—thus concluding that Times Square may have once been home to a beaver pond, along with all the plants and animals associated with beavers.

BEAVER PROBABILITY

More probable

Less probable

Contemporary street grid

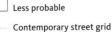

0   0.5   1
MILES

the—literally—tens of thousands of landscape relationships existing between thousands of species and millions of individual plants and animals, representing the original ecology of an island, on a hot and fair summer afternoon, four hundred years before.

It was these maps that, in the end, I gave to Mark to create the images in this book. He took the computer files from the GIS and applied digital tools that know the shape and size of trees and the way the grass bends and how the light refracts over water, tools that allow us to drape the Mannahatta landscape with a forgotten ecology. The images are like maps in their geographic precision, which enables us to match them exactly to modern photographs of the city; they are like scientific charts, filled with careful measurements backed up by deep documentation; and they are like paintings in that they reflect not only their subject but also our sensibilities of the natural world.

These images of Manhattan's past and present stand as symbols of the great tension at the heart of twenty-first-century humanity's relationship with the natural world. On one side, Mannahatta represents the best of nature's resilience and abundance—the ecological fundamentals of civilization before they had been largely entrained to our needs and desires. On the other side, Manhattan represents what might be the most exciting and stimulating city that has ever existed, providing home and satisfaction to extraordinary numbers of people, with previously unknown levels of knowledge, power, and freedom to make choices about the kind of lives they want to lead. The success of Manhattan is directly related to our success harnessing the natural potential of the planet that Mannahatta represents. The risk is that in this era of unprecedented population and consumption, with the resulting climate change, species extinctions, and habitat destruction, we are overwhelming the same planetary systems that made our achievement possible in the first place.

For my part, I look forward to a world with both Mannahattas and Manhattans. Choosing certain parts of the human footprint that we dedicate to people, where we create great places to live, will free other parts of the planet to thrive as Mannahatta once did. And cities, infused with a spirit of Mannahatta, can be ecologically efficient habitats for people and thus demand fewer resources from a planet under strain. With wisdom we can find a way of life, not unlike what the Lenapes knew, where respect and community balance ambition and self-grandeur, living in landscapes that we love, and in a manner that reinforces the continuity of life. I've come to believe that cities are the best place to create this kind of living. In the final chapter, I will try to explain why.

following pages

Both Mannahatta and Manhattan are extraordinary in their own terms. Going forward, doing cities right may be the key to saving the nature that Mannahatta represents. Midtown Manhattan circa 2009 and 1609.

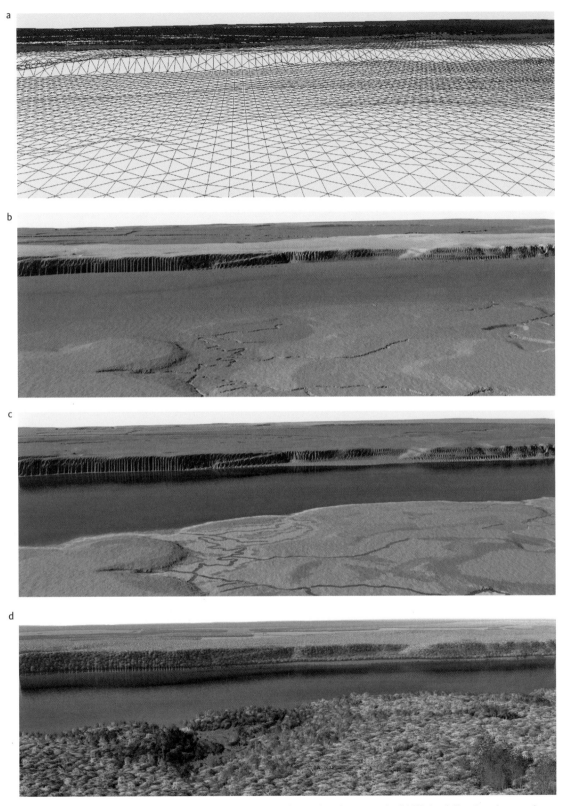

Our landscape views are composited from (a) wire-frame models of Mannahatta's topography, (b) filled and illuminated textured surfaces, and (c) georeferenced ecological community maps. Together with properly placed three-dimensional models of trees and other species, these layers produce (d) the final view of Mannahatta in 1609. Since these views are georeferenced, they can be matched to any place on Manhattan today.

Chapter Seven

Manhattan 2409

Others will see the islands large and small,
Fifty years hence, others will see them as they cross,
     the sun half an hour high,
A hundred years hence, or ever so many hundred
     years hence, others will see them,
Will enjoy the sunset, the pouring in of the flood-tide,
     the falling back to the sea of the ebb-tide.

.   .   .   .

Just as you feel when you look on the river and sky,
     so I felt,
Just as any of you is one of a living crowd, I was one
     of a crowd . . .

— Walt Whitman, "Crossing Brooklyn Ferry,"
    Leaves of Grass 1860

Four hundred years separate the biodiverse and productive
ecological landscape of Mannahatta from the culturally
diverse and thriving cityscape of Manhattan today. What
will Manhattan be like four hundred years from now?

Cities are constructed habitat for people—a lot of people. People, just like every other creature in the Muir web of ecological relationships, have habitat requirements; these include food, water, shelter, and reproductive resources (i.e., what we need to have and raise the kids, including not only wine bars and nightclubs, but also playgrounds and schools). But that's not enough. People, perhaps uniquely in the natural world, require something else: We need a sense of meaning. And meaning is what cities are uniquely designed to provide, meaning of many kinds to many kinds of people.

Twenty-first-century Manhattan is the quintessential example of a meaningful city. It takes eleven pages of eight-point type in an average *New Yorker* magazine to describe just some of the art, dance, music, and movie events going on in the city each week. Manhattan has over 1,200 churches, synagogues, and other places of worship. A recent summer spawned 124 street fairs and festivals, 36 parades, and at least 85 free outdoor concerts; there are over 18,000 places to eat out in the city. New York City provides extraordinary opportunities for epicures, sports fans, dog lovers, film buffs, art viewers, audiophiles, ball players, hipsters, and parents. Of all the ways in which people find meaning in the world, perhaps the only one that is not satisfied to the hilt in Manhattan is the one that the city's earliest residents, the Lenape, found most important: a connection to nature.

It's not that the connection to nature is entirely absent in the city. What would Manhattan be without its great Central Park, a respite of greenness in the stony city? Or the forests of Inwood? Or the stirring waters of the harbor and rivers? All the parks and open places give those consciously looking some sense of the natural world. Even for those who choose not to look, the natural world unceasingly asserts itself in thunderstorms and snowdrifts, in bird migrations (and collisions—damn those glass-walled buildings), in coyotes and turkeys (or a beaver!) sneaking back into the city. Nature lurks, offers herself, pirouettes in small, quiet places, even while we rush on to our next appointment.

The problem is that the task of meeting the basic requirements—of food, water, and shelter—for 1.5 million people, plus accommodating another million workers and perhaps 120,000 tourists per day, gets in the way of whatever the rest of nature might want to do. Not only are the material requirements for that large number of people huge, but the costs of getting the materials to an island of concentrated humanity magnify the requirements exponentially. We have dedicated large swaths of the city to transportation and extended New York's reach until it embraces literally the entire world.

top Central Park is the green heart of Manhattan Island, an essential component of habitat for Manhattan's people and wildlife. Many New Yorkers feel that life in the city would not be tenable without its parks. *bottom* The Bronx River, the city's last remaining freshwater river, has benefited from more than thirty years of cleaning and restoration. In 2007 a beaver returned on its own to the river—the first instance of beavers living in the New York City region in more than two hundred years.

On Mannahatta the Lenape satisfied nearly all their requirements from within their immediate environs, as their ancestors had for ten thousand years prior to Hudson's arrival. Their resource-shed, in analogy to a watershed, was Mannahatta and the local waters. They found their food in the wild-growing plants and animals and in the crops they grew; they drank local waters supplied by local rain; they built shelters from the trees that sheltered the island. If they peeled the bark of too many trees, if they burned the land too harshly, if they overextended their harvest of deer, they knew it because they lived with scant margin for second chances. As a result, they were not wasteful, they were careful, and they found meaning in living and supporting a world that lived and supported them.

There is no going back, but there is going forward. The conundrum of the modern world, the most important challenge of the twenty-first century, is how to provide habitat requirements for 6.7 billion people (and rising) while ensuring that the ecological systems of the planet, on which we and the rest of life, depend, are sustained. So far we have only taken the first part of that challenge seriously, developing a truly remarkable economic system that, by and large, delivers the goods, though not in a particularly equitable fashion. And many humanitarians are focused this very moment on bringing more people into that system, so that we can vanquish poverty, hunger, and thirst from the human population forever.

However, in our rush to secure the basic requirements, we have largely neglected the second part of that challenge: sustaining the planet. No self-respecting Lenape would cut down three trees when just one would do—what would be the point?—but our modern way of life seems predicated on doing just that, much to the consternation of many of us who, having secured the basic habitat requirements, want less smog, congestion, and disposable shrink-wrap plaguing our lives. As the recent outrageous success of hybrid cars has shown, all other things being equal, why wouldn't you pick a car that uses less gas, produces less pollution, and still gets you to work?

In no place are these choices clearer or more compelling than in cities. Cities with their über-populations face these questions every day, and cities with wealth have the opportunity to try new solutions to old problems. And cities are becoming the way of the world. For the first time in history in 2007, there were more people dwelling in urban communities than in rural ones globally. The number of cities on Earth with more than half a million people will top five hundred in 2009. In America, three-quarters of the population already lives in metropolitan areas; more than half of the population lives in large cities of more than a million people. The question before us is, can the relentless energy and drive to create the future, which has characterized New York since the days of the Dutch, be harnessed to create cities that are livable and sustainable for all?

Fortunately for Manhattan, many of the fundamentals are still in place—New York is not only endowed with a gorgeous and recovering estuary, diverse flora and fauna, and more than a few green corners, but is also blessed with a well-educated and affluent populace, a bully pulpit in media and communications, and a diversity of perspectives and experiences drawn from all over the world. No one loves their place as much as New Yorkers do; so how shall we express our love for our city? One way is to look at how New Yorkers past and present have found their food, water, shelter, and reproductive resources (and the two other essentials of modern life—energy and transportation) and think long and hard about what we want for the future. Luckily, looking forward over the next four hundred years, there are lots of good ideas coming over the horizon to bring a little Mannahatta back to Manhattan.

Food

We all have to eat, and getting food into the great metropolis, and all the crumbs, fruit rinds, wrappers, and other waste out afterward is one of our greatest challenges. In this respect, the Lenape had it relatively easy; the local environment was so fecund that food was broadly available, if somewhat harder to acquire than through a trip to the grocery store. As for getting the leftover shells, bones, and acorn caps out afterward, they had middens scattered conveniently outside their wigwams. It has been said that if you dig deep enough anywhere in Lower Manhattan, you will hit shells. Not a solution that would work well in the modern day—the refuse of the typical fast-food restaurant, left in the street for a week, would form a pile fifteen feet wide and over one story tall.

One lesson we can learn from the Lenape is the importance of local foods. Getting your food locally confers several advantages: The transportation costs are lower, because distances are shorter; the food is fresher, because transportation times are less; and the food is cheaper, because there are fewer links between the producer and the consumer. From the perspective of

top New soil composted by the New York City Department of Sanitation from fallen leaves and chipped Christmas trees. *bottom* During World War II, the U.S. government encouraged private citizens to plant Victory gardens near their homes. More than 20 million Americans answered the call, including these kids tending a garden along First Avenue in 1943. During the war, up to 44 percent of the nation's fresh-vegetable supply came from private gardens like this one.

sustainability, buying local foods also means that eaters (that is, all of us) are invested in the health and productivity of the lands and waters around us. Keeping our farms close means that we can better appreciate nearby agrarian landscapes (think apple picking in the Hudson Valley or fishing off Long Island's South Shore) and consider them, not as opposed to, but as part of, the urban landscape. No wonder farmers' markets are thriving across New York City, local areas are seeing a resurgence of farm restorations, and the city's finest restaurants are featuring regional specialties.

Although this fact seems to have been largely forgotten, in the past a major advantage of New York was its proximity to productive farms in the Hudson Valley, in New Jersey, and on Long Island, including in the city itself. Queens boasted small farms (called truck gardens) that grew sundry vegetables into the 1930s. Manhattan too had farms, including some in northern Manhattan that lasted until the 1910s. In the 1870s the number one most productive agricultural county in the nation was Queens County; number three was Kings County (Brooklyn). Even in the midst of the Industrial Revolution, the combined benefit of quality soils, local markets, and abundant sources of fertilizers (both animal manure and human "night soil") made agriculture a paying business in what soon became the Greater City of New York.

This fundamental fact has not changed, though suburban sprawl has taken much good land out of production. Today 10 percent of the land within a hundred miles of Central Park's Umpire Rock remains in pasture or agriculture; 26 percent in forest; and 8 percent in developed open space, like ball fields and gardens. The list of agricultural products produced locally is mouthwatering: apples, peaches, nectarines, plums, grapes, cherries, blueberries, blackberries, strawberries, lettuce, spinach, cucumbers, tomatoes, sweet corn, peas, peppers, asparagus, broccoli, potatoes, pumpkins, squash, and more. The Hudson River valley is a leader in developing organic products for a ready market, and Long Island, the birthplace of suburbia, has over forty-six farm stands open every summer. Community gardens and even small-scale farming has come back to town. One field in Red Hook thrives over a former asphalt parking lot on compost provided by the Bronx Zoo.

And let's not forget the fruits of the sea. Fish and shellfish are New York's last main wildlife food resource and, thanks to waters cleansed through the Clean Water Act (more on this shortly), fish are returning to New York Harbor and the Hudson River estuary in record numbers each year. Although like any wild food resource, fisheries can be and often are overexploited, good management, including habitat restoration (recall all the baby fish cradled in the region's salt marshes) and designated no-take areas, can restore food from New York's abundant waters once again to our dinner menus. Former catches were prodigious—at one point 765 million oysters per year were harvested from New York's waters. One haul of the net in the harbor during 1770 brought in 11,500 shad. In the 1890s the Hudson River estuary produced a catch of over 220 tons of sturgeon—known then as "Albany beef" because it was so common.

A major constraint of local food is seasonality and diversity, some say. A major advantage of local food is seasonality and diversity, others say. To my mind, asparagus in January reduces the pleasure of asparagus in June, because seasonal specialties available year-round are no longer special. New York has a four-season climate, and during winter, agricultural productivity is low, so storage is required. The Lenape solved this problem by storing dried corn and beans in grass-lined pits, preserving squash, smoking fish, and, when all else gave out, wading into the cold coastal waters to find clams and oysters. Colonial New Yorkers in midwinter ate breads made from dried grains, and boiled potatoes, squash, and peas, sometimes with meat (especially among the wealthy) and generous portions of distilled liquor. Later, in the nineteenth century, New Yorkers ate factory-processed foods from cans and tins. Today, with modern advances in refrigeration and processing, we can store what we need to from the spring, summer, and fall.

What is less than surprising is that seasonal food, grown locally and supplied over short economic chains, is actually better for us than food transported over thousands of miles any time of the year from distant parts of the planet. It not only tastes fresher (because it is) but it retains more of the complex nutrients that human beings need to thrive. These foods are healthier, because they require less in the way of preservatives and agricultural chemicals in their production and delivery to market. And, minus the middleperson, consumers can look the producer directly in the eye—we can see from where and from whom our food comes. In other words, like the Lenape sharing a freshly killed deer around camp, we become a community of people drawn together around food, not just links in a personless and placeless food chain. We remember what worked before, who can be trusted, and who supplies the freshest peaches in August.

Water

As we all know, Manhattan is an island surrounded by water—but not a drop to drink. This insular conundrum wasn't a problem at all to the Lenape—they just drank from the freshwater streams, springs, and ponds that surrounded them, which were filled with satisfying regularity by the rain and snowmelt that Mannahatta received, retained through groundwater aquifers, and then released to quench their thirst. Drinking water did become a problem for New York City, though, as already discussed, when a tannery set up shop beside the Collect Pond in the early nineteenth century, ruining in a couple of years what had taken thousands of years to form. Nearby springs were tapped and small fortunes made by carting water around the city—but water sold by the cupful is insufficient when a fire breaks out. It wasn't until, through heroic efforts, the Croton water system was completed in 1842 to bring water from thirty miles away that the city's water worries were (for the moment) assuaged. Today New Yorkers still drink from an one-hundred-mile extension of the same system, expanded to nineteen reservoirs, three controlled lakes, and a total storage capacity of approximately 580 billion gallons.

New York's solution to its water requirement—bringing water from distant lands—does create certain ironies, as well as some unexpected opportunities. One irony is that when people walk along what otherwise looks like a natural-looking stream in northern Central Park, the water beside them has actually already traveled 125 miles in a pipe, before being released into a constructed pond (the Loch). The Loch supplies Montayne's Rivulet, to give the stream its old name, which runs about a quarter mile downhill in its ancient stream course until it reaches another constructed lake (the Harlem Meer), pours into the sewer, and then finally after treatment reaches the sea.

An unexpected opportunity came along in the mid-1990s when the U.S. Environmental Protection Agency determined that New York City's water supply was not compliant with federal water-quality standards. The conventional response would be to build a multibillion-dollar water filtration facility, but city leaders discovered that it would be cheaper to instead protect the watershed that fed water into the water supply. A nearly $1 billion investment in land protection in the Catskill/Delaware Watersheds ensued, thus preserving land and saving $6–8 billion in the process. Now when the water emerges from the pipe, it is drinkable and natural lands are preserved as a result. The irony of all this is that continuing suburban development in the vicinity of the

Croton Watershed (i.e., Westchester and Putnam counties), which is closer to the city and which cannot be so simply bought off, now necessitates constructing a water filtration plant after all. And where is it sited? In a park (in the Bronx), on top of an old stream that threatens daily to fill the water filtration plant with springwater, thus requiring twenty-four-hour pumping to take the water from the site of a water filtration plant to a sewer and then again to the sea.

Storm drains and sewers are effectively the streams of the modern city. One function, of course, of streams is to help channel water to the ocean. Streams gather the flow from the vegetation, through the soil, and over the land into bubbling brooks and churning rivers before releasing their charge into the sea—creating along the way habitats for humankind and beast alike. That's what water pipes do too, sort of (at least for the rats). Storm drains have some problems to contend with, though, that streams don't. For one, storm drains catch flow off a city that doesn't really like or want the water. Cities are constructed, to borrow a term from art, of "impermeable surfaces" (e.g., concrete, asphalt, building stone), surfaces that, unlike the soil, resist the water infiltrating into them. The result is that the surface flow created after a rainstorm is much greater on Manhattan today than it was four hundred years ago. Back then, some of the water was caught by the leaves of trees (up to a quarter inch), but more of the water infiltrated into the soil, feeding the root zone that watered the plants. Some of the water, too, was held back by the soil and then slowly released into the streams.

Very little of this happens today. As any Manhattanite can tell you, after a decent-sized rain event, the streets themselves stream with water, flooding toward the drains. Paper, cardboard, and Styrofoam back up in the entrances—forming the modern equivalent of the beaver dam—which creates pools, then ponds. Not only is there more water on the surface now than in the past, but that water is moving faster. "More water, moving faster" has another name: a flood. And as urban hydrographs (which plot water flow over time) show, in fact, floods are exactly what city dwellers experience.

What is the solution to floods in the city? Not surprisingly, the answer is the same that forests came up with long ago: soil, vegetation, and streams. The South Richmond section of Staten Island is being outfitted with restored streams that provide not only runoff and flood control, but also additional parkland and wildlife habitats, together creating a "bluebelt." Water gardens can be constructed in tiny backyards or in massive parking lots, as a way to sop up water and return it to the natural hydrological cycle; several experimental ones are scattered around the city. Some novel solutions to the problem of impermeable surfaces have also been emerging—new paving materials actually allow water to soak through the parking lot to the earth below. Paving stones, rather than monotonous asphalt, give herbs a place to grow underfoot, and water a conduit to return to the earth.

On top of impermeable buildings, the latest invention is the green roof. A green roof is simply a thin layer of soil planted with grasses and flowers that can make do on what the climate provides. As New Yorkers have long known, rooftop gardens provide a delightful respite—separated from and quieter than the city at large, yet like aeries commanding an eagle's view of the landscape. A highly urbanized friend recently told me a story of sitting in his office, overlooking a green roof immediately outside his window, delighting unexpectedly in the birds that swooped down to pluck insects from the air. Green roofs not only provide city dwellers with gardens, but they also slow the water flow and cool the buildings on which they are built.

Green roofs can also be rain gardens—gardens that collect water for reuse. Some say a dollar invested in the economy creates five dollars of additional economic activity; so it is with water in ecosystems. Most of the water that falls on the city today, though, is thrown away, literally drained from Manhattan as fast as possible, and replaced largely with water transported from the Catskills, which does seem something of a waste as the annual precipitation, even at current levels of consumption, would still be sufficient to supply over 36 percent of our needs. Former New Yorkers knew this—the period after the demise of the Collect Pond and before the advent of the Croton water supply saw a flourishing of cisterns throughout the city.

Collecting and recycling water several times through the city ecosystem can potentially provide an additional benefit: clean water. The Lenape didn't have sewage treatment plants, because they didn't need them; the natural microbial processes of soil were sufficient, given that wastes were properly handled. For most of New York City's history, dumping in the ocean was our preferred treatment solution, and for some time in some ways, the old dictum of pollution scientists held up: "The solution to pollution is dilution." Eventually, though, even the mighty New York Harbor, washed by the Hudson and swept by the tides, could not absorb without consequence the millions of gallons of untreated waste released daily into the local waters. Fortunately, public advocates and government leaders literally got wind of the filth ensconcing the city and acted for change; the federal Clean Water Act was passed

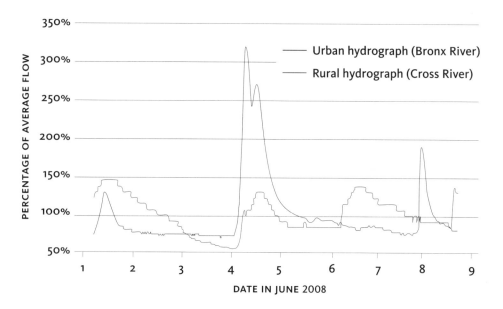

Hydrographs show water flow over time. This simultaneous comparison of the watersheds of the urban Bronx River and the rural Cross River (in northern Westchester County) shows that the Bronx River experiences faster flows and greater volume because of a greater proportion of impermeable surfaces in the urban watershed (values are adjusted for watershed areas).

in 1972, the necessary money was spent, and the result today is much, much cleaner waters.

Except right after it rains. Although New York City has generally made great strides in treating its wastewater, when it rains the stormwaters combine with the sewers and overwhelm the treatment facilities; the result is raw sewage, on the order of 27 billion gallons per year, still entering New York Harbor, albeit in a somewhat diluted form. New York City is one of the cities in the country with so-called combined sewer overflows (CSOs). Sewage in the water means that the waterfront is unsafe for recreation after stormy weather, thus depriving New York of one of its first and greatest assets, its proximity to water.

Perhaps the waterfront is the best evidence of New Yorkers' ability to reimagine and reuse our place. For the Lenape, the beaches, shores, and tidal pools were where food came from, both what could be gathered and caught and also what could be traded; corn, pottery, and wampum all traveled across the harbor waters. For the Dutch and then the British colonials, the waterfront was about trade and garbage. Furs and raw materials went out; manufactured goods came in; and the garbage went into the water. Nineteenth-century industrialists exploited the water's edge not only for trade—creating the forest

top Green roofs, like this one in the East Village, cool buildings, slow runoff, and provide green habitats for people and wildlife. *bottom* Sometimes wildlife species need help from people. In this case, young alewife herring, a fish that breeds in freshwater and then returns to the ocean, were introduced to the Bronx River in 2007, with the expectation that after two years the reintroduced fry will return to New York City as adults to take their turn at the game of life.

of ship masts of Walt Whitman's era—but also as the site for new factories. Raw materials came in; manufactured goods went out; and new industrial wastes went into the water. By the time of Robert Moses in the early twentieth century, these factories had left for more suburban and rural locales, leaving space for new highways. For Moses, the waterfront was about transportation, and thus he encircled Manhattan Island with black asphalt belts, ushering New York into the age of the automobile.

As we stand on the waterfront today, looking into the twenty-first century, New Yorkers are once again reimagining their waterfront, but this time they look to the harbor for recreation. Plans are under way to embrace Manhattan Island with greenways that will carry bicycles and skaters, not just cars; kayaks and recreational watercraft are reclaiming the Hudson and Upper Harbor with new put-in points; and parks are blossoming where factories and military bases once stood: Battery Park, Brooklyn Bridge Park, Liberty State Park, Governors Island, and a new harbor district that will become yet another major New York City attraction. Meanwhile, however, the waters creep closer as the climate changes and ice melts elsewhere; soon a different kind of accommodation will be required, for seawaters surging back to reclaim the island.

Shelter

Looking down on the water from immense heights are people living, working, and playing in buildings. Buildings, as a component of habitat, satisfy several requirements of the human animal. First and foremost they provide shelter from the extremes of climate. People are, after all, mostly furless primates that originally evolved in the tropics, and our bare skin provides scant protection from the cold winds of an arctic blast. In the summer, although our local New York climate is salubrious for trees and vines, it is distinctly uncomfortable for people and can be made all the more unpleasant in buildings that collect solar heat without discharging it and that are closed to ventilation beyond what machines provide. Buildings are also conduits for receiving and dispensing food and water and for removing wastes from our living spaces; in this sense, they are important harbors for our health. Most importantly, though, buildings and the built environment are places whose composition and arrangement influences how we feel and what we do within them. Much as a natural landscape is composed of ecosystems in distinctive arrangements that determine

Green buildings, like the Hearst Tower on West Fifty-seventh Street, are designed to provide comfortable habitats for people, use less resources, and encourage positive environmental values.

the landscape ecology of a place, the design of our cities determines much about the urban ecology and behavior of people; our built spaces set the stage for business, leisure, education, eating, and sleeping—the encounters that are life itself.

So what kind of stage have we set? We are perhaps nowhere as far removed from the 1609 Lenape as we are in our built environment. Wigwams and longhouses, which may be applauded for their construction from entirely renewable and locally harvested materials and for their elegant tensile and curvilinear design, were probably not in the final analysis very comfortable; their greatest virtue may have been that they encouraged their residents to spend time out of doors, where it was not dark, smoky, and crowded.

Today most buildings are very comfortable, at least by Lenape standards, fitted with lights, air-conditioning, and luxuriant space and privacy, but we typically construct our buildings from nonrenewable materials collected from anywhere but Manhattan. The modernist idea was to build structures that transcended time and place, and as a result, much of late-twentieth-century architecture could have been built anywhere. Architects today, fortunately, are beginning to think of buildings as the organic structures they are, of and for the places in landscapes they create: habitats for people, both responsible to and dependent on the larger ecosystem.

Like a lizard basking on a sunny rock or a dragonfly poised on a marsh reed, a building's first responsibility is that of thermoregulation, or maintaining warmth when it's cold and maintaining coolness when it's hot. Buildings designed to take advantage of passive temperature regulation can help reduce the heat load of summer and access solar heating in winter. How? First, by facing south to catch the sun's rays, and then by allowing the sides to be shaded when the light is too bright. New green buildings are built with second skins that can both shade and insulate, opening and closing depending on the season. These buildings also reach into the ground with geothermal wells, relying on the consistent temperature of the earth to offset the vicissitudes of the air. Yet others plant sky gardens throughout, taking advantage of the properties of vegetation and soil to modulate the atmosphere and climate not only at ground level but throughout a building; bringing in the plants also necessitates bringing in appropriate lighting, so that soft, natural light is drawn deep into the architecture.

Buildings also need to breathe, to take out the old air and bring in the new—think of summer breezes wafting over a pass in the hills, stirring forest leaves, scented by the sea. The weather sets the air in motion, but it is the

top Skyscrapers, like everything else in our landscapes, are not permanent. Over the next four hundred years, nearly all the buildings on Manhattan will be torn down and rebuilt, not through whole-scale change, but block by block, building by building. In this patchwork of opportunities lies the possibility of creating a more sustainable city. *top* Workers tear down the Hanover National Bank building in 1931. *bottom* A new skyscraper rises in Midtown.

architecture of the topography and vegetation that directs the winds. Similarly, buildings can shape the wind for good or ill, both inside and out (in the 1920s, the Flatiron Building at Twenty-third Street was famous for blowing down to street level fierce winds that stirred men's hats and women's skirts). Wind scoops are structures that reach into the wind and divert it into living spaces; earth tubes can channel air through the cooling ground. Many green buildings today are designed to take advantage of what air wants to do anyway—as the warm air rises, fresh air is brought in beneath it. This fresh air is often enlivened and cooled with water features, which also serve to humidify and refresh the air. These kinds of architectural features are new only in the sense of having been forgotten in modern cities; people in the tropics and Middle East were cooling their houses in these ways back when the Lenape were still building their wigwams in Foley Square.

In breathing, buildings also need to take care not to poison the air. Although that may seem so obvious as to not need saying, an unintended property of some twentieth-century building materials is that they "off-gas" substances that we shouldn't breathe in. The materials can't help it, but we can help what materials we use. We can, for example, choose materials devoid of toxic substances. And we can consider the life-span of the nontoxic materials, using building blocks that participate in cycles of use and reuse, what William McDonough has called "cradle-to-cradle" cycles, rather than "cradle-to-grave" linear processes, in which something is used only once and then thrown away. Like the nutrients that cycled through Mannahatta's ecosystems, the stone, wood, metal, and even plastics of our buildings should be designed for use and reuse.

Each building is not an island unto itself; it is a part of the main— that is, buildings, like the individual forests, streams, and grasslands of the landscape, create contexts for other things to happen. Jane Jacobs famously lectured New York in the 1960s on the value of mixed-use neighborhoods, where people can work, shop, and live in close proximity. She should have asked deer to show the way—white-tailed deer know that the best way to live is close to the grasses you love, near the shrubs that shelter, and beside the stream to drink. The same goes for people—we live best, our communities thrive most, when everything we need, including family, friends, home, and work, is near at hand.

Energy and Transportation

The Lenape had two answers to their energy and transportation needs: wood and muscle. Like the millions of New Yorkers who exercise regularly, the Lenape had a regular workout, but their workout consisted of felling trees, paddling canoes, hoeing fields, and, like New Yorkers today, walking—lots of walking. They probably used a prodigious amount of firewood, but since the forests were many and the people few, there was always more where that came from. The Lenape did not have natural gas from the Gulf Coast or petroleum from the Middle East, nor did they have electricity, except in spectacular lightning storms—but modern society would be lost without the patient, noiseless electrons that stream down the line and power our lights, computers, televisions, and industries.

New York City today uses a monumental amount of electricity: 11,020 megawatts daily at peak draw, equivalent to 3.7 billion Lenape braves doing push-ups. The great majority of that power is currently garnered from fossil fuels, nature's idea of storage for a long winter's night. Unfortunately, we've been using our winter supply in the middle of summer, as it were, which is a first-order problem in that it diminishes our supply of a nonrenewable fuel, and a second-order problem in that it encourages us to neglect better solutions. Currently New York City's electricity is generated both locally and remotely, as far away as Quebec. However, because New York sits in a "transmission pocket" (which means that, even with a massive system of power lines directed toward the city, we cannot get all the power we want from outside), we have to generate some ourselves.

At the moment, most of our heat and electricity is derived from petroleum, natural gas, and nuclear power; only a small fraction (less than 1 percent) is derived from renewable sources like the sun, the wind, the tides, and the earth's heat. It hasn't always been that way. Dutch New Amsterdam was famous for its windmills—one stood beside the fort where State Street today meets Broadway; another stood on the Commons in what is now City Hall Park; yet another, Bayard's windmill, stood for nearly 150 years on the west side of Bowery Lane, about a hundred feet north of Canal Street. Water mills also provided power—one, for example, churned in Lower Manhattan, where the Old Wreck Brook met the East River; another stood along Harlem Creek at 105th Street, near Third Avenue. Saw Kill, the stream that once drained through Central Park, derived its name from a water-driven sawmill located at East Seventy-fifth Street.

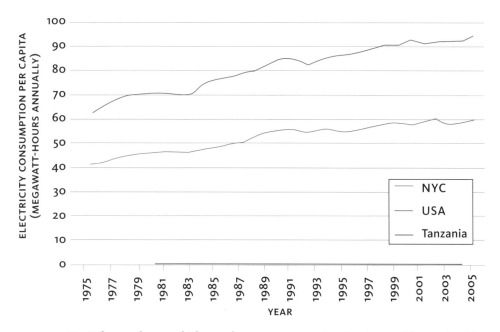

New Yorkers use about two-thirds as much energy per person as Americans in general, because they drive less and live closer together. However each American uses nearly a thousand times as much energy each year as an average Tanzanian, reflecting disparities in ways that different groups of people meet their energy demands on the planet today.

New York was also home to tidal mills, an invention over a thousand years old. On the high tide, the water comes in, driven by the tides, and then a gate closes. On the low tide, the water is released through a conduit that turns a wheel. Absolutely free, driven by the push and pull of the moon, tidal mills are perfect for cities built near estuaries—though they're not ideal for salt marshes, which also enjoy the regular cycles of the tides.

On a small scale, these lessons have not been lost. In 2007 Mayor Bloomberg switched on six tidal turbines that had been situated near Roosevelt Island in the East River; they are now generating a thousand kilowatts of power a day. Eventually the site could generate ten megawatts a day, enough to power eight hundred homes. In terms of wind power, Manhattan is not ideally placed, but nearby offshore breezes provide the steady, punishing winds that can turn multiple-megawatt wind turbines. Plans have been made and then scrubbed for large wind farms in the coastal waters off Long Island, but still the winds blow. (The U.S. Government estimates that the offshore wind-power capacity of the United States is in itself sufficient to supply electricity for the entire nation.) And then there's solar power. Recall that New York is relatively sunny. In an average year, New York has 232 sunny days (the nationwide average is 212); new sun-collecting technologies are enabling not only solar panels but also solar shingles to allow buildings to collect energy as plants do.

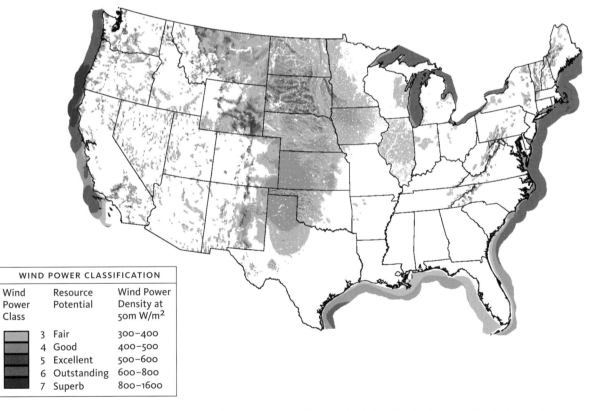

WIND POWER CLASSIFICATION		
Wind Power Class	Resource Potential	Wind Power Density at 50m W/m^2
3 Fair		300–400
4 Good		400–500
5 Excellent		500–600
6 Outstanding		600–800
7 Superb		800–1600

top As this detail from the Visscher Map shows, windmills were a prominent feature of the city's skyline for the first two hundred years of European settlement. *bottom* The U.S. National Renewable Energy Laboratory produced this map of wind-power potential in the United States. The power potential of offshore winds has been estimated at more than a thousand gigawatts—more than the current national annual electricity usage; half of this potential lies off of New England and the mid-Atlantic states.

To date, many of these projects are really just demonstrations, but over the long term the hope is that these demonstrations will collectively inform something significant and tangible, particularly as cheap oil runs out and the dire predictions surrounding climate change become a reality. We are a long way from having all the answers, but one thing everyone agrees on is that we need to wean ourselves off of our current fossil fuel addiction by better managing our energy and, particularly, our transportation.

It can be fairly said that many New Yorkers are already doing their share when it comes to getting around efficiently. Over one-third of the mass transit trips made each day in the United States are made in New York City; the city's subway system transports people on over 1.5 billion trips annually. During a busy evening rush hour, a population equivalent to Seattle's can be found on the move in our transit system. Such heavy transit use is the consequence not only of enlightened city planning and investment—dating back to the nineteenth century—but also of the city's population density, which makes commuting by public transit practical. Because of this, the average New Yorker is responsible for producing three-tenths as much carbon dioxide in a year as the average American.

Nevertheless, New York faces serious transportation problems that will stymie further growth and development if not solved—not to mention the great costs already borne in terms of quality of life and land use. Nearly 20 percent of Manhattan's real estate is currently allocated to transportation (sidewalks and streets). Those streets are continuously full of cars, even late into the night, which are noisy, dangerous, and polluting. For many of its residents, the least appealing aspect of living in twenty-first-century New York is the traffic. That's why in 2008 Mayor Bloomberg and the federal government put forward plans for congestion pricing, to literally raise the cost of operating a car in the southern half of Manhattan. Some argue that congestion pricing has worked very effectively for other cities, like London, to reduce traffic. Others argue that it is an expensive and inequitable Band-Aid. Ultimately, we need to look to solutions that simply do not depend on the automobile (and, by implication, the automobile's dependence on fossil fuels). After an one-hundred-year experiment, we can conclude that cars in cities just don't work that well.

Many Asian and European cities have found that the personal transportation mode most in keeping with urban life is bicycle riding. Bicycles are ideally suited to New York, which has a moderate climate, mainly flat topography (thanks to the street engineering of the nineteenth century),

top Manhattan is well suited to bicycles, as this bike messenger circa 1896 was aware. *bottom* New Yorkers have rediscovered the bicycle as a means of getting around. These commuters are traveling to Lower Manhattan over the Brooklyn Bridge.

Streetcars were once a feature of every major street in Manhattan. In this photograph of Broadway circa 1895 near City Hall Park, streetcars are visible on nearly every block.

Table V.

Population, miles of track, and number of passengers on streetcars and electric railways for selected cities, 1902

CITY	POPULATION	MILES OF TRACK	NUMBER OF PASSENGERS
Boston, Brookline, Cambridge, Chelsea, Everett, Malden, Newton, Somerville, Waltham, MA	927,944	452	228 million
Chicago, IL; Hammond, IN	1,769,951	1,036	410 million
Dayton, OH	85,333	53	15 million
Denver, CO	133,859	150	31 million
Little Rock, AR	38,307	21	4 million
Los Angeles, Orange, Pasadena, Santa Ana, CA	118,746	164	31 million
New Orleans, LA	287,104	180	53 million
New York, Mt. Vernon, New Rochelle, Pelham, White Plains, Yonkers, NY	3,548,096	1,299	944 million
Philadelphia, PA	1,293,697	518	331 million
San Antonio, TX	53,321	46	5 million
San Francisco, San Mateo, CA	344,614	277	117 million
Sioux City, IA; South Sioux City, NE	34,000	43	4 million
Springfield, MO	23,267	19	2 million
Spokane, WA	36,848	37	5 million
Washington, DC	279,940	140	63 million
U.S. TOTAL	76.2 million	22, 577	4,774 million

dense land use, a spectacular waterfront, and extensive linear parks. As the Bicycle Master Plan for New York City states, "[M]ore and more New Yorkers are embracing the bicycle as a liberating, healthy, inexpensive, environmentally beneficial and, in general, fun way to travel." The Greenway Plan for New York City lays out over 350 miles of bicycle and pedestrian paths, including a greenway that would completely circle Manhattan Island.

Although by many measures bicycles are as sweet an invention as humankind has ever known, they are not for everyone; other transit solutions are needed for winter and for those who can't ride. My favorite urban mass-transit solution is the streetcar (also known as the trolley or the tram), whose virtues are nearly as numerous as the bicycle's. Streetcars are cheaper to build than other modes of transit ($12–15 million/mile vs. $30–50 million/mile for light rail, $150–200 million/mile for underground subways, or as much as $1 billion/mile for urban highways); they are faster, more comfortable, and more genteel than buses; they can readily adjust to traffic load (by adding or removing tram cars); they can stop at every block or run "express"; and they are compatible with pedestrians and bicycles because they move at low speeds on dedicated rights-of-way. Manhattan once had extensive fleets of streetcars (also known as the "urban railway"), which is why the avenues, and some streets (e.g., Twenty-third, Thirty-fourth, Forty-second, and Fifty-ninth) are wider than others. In 1902 one could travel from Manhattan to White Plains, in Westchester County, more than thirty miles, by trolley; the average New Yorker that year made more than 250 journeys by streetcar, and in total, more than 950 million trips were taken. New York wasn't alone in this; a hundred years ago nearly all American cities had streetcars. Then they tore them out—competition, poor regulation, and connivance on the part of bus and car companies led to their demise. Many cities (e.g., Portland, San Francisco, Little Rock) have found that restoring streetcars provides a no-nonsense, attractive, and economical means of transit. Deployed *instead of* cars rather than *among* them, streetcars could be revolutionary.

Streetcars and bicycles, and of course pedestrian walkways, can get most of us around, but they still leave the task of getting our stuff around unresolved. The city's food and material requirements and its exports and waste streams also need transportation. The best idea for New York is probably to move these nonhuman flows underground, into the subway tunnels. Once the people are aboveground, breathing the fresh air, the warren of tunnels that infiltrate the city will be available for locomotives that can transport and distribute loads throughout the city. Manhattan has sixty-seven miles of underground track, reaching to most parts of the island and already connected with railway systems from New Jersey, Long Island, and northern New York. Some further tunnels will be required, and subway stations will need to be reconfigured for loading and unloading, and for marshaling the goods to be delivered throughout the city by a new fleet of speedy-delivery pedicabs on the streets above. The result will be a new way of living and moving in the city.

Raising the Kids

In the game of life, acquiring food, water, and shelter is just a prelude to the final scoring round for adults: reproduction. Success in the game of life is measured in terms of how many genes get passed on to the next round and have their chance to get passed on again. Although fortunately human beings have many other ways of keeping score today, part of our evolutionary baggage is the extraordinarily long time it takes us to grow up; human children are the slowest to develop and most dependent young animals in the natural world.

Caring for our kids and educating them in the ways of the world is a major social responsibility for individuals and cities alike. The Lenape were very lucky in this regard—they lived and worked with their kids in regular company; they enjoyed extended family units that provided support and assistance; and their kids had a lot of time outdoors. Parks commissioners since the days of Olmsted have been successfully creating parklands for New Yorkers and populating them with ball fields, running tracks, and, occasionally, swimming pools, but many city children don't have a grassy hill or woodlot to run in, a place to have what child psychologists call "unstructured outdoor play." It turns out it is exactly that kind of play that helps kids learn to love nature in the deepest recesses of their hearts.

We need not only parks that are safe but more parks where nature is the first priority. My conservation colleagues think I'm crazy when I advocate for more nature in cities, because from the "perspective of nature" (if one can speak in such a way), cities are really not very good habitat for lots of things. Black bears, wolves, and timber rattlesnakes are not coming back to Manhattan, nor would we want them to—they would be unhappy, and so would we. Moreover, nature conservation in cities is incredibly expensive. One study placed it at over $1 million per acre—as compared with $1 per acre in some of the wildest parts of the planet. Since big nature needs big places, the argument goes, we should look to conserve it where we can afford it.

top After becoming endangered by the use of DDT, the peregrine falcon has staged a recovery and now nests in several places in New York City, including on the Brooklyn Bridge. *bottom* Manhattan's location on the Atlantic Flyway makes for great birdwatching for young and old alike, especially during the spring and fall migrations. More than 350 species of birds can be seen in the New York City metropolitan area today.

But we need more nature in cities for exactly the opposite reason—not because it's good for nature per se (though the birds migrating through Central Park are mighty glad for the Ramble), but because it's good for us. We need to be close to nature in order to be inspired by it. So if people are going to live in cities, then nature had better come to the party too. Most of this chapter has dealt with the abiotic side of nature—air, water, energy, and waste—but it is the biota that we most love: warblers singing, flowers blooming, whales breaching, ducks angling in the fall sky. We don't need all of nature, just the nature that we can accommodate by making good and imaginative choices. Mountain lions on Murray Hill?—not likely. Brook trout in Minetta Brook?—maybe. Red-tails in love?—that's the life we need.

Manhattan 2409

So what will Manhattan look like four hundred years from now? My crystal ball is probably just as foggy as Henry Hudson's would have been looking forward to our time (he might have had us all wearing large neck frills and drinking from cheap Chinese tea sets—and he would have been half right!). Sometimes when I contemplate the future, I feel a common bond with John Randel, Jr., the nineteenth-century land surveyor who plotted the street grid Manhattan has today. How strange it must have been for him, stomping through woodlands and marshes, laying measurement chains over hills, and marking boulders for demolition where eventually streets would pass, to imagine our city of skyscrapers and automobiles.

One thing is certain: The city of the future will be different from the city of today. Our current way of living is patently unsustainable and will have to change. Moreover, whatever solutions we come up with will need to be implemented piecemeal, rather than as whole-scale reconstructions. Over the next four hundred years, all the buildings in the city will be rebuilt in one form or another. In the spaces created by these disturbance events, a new city will be designed and crafted from the old. The new New York City will rediscover some of Mannahatta's most cherished fundamentals and thus find a way for long-term success.

Or we will perish in the attempt. It has been estimated that if the entire world lived the way Americans do today, it would take four planet Earths to supply the global population's resource requirements. Unfortunately, we

By 2409 Manhattan will have reinvented street life. While today Fifth Avenue is dedicated to cars and trucks, in four hundred years, streetcars, bicycles, pedestrians, and streams will all flow through quiet streetscapes designed for people.

From the air, the future Manhattan will present a carpet of green roofs and parklands, powered by food and electricity from the region. Manhattan will be an exemplar physically and functionally of the green city.

don't have four Earths to give—and equality will be demanded—therefore just as we have solved other problems in the past, we will solve this one too; the only question is how much pain we will need to suffer before we apply ourselves to the task. Plato wrote cogently on what happens to city-states when they outgrow their available resources—they attack the next city-state to get more—and I am none too eager to live through his predictions, extrapolated into the nuclear era. But I know enough of history to temper my expectations, while reveling in past "impossibilities" that came to pass in New York City. After all, the Empire State Building was built in only thirteen months, the harbor is cleaner now than it has been in a century, and a beaver has lately returned to a revitalized Bronx River. It's remarkable what people and nature can do when given a chance.

Looking ahead four hundred years, one reward is that we will no longer be worrying about cars plaguing our streets, having long ago exhausted our fossil fuel supply. Instead the city will run on renewable energies, perhaps captured and transported as hydrogen and derived from the windmills, tidal mills, and solar panels of the future. Many of these will be local, built into the fabric of the city, powering lights and industry with as yet untold efficiency. The buildings will be layered with gardens and designed to passively collect sunlight and passively shed excesses of it and to breathe deeply of the quiet, smog-free air. Our habitats will be nucleated around transportation stops, served by old-fashioned streetcars that run along greenways thick with trees and bushes, interwoven with pedestrian paths and bikeways. Our goods will pass unseen through the old subway tunnels, expanded slightly to better serve their new mission and interconnected with cellars beneath the buildings—people reclaim the surface, materials move underground.

Those foods and materials being transported will be harvested locally—New Jersey, Long Island, and the Hudson Valley will return to their agrarian ways; suburban sprawl will be replaced with complex, dense cities and agricultural belts that extend into the city. Bright patchworks of small farms will produce a diversity of crops year-round for a network of towns connected by high-speed magnetically levitated railways. Farms will be organized by cooperatives (rather than corporations) and will deliver their food into the city again, relinking the consumer directly with the producer, which will reward both. We will of course produce a few more apples and potatoes than needed and trade them, along with our art, science, business, and media savvy, for sustainable coffee shipped into a revitalized harbor. We must have our coffee!

preceding pages

left From a satellite, it is clear how the New York City metroplex dominates the landscape today, providing home to more than twelve million people, as in this NASA image from 2002. *right* By 2409, popular demand for sustainability will have reshaped the landscape to support its twelve million people, who will live in a necklace of unique and extraordinary cities on only 36 percent of the land (assuming the same density as modern Manhattan), surrounded by farms, wildlands, and a restored and thriving estuary, with boundaries redrawn by climate change.

Between the boats bringing in the coffee, small fishing and oyster crews will once again make their living on New York Harbor and out in the waters of the Atlantic and Long Island Sound, sustainably harvesting the wealth of rebuilt ocean ecosystems. Coming back to land they will pass the gold-green swards of salt marshes and marvel at the beauty of streams opening at the sandy shores on the edge of the magnificent city. The streams will have their headwaters in green rooftops and rain gardens and will have run through waterfalls and buildings and parklands multiple times before reaching the sea, where the children swim with their parents. Pure, clean water will continue to flow from the tap, some garnered locally, but most still drawn from protected wildernesses upstate (we will still live on an archipelago in an estuary, after all, on islands narrowed by the rising tide).

In the parks, parents will teach kids about the enormous abundance and diversity of our home. Beavers will have returned to Central Park to build their lodges; birds will nest in the forest; and kids will play on the undulations of Battery Park, Marcus Garvey Park, and Inwood Hill, building forts, mapping trails, and fishing in the local ponds. Canoes and kayaks will be as common as today's iPods, boats chasing one another in laps around a new landscape, constructed out of native ecosystems on the refurbished Governors Island. Since streams will be winding through the city, providing homes for brook trout, a Manhattan businesswoman will be able to spend her fall evenings fly-fishing in Minetta Water, down the street from the office before heading out to the opera or the baseball game. Regional planning will ensure that nearby there are vast swaths of nature for weekend hiking, and safe, clean, cheap public transportation to get there.

New Yorkers in 2409 will still be loud, direct, and pushy; I have no doubt. In 2409, we will also still be warm and generous and involved in what happens in the world. More than ever, we will be a city of walkers and talkers, drawn from cultures all over the globe. The city will sing with art and music, good life and braggadocio. The difference will be that the thrill of the big city will not, philosophically or practically, preclude nature; rather nature will be integrated into our lives and how we imagine ourselves. New Yorkers will live in communities and cycles of life that extend beyond their city, knowing that they are playing productive roles in the global ecological economy and that the world is assured for their children, and their children's children. Mannahatta will be back for all of us, a land as pleasant as one can tread upon, a city that all the people have created, connected by a thousand invisible cords, the fresh, green breast of a world that will thrive for another four hundred years, and then some.

APPENDIX A.
Selected natural features of Mannahatta, with historical descriptions from various sources, arranged approximately from Downtown to Uptown. Author's comments, including suggested names for features whose historical names have been lost, are enclosed in square brackets.

Name(s)	Feature Type(s)	Selected Descriptions, with Modern Location	Additional Descriptions
[Fraunces Tavern Spring]	Spring	"A 1781 advertisement describes the house [Fraunces Tavern] as having '9 spacious rooms plus 5 bedchambers, 13 fireplaces . . . and an exceeding good kitchen, and a spring of remarkable fine water therein'" (von Pressentin Wright, Miller, and Seitz 2002). [Fraunces Tavern stands at the southeast corner of Broad and Pearl streets.]	
Heere Gracht; Heere Graft; Graught; The Ditch	Stream	"An inlet of the bay [New York Harbor], which could be made to do duty as a canal, extended inland for about a quarter of a mile on a line of the present Broad Street. This ditch was the natural outlet for a marshy section of considerable size lying above. . . . A brook trickled through this marsh, from the common lying north of it, called Schaape Waytie . . . , and received the flow of a small stream which ran through the Company's Valley [known to the Dutch as Blommaert's Vly], as that portion of the Beaver Path was named. . . . [F]rom that point, the Heere Gracht or Heere Graft as it was soon called, stretched its odorous length to the bay" (Hill and Waring 1897).	Buttenweiser (1987); Dunshee (1952); Janvier (1894); Stokes (1915–28); Waldman (1999)
Prince Graft, Beaver's Gracht	Stream	"Intersecting the Ditch, the industrious burghers dug out a smaller canal called the Beaver's Gracht (now Beaver Street), draining off a marsh fed by two small streams from which trappers had wiped out their first bounty" (Koeppel 2000).	Janvier (1894); Waldman (1999)
Verlettenberg; Flat and Barrack Hill	Hill	"In the winter [c. 1670s] the boys of the town improved so well the coasting [i.e., sledding] facilities afforded by the hill from Broadway to the bridge [across the Heere Gracht, near today's Exchange Place] that the merchants were obliged to ask for protection [from them]" (Hill and Waring 1897).	Dunshee (1952); Haswell (1896)

Name(s)	Feature Type(s)	Selected Descriptions, with Modern Location	Additional Descriptions
[Maiden Spring]	Spring	"Little Miss Havens recorded her mother's description of what was perhaps the earliest use of running water in a house in the city [in 1799]: 'Everybody had a cistern of rain water for washing, in the back yard. And when she (my mother) lived in Maiden Lane, the servants had to go up to the corner of Broadway and get the drinking water from the pump there. It was a great bother, and so when my grandfather built his new house at 19 Maiden Lane he asked the alderman if he might run a pipe to the kitchen of the house from the pump at the corner of Broadway, and they said he could, and he had a faucet in the kitchen, and it was the first house in the city have drinking (running) water in it.' During the water shortage in New York City in 1950, the need for a supply of water for air conditioning prompted Barthman and Company, the well-known jewelers on the northeast corner of Maiden Lane and Broadway, to seek water where the old pump described by Miss Havens once stood. After several weeks their workmen were successful in locating a good supply of water 22 feet below the floor of their subcellar. This water lay in a deep bed of brownish sand which contained a great deal of mica, and has been identified as a type of sand native to this vicinity. The flow of water, while bounteous at first, finally leveled off to little more than one gallon per minute, which, while steady, was insufficient for the purpose in mind" (Dunshee 1952).	Hill and Waring (1897); Smith (1938)
Maagde Paetje [Kill] *and* Smith's Valley; Smit's Vly	Stream and Valley	"The Maagde Paetje, the Maiden's Path, was originally in a valley which Maiden Lane now traverses. The path followed a charming rivulet which ran through the little vale towards the East River. The stream, fed by a living spring, came tumbling down over the rocks, forming a series of pools. It descended on the north side of the valley as far as the spot now crossed by William Street. An early map shows it forming a fair-sized pond at that point, from which it made its way to the East River. The entire area was one of pastoral beauty and was one of the most picturesque spots in the city" (Dunshee 1952).	Hill and Waring (1897); Koeppel (2000); Stokes (1915–28)

Name(s)	Feature Type(s)	Selected Descriptions, with Modern Location	Additional Descriptions
Golden Hill; Gouwenberg; Gouden Bergh	Hill	"Gold Street is named after Golden Hill Street, a pasture that glowed with yellow flowers. The Dutch called the flower, apparently the celandine (*Chelidonium majus*), the *gouwe*, and the area the *Gouwenberg*: the British anglicized the name to Golden Hill" (Moscow 1978). [Golden Hill was the scene of the "Battle of Golden Hill," described in Chapter 2.]	Haswell (1896); Stokes (1915–28)
[Ablution Spring]	Spring	"The earliest Jewish synagogue in New York was also located in South William Street. Some years later this site, which contained a fresh spring where ritual cleansings and ablutions had been performed, became a mill seat. The bark mill of Ten Eyck, a Dutch settler, is believed to have stood there" (Dunshee 1952).	
Mount Pitt; Jones Hill	Hill	"[In 1816,] at the intersection of Grand Street and East Broadway (Herman Street) was the hill known as Mount Pitt" (Haswell 1896).	Gilmore (1995); Stokes (1915–28)
Tea Water Pump; Tea Water Spring	Spring	"[In 1816] in Chatham Street, at the corner of Roosevelt, stood the celebrated Tea Water Pump, of which it was alleged by the housekeepers who drew from it, that it made better tea than any other water" (Haswell 1896).	Smith (1938)
Kalck Hoek; Catiemuts Hill; The Windmill Hill; Lime-shell Point; Gallows Hill; Potbaker's Hill; Potter-Hill	Hill	"A hill whose substratum forms the down grade to Broadway toward Canal Street, rose at Franklin Street and declined towards the still obvious hollow of Centre Street, commanding the Collect Pond, and the inconspicuous city to the south" (Gratacap 1904). "The vicinity of Chatham Street, south of Pearl Street was in its natural condition a considerable eminence, called in early times Catiemuts Hill. Whether the name is of Indian derivation or not is uncertain. . . . The earliest indication of any improvement in that vicinity was the erection of a windmill west of present Chatham Street and a little north of Duane Street. The earliest [known] mention of the mill [was] in 1662" (New York Common Council 1842–70).	Bolton (1922); Finch (1909); Stokes (1915–28)

Name(s)	Feature Type(s)	Selected Descriptions, with Modern Location	Additional Descriptions
Lispenard's Creek	Stream	"East of the Church Street of today, its [Lispenard's Creek's] course lay through a low, but rather narrow, marshy valley, between rolling land, topped here and there with conical sand-hills on the north, and the Kalch Hoek, which rose to a considerable elevation on the south. Beyond this hill and following the curve of its base, there spread the broad pasture land, swamps, and salt marshes of the Lispenard Meadows. . . . Through these meadows the stream flowed sluggishly, spreading out over the low land, but maintaining enough of a channel to permit the passage of small boats from the river to the pond. A little brook entered nearly at [a] right angle and from the north side a tiny rivulet trickled down from a fine spring" (Hill and Waring 1897). [This west-flowing outlet of the Collect Pond was enlarged to drain the pond, creating the "canal" that eventually gave its name to Canal Street.]	Barlow (1969); Cozzens (1843); Randel (1864); Stokes (1915–28)
Old Wreck Brook; Wreck Brook; Old Kill; Fresh Water; Little Creek; Wolfert's Creek	Stream	"The northern limit of the map [the Duke's Plan] is about the present Roosevelt Street, where Old Wreck Brook (as it was called later) discharged the waters of the Fresh Water pond into the East River across the region which is still known as 'The Swamp'" (Janvier 1894). "The eastern outlet of the Collect Pond which made its way to the East River practically on the line of present day Roosevelt Street, through a swampy valley known as Wolfert's Marsh" (Hill and Waring 1897).	Cohen and Augustyn (1997); Haswell (1896); Waldman (1999)
Rutgers Hill	Hill	"[J]ust north of the Kissing Bridge over the Old Kill, the High Road ascended a hill so steep that a circuitous route was necessary, and the loop formed in the effort to secure a better grade still exists as Chatham Square [at Market and Madison streets]. . . . Close to the road stood Wolfert's Webber's tavern, for a long time the farthest outlying dwelling on the east side" (Hill and Waring 1897).	Dunshee (1952); Gilmore (1995)

Name(s)	Feature Type(s)	Selected Descriptions, with Modern Location	Additional Descriptions
Collect Pond; Collect, the; Calck; Kalch; Kolck; Freshwater Pond; Fresh Water	Pond	"[T]his clear and sparkling pond was fed by large springs of great reputed purity. Its depth was uncertain, the records ranging from 40 to 70 feet, but it was undoubtedly very deep, and was currently reported to be bottomless. . . . [I]t was said to be the abode of hideous and terrible sea-monsters which were seen at intervals by solitary individuals and which seized a Hessian trooper during the revolution" (Hill and Waring 1897). "The common traces of native residence were observed in later times under the shelter of the eminence known to the Dutch as the Kalch Hoek, at which place there was the most abundant supply of fresh water in the locality, provided by the springs which filled the 'Fresh Water' pond occupying the low ground now traversed by Centre Street. Around this sheltered spot, discarded oyster-shells, the unfailing sign of local aboriginal occupancy, were at one time observable in great abundance" (Bolton 1922). "In these ponds, were several kinds of fish, one peculiar to fresh water—viz. (*Labrus Auritus* . . .) or fresh water sun-fish; the other species were common to both fresh and salt water. The common eel (*Anguilla Vulgaris* . . .) three varieties of Killifish, (*Esox pisculentus* . . .) one of which, I do not recollect having seen any where else, it was called by the boys, 'Yellow-bellied Cobbler' on account of its abdomen being of a golden color. The 'stickle back' (*Gasterosteus quadracus* . . .) was found in the powder-house pond [the Little Collect], but did not inhabit 'the Collect'" (Cozzens 1843).	Anbinder (2001); Dunshee (1952); Gratacap (1904); Koeppel (2000); Stokes (1915–28)
[Twentieth Street Spring]	Spring	"The latter [the east branch of Minetta Water] had its origin in a spring east of 5th Avenue and above 20th Street" (Hill and Waring 1897).	

Name(s)	Feature Type(s)	Selected Descriptions, with Modern Location	Additional Descriptions
Bunker Hill; Bayard's Mount; Mallesmitsberg; Mad Smith's Hill	Hill	"[T]he highest and steepest [hill] on the south end of this island . . . was called 'Bunker Hill.' The diluvium of this hill was similar to the rest of the hills of the island. It was a steep, and somewhat pyramidal hill, about 100 feet higher than the present level of Grand Street. . . . How often have I, when a boy, stood on the breast-work of this hill, and looked, with delight, to the south, over that beautiful sheet of water, the Kolck (Collect), on the small city, with its few spires and domes. Beyond was seen the bay, with the hills of Staten Island still farther in the south; then turning to the west, the 'Noble Hudson,' with the Newark Mountains in the distance, the farm houses and country seats of the island and that stupendous work of nature the [P]alisades, on the north, and on the east the high ridge of that fertile plain, Long Island, 'all covered with their native green'" (Cozzens 1843). [Bunker Hill, or Bayard's Mount, as it is described in Chapter 3, stood between Centre Street and the Bowery, Pell, and Canal streets.]	Anbinder (2001); Gilmore (1995); Stokes (1915–28)
[Spring Street Spring]	Spring	"Spring Street is named after a spring tapped by Aaron Burr's Manhattan Water Company. . . . Local legend maintains that a well at Broadway and Spring Street became the grave of one Juliana (or Gulielma) Elmore Sands, whose body minus shoes, hat and shawl was found floating there on Jan. 2, 1800. Her fiancé was acquitted of the crime, but her ghost has been seen occasionally in the area. In 1974 a resident of 535 Broadway (at Spring Street) reported that a gray-haired apparition wearing mossy garments emerged from his waterbed. The same year the spring burst its underground channel and flooded a basement on West Broadway" (von Pressentin Wright, Miller, and Seitz 2002).	Feirstein (2001); Hill and Waring (1897); Smith (1938)
Rose Hill	Hill	"[A] wooded height, though less high than Murray Hill" (Hill and Waring 1897) "[In 1816] a lane, the Rose Hill, from Eighth Avenue [ran] between 21st and 22nd streets to Broadway, [then] to 23rd and Third Avenue" (Haswell 1896).	

Name(s)	Feature Type(s)	Selected Descriptions, with Modern Location	Additional Descriptions
Richmond Hill; Zandtberg	Hill	"From this crossing-place [at Lispenard's Creek] I followed a well-beaten path, leading from the city to the then village of Greenwich, passing over open and partly fenced lots and fields, not at that time under cultivation, and remote from any dwelling house, now remembered by me, except Col. Aaron Burr's former country seat, on elevated ground, called 'Richmond Hill,' which was then 100 to 150 yards west of this path, and was then occupied as a place of refreshment for gentlemen taking a drive from the city" (Randel 1864). "West of Broadway to Fourth Street [the] range of hills extended, apparently similar in character to the cobble-stone heaps that prevail in and around Brooklyn to-day. These hills were remarkable for the abundance of quail and woodcock found in their shelters" (Gratacap 1904). [The former location of Richmond Hill is approximately Chatham and Varick streets. The Sand Hills extended from Richmond Hill up to today's Astor Place.]	Hill and Waring (1897);
Minetta Water; Minetta Brook; Minetta Stream; Manetta Water; Bestevaer's Killetje	Stream	"In this year [1816] Minetta stream was fully apparent; and as it was and is of considerable volume, it has been [a] very important and expensive factor in the construction of the foundations along its line, from its main source, near the site of the Union Club, to its discharge in the North River. Its other branch had its source at Sixth Avenue and Sixteenth Street, the two joining between Eleventh and Twelfth streets and Fifth and Sixth avenues; its course thence being irregular to Minetta Lane and Bleecker Street, thence direct to Hudson Street at King Street; then bifurcating and joining at Greenwich Street, thence to the river by Charlton Street" (Haswell 1896). "[A] brisk little brook full of trout, in places a foamy rush through [a] narrow channel, elsewhere 'sulking under the shadow of the bank in the quiet pool below'" (Hill and Waring 1897). "In 1820, there was still a small colony of muskrats, bordering this creek. The brook passed along the lower end of Potters' Field [now Washington Square Park], and formed a large pond called Bollus's pond, where Downing Street now is; the low swampy grounds that were filled up caused this pond, which lay a little north-west of Richmond Hill" (Cozzens 1843).	Janvier (1894); Randel (1864); Stokes (1915–28)

Name(s)	Feature Type(s)	Selected Descriptions, with Modern Location	Additional Descriptions
Knapp's Spring	Spring	"A scanty supply of tea and drinking water [was] obtained from 'Knapp's Spring' . . . and other springs" (Randel 1864). "[In 1816] near Bethune (West Fourth Street), also was a spring of exceptionally pure water, owned by a Mr. Knapp, who distributed the product from carts at two cents a pail" (Haswell 1896).	Smith (1938)
Stuyvesant's Creek *and* [Ninth Street Creek]	Streams	"[Stuyvesant Creek] rose in the neighborhood of Rivington and Suffolk streets . . . one of two main creeks that drained through Stuyvesant's Meadows . . . emptying into the [East] river at the foot of Third Street. [The other had] its origin near First Avenue and Sixth Street, crossed Tompkins Square, and flowed diagonally to its outlet near the foot of Ninth Street. Both were home of countless eels" (Hill and Waring 1897).	
"Manhattan Island"	Hill	"[Stuyvesant Creek] At the southern end of the region of wetness [Stuyvesant's Meadows] near the shore (on the spot of Manhattan Street [now Houston Street, between Third and Lewis streets]) rose a little knoll, covering about an acre, cut off by creeks and marshes from the dryland, and completely surrounded by open water during exceptionally high tides, called by some 'Manhattan Island'" (Hill and Waring 1897).	
Cedar Creek; Krom Moerasje	Stream	"The Dutch named the locality [Cedar Creek] Krom Moerasje, meaning 'little crooked swamp,' which also designated the brook that used to twist from Madison Square to the East River near 18th Street" (The Federal Writers' Project 1939).	Haswell (1896); Koeppel (2000); Stokes (1915–28); von Pressentin Wright, Miller, and Seitz (2002)
Ash Brook	Stream	"At the foot of east 25th Street was the estate of John Lawrence, where lay a miniature pond fed by a spring and from this ran a tiny rill called Ash Brook" (Hill and Waring 1897).	Barlow (1969)

Name(s)	Feature Type(s)	Selected Descriptions, with Modern Location	Additional Descriptions
[Iron Spring]	Spring	"There were some few wells and springs on the Island, which were somewhat charged with iron, making them Chalybeate; the one near where 24th Street crosses the 8th Avenue, is so strong with iron, that it could not be used, for nay useful purpose, either had it any medicinal quality" (Cozzens 1843).	
Sun-fish Pond	Pond	"[A]t Madison Avenue and 32nd Street the stream expanded into a pond, which extended to 4th Avenue (Sun-fish Pond), famous as a fishing ground, although on several occasions during protracted drought, it nearly disappeared, for the stream which fed it received very little spring water and often in summer, its bed was nearly dry. In times of heavy rains though it overflowed its banks and spread from Murray Hill to Rose Hill" (Hill and Waring 1897).	Haswell (1896)
Murray Hill; Inclenberg; Fire-beacon Hill	Hill	"[Murray Hill was a] hill of the rudest and most hetero-geneous mixture of stones and gravel and boulders, cemented together into a matrix of almost impenetra-ble density existed, crowning the underlying schist. . . . It had a natural rise from 34th Street, sinking towards 42nd Street and reaching from Lexington Avenue to Broadway, with an imperceptible prolongation north-ward, melting into the surfaces of Central Park" (Gratacap 1904). "A magnificent place altogether was Inclenberg [where the Murrays of Murray Hill lived], approached by an avenue of magnolias, elms, spruce and Lombardy poplars, which led to a wide lawn bordered on either side by extensive gardens. The spacious, two-story mansion had a broad veranda extending around three sides, and . . . front windows commanding a view of Kip's Bay and the East River. Inclenberg was frequently spoken of by chroniclers as one of the loveliest spots on the island" (Monaghan 1998).	Cozzens (1843); Haswell (1896); Hill and Waring (1897); von Pressentin Wright, Miller, and Seitz (2002)
[Marston Spring]	Spring	"A spring at East End Avenue and 79th Street flowed into Marston's Creek which used to flow on the east side of Manhattan. Another spring feeding Marston's Creek began at [the future location of] 'Sloan's Supermarket'" (Barlow 1969).	

Name(s)	Feature Type(s)	Selected Descriptions, with Modern Location	Additional Descriptions
Kill of Schepmoes	Stream	"[The Kill of Schepmoes was a] stream north of Murray Hill and Kip's Farm. It collected the flow of several streams among the rocks in the vicinity of 46th Street, between 5th and 6th avenues, and flowed, almost due east, to a point near 4th Avenue, where it curved towards the south and passed through the valley between Murray and Dutch Hills to its outlet at 36th Street at Kip's Bay on the East River" (Hill and Waring 1897).	Grumet (1981); Koeppel (2000); Stokes (1915–28)
Great Kill; Grote Kill	Stream	"Three small streams, running north, south and west united near present 10th Avenue and 40th Street [to form Great Kill], then wound through a marshy valley (Reed Valley) to a deep bay on the Hudson River at present 42nd Street and 11th Avenue . . . a wonderful fishing and hunting ground" (Stokes 1915–28). [Great Kill ran through what is today's Times Square.]	Hill and Waring (1897); Koeppel (2000); The Federal Writers' Project (1939); Waldman (1999)
Coale Kill; Coble Kill; Duffore's Mill Stream	Stream	"As a tiny rivulet, this brook rose among the rocks on high ground near Ninth Avenue and 72nd Street and ran, southeasterly, in a narrow stony channel to Eighth Avenue and 65th street. Here it entered a wider valley and its bed lay for a considerable distance through alluvial deposit. The banks were more or less boggy and just east of the point where the projections of Sixth Avenue and 63rd Street would cross, the stream formed a lake. . . . Continuing in a southeasterly direction in the valley, the stream flowed sluggishly through a swampy area . . . the stream crossed 59th Street between Fifth and Sixth avenues, turned to the east, recrossed 59th Street near Madison Avenue, and at Fourth Avenue curved again to the southeast, maintaining a fairly constant course to 2nd Avenue and 51st Street, and flowing south parallel to 2nd Avenue, to 48th Street where it turned sharply east until the line of 5th Avenue, where it turned again to the southeast finding its outlet at 47th Street in Turtle Bay" (Hill and Waring 1897).	Koeppel (2000)
[Milkman Spring]	Spring	"Along the west side of the Boulevard [Broadway] between 61st and 62nd streets . . . there is a spring. The level of the water never changes. It never dries up, never freezes, and it is cold in summer and warm in winter. . . . I drank of the water from a milk can (for of course there is a milkman here and his shed and cans are within a few yards of the spring). It was colder than Croton [water supply], but not very cold, and it had a slight salty taste" (Smith 1938).	

Name(s)	Feature Type(s)	Selected Descriptions, with Modern Location	Additional Descriptions
Saw Kill; Sawmill Creek; Arch Brook; Old Arch Brook; Marston's Creek	Stream	"A rill flowing east from the rocky ridge overlooking Bloomingdale Village, which rose near Ninth Avenue and 85th Street, flowed in a southerly direction through Manhattan Square [where the American Museum of Natural History is today], where it spread into a little pond, and then turned east, crossing Central Park to Fifth Avenue and 75th Street, receiving three tributaries within its [Central Park's] limits, two from the north and one from the south. At 75th Street near Third Avenue it was joined by another stream [name unknown]. Near this junction the old Boston Post Road crossed it, and then from this point, the stream ran due east to its outlet near the foot of 75th Street [into the East River]. Near Avenue A it received a short superficial tributary from the northwest" (Hill and Waring 1897).	Barlow (1969); Haswell (1896); Koeppel (2000)
[Ninety-eighth Street Spring]	Spring	"[A] little stream which led from a spring in Central Park near the imaginary intersection of Sixth Avenue and 98th Street, skirted the north end of the high ground lying west of and emptied into one of the inlets [on the East River]" (Hill and Waring 1897).	
Tanner's Spring	Spring	"In July, 1880, while Dr. Henry S. Tanner was giving public exhibitions of going without solid food for forty days, he made almost daily visits to this spring, it is said, and drew from it such liquid sustenance as he was allowed to consume during his public fast. In consequence of these visitations, it became known as 'Tanner's Spring' and has ever since retained that designation. Perhaps Tanner's apparent ability to live without eating was attributed to some nourishing element in this spring. At any rate, people came even from distant parts of the town with bottles, pitchers, and pails, which they filled here and carried to their homes. In those days, this spring had an extensive reputation as a specific for rheumatism" (Smith 1938). [Tanner's Spring is in Central Park, north of the line of West 82nd Street.]	
[Unquenchable Spring]	Spring	"[O]n the Hudson River shore at West 104th Street. . . [there is] a persistent, unquenchable spring" (Smith 1938).	

Name(s)	Feature Type(s)	Selected Descriptions, with Modern Location	Additional Descriptions
[Ramble Spring]	Spring	"April 2, 1898. There is a quiet spring about one hundred and sixty feet west of the East Drive, just about opposite the Jewish Temple Beth-El on Fifth Avenue. It is near the foot of the slope that rises to that part [of] the Ramble which contains the Park's giant boulders, some of which were rocking stones less than forty years ago. Leeks and dandelions are growing around the spring, and a little stream running from it, in a southwesterly direction, loses itself in the grass. . . . Its water is cold and pleasant to the taste, and there is ample testimony that it is a good, potable spring, in the healthy frames of Park employees of seventy years of age who drink from it daily" (Smith 1938).	
[Children's Spring]	Spring	"March 8, 1898. On the north side of East 79th Street, about one hundred and ffifty feet west of East End Avenue . . . there appears a little spring, protected by planks from the sand over it. The water boils up lustily, and does not congeal even when the hydrants of the vicinity are frozen solid, as they were last winter. The children of the neighborhood are its constant patrons" (Smith 1938).	
Montayne's Rivulet	Stream	"Montayne's Rivulet rose in the rocks east of Bloomingdale, entered what is now Central Park near the line of 101st Street, then curved northeast and east, and joined the main stream near where 109th Street now enters Fifth Avenue. In its course, it flowed through McGowan's Pass and then drained into Harlem Creek" (Hill and Waring 1897).	Mittelbach and Crewdson (1997); von Pressentin Wright, Miller, and Seitz (2002)
[Lamplighter Spring]	Spring	"On the north side of West 115th Street, between Fifth and Lenox avenues, right against the eastern wall of No. 27 is a pump with a latticed house over it. This pump is supplied by a spring which ten years ago welled up out of the ground and gave the contractor a good deal of trouble. The German lamplighter, who lives nearby on the south side of 115th Street near Lenox Avenue, says that it used to come up in a sandy place under a little overhang, bubbling up in four or five places. An Irishman who lives in the little house east of Grant's Tomb says the owners of the two houses wished to have the spring preserved, and that he superintended the building of the spring house" (Smith 1938).	

Name(s)	Feature Type(s)	Selected Descriptions, with Modern Location	Additional Descriptions
Harlem Creek; Rechgawac's Creek; Kill of Rechawanis; Benson's Creek; Benson's Mill Creek; Mill Creek	Stream	"There were many small streams or brooks on the Island, but none of importance, if we except the one called Harlem Creek, which runs through the salt marsh, at the six mile stone; this creek has two or three branches, one of which follows along the low-lands to near Manhattanville, where some projectors in a speculation commenced a few years since, a canal, which they left when partly finished" (Cozzens 1843). "[A] considerable creek, twenty feet deep and one hundred feet wide where it emptied into Hell Gate Bay" (Hill and Waring 1897).	Grumet (1981); Haswell (1896); Koeppel (2000)
Round Hills; Ronde Gebergte; Mount Morris; Slang Berg; Snake Hill *and* Little Hill	Hills	"[P]artially hidden from view [from McGown's Pass] by the Ronde Gebergte, or Round Hills. . . . [o]ne is an abrupt wooded eminence, by modern innovation styled Mount Morris, but which the Dutch called the Slang Berg, or Snake Hill, from the reptile tribes that infested its cleft rocks and underbrush even within memory of the living. Southerly from it the gneiss rock crops out in huge, disordered masses. A little way to the right is the other, a lesser height or ridge, and which to the inhabitants came to be known as the Little Hill, when was built opposite to it (Kingsbridge Road only parting them) the goodly Dutch farm-house of Johannes Sickels, still standing in 123rd Street" (Riker 1881). [Mount Morris still stands in Marcus Garvey Park; Little Hill, just to the east, was destroyed during the construction of Park Avenue.]	Hill and Waring (1897); Randel (1864); Stokes (1915–28); von Pressentin Wright, Miller, and Seitz (2002)
[Grant's Spring]	Spring	"November 16, 1898. This spring bubbles up a few feet east of the New York Central Railroad tracks on the Hudson River shore, between 122nd and 123rd streets. It is at the western base of the high hill sloping down from Grant's Tomb. . . . Those who knew this spring forty years ago before the wall was built say that the water comes from a cleft in a rock underlying the wall, and that it bubbles up through a sandy bottom when the spring is newly cleaned. The surface of the water is about six feet along the wall and about three feet wide and two feet deep" (Smith 1938).	

Name(s)	Feature Type(s)	Selected Descriptions, with Modern Location	Additional Descriptions
Mount Washington	Hill	"The highest natural elevation in Manhattan (267.75 feet) is attained at a point near the intersection of Fort Washington Avenue and 183rd Street [It is the] former site of Fort Washington during the American Revolution" (The Federal Writers' Project 1939). [Mount Washington is labeled FORT KNYPHAUSEN on the British Headquarters Map; Knyphausen was the Hessian general in charge of northern Manhattan during the Revolution.]	Bolton (1924); Grumet (1981); Schecter (2002)
Mount Washington Spring	Spring	"At 161st Street the Kingsbridge Road [i.e., Broadway] passed east of and opposite to Mount Washington spring" (Randel 1864).	
Laurel Hill; Ronde-Vly-Berg	Hill	"The former site of Fort George [, Laurel Hill is] about two hundred feet high" (Hill and Waring 1897).	Schecter (2002); The Federal Writers' Project (1939)
Half Kill; Sherman's Creek; Sherman Creek	Stream	"The Sherman family were early residents of this location, residing in what one source describes as a fisherman's dwelling erected circa 1815 at the foot of Fort George Hill. The creek which took the family name emptied into the Harlem River approximately between Dyckman and Academy streets" (Feirstein 2001).	Barlow (1969); Buttenweiser (1987); Hill and Waring (1897)
Inwood Hill; Cox's Hill; Cocks Hill	Hill	"At 216th Street the [Kingsbridge] road was 33 yards west of 10th Avenue, and 1070 yards east of Cock Hill Fort, on high ground, between Spuyten Duyvil (Spiteing Devil) creek and Hudson's River" (Randel 1864). [Inwood Hill is now a forested reserve in Inwood Hill Park. It includes the most intact forest ecosystem on the island.]	Horenstein (2007); Riker (1904)
Marble Hill; Papperimemin; Saperewack	Hill	"A rocky promontory called Marble Hill referring to the marble and limestone quarries around its base, Spuyten Duyvil Creek wound around Marble Hill's northern protuberance, connecting the Harlem and the Hudson Rivers" (Feirstein 2001). [After the Harlem Ship Canal was completed in the 1890s, modifying the path of Spuyten Duyvil Creek, Marble Hill became physically part of the Bronx, though politically its citizens still vote with Manhattan.]	Bolton (1934); Grumet (1981); Horenstein (2007)

APPENDIX B.

Late Woodland Lenape sites and place-names on Mannahatta and harbor islands, with evidence and sources, arranged approximately from Uptown to Downtown. Places for which the Lenape name is unknown are supplied with historical place-names in square brackets (see Appendix A); Native American names of a later date are shown in quotation marks, with source, and may not be authentic. For a detailed analysis of Native American place-names in New York City, see Grumet (1981).

Place	Approximate Modern Location	Evidence
Saperewack	220th Street and Broadway (formerly Kingsbridge Road), on Marble Hill	*Artifacts:* Shell middens, soapstone pipe (Bolton 1909, 1934). *Name:* The site was located in the March 4, 1669, deed to the Fordham section in the Bronx as being on the "Harlem Ryver at ye Hook called Saperewack" (Bolton 1881). *History:* This is the approximate location of the "Wading Place" that was used by the Lenape as well as later European colonists as the easiest place to cross Spuyten Duyvil Creek prior to the first bridge (Bolton 1922).
[Cold Spring Hollow]	Cold Spring Hollow, within Inwood Hill Park	*Artifacts:* Shell middens, rock shelters, fire pits, animal remains (turkey, deer), broken pottery, and projectile points (Finch 1909; Bolton 1909; Harrington 1909). *History:* One reputed location of the "sale" of Manhattan to the Dutch.
Shorakapok	Along Seaman Avenue, between Isham Park and Inwood Park	*Artifacts:* Human remains, animal remains (sturgeon, deer, dog—including two puppies), numerous shell middens, stone axe, club-stone, projectile points, hammer stones, sinkers, pestle, pottery, fire stones, and charcoal (Bolton 1909; Skinner 1909; Parker 1920). *Name:* Forms of "Shorakapok" used in colonial manuscripts from 1646, 1666, and 1693 (Grumet 1981). Name survives in abbreviated form as "Kappok Street" in the Spuyten Duyvil section of the Bronx. *History:* "On January 7, 1676, eighteen Lenape from northern Manhattan met with the British governor at the fort, presenting deer skins and venison, after which the Governor declared, 'Resolved, That the Wickers-creek Indians, if they desire it, be admitted with their wives and children, to plant upon this Island, but nowhere else, if they remove, and that it be upon the north point of the Island near Spuyten Duyvil'" (Bolton 1909). *Inference:* Bolton (1924) concluded that this site was long inhabited, with planting fields nearby.

Place	Approximate Modern Location	Evidence
Muscoota	Three sites along the Harlem River in northern Manhattan: between West 196th and 201st streets, West 209th and 211th streets, and West 213 and 214th streets, all east of 10th Avenue	*Artifacts:* Human remains, numerous shell middens, "ceremonial" food pits, animal remains (dog, deer, turtle, snake, sturgeon), breast ornament made of fish bones, a "fine Iroquoian vessel," paint cups, pestles, a "tomahawk," and a bone needle (Finch 1909; Bolton 1909; Skinner 1909; Parker 1920; Bolton 1922, 1934). *Name:* The name appears in documents from August 25, 1655 (Gehring 1980), September 1, 1671 (Fauconnier cited in Grumet 1981), and 1696 (Bolton 1881). Both the Harlem River and adjacent areas on shore have been referred to as "Muscoota." Bolton (1922) located "Muscoota" as the Dyckman and Nagel farm properties north of Sherman Creek. Grumet (1981) gives this as a name for the Harlem Flats, similar to "Schorakin." *Inference:* Bolton (1909) thought that, given the nature of the finds at this site and its easy visibility from the settlement of Nipnichsen (on the heights of Spuyten Duyvil), the site may have been used ceremonially. Grumet (1981), however, locates "Nip Nickson" in New Jersey.
[Tubby Hook]	Dyckman Street at the Hudson River, within Inwood Hill Park	*Artifacts:* Shell middens, charcoal and ashes (up to five feet deep), animal remains (elk, bear), human remains, and stone pipe (Bolton 1909; Harrington 1909; Skinner 1909; Bolton 1922, 1934; Smith 1950; Cantwell and Wall 2001).
[Forest Hill]	Dongan Place and Broadway, within Fort Tryon Park	*Artifacts:* Native objects found in former truck garden on this site (Bolton 1922), shell middens (from Cohn 1976, cited in New York State Historical Preservation Office Records, Waterford, New York).
[Laurel Hill]	Between 191st and 196th streets, and Amsterdam and Eleventh (or St. Nicholas) avenues	*Artifacts:* Native objects found (Bolton 1909).
"Great Maize Land"	Between West 176th and 181st streets, and Broadway and Wadsworth Avenue	*Name:* Mentioned in a lease to Jan Kiersen and Jan Gerritsen Van Dalsen on March 30, 1686 (Bolton 1909, 1922).

Place	Approximate Modern Location	Evidence
[Jeffrey's Hook]	Promontory beneath the George Washington Bridge, south to 156th Street	*Artifacts:* Shell middens, wood ashes, projectile points in various rock shelters (Bolton 1909, 1922, 1934). *History:* Jeffrey's Hook may have been the location where Hudson's ship was attacked by Lenape from Manhattan in October 1609 (Johnson 1993; Bolton 1909).
Schorrakin	Plain between East 135th and 150th streets along the Harlem River	*Name:* Mentioned in document from March 9, 1644, cited in Grumet (1981), and again in 1650 (Riker 1881). Bolton (1934) also considered "Schorrakin" a name for the site on Conykeest.
[North Harlem]	152nd Street and Bradhurst Avenue	*History:* Supposed cave with campsite (Bolton 1934). *Inference:* Maximum Entropy (MAXENT) model of Lenape site suitability; the model result is shown on page 111 and explained in the notes for Chapter 4.
[Hollow Way]	Approximately 131st Street and Broadway	*Inference:* MAXENT model. This location typifies the kind of place the Lenape would have found attractive: mainly flat, with ample freshwater and access to the Hudson River.
Tenkenas	Ward's Island	*Name:* First recorded use on July 16, 1637 (Gehring 1980).
Minnahanock	Randall's Island	*Name:* First recorded use on July 16, 1637 (Gehring 1980).
Conykeekst	On the neck of land between East 108th and 123rd streets, east of Fifth Avenue to the East River; potentially multiple sites	*Artifacts:* Shell middens, projectile points, flakes, and rejects found at East 121st Street and Pleasant Avenue (Riker 1881; Bolton 1922). *Name:* "Conykeekst" is mentioned in a Dutch deed from 1639 (Riker 1881). Formerly, a local street in the area was called "Conkeek Street" (Bolton 1922). Also see Grumet (1981). *Inference:* Parker (1920) indicates that a large fishing camp was found at Montagne's Point, on the shore of Hellgate Bay, at 110th Street. Bolton (1909) places this camp across the mouth of Harlem Creek, at about 106th Street. The MAXENT model supports the 106th Street location, though both are possible.

Place	Approximate Modern Location	Evidence
Rechgawanes	On the point of land between East 102nd and East 103rd streets	*Name:* "Rechgawanes," mentioned in the May 9, 1647, sale of land in northern Manhattan, referred to a "certain point extending between two creeks" (Gehring 1980; Grumet 1981), which may be the same as "Conykeekst." Bolton (1909) cites a deed from August 20, 1669, referring to "the Point named Rechwanis" between a creek [possibly Harlem Creek] and hills [possibly the Round Hills]. *History:* Riker (1881) cites an order given in 1675 requiring the Lenape "to remove within a fortnight to their usual winter quarters *within Hellgate* upon this island [Manhattan]." *Inference:* "This winter retreat [where the Lenape were to remove in 1675, interprets Riker] was either the woodlands between Harlem Plains and Kingsbridge at that date still claimed by these Indians as hunting grounds, or Rechewanes on the Bay of Hellgate" (Riker 1881).
Konaande Kongh	On high ground between Madison and Lexington avenues at East 98th to 100th streets	*Name:* "Konaande Kongh" was named in a deed from August 4, 1669, as a locale near "the Point named Rechwanis" (cited in Riker 1881). The original document has not been found. Also see discussion in Grumet (1981). *History:* A Lenape chief, Reckgawanc, abandoned this site in 1669 (Bolton 1922).
[Stryker's Bay]	Upper West Side, 96th Street	*Artifacts:* Shell middens (Bolton 1922). *Inference:* The MAXENT model supports this location.
[East River fishing camps]	From East 36th to 79th streets, along the East River	*Inference:* Bolton (1922) inferred from their protected locales and access points to the East River that there were probably several fishing camps on the eastern side of Mannahatta. Our MAXENT model supports this inference at six potential locations: Kip's Bay, Turtle Bay, and the mouths of streams at East 53rd, East 62nd, East 74th (Saw Kill), and East 80th streets.
Sapokanikan	Gansevoort Street, near the Hudson River	*Name:* The name is mentioned in several documents from the 1640s and was also used in Brooklyn (James and Jameson 1913; Gehring 1980). In Dutch times, the area that would one day be known as Greenwich Village was commonly referred to as "Sapokanikan" (Janvier 1894; Finch 1909). *History:* Bolton (1909) believed that Lenape from Sapokanikan "brought great store of very good oysters aboard, which were bought for trifles" to trade with Hudson's crew (Benson 1849; Bolton 1922, 1934). Also see Grumet (1981) for discussion.

Place	Approximate Modern Location	Evidence
"Schepmoes"	East 14th Street and 2nd Avenue	*Name:* Beauchamp (1900) identified the "Kil of Schepmoes" as a stream mentioned in a November 15, 1639, deed to land in Lower Manhattan; Bolton (1920) claims there was a small habitation site there. Grumet (1981) suggests that the name likely follows from Jan Jansen Schepmoe, a prominent Dutch landowner, and may not have been of Native American origin.
"Minetta"	Greenwich Village, including running through the modern location of Washington Square Park	*Name:* Grumet (1981) attributes this name for the stream to Bolton (1905), though that seems unlikely since it is also referred to in nineteenth-century sources (Haswell 1896; Hill and Waring 1897). Also see Stokes (1915–28). Feirstein (2001) indicates that *Minetta* means "small stream" in Dutch. *History:* Nineteenth-century accounts suggest this area was used by the Lenape to grow their tobacco (Hill and Waring 1897).
"Werpoes"	Between Lafayette and Centre streets and between Duane and Worth streets, approximately within the bounds and to the north of today's Foley Square, neighboring the Collect Pond	*Artifacts:* Abundant shell middens (Bolton 1922). *Name:* Bolton (1922) believed that "Werpoes" was the name of a Lenape settlement site at the Collect Pond, in the lee of the Kalch Hoek, citing a deed to Augustine Heermans in 1651 for "the land of Werpoes." Gehring (1980), however, indicates that "Werpoes" refers to a site in what is now downtown Brooklyn, based on a document from May 27, 1640. It is possible that the name was used formerly on Manhattan and later used again in Brooklyn, after European settlement. *History:* Bolton (1922) wrote that the people of "Werpoes" sold Manhattan to the Dutch in 1626, then moved to Brooklyn to live with their kinspeople, the Carnarsee. *Inference:* Bolton (1922) inferred from the abundance of freshwater and the flat, cultivable land nearby (e.g., City Hall Park, Chinatown) that Werpoes was the most important habitation site in Lower Manhattan. The MAXENT model supports the quality of this site.
Nechtanc	Jefferson, Henry, Clinton, and Madison streets	*Name:* The name appears in colonial manuscripts from 1640 and 1683. "Nechtanc" is the Lenape name for Corlear's Hook, a hill on the East River shore, and the habitation site below it (Scott and Stryker-Rodda 1974; Grumet 1981). *History:* It was the site of the massacre of approximately forty Lenape by Dutch settlers on February 25, 1642 (De Vries 1655; Bolton 1934).

Place	Approximate Modern Location	Evidence
[Southern Mannahatta, East River shore]	Pearl Street, from Peck Slip to Broad Street	*Artifacts:* Shell middens (Bolton 1922; Kardas and Larrabee 1976) *Name:* Pearl Street takes its name from the abundant shells found on the shore of Lower Manhattan; Pearl Street once marked the strand (Feirstein 2001). E. Boesch, a long-time archaeologist in Manhattan, said that under most of Lower Manhattan is a stratum of shell fragments (pers. comm.).
Kapsee	Ledge of rocks off the southern tip of Manhattan Island	*Name:* The name was first used in 1693 (Ruttenber 1906, cited in Grumet 1981). Also see Stokes (1915–28) and Bolton (1922).
Pagganck	Three sites on Governors Island: outside the entrance to Fort Jay; beneath the parking lot of the Governors Island Library; and in Nolan Park, just south of Andes Road	*Artifacts:* Pottery fragments, storage pits, flint flakes, and charcoal (Santone and Irish 1997; Herbster et al. 1997; Wall and Cantwell 2004). *Name:* "Pagganck" is mentioned in an agreement dated June 16, 1637, between the Dutch and the "sachems from Keschaechquereren," a community of Carnarsee Lenape living in northern Brooklyn (Gehring 1980; Grumet 1981).
[Ellis Island] or "Kioshk," suggested by Schoolcraft (1845)	Near Immigration Museum, Ellis Island	*Artifacts:* Human remains, pottery fragments, shell middens (Kardas and Larrabee 1976; Pousson 1986; Wall and Cantwell 2004).
[Liberty Island] or "Minnisais," according to Schoolcraft (1845)	Below the Statue of Liberty	*Artifacts:* Shell middens (oysters, soft-shelled clams, mussels), animal remains (canvasback duck, quail, oyster toadfish, white perch, turtle), hickory nuts, pottery fragments, charcoal, spear point (State Historical Preservation Office Records, Waterford, New York; Wall and Cantwell 2004; Griswold 2003).

APPENDIX C.
Flora and Fauna. A list of ecological communities, native plants, and vertebrate animal species possibly found on Mannahatta in September 1609. Communities and species are organized by family. The probability of different species occurring on Mannahatta is indicated with superscripts to the common name:

*** = likely
** = probable
* = possible
° = remotely possible

Sources and methods are described in the notes to Chapter 6. This list is subject to further revisions as more information becomes available.

ECOLOGICAL COMMUNITIES

Marine
Marine deepwater community***
Marine gravel–sand beach community***
Marine intertidal mudflat community***
Marine rocky intertidal community***
Marine eelgrass meadow**

Estuarine
High salt marsh***
Low salt marsh***
Salt shrub community***
Tidal creek community***
Tidal river community***
Brackish intertidal mudflat community**
Brackish intertidal shore community**
Brackish subtidal aquatic bed community**
Brackish tidal marsh**
Coastal salt pond community**
Salt panne community**

Palustrine
Red maple–hardwood swamp***
Shallow emergent marsh***
Shrub swamp***
Vernal pool community***
Coastal plain Atlantic white cedar swamp**
Coastal plain pond-shore community**
Deep emergent marsh**
Floodplain forest**
Highbush blueberry bog thicket**

Lacustrine
Eutrophic pond community***
Coastal plain pond community**

Riverine
Intermittent stream community***
Marsh headwater stream community***
Rocky headwater stream community***
Coastal plain stream community**
Midreach stream community**

Terrestrial
Coastal Appalachian oak-pine forest***
Coastal oak-hickory forest***
Maritime beach community***
Oak-tulip tree forest***
Successional old field community***
Successional shrubland***
Chestnut oak forest**
Cliff community**
Coastal oak-beech forest**
Hemlock–northern hardwood forest**
Hempstead Plains grassland**
Maritime dunes community**
Maritime shrubland**
Pitch pine–scrub oak barrens**
Serpentine barrens**
Shoreline outcrop community**
Calcareous cliff community*
Calcareous shoreline outcrop community*
Lenape horticulture community***
Lenape shell-middens community***
Lenape trail community***
Lenape village-site community***
Lenape wigwams and longhouses
  community***

PLANTS

Acanthaceae
American water willow* *Justicia americana*

Aceraceae
Box elder*** *Acer negundo*

Red maple*** *Acer rubrum*
Silver maple*** *Acer saccharinum*
Sugar maple*** *Acer saccharum*
Black maple* *Acer nigrum*
Striped maple* *Acer pensylvanicum*

Acoraceae
Sweetflag*** *Acorus americanus*

Alismataceae
Northern water plantain*** *Alisma triviale*
Grassy arrowhead*** *Sagittaria graminea*
Broadleaf arrowhead*** *Sagittaria latifolia*
Hooded arrowhead* *Sagittaria calycina*
Awl-leaf arrowhead* *Sagittaria subulata*

Amaranthaceae
Tidal-marsh amaranth* *Amaranthus cannabinus*
Seaside amaranth* *Amaranthus pumilus*

Anacardiaceae
Fragrant sumac*** *Rhus aromatica*
Flameleaf sumac*** *Rhus copallinum*
Eastern poison ivy*** *Toxicodendron radicans*
Poison sumac*** *Toxicodendron vernix*

Apiaceae
Spotted water hemlock*** *Cicuta maculata*
Eastern grasswort*** *Lilaeopsis chinensis*
Purple meadow parsnip*** *Thaspium trifoliatum*
Purplestem angelica* *Angelica atropurpurea*
Hairy angelica* *Angelica venenosa*
Bulblet-bearing water hemlock* *Cicuta bulbifera*
Canadian honewort* *Cryptotaenia canadensis*
Rattlesnake master* *Eryngium aquaticum*
Common cow parsnip* *Heracleum maximum*
American marsh pennywort* *Hydrocotyle americana*
Manyflower marsh pennywort* *Hydrocotyle umbellata*
Longstyle sweetroot* *Osmorhiza longistylis*
Stiff cowbane* *Oxypolis rigidior*
Herbwilliam* *Ptilimnium capillaceum*
Canadian black snakeroot* *Sanicula canadensis*
Maryland sanicle* *Sanicula marilandica*
Hemlock water parsnip* *Sium suave*
Yellow pimpernel* *Taenidia integerrima*
Meadow Zizia* *Zizia aptera*
Golden Zizia* *Zizia aurea*

Apocynaceae
Spreading dogbane*** *Apocynum androsaemifolium*
Indian hemp*** *Apocynum cannabinum*

Aquifoliaceae
Smooth winterberry*** *Ilex laevigata*
Mountain holly*** *Ilex montana*
Common winterberry*** *Ilex verticillata*
Inkberry* *Ilex glabra*

Araceae
Green dragon*** *Arisaema dracontium*
Jack-in-the-pulpit*** *Arisaema triphyllum*
Goldenclub*** *Orontium aquaticum*
Skunk cabbage*** *Symplocarpus foetidus*
Green arrow arum* *Peltandra virginica*

Araliaceae
Wild sarsaparilla*** *Aralia nudicaulis*
American spikenard*** *Aralia racemosa*
American ginseng*** *Panax quinquefolius*
Bristly sarsaparilla* *Aralia hispida*
Dwarf ginseng* *Panax trifolius*

Aristolochiaceae
Canadian wild ginger* *Asarum canadense*

Asclepiadaceae
Swamp milkweed*** *Asclepias incarnata*
Purple milkweed*** *Asclepias purpurascens*
Common milkweed*** *Asclepias syriaca*
Butterfly milkweed*** *Asclepias tuberosa*
Redring milkweed*** *Asclepias variegata*
Clasping milkweed* *Asclepias amplexicaulis*
Poke milkweed* *Asclepias exaltata*
Fourleaf milkweed* *Asclepias quadrifolia*
Red milkweed* *Asclepias rubra*
Whorled milkweed* *Asclepias verticillata*
Green comet milkweed* *Asclepias viridiflora*

Aspleniaceae
Ebony spleenwort*** *Asplenium platyneuron*
Walking fern*** *Asplenium rhizophyllum*
Maidenhair spleenwort*** *Asplenium trichomanes*
Wallrue* *Asplenium ruta-muraria*

Asteraceae
Annual ragweed*** *Ambrosia artemisiifolia*
Great ragweed*** *Ambrosia trifida*

Western pearly everlasting*** *Anaphalis margaritacea*
Field pussytoes*** *Antennaria neglecta*
Woman's tobacco*** *Antennaria plantaginifolia*
Eastern Baccharis*** *Baccharis halimifolia*
Spanish needles*** *Bidens bipinnata*
Nodding beggar-ticks*** *Bidens cernua*
Purplestem beggar-ticks*** *Bidens connata*
Crowned beggar-ticks*** *Bidens coronata*
Devil's beggar-ticks*** *Bidens frondosa*
Maryland golden aster*** *Chrysopsis mariana*
Yellow thistle*** *Cirsium horridulum*
Swamp thistle*** *Cirsium muticum*
Pasture thistle*** *Cirsium pumilum*
Canadian horseweed*** *Conyza canadensis*
American burnweed*** *Erechtites hieraciifolia*
Eastern daisy fleabane*** *Erigeron annuus*
Philadelphia fleabane*** *Erigeron philadelphicus*
Prairie fleabane*** *Erigeron strigosus*
Hyssopleaf thoroughwort*** *Eupatorium hyssopifolium*
Spotted Joe-Pye weed*** *Eupatorium maculatum*
Common boneset*** *Eupatorium perfoliatum*
Sweet-scented Joe-Pye weed*** *Eupatorium purpureum*
Roundleaf thoroughwort*** *Eupatorium rotundifolium*
White wood aster*** *Eurybia divaricata*
Bigleaf aster*** *Eurybia macrophylla*
Flat-top goldentop*** *Euthamia graminifolia*
Slender goldentop*** *Euthamia tenuifolia*
Thinleaf sunflower*** *Helianthus decapetalus*
Giant sunflower*** *Helianthus giganteus*
Queendevil*** *Hieracium gronovii*
Allegheny hawkweed*** *Hieracium paniculatum*
Rough hawkweed*** *Hieracium scabrum*
Rattlesnake weed*** *Hieracium venosum*
Flaxleaf whitetop aster*** *Ionactis linariifolius*
Jesuit's bark*** *Iva frutescens*
Tall blue lettuce*** *Lactuca biennis*
Canada lettuce*** *Lactuca canadensis*
Devil's bite*** *Liatris scariosa*
Climbing hempvine*** *Mikania scandens*
Whorled wood aster*** *Oclemena acuminata*
Stiff goldenrod*** *Oligoneuron rigidum*
Golden ragwort*** *Packera aurea*
Sweetscent*** *Pluchea odorata*
Tall rattlesnake root*** *Prenanthes altissima*

Macoun's cudweed*** *Pseudognaphalium macounii*
Rabbittobacco*** *Pseudognaphalium obtusifolium*
Narrowleaf whitetop aster*** *Sericocarpus linifolius*
White goldenrod*** *Solidago bicolor*
Canada goldenrod*** *Solidago canadensis*
Zigzag goldenrod*** *Solidago flexicaulis*
Gray goldenrod*** *Solidago nemoralis*
Anisescented goldenrod*** *Solidago odora*
Roundleaf goldenrod*** *Solidago patula*
Seaside goldenrod*** *Solidago sempervirens*
Showy goldenrod*** *Solidago speciosa*
Common blue wood aster*** *Symphyotrichum cordifolium*
White heath aster*** *Symphyotrichum ericoides*
White panicle aster*** *Symphyotrichum lanceolatum*
Lowrie's blue wood aster*** *Symphyotrichum lowrieanum*
New England aster*** *Symphyotrichum novae-angliae*
New York aster*** *Symphyotrichum novi-belgii*
Purplestem aster*** *Symphyotrichum puniceum*
Smooth white oldfield aster*** *Symphyotrichum racemosum*
Shore aster*** *Symphyotrichum tradescantii*
New York ironweed*** *Vernonia noveboracensis*
Trumpetweed** *Eupatorium fistulosum*
Kalm's hawkweed** *Hieracium kalmii*
White snakeroot* *Ageratina altissima*
Small beggar-ticks* *Bidens discoidea*
Smooth beggar-ticks* *Bidens laevis*
Threelobe beggar-ticks* *Bidens tripartita*
Tall thistle* *Cirsium altissimum*
Field thistle* *Cirsium discolor*
Blue mistflower* *Conoclinium coelestinum*
Cornel-leaf whitetop* *Doellingeria infirma*
Parasol whitetop* *Doellingeria umbellata*
Robin's plantain* *Erigeron pulchellus*
White thoroughwort* *Eupatorium album*
Justiceweed* *Eupatorium leucolepis*
Pine-barren thoroughwort* *Eupatorium resinosum*
Low rough aster* *Eurybia radula*
Western showy aster* *Eurybia spectabilis*
Spoonleaf purple everlasting* *Gamochaeta purpurea*

Common sneezeweed* *Helenium autumnale*
Swamp sunflower* *Helianthus angustifolius*
Woodland sunflower* *Helianthus divaricatus*
Paleleaf woodland sunflower* *Helianthus strumosus*
Smooth oxeye* *Heliopsis helianthoides*
Canadian hawkweed* *Hieracium canadense*
Twoflower dwarf dandelion* *Krigia biflora*
Virginia dwarf dandelion* *Krigia virginica*
Woodland lettuce* *Lactuca floridana*
Hairy lettuce* *Lactuca hirsuta*
Dense blazing star* *Liatris spicata*
Bog aster* *Oclemena nemoralis*
Roundleaf ragwort* *Packera obovata*
Balsam groundsel* *Packera paupercula*
Sickleleaf silk grass* *Pityopsis falcata*
White rattlesnake root* *Prenanthes alba*
Purple rattlesnake root* *Prenanthes racemosa*
Cankerweed* *Prenanthes serpentaria*
Gall of the earth* *Prenanthes trifoliolata*
Cutleaf coneflower* *Rudbeckia laciniata*
Toothed whitetop aster* *Sericocarpus asteroides*
Atlantic goldenrod* *Solidago arguta*
Wreath goldenrod* *Solidago caesia*
Giant goldenrod* *Solidago gigantea*
Hairy goldenrod* *Solidago hispida*
Early goldenrod* *Solidago juncea*
Elliott's goldenrod* *Solidago latissimifolia*
Downy goldenrod* *Solidago puberula*
Wrinkleleaf goldenrod* *Solidago rugosa*
Stout goldenrod* *Solidago squarrosa*
Bog goldenrod* *Solidago uliginosa*
Elmleaf goldenrod* *Solidago ulmifolia*
Rice button aster* *Symphyotrichum dumosum*
Smooth blue aster* *Symphyotrichum laeve*
Calico aster* *Symphyotrichum lateriflorum*
Late purple aster* *Symphyotrichum patens*
Pringle's aster* *Symphyotrichum pilosum*
Willowleaf aster* *Symphyotrichum praealtum*
Eastern annual saltmarsh aster* *Symphyotrichum subulatum*
Perennial saltmarsh aster* *Symphyotrichum tenuifolium*
Waxyleaf aster* *Symphyotrichum undulatum*
Wingstem* *Verbesina alternifolia*

Azollaceae
Carolina mosquito fern* *Azolla caroliniana*

Balsaminaceae
Jewelweed*** *Impatiens capensis*
Pale touch-me-not*** *Impatiens pallida*

Berberidaceae
Blue cohosh*** *Caulophyllum thalictroides*
Mayapple*** *Podophyllum peltatum*

Betulaceae
Speckled alder*** *Alnus incana ssp. rugosa*
Hazel alder*** *Alnus serrulata*
Yellow birch*** *Betula alleghaniensis*
Sweet birch*** *Betula lenta*
River birch*** *Betula nigra*
Paper birch*** *Betula papyrifera*
Gray birch*** *Betula populifolia*
American hornbeam*** *Carpinus caroliniana*
American hazelnut*** *Corylus americana*
Hophornbeam*** *Ostrya virginiana*
Beaked hazelnut* *Corylus cornuta*

Blechnaceae
Netted chain fern*** *Woodwardia areolata*
Virginia chain fern*** *Woodwardia virginica*

Boraginaceae
Spring forget-me-not*** *Myosotis verna*
Wild Job's tears*** *Onosmodium virginianum*
Wild comfrey* *Cynoglossum virginianum*
Beggarslice* *Hackelia virginiana*
Virginia bluebells* *Mertensia virginica*
Bay forget-me-not* *Myosotis laxa*

Brassicaceae
Sicklepod*** *Arabis canadensis*
Tower rock cress*** *Arabis glabra*
Smooth rock cress*** *Arabis laevigata*
Bulbous bittercress*** *Cardamine bulbosa*
Cutleaf toothwort*** *Cardamine concatenata*
Crinkleroot*** *Cardamine diphylla*
Sand bittercress*** *Cardamine parviflora*
Carolina draba*** *Draba reptans*
Hairy rock cress* *Arabis hirsuta*
Lyrate rock cress* *Arabis lyrata*
American searocket* *Cakile edentula*
Pennsylvania bittercress* *Cardamine pensylvanica*
Cuckooflower* *Cardamine pratensis*
Bog yellowcress* *Rorippa palustris*

Cabombaceae
Watershield* *Brasenia schreberi*

Cactaceae
Devil's-tongue*** *Opuntia humifusa*

Callitrichaceae

Northern water starwort*** *Callitriche hermaphroditica*
Twoheaded water starwort* *Callitriche heterophylla*
Vernal water starwort* *Callitriche palustris*
Terrestrial water starwort* *Callitriche terrestris*

Campanulaceae

Cardinal flower*** *Lobelia cardinalis*
Indian tobacco*** *Lobelia inflata*
Ontario lobelia*** *Lobelia kalmii*
Nuttall's lobelia*** *Lobelia nuttallii*
Great blue lobelia*** *Lobelia siphilitica*
Palespike lobelia*** *Lobelia spicata*
Clasping Venus's looking-glass*** *Triodanis perfoliata*
Marsh bellflower* *Campanula aparinoides*
American bellflower* *Campanulastrum americanum*

Capparaceae

Redwhisker clammyweed* *Polanisia dodecandra*

Caprifoliaceae

Northern bush honeysuckle*** *Diervilla lonicera*
Limber honeysuckle*** *Lonicera dioica*
Trumpet honeysuckle*** *Lonicera sempervirens*
Common elderberry*** *Sambucus nigra ssp. canadensis*
Feverwort*** *Triosteum perfoliatum*
Mapleleaf Viburnum*** *Viburnum acerifolium*
Southern arrowwood*** *Viburnum dentatum*
Hobblebush*** *Viburnum lantanoides*
Blackhaw*** *Viburnum prunifolium*
Orangefruit horse gentian** *Triosteum aurantiacum*
Twinflower* *Linnaea borealis*
Red elderberry* *Sambucus racemosa*
Nannyberry* *Viburnum lentago*
Possumhaw* *Viburnum nudum*

Caryophyllaceae

Seaside sandplant*** *Honckenya peploides*
Sleepy Silene*** *Silene antirrhina*
Pennsylvania catchfly*** *Silene caroliniana ssp. pensylvanica*
Widowsfrill*** *Silene stellata*
Nodding chickweed* *Cerastium nutans*
Pine-barren stitchwort* *Minuartia caroliniana*
Bluntleaf sandwort* *Moehringia lateriflora*

Smooth forked nailwort* *Paronychia canadensis*
Trailing pearlwort* *Sagina decumbens*
Bog chickweed* *Stellaria alsine*
Longleaf starwort* *Stellaria longifolia*

Celastraceae

American bittersweet*** *Celastrus scandens*
Strawberry bush*** *Euonymus americana*
Eastern wahoo* *Euonymus atropurpurea*
Running strawberry bush* *Euonymus obovata*

Ceratophyllaceae

Coon's tail* *Ceratophyllum demersum*
Spineless hornwort* *Ceratophyllum echinatum*

Chenopodiaceae

Crested saltbush*** *Atriplex cristata*
Mapleleaf goosefoot*** *Chenopodium simplex*
Chickenclaws (pickleweed)*** *Sarcocornia perennis*
Red goosefoot* *Chenopodium rubrum*
Standley's goosefoot* *Chenopodium standleyanum*
Dwarf saltwort* *Salicornia bigelovii*
Annual seepweed* *Suaeda linearis*

Cistaceae

Hairy pinweed*** *Lechea mucronata*
Illinois pinweed*** *Lechea racemulosa*
Hoary frostweed* *Helianthemum bicknellii*
Longbranch frostweed* *Helianthemum canadense*
Pine-barren goldenheather* *Hudsonia ericoides*
Woolly beach heather* *Hudsonia tomentosa*
Largepod pinweed* *Lechea intermedia*
Beach pinweed* *Lechea maritima*
Thymeleaf pinweed* *Lechea minor*
Leggett's pinweed* *Lechea pulchella*
Narrowleaf pinweed* *Lechea tenuifolia*

Clethraceae

Coastal sweet pepperbush*** *Clethra alnifolia*

Clusiaceae

Lesser Canadian St. John's wort*** *Hypericum canadense*
Spotted St. John's wort*** *Hypericum punctatum*
Virginia Marsh St. John's wort*** *Triadenum virginicum*
Pale St. John's wort* *Hypericum ellipticum*
Orange grass* *Hypericum gentianoides*

Large St. John's wort*   *Hypericum majus*
Dwarf St. John's wort*   *Hypericum mutilum*

Commelinaceae
Whitemouth dayflower***   *Commelina erecta*

Convolvulaceae
Low false bindweed***   *Calystegia spithamaea*
Man-of-the-earth***   *Ipomoea pandurata*

Cornaceae
Alternateleaf dogwood***   *Cornus alternifolia*
Silky dogwood***   *Cornus amomum*
Flowering dogwood***   *Cornus florida*
Stiff dogwood***   *Cornus foemina*
Gray dogwood***   *Cornus racemosa*
Roundleaf dogwood***   *Cornus rugosa*
Redosier dogwood***   *Cornus sericea*
Bunchberry dogwood*   *Cornus canadensis*

Crassulaceae
Ditch stonecrop***   *Penthorum sedoides*

Cucurbitaceae
Wild cucumber***   *Echinocystis lobata*
Oneseed burr cucumber***   *Sicyos angulatus*

Cupressaceae
Atlantic white cedar***   *Chamaecyparis thyoides*
Eastern red cedar***   *Juniperus virginiana*
Common juniper*   *Juniperus communis*

Cuscutaceae
Scaldweed***   *Cuscuta gronovii*
Fiveangled dodder**   *Cuscuta pentagona*
Buttonbush dodder*   *Cuscuta cephalanthi*
Compact dodder*   *Cuscuta compacta*
Hazel dodder*   *Cuscuta coryli*

Cyperaceae
Densetuft hairsedge***   *Bulbostylis capillaris*
Thicket sedge***   *Carex abscondita*
Emmons' sedge***   *Carex albicans*
Oval-leaf sedge***   *Carex cephalophora*
Bristleleaf sedge***   *Carex eburnea*
Hitchcock's sedge***   *Carex hitchcockiana*
Hop sedge***   *Carex lupulina*
Muhlenberg's sedge***   *Carex muehlenbergii*
Pennsylvania sedge***   *Carex pensylvanica*
Broadleaf sedge***   *Carex platyphylla*
Schweinitz's sedge***   *Carex schweinitzii*

Squarrose sedge***   *Carex squarrosa*
Parasol sedge***   *Carex umbellata*
Fox sedge***   *Carex vulpinoidea*
Globe flatsedge***   *Cyperus echinatus*
Great Plains flatsedge***   *Cyperus lupulinus*
Fragrant flatsedge***   *Cyperus odoratus*
Bearded flatsedge***   *Cyperus squarrosus*
Strawcolored flatsedge***   *Cyperus strigosus*
Threeway sedge***   *Dulichium arundinaceum*
Elliptic spike rush***   *Eleocharis elliptica*
Bald spike rush***   *Eleocharis erythropoda*
Dwarf spike rush***   *Eleocharis parvula*
Beaked spike rush***   *Eleocharis rostellata*
Hairy umbrella sedge***   *Fuirena squarrosa*
White beak sedge***   *Rhynchospora alba*
Brownish beak sedge***   *Rhynchospora capitellata*
Chairmaker's bulrush***   *Schoenoplectus americanus*
River bulrush***   *Schoenoplectus fluviatilis*
Softstem bulrush***   *Schoenoplectus tabernaemontani*
Woodland bulrush***   *Scirpus expansus*
Whip nut rush***   *Scleria triglomerata*
Bashful bulrush***   *Trichophorum planifolium*
Thinleaf sedge**   *Carex cephaloidea*
New England bulrush**   *Schoenoplectus novae-angliae*
Panicled bulrush**   *Scirpus microcarpus*
Broadwing sedge*   *Carex alata*
Greenwhite sedge*   *Carex albolutescens*
White bear sedge*   *Carex albursina*
Eastern narrowleaf sedge*   *Carex amphibola*
Yellowfruit sedge*   *Carex annectens*
Water sedge*   *Carex aquatilis*
Hay sedge*   *Carex argyrantha*
Prickly bog sedge*   *Carex atlantica*
Barratt's sedge*   *Carex barrattii*
Eastern woodland sedge*   *Carex blanda*
Bromelike sedge*   *Carex bromoides*
Button sedge*   *Carex bullata*
Bush's sedge*   *Carex bushii*
Buxbaum's sedge*   *Carex buxbaumii*
Silvery sedge*   *Carex canescens*
Fibrousroot sedge*   *Carex communis*
Longhair sedge*   *Carex comosa*
Hirsute sedge*   *Carex complanata*
Openfield sedge*   *Carex conoidea*
Fringed sedge*   *Carex crinita*
White edge sedge*   *Carex debilis*
Slender woodland sedge*   *Carex digitalis*
Softleaf sedge*   *Carex disperma*

Star sedge* *Carex echinata*
Thinfruit sedge* *Carex flaccosperma*
Dryspike sedge* *Carex foenea*
Northern long sedge* *Carex folliculata*
Graceful sedge* *Carex gracillima*
Limestone meadow sedge* *Carex granularis*
Gray's sedge* *Carex grayi*
Nodding sedge* *Carex gynandra*
Fuzzy Wuzzy sedge* *Carex hirsutella*
Pubescent sedge* *Carex hirtifolia*
Bottlebrush sedge* *Carex hystericina*
Greater bladder sedge* *Carex intumescens*
Spreading sedge* *Carex laxiculmis*
Broad looseflower sedge* *Carex laxiflora*
Bristlystalked sedge* *Carex leptalea*
False hop sedge* *Carex lupuliformis*
Shallow sedge* *Carex lurida*
Black edge sedge* *Carex nigromarginata*
Greater straw sedge* *Carex normalis*
Pale sedge* *Carex pallescens*
Woolly sedge* *Carex pellita*
Variable sedge* *Carex polymorpha*
Drooping sedge* *Carex prasina*
Cypresslike sedge* *Carex pseudocyperus*
Reflexed sedge* *Carex retroflexa*
Knotsheath sedge* *Carex retrorsa*
Rosy sedge* *Carex rosea*
Eastern rough sedge* *Carex scabrata*
Broom sedge* *Carex scoparia*
Beach sedge* *Carex silicea*
Burr reed sedge* *Carex sparganioides*
Dioecious sedge* *Carex sterilis*
Owlfruit sedge* *Carex stipata*
Eastern straw sedge* *Carex straminea*
Upright sedge* *Carex stricta*
Bent sedge* *Carex styloflexa*
Swan's sedge* *Carex swanii*
Rigid sedge* *Carex tetanica*
Blunt broom sedge* *Carex tribuloides*
Hairyfruit sedge* *Carex trichocarpa*
Threeseeded sedge* *Carex trisperma*
Velvet sedge* *Carex vestita*
Ribbed sedge* *Carex virescens*
Willdenow's sedge* *Carex willdenowii*
Smooth saw grass* *Cladium mariscoides*
Slender flatsedge* *Cyperus bipartitus*
Toothed flatsedge* *Cyperus dentatus*
Umbrella flatsedge* *Cyperus diandrus*
Redroot flatsedge* *Cyperus erythrorhizos*
Yellow flatsedge* *Cyperus flavescens*
Gray's flatsedge* *Cyperus grayi*
Needle spike rush* *Eleocharis acicularis*

Engelmann's spike rush* *Eleocharis engelmannii*
Blackfruit spike rush* *Eleocharis melanocarpa*
Blunt spike rush* *Eleocharis obtusa*
Bright green spike rush* *Eleocharis olivacea*
Ovate spike rush* *Eleocharis ovata*
Common spike rush* *Eleocharis palustris*
Squarestem spike rush* *Eleocharis quadrangulata*
Cone-cup spike rush* *Eleocharis tuberculosa*
Slender cotton grass* *Eriophorum gracile*
Tawny cotton grass* *Eriophorum virginicum*
Slender fimbry* *Fimbristylis autumnalis*
Marsh fimbry* *Fimbristylis castanea*
Brown beak sedge* *Rhynchospora fusca*
Common threesquare* *Schoenoplectus pungens*
Weakstalk bulrush* *Schoenoplectus purshianus*
Sturdy bulrush* *Schoenoplectus robustus*
Torrey's bulrush* *Schoenoplectus torreyi*
Wool grass* *Scirpus cyperinus*
Rufous bulrush* *Scirpus pendulus*
Leafy bulrush* *Scirpus polyphyllus*
Netted nut rush* *Scleria reticularis*
Low nut rush* *Scleria verticillata*

Dennstaedtiaceae
Eastern hay-scented fern*** *Dennstaedtia punctilobula*
Western bracken fern*** *Pteridium aquilinum*

Dioscoreaceae
Wild yam*** *Dioscorea villosa*

Droseraceae
Threadleaf sundew* *Drosera filiformis*
Spoonleaf sundew* *Drosera intermedia*
Roundleaf sundew* *Drosera rotundifolia*

Dryopteridaceae
Common lady fern*** *Athyrium filix-femina*
Bulblet bladder fern*** *Cystopteris bulbifera*
Brittle bladder fern*** *Cystopteris fragilis*
Silver false spleenwort*** *Deparia acrostichoides*
Spinulose wood fern*** *Dryopteris carthusiana*
Crested wood fern*** *Dryopteris cristata*
Intermediate wood fern*** *Dryopteris intermedia*
Marginal wood fern*** *Dryopteris marginalis*
Ostrich fern*** *Matteuccia struthiopteris*
Sensitive fern*** *Onoclea sensibilis*
Christmas fern*** *Polystichum acrostichoides*

Rusty Woodsia*** *Woodsia ilvensis*
Bluntlobe cliff fern*** *Woodsia obtusa*
Mountain wood fern* *Dryopteris campyloptera*
Clinton's wood fern* *Dryopteris clintoniana*
Goldie's wood fern* *Dryopteris goldiana*
Western oak fern* *Gymnocarpium dryopteris*

Ebenaceae
Common persimmon*** *Diospyros virginiana*

Elatinaceae
American waterwort* *Elatine americana*

Equisetaceae
Field horsetail*** *Equisetum arvense*
Scouringrush horsetail*** *Equisetum hyemale*
Water horsetail* *Equisetum fluviatile*
Woodland horsetail* *Equisetum sylvaticum*

Ericaceae
Creeping snowberry*** *Gaultheria hispidula*
Eastern teaberry*** *Gaultheria procumbens*
Black huckleberry*** *Gaylussacia baccata*
Blue huckleberry*** *Gaylussacia frondosa*
Mountain laurel*** *Kalmia latifolia*
Swamp dog hobble*** *Leucothoe racemosa*
Maleberry*** *Lyonia ligustrina*
Piedmont staggerbush*** *Lyonia mariana*
Swamp azalea*** *Rhododendron viscosum*
Lowbush blueberry*** *Vaccinium angustifolium*
Highbush blueberry*** *Vaccinium corymbosum*
Cranberry*** *Vaccinium macrocarpon*
Blue Ridge blueberry*** *Vaccinium pallidum*
Deerberry*** *Vaccinium stamineum*
Kinnikinnick* *Arctostaphylos uva-ursi*
Leatherleaf* *Chamaedaphne calyculata*
Trailing arbutus* *Epigaea repens*
Dwarf huckleberry* *Gaylussacia dumosa*
Sheep laurel* *Kalmia angustifolia*
Rhodora* *Rhododendron canadense*
Great laurel* *Rhododendron maximum*

Eriocaulaceae
Sevenangle pipewort* *Eriocaulon aquaticum*

Euphorbiaceae
Slender three-seed mercury*** *Acalypha gracilens*
Virginia three-seed mercury*** *Acalypha virginica*
Spotted sand mat*** *Chamaesyce maculata*
Eyebane*** *Chamaesyce nutans*

Seaside sand mat*** *Chamaesyce polygonifolia*
Wormseed sand mat** *Chamaesyce vermiculata*
Ribseed sand mat* *Chamaesyce glyptosperma*
Flowering spurge* *Euphorbia corollata*
American ipecac* *Euphorbia ipecacuanhae*

Fabaceae
American hog peanut*** *Amphicarpaea bracteata*
Groundnut*** *Apios americana*
Eastern redbud*** *Cercis canadensis*
Sleepingplant*** *Chamaecrista fasciculata*
Partridge pea*** *Chamaecrista nictitans*
Arrowhead rattlebox*** *Crotalaria sagittalis*
Showy tick trefoil*** *Desmodium canadense*
Hoary tick trefoil*** *Desmodium canescens*
Dillenius' tick trefoil*** *Desmodium glabellum*
Smooth tick trefoil*** *Desmodium laevigatum*
Smooth small-leaf tick trefoil*** *Desmodium marilandicum*
Nakedflower tick trefoil*** *Desmodium nudiflorum*
Nuttall's tick trefoil*** *Desmodium nuttallii*
Stiff tick trefoil*** *Desmodium obtusum*
Panicledleaf tick trefoil*** *Desmodium paniculatum*
Prostrate tick trefoil*** *Desmodium rotundifolium*
Downy milk pea*** *Galactia volubilis*
Marsh pea*** *Lathyrus palustris*
Roundhead Lespedeza*** *Lespedeza capitata*
Hairy Lespedeza*** *Lespedeza hirta*
Trailing Lespedeza*** *Lespedeza procumbens*
Violet Lespedeza*** *Lespedeza violacea*
Thicket bean*** *Phaseolus polystachios*
Trailing fuzzybean*** *Strophostyles helvula*
Carolina vetch*** *Vicia caroliniana*
Horseflyweed* *Baptisia tinctoria*
Atlantic pigeonwings* *Clitoria mariana*
Hairy small-leaf tick trefoil* *Desmodium ciliare*
Largebract tick trefoil* *Desmodium cuspidatum*
Pointedleaf tick trefoil* *Desmodium glutinosum*
Beach pea* *Lathyrus japonicus*
Narrowleaf Lespedeza* *Lespedeza angustifolia*
Creeping Lespedeza* *Lespedeza repens*
Tall Lespedeza* *Lespedeza stuevei*
Sundial lupine* *Lupinus perennis*
American senna* *Senna hebecarpa*
Pink fuzzybean* *Strophostyles umbellata*
Virginia Tephrosia* *Tephrosia virginiana*

Fagaceae
American chestnut*** *Castanea dentata*
American beech*** *Fagus grandifolia*
White oak*** *Quercus alba*
Swamp white oak*** *Quercus bicolor*
Scarlet oak*** *Quercus coccinea*
Bur oak*** *Quercus macrocarpa*
Pin oak*** *Quercus palustris*
Dwarf chinkapin oak*** *Quercus prinoides*
Chestnut oak*** *Quercus prinus*
Northern red oak*** *Quercus rubra*
Post oak*** *Quercus stellata*
Black oak*** *Quercus velutina*
Blackjack oak* *Quercus marilandica*
Willow oak* *Quercus phellos*

Fumariaceae
Rock harlequin*** *Corydalis sempervirens*
Dutchman's-breeches*** *Dicentra cucullaria*
Yellow fumewort* *Corydalis flavula*
Squirrel corn* *Dicentra canadensis*

Gentianaceae
Twining screwstem*** *Bartonia paniculata*
Closed bottle gentian*** *Gentiana andrewsii*
Harvestbells*** *Gentiana saponaria*
Greater fringed gentian*** *Gentianopsis crinita*
Rosepink*** *Sabatia angularis*
Slender rose gentian*** *Sabatia campanulata*
Marsh rose gentian*** *Sabatia dodecandra*
Yellow screwstem* *Bartonia virginica*
Rose of Plymouth* *Sabatia stellaris*

Geraniaceae
Carolina geranium*** *Geranium carolinianum*
Spotted geranium*** *Geranium maculatum*

Grossulariaceae
American black currant*** *Ribes americanum*
Eastern prickly gooseberry* *Ribes cynosbati*
Hairystem gooseberry* *Ribes hirtellum*
Appalachian gooseberry* *Ribes rotundifolium*

Haloragaceae
Marsh mermaid weed*** *Proserpinaca palustris*
Low water milfoil* *Myriophyllum humile*
Cutleaf water milfoil* *Myriophyllum pinnatum*
Slender water milfoil* *Myriophyllum tenellum*

Hamamelidaceae
American witch hazel*** *Hamamelis virginiana*
Sweetgum*** *Liquidambar styraciflua*

Hydrangeaceae
Wild hydrangea* *Hydrangea arborescens*

Hydrocharitaceae
Canadian waterweed* *Elodea canadensis*
American eelgrass* *Vallisneria americana*

Hydrophyllaceae
Bluntleaf waterleaf*** *Hydrophyllum canadense*
Shawnee salad* *Hydrophyllum virginianum*

Iridaceae
Common goldstar*** *Hypoxis hirsuta*
Harlequin blueflag*** *Iris versicolor*
Narrowleaf blue-eyed grass*** *Sisyrinchium angustifolium*
Slender blue iris* *Iris prismatica*
Eastern blue-eyed grass* *Sisyrinchium atlanticum*
Coastalplain blue-eyed grass* *Sisyrinchium fuscatum*
Needletip blue-eyed grass* *Sisyrinchium mucronatum*

Isoetaceae
Appalachian quillwort* *Isoetes engelmannii*
Shore quillwort* *Isoetes riparia*

Juglandaceae
Mockernut hickory*** *Carya alba*
Bitternut hickory*** *Carya cordiformis*
Pignut hickory*** *Carya glabra*
Shellbark hickory*** *Carya laciniosa*
Red hickory*** *Carya ovalis*
Shagbark hickory*** *Carya ovata*
Butternut*** *Juglans cinerea*
Black walnut*** *Juglans nigra*

Juncaceae
Tapertip rush*** *Juncus acuminatus*
Jointleaf rush*** *Juncus articulatus*
Common rush*** *Juncus effusus*
Saltmeadow rush*** *Juncus gerardii*
Grassleaf rush*** *Juncus marginatus*
Knotted rush*** *Juncus nodosus*
Poverty rush*** *Juncus tenuis*
Torrey's rush*** *Juncus torreyi*
Baltic rush* *Juncus balticus*
Bog rush* *Juncus biflorus*
Toad rush* *Juncus bufonius*
Canadian rush* *Juncus canadensis*

Weak rush* *Juncus debilis*
Forked rush* *Juncus dichotomus*
Brownfruit rush* *Juncus pelocarpus*
Needlepod rush* *Juncus scirpoides*
Lopsided rush* *Juncus secundus*
Hairy woodrush* *Luzula acuminata*

Juncaginaceae
Seaside arrowgrass*** *Triglochin maritimum*

Lamiaceae
Yellow giant hyssop*** *Agastache nepetoides*
Richweed*** *Collinsonia canadensis*
Northern bugleweed*** *Lycopus uniflorus*
Basil mountain mint*** *Pycnanthemum clinopodioides*
Hoary mountain mint*** *Pycnanthemum incanum*
Clustered mountain mint*** *Pycnanthemum muticum*
Narrowleaf mountain mint*** *Pycnanthemum tenuifolium*
Torrey's mountain mint*** *Pycnanthemum torrei*
Virginia mountain mint*** *Pycnanthemum virginianum*
Lyreleaf sage*** *Salvia lyrata*
Hairy skullcap*** *Scutellaria elliptica*
Marsh skullcap*** *Scutellaria galericulata*
Blue skullcap*** *Scutellaria lateriflora*
Hyssopleaf hedge nettle*** *Stachys hyssopifolia*
Smooth hedge nettle*** *Stachys tenuifolia*
Canada germander*** *Teucrium canadense*
Forked bluecurls*** *Trichostema dichotomum*
Purple giant hyssop* *Agastache scrophulariifolia*
Common dittany* *Cunila origanoides*
American false pennyroyal* *Hedeoma pulegioides*
American water horehound* *Lycopus americanus*
Clasping water horehound* *Lycopus amplectens*
Taperleaf water horehound* *Lycopus rubellus*
Virginia water horehound* *Lycopus virginicus*
Scarlet beebalm* *Monarda didyma*
Wild bergamot* *Monarda fistulosa*
Spotted beebalm* *Monarda punctata*
Whorled mountain mint* *Pycnanthemum verticillatum*
Helmetflower* *Scutellaria integrifolia*
Marsh hedge nettle* *Stachys palustris*
Narrowleaf bluecurls* *Trichostema setaceum*

Lauraceae
Northern spicebush*** *Lindera benzoin*
Sassafras*** *Sassafras albidum*

Lemnaceae
Common duckweed*** *Lemna minor*
Minute duckweed* *Lemna perpusilla*
Star duckweed* *Lemna trisulca*
Valdivia duckweed* *Lemna valdiviana*
Common duckmeat* *Spirodela polyrrhiza*
Columbian watermeal* *Wolffia columbiana*

Lentibulariaceae
Hiddenfruit bladderwort* *Utricularia geminiscapa*
Humped bladderwort* *Utricularia gibba*
Common bladderwort* *Utricularia macrorhiza*
Lesser bladderwort* *Utricularia minor*
Eastern purple bladderwort* *Utricularia purpurea*
Striped bladderwort* *Utricularia striata*

Liliaceae
White colicroot*** *Aletris farinosa*
Meadow garlic*** *Allium canadense*
Fairywand*** *Chamaelirium luteum*
Dogtooth violet*** *Erythronium americanum*
Canada lily*** *Lilium canadense*
Wood lily*** *Lilium philadelphicum*
Turk's-cap lily*** *Lilium superbum*
Canada mayflower*** *Maianthemum canadense*
Feathery false lily of the valley*** *Maianthemum racemosum*
Indian cucumber*** *Medeola virginiana*
Hairy Solomon's seal*** *Polygonatum pubescens*
Red Trillium*** *Trillium erectum*
Perfoliate bellwort*** *Uvularia perfoliata*
Sessileleaf bellwort*** *Uvularia sessilifolia*
Green false hellebore*** *Veratrum viride*
Wild leek* *Allium tricoccum*
Flypoison* *Amianthium muscitoxicum*
White fawn lily* *Erythronium albidum*
Swamp pink* *Helonias bullata*
Starry false lily of the valley* *Maianthemum stellatum*
Slender bunchflower* *Melanthium latifolium*
Virginia bunchflower* *Melanthium virginicum*
Smooth Solomon's seal* *Polygonatum biflorum*
Whip-poor-Will flower* *Trillium cernuum*

Painted Trillium* *Trillium undulatum*
Pine-barren death camas* *Zigadenus leimanthoides*

Limnanthaceae
False mermaid weed* *Floerkea proserpinacoides*

Linaceae
Woodland flax*** *Linum virginianum*
Ridged yellow flax* *Linum striatum*
Grooved flax* *Linum sulcatum*

Lycopodiaceae
Shining clubmoss*** *Huperzia lucidula*
Groundcedar*** *Lycopodium complanatum*
Rare clubmoss*** *Lycopodium obscurum*
Foxtail clubmoss* *Lycopodiella alopecuroides*
Slender clubmoss* *Lycopodiella caroliniana*
Inundated clubmoss* *Lycopodiella inundata*
Stiff clubmoss* *Lycopodium annotinum*
Running clubmoss* *Lycopodium clavatum*

Lygodiaceae
American climbing fern* *Lygodium palmatum*

Lythraceae
Blue waxweed*** *Cuphea viscosissima*
Swamp loosestrife* *Decodon verticillatus*
Winged lythrum* *Lythrum alatum*
Lowland rotala* *Rotala ramosior*

Magnoliaceae
Tulip tree*** *Liriodendron tulipifera*
Cucumber tree** *Magnolia acuminata*
Sweetbay* *Magnolia virginiana*

Malvaceae
Crimsoneyed rose mallow*** *Hibiscus moscheutos*

Melastomataceae
Handsome Harry*** *Rhexia virginica*

Menispermaceae
Common moonseed*** *Menispermum canadense*

Monotropaceae
Pinesap*** *Monotropa hypopithys*
Indianpipe*** *Monotropa uniflora*

Moraceae
Red mulberry*** *Morus rubra*

Myricaceae
Sweet fern*** *Comptonia peregrina*
Northern bayberry*** *Morella pensylvanica*
Sweetgale* *Myrica gale*

Najadaceae
Nodding waternymph* *Najas flexilis*

Nymphaeaceae
Yellow pond lily*** *Nuphar lutea*
American white water lily*** *Nymphaea odorata*

Nyssaceae
Blackgum*** *Nyssa sylvatica*

Oleaceae
White ash*** *Fraxinus americana*
Black ash*** *Fraxinus nigra*
Green ash*** *Fraxinus pennsylvanica*

Onagraceae
Broadleaf enchanter's nightshade*** *Circaea lutetiana*
Purpleleaf willow herb*** *Epilobium coloratum*
Bog willow herb*** *Epilobium leptophyllum*
Marsh willow herb*** *Epilobium palustre*
Seedbox*** *Ludwigia alternifolia*
Marsh seedbox*** *Ludwigia palustris*
Common evening primrose*** *Oenothera biennis*
Northern evening primrose*** *Oenothera parviflora*
Cutleaf evening primrose** *Oenothera laciniata*
Fireweed* *Chamerion angustifolium*
Downy willow herb* *Epilobium strictum*
Globefruit primrose willow* *Ludwigia sphaerocarpa*
Narrowleaf evening primrose* *Oenothera fruticosa*
Little evening primrose* *Oenothera perennis*

Ophioglossaceae
Cutleaf grape fern*** *Botrychium dissectum*
Rattlesnake fern*** *Botrychium virginianum*
Northern adderstongue*** *Ophioglossum pusillum*
Lanceleaf grape fern* *Botrychium lanceolatum*

Matricary grape fern*   *Botrychium matricariifolium*
Leathery grape fern*   *Botrychium multifidum*
Little grape fern*   *Botrychium simplex*

Orchidaceae
Summer coralroot***   *Corallorrhiza maculata*
Autumn coralroot***   *Corallorrhiza odontorhiza*
Moccasin flower***   *Cypripedium acaule*
Lesser yellow lady's slipper***   *Cypripedium parviflorum*
Showy orchid***   *Galearis spectabilis*
Downy rattlesnake plantain***   *Goodyera pubescens*
Brown widelip orchid***   *Liparis liliifolia*
Yellow widelip orchid***   *Liparis loeselii*
Yellow fringed orchid***   *Platanthera ciliaris*
Palegreen orchid***   *Platanthera flava*
Green fringed orchid***   *Platanthera lacera*
Nodding ladies' tresses***   *Spiranthes cernua*
Northern slender ladies' tresses***   *Spiranthes lacera*
Crippled crane fly***   *Tipularia discolor*
Threebirds***   *Triphora trianthophora*
Adam-and-Eve*   *Aplectrum hyemale*
Dragon's-mouth*   *Arethusa bulbosa*
Tuberous grass pink*   *Calopogon tuberosus*
Longbract frog orchid*   *Coeloglossum viride*
Showy lady's slipper*   *Cypripedium reginae*
Purple fiveleaf orchid*   *Isotria verticillata*
Heartleaf twayblade*   *Listera cordata*
Green adder's mouth orchid*   *Malaxis unifolia*
White fringed orchid*   *Platanthera blephariglottis*
Small green wood orchid*   *Platanthera clavellata*
Scentbottle*   *Platanthera dilatata*
Lesser purple fringed orchid*   *Platanthera psycodes*
Snakemouth orchid*   *Pogonia ophioglossoides*
Little ladies' tresses*   *Spiranthes tuberosa*
Spring ladies' tresses*   *Spiranthes vernalis*

Orobanchaceae
American squawroot***   *Conopholis americana*
Beechdrops***   *Epifagus virginiana*
Oneflowered broomrape***   *Orobanche uniflora*

Osmundaceae
Cinnamon fern***   *Osmunda cinnamomea*
Interrupted fern***   *Osmunda claytoniana*
Royal fern***   *Osmunda regalis*

Oxalidaceae
Mountain wood sorrel***   *Oxalis montana*
Common yellow oxalis***   *Oxalis stricta*
Violet wood sorrel***   *Oxalis violacea*

Papaveraceae
Bloodroot***   *Sanguinaria canadensis*

Phytolaccaceae
American pokeweed***   *Phytolacca americana*

Pinaceae
Tamarack***   *Larix laricina*
Black spruce***   *Picea mariana*
Red pine***   *Pinus resinosa*
Pitch pine***   *Pinus rigida*
Eastern white pine***   *Pinus strobus*
Eastern hemlock***   *Tsuga canadensis*
Balsam fir*   *Abies balsamea*
Shortleaf pine*   *Pinus echinata*
Virginia pine*   *Pinus virginiana*

Plantaginaceae
Heartleaf plantain***   *Plantago cordata*
Goose tongue***   *Plantago maritima*
Dwarf plantain**   *Plantago pusilla*
Blackseed plantain*   *Plantago rugelii*
Virginia plantain*   *Plantago virginica*

Platanaceae
American sycamore***   *Platanus occidentalis*

Plumbaginaceae
Carolina sea lavender***   *Limonium carolinianum*

Poaceae
Winter bentgrass***   *Agrostis hyemalis*
Upland bentgrass***   *Agrostis perennans*
American beachgrass***   *Ammophila breviligulata*
Bushy bluestem***   *Andropogon glomeratus*
Broomsedge bluestem***   *Andropogon virginicus*
Slimspike three-awn***   *Aristida longispica*
Fringed brome***   *Bromus ciliatus*
Hairy woodland brome***   *Bromus pubescens*
Mat sandbur***   *Cenchrus longispinus*
Sanddune sandbur***   *Cenchrus tribuloides*
Sweet woodreed***   *Cinna arundinacea*
Flattened oat grass***   *Danthonia compressa*
Poverty oat grass***   *Danthonia spicata*
Wavy hair grass***   *Deschampsia flexuosa*

Deertongue*** *Dichanthelium clandestinum*
Starved panic grass*** *Dichanthelium depauperatum*
Velvet Panicum*** *Dichanthelium scoparium*
Inland salt grass*** *Distichlis spicata*
Canada wildrye*** *Elymus canadensis*
Eastern bottlebrush grass*** *Elymus hystrix*
Virginia wild rye*** *Elymus virginicus*
Lace grass*** *Eragrostis capillaris*
Teal lovegrass*** *Eragrostis hypnoides*
Tufted lovegrass*** *Eragrostis pectinacea*
Red fescue*** *Festuca rubra*
Creeping manna grass*** *Glyceria acutiflora*
Rattlesnake manna grass*** *Glyceria canadensis*
Vanilla grass*** *Hierochloe odorata*
White grass*** *Leersia virginica*
Nimblewill*** *Muhlenbergia schreberi*
Rock muhly*** *Muhlenbergia sobolifera*
Witchgrass*** *Panicum capillare*
Warty panic grass*** *Panicum verrucosum*
Switch grass*** *Panicum virgatum*
Thin Paspalum*** *Paspalum setaceum*
Common reed*** *Phragmites australis*
Little bluestem*** *Schizachyrium scoparium*
Smooth cordgrass*** *Spartina alterniflora*
Big cordgrass*** *Spartina cynosuroides*
Shiny wedgescale*** *Sphenopholis nitida*
Prairie wedgescale*** *Sphenopholis obtusata*
Swamp wedgescale*** *Sphenopholis pensylvanica*
Composite dropseed*** *Sporobolus compositus*
Pale false manna grass*** *Torreyochloa pallida*
Purpletop Tridens*** *Tridens flavus*
Purple salt grass*** *Triplasis purpurea*
Eastern gama grass*** *Tripsacum dactyloides*
Sixweeks fescue*** *Vulpia octoflora*
Tapered rosette grass** *Dichanthelium acuminatum*
Variable panic grass** *Dichanthelium commutatum*
Slimleaf panic grass** *Dichanthelium linearifolium*
Roundseed panic grass** *Dichanthelium sphaerocarpon*
Wirestem muhly** *Muhlenbergia frondosa*
Prairie cordgrass** *Spartina pectinata*
Puffsheath dropseed** *Sporobolus neglectus*
Rough bentgrass* *Agrostis scabra*
Creeping bentgrass* *Agrostis stolonifera*
Big bluestem* *Andropogon gerardii*
Churchmouse three-awn* *Aristida dichotoma*
Arrowfeather three-awn* *Aristida purpurascens*

Seaside three-awn* *Aristida tuberculosa*
Bearded shorthusk* *Brachyelytrum erectum*
Bluejoint* *Calamagrostis canadensis*
Arctic reed grass* *Calamagrostis coarctata*
Slender woodoats* *Chasmanthium laxum*
Tufted hair grass* *Deschampsia caespitosa*
Bosc's panic grass* *Dichanthelium boscii*
Broadleaf rosette grass* *Dichanthelium latifolium*
Heller's rosette grass* *Dichanthelium oligosanthes*
Addison's rosette grass* *Dichanthelium ovale*
Hairy wild rye* *Elymus villosus*
Purple lovegrass* *Eragrostis spectabilis*
American manna grass* *Glyceria grandis*
Atlantic manna grass* *Glyceria obtusa*
Floating manna grass* *Glyceria septentrionalis*
Fowl manna grass* *Glyceria striata*
Rice cut-grass* *Leersia oryzoides*
Bearded sprangletop* *Leptochloa fusca*
Mexican muhly* *Muhlenbergia mexicana*
Woodland muhly* *Muhlenbergia sylvatica*
Slender muhly* *Muhlenbergia tenuiflora*
Bitter panic grass* *Panicum amarum*
Redtop panic grass* *Panicum rigidulum*
Field paspalum* *Paspalum laeve*
Blackseed spear grass* *Piptochaetium avenaceum*
Grove bluegrass* *Poa alsodes*
Fowl bluegrass* *Poa palustris*
Woodland bluegrass* *Poa sylvestris*
Saltmarsh alkali grass* *Puccinellia fasciculata*
Shore little bluestem* *Schizachyrium littorale*
Marsh bristlegrass* *Setaria parviflora*
Indian grass* *Sorghastrum nutans*
Saltmeadow cordgrass* *Spartina patens*
Slender wedgescale* *Sphenopholis intermedia*
Poverty dropseed* *Sporobolus vaginiflorus*
Annual wild rice* *Zizania aquatica*

Polemoniaceae
Wild blue phlox* *Phlox divaricata*
Moss phlox* *Phlox subulata*
Greek valerian* *Polemonium reptans*

Polygalaceae
Procession flower*** *Polygala incarnata*
Purple milkwort*** *Polygala sanguinea*
Whorled milkwort*** *Polygala verticillata*
Whorled milkwort* *Polygala ambigua*
Drumheads* *Polygala cruciata*
Orange milkwort* *Polygala lutea*
Nuttall's milkwort* *Polygala nuttallii*

Gaywings*   *Polygala paucifolia*
Racemed milkwort*   *Polygala polygama*

Polygonaceae
Water knotweed***   *Polygonum amphibium*
Halberdleaf tearthumb***   *Polygonum arifolium*
Carey's smartweed***   *Polygonum careyi*
Erect knotweed***   *Polygonum erectum*
Swamp smartweed***   *Polygonum hydropiperoides*
Pennsylvania smartweed***   *Polygonum pensylvanicum*
Dotted smartweed***   *Polygonum punctatum*
Bushy knotweed***   *Polygonum ramosissimum*
Arrowleaf tearthumb***   *Polygonum sagittatum*
Climbing false buckwheat***   *Polygonum scandens*
Pleatleaf knotweed***   *Polygonum tenue*
Jumpseed***   *Polygonum virginianum*
Greater water dock***   *Rumex orbiculatus*
Coastal jointweed*   *Polygonella articulata*
Fringed black bindweed*   *Polygonum cilinode*
Seaside knotweed*   *Polygonum glaucum*
Pale dock*   *Rumex altissimus*
Heartwing sorrel*   *Rumex hastatulus*
Golden dock*   *Rumex maritimus*
Swamp dock*   *Rumex verticillatus*

Polypodiaceae
Rock polypody***   *Polypodium virginianum*

Pontederiaceae
Grassleaf mud plantain*   *Heteranthera dubia*
Pickerelweed*   *Pontederia cordata*

Portulacaceae
Virginia spring beauty***   *Claytonia virginica*
Carolina spring beauty*   *Claytonia caroliniana*

Potamogetonaceae
Largeleaf pondweed*   *Potamogeton amplifolius*
Waterthread pondweed*   *Potamogeton diversifolius*
Variableleaf pondweed*   *Potamogeton gramineus*
Floating pondweed*   *Potamogeton natans*
Longleaf pondweed*   *Potamogeton nodosus*
Claspingleaf pondweed*   *Potamogeton perfoliatus*
Spotted pondweed*   *Potamogeton pulcher*
Small pondweed*   *Potamogeton pusillus*
Spiral pondweed*   *Potamogeton spirillus*
Flatstem pondweed*   *Potamogeton zosteriformis*
Sago pondweed*   *Stuckenia pectinatus*

Primulaceae
Fringed loosestrife***   *Lysimachia ciliata*
Earth loosestrife***   *Lysimachia terrestris*
Tufted loosestrife***   *Lysimachia thyrsiflora*
Starflower***   *Trientalis borealis*
American featherfoil*   *Hottonia inflata*
Lowland yellow loosestrife*   *Lysimachia hybrida*
Whorled yellow loosestrife*   *Lysimachia quadrifolia*
Seaside brookweed*   *Samolus valerandi ssp. parviflorus*

Pteridaceae
Northern maidenhair***   *Adiantum pedatum*
Hairy lip fern***   *Cheilanthes lanosa*
Purple cliff brake***   *Pellaea atropurpurea*

Pyrolaceae
Striped prince's pine***   *Chimaphila maculata*
Pipsissewa***   *Chimaphila umbellata*
American wintergreen***   *Pyrola americana*
Sidebells wintergreen*   *Orthilia secunda*
Waxflower shinleaf*   *Pyrola elliptica*

Ranunculaceae
White baneberry***   *Actaea pachypoda*
Red baneberry***   *Actaea rubra*
Canadian anemone***   *Anemone canadensis*
Candle anemone***   *Anemone cylindrica*
Nightcaps***   *Anemone quinquefolia*
Tall thimbleweed***   *Anemone virginiana*
Red columbine***   *Aquilegia canadensis*
Yellow marsh marigold***   *Caltha palustris*
Black bugbane***   *Cimicifuga racemosa*
Devil's darning needles***   *Clematis virginiana*
Roundlobe Hepatica***   *Hepatica nobilis*
Littleleaf buttercup***   *Ranunculus abortivus*
Greater creeping spearwort***   *Ranunculus flammula*
Pennsylvania buttercup***   *Ranunculus pensylvanicus*
Low spearwort***   *Ranunculus pusillus*
Blisterwort***   *Ranunculus recurvatus*
Cursed buttercup***   *Ranunculus sceleratus*
Purple meadow rue***   *Thalictrum dasycarpum*
Early meadow rue***   *Thalictrum dioicum*
Rue anemone***   *Thalictrum thalictroides*
Curlyheads*   *Clematis ochroleuca*
Threeleaf goldthread*   *Coptis trifolia*
Waterplantain spearwort*   *Ranunculus ambigens*
Alkali buttercup*   *Ranunculus cymbalaria*
Early buttercup*   *Ranunculus fascicularis*

Yellow water buttercup* *Ranunculus flabellaris*
Bristly buttercup* *Ranunculus hispidus*
Rock buttercup* *Ranunculus micranthus*
Threadleaf crowfoot* *Ranunculus trichophyllus*
King of the meadow* *Thalictrum pubescens*
Waxyleaf meadow rue* *Thalictrum revolutum*
American globeflower* *Trollius laxus*

Rhamnaceae
New Jersey tea*** *Ceanothus americanus*

Rosaceae
Harvestlice*** *Agrimonia parviflora*
Canadian serviceberry*** *Amelanchier canadensis*
Cockspur hawthorn*** *Crataegus crus-galli*
Scarlet hawthorn*** *Crataegus pedicellata*
Waxyfruit hawthorn*** *Crataegus pruinosa*
Shrubby cinquefoil*** *Dasiphora floribunda*
Virginia strawberry*** *Fragaria virginiana*
Spring avens*** *Geum vernum*
Cream avens*** *Geum virginianum*
Sweet crabapple*** *Malus coronaria*
Black chokeberry*** *Photinia melanocarpa*
Red chokeberry*** *Photinia pyrifolia*
Dwarf cinquefoil*** *Potentilla canadensis*
Norwegian cinquefoil*** *Potentilla norvegica*
Common cinquefoil*** *Potentilla simplex*
Beach plum*** *Prunus maritima*
Pin cherry*** *Prunus pensylvanica*
Black cherry*** *Prunus serotina*
Chokecherry*** *Prunus virginiana*
Carolina rose*** *Rosa carolina*
Swamp rose*** *Rosa palustris*
Virginia rose*** *Rosa virginiana*
Allegheny blackberry*** *Rubus allegheniensis*
Smooth blackberry*** *Rubus canadensis*
Sand blackberry*** *Rubus cuneifolius*
Northern dewberry*** *Rubus flagellaris*
Bristly dewberry*** *Rubus hispidus*
Black raspberry*** *Rubus occidentalis*
Purple-flowering raspberry*** *Rubus odoratus*
American mountain ash*** *Sorbus americana*
Steeplebush*** *Spiraea tomentosa*
Common serviceberry** *Amelanchier arborea*
Running serviceberry** *Amelanchier stolonifera*
Copenhagen hawthorn** *Crataegus intricata*
Tall hairy agrimony* *Agrimonia gryposepala*
Soft agrimony* *Agrimonia pubescens*
Silverweed cinquefoil* *Argentina anserina*
Dwarf hawthorn* *Crataegus uniflora*

Yellow avens* *Geum aleppicum*
White avens* *Geum canadense*
Purple chokeberry* *Photinia floribunda*
Common ninebark* *Physocarpus opulifolius*
American plum* *Prunus americana*
Sandcherry* *Prunus pumila*
Climbing rose* *Rosa setigera*
Grayleaf red raspberry* *Rubus idaeus ssp. strigosus*
Pennsylvania blackberry* *Rubus pensilvanicus*
Canadian burnet* *Sanguisorba canadensis*
White meadowsweet* *Spiraea alba*

Rubiaceae
Common buttonbush*** *Cephalanthus occidentalis*
Rough bedstraw*** *Galium asprellum*
Northern bedstraw*** *Galium boreale*
Lanceleaf wild licorice*** *Galium lanceolatum*
Fragrant bedstraw*** *Galium triflorum*
Partridgeberry*** *Mitchella repens*
Clustered mille graines*** *Oldenlandia uniflora*
Common marsh bedstraw** *Galium palustre*
Poorjoe* *Diodia teres*
Stickywilly* *Galium aparine*
Licorice bedstraw* *Galium circaezans*
Hairy bedstraw* *Galium pilosum*
Stiff marsh bedstraw* *Galium tinctorium*
Threepetal bedstraw* *Galium trifidum*
Azure bluet* *Houstonia caerulea*
Longleaf summer bluet* *Houstonia longifolia*

Ruppiaceae
Widgeongrass* *Ruppia maritima*

Rutaceae
Common hop tree*** *Ptelea trifoliata*
Common pricklyash* *Zanthoxylum americanum*

Salicaceae
Balsam poplar*** *Populus balsamifera*
Bigtooth aspen*** *Populus grandidentata*
Swamp cottonwood*** *Populus heterophylla*
Quaking aspen*** *Populus tremuloides*
Sageleaf willow*** *Salix candida*
Pussy willow*** *Salix discolor*
Missouri river willow*** *Salix eriocephala*
Prairie willow*** *Salix humilis*
Black willow*** *Salix nigra*
Silky willow*** *Salix sericea*
Eastern cottonwood** *Populus deltoides*
Bebb willow* *Salix bebbiana*

Heartleaf willow*   *Salix cordata*
Narrowleaf willow*   *Salix exigua*
Meadow willow*   *Salix petiolaris*

Santalaceae
Bastard toadflax*   *Comandra umbellata*

Sarraceniaceae
Purple pitcher plant*   *Sarracenia purpurea*

Saururaceae
Lizard's-tail***   *Saururus cernuus*

Saxifragaceae
American golden saxifrage***
   Chrysosplenium americanum
Fen grass of Parnassus***   *Parnassia glauca*
Eastern swamp saxifrage***   *Saxifraga
   pensylvanica*
Early saxifrage***   *Saxifraga virginiensis*
American alumroot*   *Heuchera americana*
Twoleaf miterwort*   *Mitella diphylla*
Heartleaf foamflower*   *Tiarella cordifolia*

Schizaeaceae
Little curly grass fern*   *Schizaea pusilla*

Scrophulariaceae
Saltmarsh false foxglove***   *Agalinis maritima*
Smallflower false foxglove***   *Agalinis
   paupercula*
Purple false foxglove***   *Agalinis purpurea*
Slenderleaf false foxglove***   *Agalinis tenuifolia*
Smooth yellow false foxglove***   *Aureolaria
   flava*
Downy yellow false foxglove***   *Aureolaria
   virginica*
White turtlehead***   *Chelone glabra*
Yellowseed false pimpernel***   *Lindernia dubia*
Sharpwing monkeyflower***   *Mimulus alatus*
Allegheny monkeyflower***   *Mimulus ringens*
Canadian lousewort***   *Pedicularis canadensis*
Swamp lousewort***   *Pedicularis lanceolata*
Carpenter's square***   *Scrophularia marilandica*
Culver's root***   *Veronicastrum virginicum*
Fernleaf yellow false foxglove*   *Aureolaria
   pedicularia*
Scarlet Indian paintbrush*   *Castilleja coccinea*
Golden hedge hyssop*   *Gratiola aurea*
Clammy hedge hyssop*   *Gratiola neglecta*
Welsh mudwort*   *Limosella australis*
Narrowleaf cowwheat*   *Melampyrum lineare*

Hairy beardtongue*   *Penstemon hirsutus*
Lanceleaf figwort*   *Scrophularia lanceolata*
American speedwell*   *Veronica americana*
Neckweed*   *Veronica peregrina*
Skullcap speedwell*   *Veronica scutellata*

Selaginellaceae
Meadow spikemoss***   *Selaginella apoda*
Northern Selaginella***   *Selaginella rupestris*

Smilacaceae
Cat greenbrier***   *Smilax glauca*
Smooth carrion flower***   *Smilax herbacea*
Roundleaf greenbrier***   *Smilax rotundifolia*

Solanaceae
Clammy ground-cherry***   *Physalis
   heterophylla*
Virginia ground-cherry***   *Physalis virginiana*
Longleaf ground-cherry**   *Physalis longifolia*
Husk tomato*   *Physalis pubescens*

Sparganiaceae
Branched bur-reed***   *Sparganium
   androcladum*
American bur-reed*   *Sparganium americanum*
Broadfruit bur-reed*   *Sparganium eurycarpum*

Staphyleaceae
American bladdernut***   *Staphylea trifolia*

Taxaceae
Canada yew***   *Taxus canadensis*

Thelypteridaceae
Long beech fern***   *Phegopteris connectilis*
Broad beech fern***   *Phegopteris hexagonoptera*
New York fern***   *Thelypteris noveboracensis*
Eastern marsh fern***   *Thelypteris palustris*
Bog fern*   *Thelypteris simulata*

Thymelaeaceae
Eastern leatherwood***   *Dirca palustris*

Tiliaceae
American basswood***   *Tilia americana*

Typhaceae
Broadleaf cattail***   *Typha latifolia*

Ulmaceae
Common hackberry***   *Celtis occidentalis*

American elm*** *Ulmus americana*
Slippery elm*** *Ulmus rubra*

Urticaceae
Smallspike false nettle*** *Boehmeria cylindrica*
Canadian woodnettle*** *Laportea canadensis*
Pennsylvania pellitory*** *Parietaria pensylvanica*
Canadian clearweed*** *Pilea pumila*
California nettle* *Urtica dioica ssp. gracilis*

Verbenaceae
American lopseed*** *Phryma leptostachya*
Swamp Verbena*** *Verbena hastata*
Narrowleaf vervain*** *Verbena simplex*
White vervain*** *Verbena urticifolia*

Violaceae
Marsh blue violet*** *Viola cucullata*
Bog white violet*** *Viola lanceolata*
Early blue violet*** *Viola palmata*
Birdfoot violet*** *Viola pedata*
Downy yellow violet*** *Viola pubescens*
Arrowleaf violet*** *Viola sagittata*
Common blue violet*** *Viola sororia*
Sand violet* *Viola affinis*
Sweet white violet* *Viola blanda*
Canadian white violet* *Viola canadensis*
American dog violet* *Viola conspersa*
Smooth white violet* *Viola macloskeyi ssp. pallens*
Roundleaf yellow violet* *Viola rotundifolia*
Striped cream violet* *Viola striata*

Viscaceae
Oak mistletoe* *Phoradendron leucarpum*

Vitaceae
Virginia creeper*** *Parthenocissus quinquefolia*
Summer grape*** *Vitis aestivalis*
Fox grape*** *Vitis labrusca*
Riverbank grape*** *Vitis riparia*

Xyridaceae
Bog yelloweyed grass* *Xyris difformis*
Slender yelloweyed grass* *Xyris torta*

Zannichelliaceae
Horned pondweed* *Zannichellia palustris*

Zosteraceae
Seawrack (eelgrass)*** *Zostera marina*

FISHES
Acipenseridae
Atlantic sturgeon*** *Acipenser oxyrinchus*
Shortnose sturgeon** *Acipenser brevirostrum*

Albulidae
Bonefish° *Albula vulpes*

Ammodytidae
American sand lance*** *Ammodytes americanus*

Anguillidae
American eel*** *Anguilla rostrata*

Atherinidae
Rough silverside*** *Membras martinica*
Inland silverside*** *Menidia beryllina*
Atlantic silverside*** *Menidia menidia*

Balistidae
Orange filefish* *Aluterus schoepfii*
Planehead filefish° *Stephanolepis hispidus*

Batrachoididae
Oyster toadfish*** *Opsanus tau*

Belonidae
Atlantic needlefish*** *Strongylura marina*
Houndfish° *Tylosurus crocodilus*

Blenniidae
Freckled blenny* *Hyposblennius ionathus*
Feather blenny° *Hypsoblennius hentz*

Bothidae
Fourspot flounder*** *Hippoglossina oblonga*
Summer flounder*** *Paralichthys dentatus*
Windowpane*** *Scophthalmus aquosus*
Gulf Stream flounder* *Citharichthys arctifrons*
Smallmouth flounder* *Etropus microstomus*

Carangidae
Crevalle jack*** *Caranx hippos*
Atlantic moonfish** *Selene setapinnis*
Lookdown** *Selene vomer*
Permit* *Trachinotus falcatus*

Carcharhinidae
Bull shark** *Carcharhinus leucas*
Smooth dogfish** *Mustelus canis*

Dusky shark* *Carcharhinus obscurus*
Sandbar shark* *Carcharhinus plumbeus*

Catostomidae
Creek chubsucker*** *Erimyzon oblongus*
White sucker*** *Catostomus commersonii*
Shorthead redhorse° *Moxostoma
  macrolepidotum*

Centrarchidae
Red-breast sunfish*** *Lepomis auritus*
Pumpkinseed*** *Lepomis gibbosus*
Banded sunfish* *Enneacanthus obesus*
Bluespotted sunfish° *Enneacanthus gloriosus*

Chaetodontidae
Foureye butterflyfish* *Chaetodon capristratus*
Spotfin butterflyfish° *Chaetodon ocellatus*

Clupeidae
Blueback herring*** *Alosa aestivalis*
Hickory shad*** *Alosa mediocris*
Alewife*** *Alosa pseudoharengus*
American shad*** *Alosa sapidissima*
Atlantic menhaden*** *Brevoortia tyrannus*
Atlantic herring*** *Clupea harengus*
Round herring*** *Etrumeus teres*

Congridae
Conger eel*** *Conger oceanicus*

Cottidae
Slimy sculpin*** *Cottus cognatus*
Sea raven*** *Hemitripterus americanus*
Grubby*** *Myoxocephalus aenaeus*
Longhorn sculpin*** *Myoxocephalus
  octodecemspinosus*

Cyclopteridae
Atlantic seasnail** *Liparis atlanticus*
Lumpfish° *Cyclopterus lumpus*

Cyprinidae
Golden shiner*** *Notemigonus crysoleucas*
Eastern blacknose dace*** *Rhinichthys atratulus*
Bridle shiner** *Notropis bifrenatus*
Satinfin shiner** *Notropis analostanus*
Spottail shiner** *Notropis hudsonius*
Common shiner** *Luxilus cornutus*
Creek chub* *Semotilus atromaculatus*
Fallfish* *Semotilus corporalis*
Cutlips minnow* *Exoglossum maxillingua*

Eastern silvery minnow* *Hybognathus regius*
Comely shiner* *Notropis amoenus*
Longnose dace* *Rhinichthys cataractae*
Bluntnose minnow° *Pimephales notatus*

Cyprinodontidae
Mummichog*** *Fundulus heteroclitus*
Spotfin killifish*** *Fundulus luciae*

Dactylopteridae
Flying gurnard* *Dactylopterus volitans*

Echeneidae
Sharksucker** *Echeneis naucrates*

Elopidae
Ladyfish° *Elops saurus*
Tarpon° *Megalops atlanticus*

Engraulidae
Striped anchovy*** *Anchoa hepsetus*
Bay anchovy*** *Anchoa mitchilli*

Ephippidae
Atlantic spadefish° *Chaetodipterus faber*

Esocidae
Redfin pickerel*** *Esox americanus*
Chain pickerel*** *Esox niger*
Northern pike° *Esox lucius*

Fistulariidae
Bluespotted cornetfish° *Fistularia tabacaria*

Fundulidae
Banded killifish*** *Fundulus diaphanus*
Striped killifish** *Fundulus majalis*

Gadidae
Atlantic cod*** *Gadus morhua*
Silver hake*** *Merluccius bilinearis*
Atlantic tomcod*** *Microgadus tomcod*
Red hake*** *Urophycis chuss*
Spotted hake*** *Urophycis regia*
Fourbeard rockling** *Enchelyopus cimbrius*
Pollack** *Pollachius virens*
White hake° *Urophycis tenuis*

Gasterosteidae
Fourspine stickleback*** *Apeltes quadracus*
Threespine stickleback*** *Gasterosteus
  aculeatus*
Ninespine stickleback*** *Pungitius pungitius*

Gerreidae
Spotfin mjorra* *Eucinostomus argenteus*

Gobiidae
Naked goby*** *Gobiosoma bosc*
Highfin goby* *Gobionellus oceanicus*

Ictaluridae
White catfish*** *Ameiurus catus*
Brown bullhead*** *Ameiurus nebulosus*
Tadpole madtom* *Noturus gyrinus*
Yellow bullhead° *Ameiurus natalis*
Margined madtom° *Noturus insignis*

Labridae
Tautog*** *Tautoga onitis*
Cunner*** *Tautogolabrus adspersus*

Lophiiformes
Goosefish*** *Lophius americanus*

Lutjanidae
Pigfish*** *Orthopristis chrysoptera*
Grey snapper** *Lutjanus griseus*
Schoolmaster° *Lutjanus apodus*

Moronidae
White perch*** *Morone americana*
Striped bass*** *Morone saxatilis*

Mugilidae
Striped mullet*** *Mugil cephalus*
White mullet*** *Mugil curema*

Odontaspididae
Sand tiger* *Odontaspis taurus*

Ophidiidae
Striped cusk-eel*** *Ophidion marginatum*

Osmeridae
Atlantic rainbow smelt*** *Osmerus mordax*

Ostraciidae
Scrawled cowfish* *Acanthostracion quadricornis*

Percidae
Tessellated darter*** *Etheostoma olmstedi*
Yellow perch*** *Perca flacescens*

Petromyzontidae
Sea lamprey*** *Petromyzon marinus*

American brook lamprey** *Lampetra appendix*

Pholidae
Rock gunnel*** *Pholis gunnellus*

Pleuronectidae
Winter flounder*** *Pseudopleuronectes americanus*
Yellowtail flounder° *Limanda ferruginea*

Pomatomidae
Bluefish*** *Pomatomus saltatrix*

Priacanthidae
Short bigeye* *Pristigenys alta*

Rachycentridae
Cobia° *Rachycentron canadum*

Rajidae
Little skate*** *Leucoraja erinacea*
Barndoor skate° *Dipturus laevis*

Salmonidae
Brook trout*** *Salvelinus fontinalis*
Atlantic salmon* *Salmo salar*

Sciaenidae
Silver perch*** *Bairdiella chrysoura*
Weakfish*** *Cynoscion regalis*
Spot*** *Leiostomus xanthurus*
Northern kingfish*** *Menticirrhus saxatilis*
Black drum*** *Pogonias cromis*
Atlantic mackeral*** *Scomber scombrus*
Atlantic croaker* *Micropogonias undulatus*
Spanish mackeral* *Scomberomorus maculatus*

Serranidae
Black sea bass*** *Centropristis striata*
Gag° *Mycteroperca microlepis*

Soleidae
Hogchoker*** *Trinectes maculatus*

Sparidae
Sheepshead*** *Archosargus probatocephalus*
Porgy (Scup)*** *Stenotomus chrysops*
Pinfish** *Lagodon rhomboides*

Sphyraenidae
Northern sennet* *Sphyraena borealis*
Guaguanche* *Sphyraena guachancho*

Squalidae
Spiny dogfish*** *Squalus acanthias*

Stromateidae
Butterfish*** *Peprilus triacanthus*

Syngnathidae
Lined seahorse*** *Hippocampus erectus*
Northern pipefish*** *Syngnathus fuscus*

Synodontidae
Inshore lizardfish*** *Synodus foetens*

Tetraodontidae
Northern puffer*** *Sphoeroides maculatus*
Smooth puffer* *Lagocephalus laevigatus*
Striped burrfish° *Chilomycterus schoepfii*

Thrichiuridae
Atlantic cutlassfish° *Trichiurus lepturus*

Triglidae
Northern searobin*** *Prionotus carolinus*
Striped searobin*** *Prionotus evolans*

Umbridae
Eastern mudminnow*** *Umbra pygmaea*

Uranoscopidae
Northern stargazer° *Astroscopus guttatus*

AMPHIBIANS
Ambystomatidae
Spotted salamander*** *Ambystoma maculatum*
Marbled salamander*** *Ambystoma opacum*
Blue-spotted salamander complex**
  Ambystoma laterale x jeffersonianum
Eastern tiger salamander** *Ambystoma tigrinum*

Bufonidae
Fowler's toad*** *Bufo fowleri*
American toad* *Bufo americanus*

Hylidae
Northern cricket frog*** *Acris crepitans*
Northern gray tree frog*** *Hyla versicolor*
Spring peeper*** *Pseudacris crucifer*

Upland chorus frog* *Pseudacris triseriata ferarium*
Pine-barrens tree frog° *Hyla andersonii*
New Jersey chorus frog° *Pseudacris triseriata kalmi*

Pelobatidae
Eastern spadefoot toad*** *Scaphiopus holbrookii*

Plethodontidae
Dusky salamander*** *Desmognathus fuscus*
Two lined salamander*** *Eurycea bislineata*
Four toed salamander*** *Hemidactylium scutatum*
Redback salamander*** *Plethodon cinereus*
Slimy salamander** *Plethodon glutinosis*
Northern red salamander** *Pseudotriton ruber*
Spring salamander* *Gyrinophilus porphyriticus*
Allegheny Mountain dusky salamander° *Desmognathus ochrophaeus*
Longtail salamander° *Eurycea longicauda*
Mud salamander° *Pseudotriton montanus*

Ranidae
Bullfrog*** *Rana catesbeiana*
Green frog*** *Rana clamitans*
Pickerel frog*** *Rana palustris*
Southern leopard frog*** *Rana sphenocephala*
Wood frog*** *Rana sylvatica*
Northern leopard frog* *Rana pipiens*
Carpenter frog° *Rana virgatipes*

Salamandridae
Red spotted newt*** *Notophlamus viridiscens*

REPTILES
Cheloniidae
Loggerhead sea turtle** *Caretta caretta*
Green turtle** *Chelonia mydas*
Atlantic ridley sea turtle** *Lepidochelys kempii*
Atlantic hawksbill sea turtle* *Eretmochelys imbricata*

Chelydridae
Snapping turtle*** *Chelydra serpentina*

Colubridae
Eastern worm snake*** *Carphophis amoenus*
Northern black racer*** *Coluber constrictor*
Northern ringneck snake*** *Diadophis punctatus edwardsi*

Eastern hognose snake*** *Heterodon platirhinos*
Eastern milk snake*** *Lampropeltis triangulum triangulum*
Northern water snake*** *Nerodia sipeodon*
Smooth green snake*** *Opheodrys vernalis*
Brown snake*** *Storeria dekayi*
Eastern ribbon snake*** *Thamnophis sauritus*
Eastern garter snake*** *Thamnophis sirtalis*
Redbelly snake** *Storeria occipitomaculata*
Black rat snake* *Elaphe obsoleta*
Rough green snake* *Opheodrys aestivus*
Northern scarlet snake° *Cemophora coccinea*
Southern ringneck snake° *Diadophis punctatus punctatus*
Corn snake° *Elaphe gutatta*
Eastern king snake° *Lampropeltis getula*
Scarlet king snake° *Lampropeltis triangulum elapsoides*
Northern pine snake° *Pituophis melanoleucus*
Queen snake° *Regina septemvittita*
Smooth earth snake° *Virginia valeriae*

Dermochylidae
Leatherback sea turtle* *Dermochelys coriacea*

Emydidae
Eastern painted turtle*** *Chrysemys picta picta*
Spotted turtle*** *Clemmys guttata*
Diamondback terrapin*** *Malaclemmys terrapin*
Eastern box turtle*** *Terrapene carolina*
Wood turtle* *Glyptemys insculpta*
Bog turtle* *Glyptemys muhlenbergii*
Common map turtle* *Graptemys geographica*
Redbelly turtle* *Pseudemys rubriventris*
Blanding's turtle° *Emydoidea blandingii*

Kinosternidae
Eastern mud turtle*** *Kinsternum subrubrum*
Common musk turtle*** *Sternothorus odoratus*

Phrynosomatidae
Northern fence lizard* *Sceloporus undulatus*

Scincidae
Five-lined skink* *Eumeces fasciatus*
Ground skink° *Scincella lateralis*

Viperidae
Timber rattlesnake*** *Crotalus horridus*
Northern copperhead* *Agkistrodon contortrix*

BIRDS
Accipitridae
Sharp-shinned hawk*** *Accipiter striatus*
Red-tailed hawk*** *Buteo jamaicensis*
Red-shouldered hawk*** *Buteo lineatus*
Broad-winged hawk*** *Buteo platypterus*
Northern harrier*** *Circus cyaneus*
Bald eagle*** *Haliaeetus leucocephalus*
Osprey*** *Pandion haliaetus*
Cooper's hawk** *Accipiter cooperii*
Northern goshawk** *Accipiter gentilis*
Golden eagle° *Aquila chrysaetos*
Rough-legged hawk° *Buteo lagopus*
Swallow-tailed kite° *Elanoides forficatus*
Mississippi kite° *Ictinia mississippiensis*

Alaudidae
Horned lark° *Eremophila alpestris*

Alcedinidae
Belted kingfisher*** *Ceryle alcyon*

Alcidae
Razorbill° *Alca torda*
Dovekie° *Alle alle*
Atlantic puffin° *Fratercula arctica*
Great auk° *Pinguinus impennis*
Common murre° *Uria aalge*
Thick-billed murre° *Uria lomvia*

Anatidae
Wood duck*** *Aix sponsa*
Blue-winged teal*** *Anas discors*
American black duck*** *Anas rubripes*
Tufted duck*** *Aythya fuligula*
Barrow's goldeneye*** *Bucephala islandica*
Snow goose*** *Chen caerulescens*
Red-breasted merganser*** *Mergus serrator*
Common merganser** *Mergus merganser*
Greater white-fronted goose** *Anser albifrons*
Tundra swan** *Cygnus columbianus*
Harlequin duck** *Histrionicus histrionicus*
King eider** *Somateria spectabilis*
Northern pintail* *Anas acuta*
Ring-necked duck* *Aythya collaris*
Greater scaup* *Aythya marila*
Brant* *Branta bernicla*
Canada goose* *Branta canadensis*
Bufflehead* *Bucephala albeola*
Common goldeneye* *Bucephala clangula*
Labrador duck* *Camptorhynchus labradorius*

Long-tailed duck (Oldsquaw)* *Clangula hyemalis*
Hooded merganser* *Lophodytes cucullatus*
White-winged scoter* *Melanitta fusca*
Black scoter* *Melanitta nigra*
Surf scoter* *Melanitta perspicillata*
Common eider* *Somateria mollissima*
American wigeon° *Anas americana*
Northern shoveler° *Anas clypeata*
Green-winged teal° *Anas crecca*
Eurasian wigeon° *Anas penelope*
Mallard° *Anas platyrhynchos*
Gadwall° *Anas strepera*
Lesser scaup° *Aythya affinis*
Redhead° *Aythya americana*
Canvasback° *Aythya valisineria*
Ruddy duck° *Oxyura jamaicensis*

Apodidae
Chimney swift** *Chaetura pelagica*

Ardeidae
American bittern*** *Botaurus lentiginosus*
Green heron*** *Butorides virescens*
Black-crowned night heron*** *Nycticorax nycticorax*
Great blue heron** *Ardea herodias*
Least bittern** *Ixobrychus exilis*
Great egret* *Ardea alba*
Snowy egret* *Egretta thula*
Little blue heron° *Egretta caerulea*
Tricolored heron° *Egretta tricolor*
Yellow-crowned night heron° *Nyctanassa violacea*

Bombycillidae
Cedar waxwing*** *Bombycilla cedrorum*

Caprimulgidae
Whip-poor-will*** *Caprimulgus vociferus*
Common nighthawk*** *Chordeiles minor*
Chuck-will's-widow° *Caprimulgus carolinensis*

Cathartidae
Turkey vulture* *Cathartes aura*
Black vulture° *Coragyps atratus*

Certhiidae
Brown creeper*** *Certhia americana*

Charadriidae
Semipalmated sandpiper*** *Calidris pusilla*

Killdeer*** *Charadrius vociferus*
Black-bellied plover*** *Pluvialis squatarola*
Piping plover** *Charadrius melodus*
American golden plover** *Pluvialis dominica*

Columbidae
Passenger pigeon*** *Ectopistes migratorius*
Mourning dove*** *Zenaida macroura*

Corvidae
American crow*** *Corvus brachyrhynchos*
Common raven*** *Corvus corax*
Blue jay*** *Cyanocitta cristata*
Fish crow° *Corvus ossifragus*
Gray jay° *Perisoreus canadensis*

Cuculidae
Black-billed cuckoo*** *Coccyzus erythropthalmus*
Yellow-billed cuckoo* *Coccyzus americanus*

Emberizidae
Saltmarsh sharp-tailed sparrow*** *Ammodramus caudacutus*
American goldfinch*** *Carduelis tristis*
Purple finch*** *Carpodacus purpureus*
Baltimore oriole*** *Icterus galbula*
Swamp sparrow*** *Melospiza georgiana*
Lincoln's sparrow*** *Melospiza lincolnii*
Song sparrow*** *Melospiza melodia*
Fox sparrow*** *Passerella iliaca*
Indigo bunting*** *Passerina cyanea*
Rose-breasted grosbeak*** *Pheucticus ludovicianus*
Eastern towhee*** *Pipilo erythrophthalmus*
Common grackle*** *Quiscalus quiscula*
American tree sparrow*** *Spizella arborea*
Clay-colored sparrow*** *Spizella pallida*
Chipping sparrow*** *Spizella passerina*
Field sparrow*** *Spizella pusilla*
White-throated sparrow*** *Zonotrichia albicollis*
White-crowned sparrow*** *Zonotrichia leucophrys*
Nelson's sharp-tailed sparrow** *Ammodramus nelsoni*
Lapland longspur** *Calcarius lapponicus*
Lark sparrow** *Chondestes grammacus*
Bobolink** *Dolichonyx oryzivorus*
Savannah sparrow** *Passerculus sandwichensis*
Snow bunting** *Plectrophenax nivalis*
Boat-tailed grackle** *Quiscalus major*

Henslow's sparrow* *Ammodramus henslowii*
Seaside sparrow* *Ammodramus maritimus*
Pine siskin* *Carduelis pinus*
Orchard oriole* *Icterus spurius*
Dark-eyed junco* *Junco hyemalis*
Red crossbill* *Loxia curvirostra*
Vesper sparrow* *Pooecetes gramineus*
Dickcissel* *Spiza americana*
LeConte's sparrow° *Ammodramus leconteii*
Grasshopper sparrow° *Ammodramus savannarum*
Northern cardinal° *Cardinalis cardinalis*
Common redpoll° *Carduelis flammea*
Evening grosbeak° *Coccothraustes vespertinus*
White-winged crossbill° *Loxia leucoptera*
Brown-headed cowbird° *Molothrus ater*
Blue grosbeak° *Passerina caerulea*
Painted bunting° *Passerina ciris*
Pine grosbeak° *Pinicola enucleator*
Western tanager° *Piranga ludoviciana*

Falconidae
Peregrine falcon*** *Falco peregrinus*
American kestrel*** *Falco sparverius*
Merlin** *Falco columbarius*
Gyrfalcon° *Falco rusticolus*

Gaviidae
Common loon* *Gavia immer*
Red-throated loon° *Gavia stellata*

Gruidae
Whooping crane° *Grus americana*

Haematopodidae
American oystercatcher* *Haematopus palliatus*

Hirundinidae
Barn swallow*** *Hirundo rustica*
Bank swallow*** *Riparia riparia*
Tree swallow*** *Tachycineta bicolor*
Cliff swallow** *Petrochelidon pyrrhonota*
Purple martin** *Progne subis*
Northern rough-winged swallow*
Stelgidopteryx serripennis

Hydrobatidae
Leach's storm petrel° *Oceanodroma leucorhoa*

Icteridae
Red-winged blackbird*** *Agelaius phoeniceus*
Eastern meadowlark** *Sturnella magna*

Yellow-headed blackbird** *Xanthocephalus xanthocephalus*
Rusty blackbird* *Euphagus carolinus*
Brewer's blackbird° *Euphagus cyanocephalus*

Laniidae
Loggerhead shrike** *Lanius ludovicianus*
Northern shrike** *Lanius excubitor*

Laridae
Ring-billed gull*** *Larus delawarensis*
Iceland gull*** *Larus glaucoides*
Black-headed gull*** *Larus ridibundus*
Common tern*** *Sterna hirundo*
Black tern** *Chlidonias niger*
Laughing gull** *Larus atricilla*
Glaucous gull** *Larus hyperboreus*
Little gull** *Larus minutus*
Bonaparte's gull** *Larus philadelphia*
Black-legged kittiwake** *Rissa tridactyla*
Least tern** *Sternula antillarum*
Sabine's gull** *Xema sabini*
Caspian tern* *Hydroprogne caspia*
Herring gull* *Larus argentatus*
Forster's tern* *Sterna forsteri*
Royal tern* *Thalasseus maximus*
Gull-billed tern° *Gelochelidon nilotica*
Lesser black-backed gull° *Larus fuscus*
Greater black-backed gull° *Larus marinus*
Roseate tern° *Sterna dougallii*
Arctic tern° *Sterna paradisaea*
Sandwich tern° *Thalasseus sandvicensis*

Mimidae
Gray catbird*** *Dumetella carolinensis*
Brown thrasher*** *Toxostoma rufum*
Northern mockingbird° *Mimus polyglottos*

Motacillidae
American pipit* *Anthus rubescens*

Odontophoridae
Northern bobwhite*** *Colinus virginianus*

Paridae
Black-capped chickadee*** *Poecile atricapillus*
White-breasted nuthatch*** *Sitta carolinensis*
Tufted titmouse° *Baeolophus bicolor*
Boreal chickadee° *Poecile hudsonica*
Red-breasted nuthatch° *Sitta canadensis*

Parulidae

Black-throated blue warbler*** *Dendroica caerulescens*
Bay-breasted warbler*** *Dendroica castanea*
Blackburnian warbler*** *Dendroica fusca*
Magnolia warbler*** *Dendroica magnolia*
Yellow warbler*** *Dendroica petechia*
Blackpoll warbler*** *Dendroica striata*
Black-throated green warbler*** *Dendroica virens*
Common yellowthroat*** *Geothlypis trichas*
Black-and-white warbler*** *Mniotilta varia*
Northern Parula*** *Parula americana*
Ovenbird*** *Seiurus aurocapilla*
Northern waterthrush*** *Seiurus noveboracensis*
American redstart*** *Setophaga ruticilla*
Nashville warbler*** *Vermivora ruficapilla*
Canada warbler*** *Wilsonia canadensis*
Wilson's warbler*** *Wilsonia pusilla*
Yellow-throated warbler** *Dendroica dominica*
Connecticut warbler** *Oporornis agilis*
Mourning warbler** *Oporornis philadelphia*
Prothonotary warbler** *Protonotaria citrea*
Tennessee warbler** *Vermivora peregrina*
Yellow-rumped warbler* *Dendroica coronata*
Palm warbler* *Dendroica palmarum*
Chestnut-sided warbler* *Dendroica pensylvanica*
Cape May warbler* *Dendroica tigrina*
Hooded warbler* *Geothlypis nelsoni*
Cerulean warbler° *Dendroica cerulea*
Prairie warbler° *Dendroica discolor*
Black-throated gray warbler° *Dendroica nigrescens*
Pine warbler° *Dendroica pinus*
Townsend's warbler° *Dendroica townsendi*
Worm-eating warbler° *Helmitheros vermivorum*
Yellow-breasted chat° *Icteria virens*
Swainson's warbler° *Limnothlypis swainsonii*
Kentucky warbler° *Oporornis formosus*
Louisiana waterthrush° *Seiurus motacilla*
Orange-crowned warbler° *Vermivora celata*
Golden-winged warbler° *Vermivora chrysoptera*
Blue-winged warbler° *Vermivora pinus*

Pelecanidae

American white pelican° *Pelecanus erythrorhynchos*
Brown pelican° *Pelecanus occidentalis*

Phaethontidae

Northern gannet* *Morus bassanus*

Phalacrocoracidae

Double-cresterd cormorant*** *Phalacrocorax auritus*
Great cormorant** *Phalacrocorax carbo*
Anhinga° *Anhinga anhinga*

Phasianidae

Ruffed grouse*** *Bonasa umbellus*
Wild turkey*** *Meleagris gallopavo*
Heath hen*** *Tympanuchus cupido*

Picidae

Northern flicker*** *Colaptes auratus*
Pileated woodpecker*** *Dryocopus pileatus*
Red-bellied woodpecker*** *Melanerpes arolinus*
Downy woodpecker*** *Picoides pubescens*
Hairy woodpecker*** *Picoides villosus*
Red-headed woodpecker* *Melanerpes erythrocephalus*
Yellow-bellied sapsucker* *Sphyrapicus varius*
Black-backed woodpecker° *Picoides arcticus*

Podicidepidae

Pied-billed grebe*** *Podilymbus podiceps*
Horned grebe** *Podiceps auritus*
Red-necked grebe** *Podiceps grisegena*
Eared grebe° *Podiceps nigricollis*

Procellariidae

Wilson's storm petrel* *Oceanites oceanicus*
Cory's shearwater° *Calonectris diomedea*
Northern fulmar° *Fulmarus glacialis*
Greater shearwater° *Puffinus gravis*
Sooty shearwater° *Puffinus griseus*

Rallidae

American coot** *Fulica americana*
Common moorhen*** *Gallinula chloropus*
Sora*** *Porzana carolina*
Virginia rail*** *Rallus limicola*
Clapper rail*** *Rallus longirostris*
King rail** *Rallus elegans*
Yellow rail* *Coturnicops noveboracensis*
Black rail* *Laterallus jamaicensis*
Purple gallinule° *Porphyrio martinica*

Recurvirostridae
Black-necked stilt° *Himantopus mexicanus*
American avocet° *Recurvirostra americana*

Regulidae
Ruby-crowned kinglet* *Regulus calendula*
Golden-crowned kinglet° *Regulus satrapa*

Rynchopinae
Black skimmer° *Rynchops niger*

Scolopacidae
Spotted sandpiper*** *Actitis macularius*
Upland sandpiper*** *Bartramia longicauda*
White-rumped sandpiper*** *Calidris fuscicollis*
Pectoral sandpiper*** *Calidris melanotos*
Least sandpiper*** *Calidris minutilla*
Semipalmated plover*** *Charadrius semipalmatus*
Hudsonian godwit*** *Limosa haemastica*
Long-billed curlew*** *Numenius americanus*
Eskimo curlew*** *Numenius borealis*
Whimbrel*** *Numenius phaeopus*
American woodcock*** *Scolopax minor*
Lesser yellowlegs*** *Tringa flavipes*
Greater yellowlegs*** *Tringa melanoleuca*
Solitary sandpiper*** *Tringa solitaria*
Ruddy turnstone** *Arenaria interpres*
Red knot** *Calidris canutus*
Curlew sandpiper** *Calidris ferruginea*
Stilt sandpiper** *Calidris himantopus*
Purple sandpiper** *Calidris maritima*
Western sandpiper** *Calidris mauri*
Red-necked stint** *Calidris ruficollis*
Long-billed dowitcher** *Limnodromus scolopaceus*
Marbled godwit** *Limosa fedoa*
Ruff** *Philomachus pugnax*
Willet** *Tringa semipalmata*
Sanderling* *Calidris alba*
Dunlin* *Calidris alpina*
Common snipe* *Gallinago gallinago*
Short-billed dowitcher* *Limnodromus griseus*
Buff-breasted sandpiper* *Tryngites subruficollis*
Baird's sandpiper° *Calidris bairdii*
Little stint° *Calidris minuta*
Red phalarope° *Phalaropus fulicarius*
Red-necked phalarope° *Phalaropus lobatus*
Wilson's phalarope° *Phalaropus tricolor*

Stercorariidae
Long-tailed jaeger° *Stercorarius longicaudatus*

Parasitic jaeger° *Stercorarius parasiticus*
Pomarine jaeger° *Stercorarius pomarinus*

Strigidae
Northern saw-whet owl*** *Aegolius acadicus*
Great horned owl*** *Bubo virginianus*
Eastern screech owl*** *Megascops asio*
Barred owl*** *Strix varia*
Short-eared owl** *Asio flammeus*
Snowy owl** *Bubo scandiacus*
Long-eared owl* *Asio otus*
Barn owl* *Tyto alba*

Thraupidae
Scarlet tanager*** *Piranga olivacea*
Summer tanager° *Piranga rubra*

Threskiornithidae
White-faced ibis° *Plegadis chihi*
Glossy ibis° *Plegadis falcinellus*

Trochilidae
Ruby-throated hummingbird*** *Archilochus colubris*

Troglodytidae
Marsh wren*** *Cistothorus palustris*
House wren*** *Troglodytes aedon*
Sedge wren** *Cistothorus platensis*
Winter wren** *Troglodytes troglodytes*
Carolina wren* *Thryothorus ludovicianus*
Blue-gray gnatcatcher° *Polioptila caerulea*
Bewick's wren° *Thryomanes bewickii*

Turdidae
Veery*** *Catharus fuscescens*
Hermit thrush*** *Catharus guttatus*
Swainson's thrush*** *Catharus ustulatus*
American robin*** *Turdus migratorius*
Eastern bluebird** *Sialia sialis*
Varied thrush** *Ixoreus naevius*
Bicknells thursh* *Catharus bicknelli*
Gray-cheeked thrush* *Catharus minimus*
Wood thrush* *Hylocichla mustelina*
Northern wheatear° *Oenanthe oenanthe*

Tyrannidae
Olive-sided flycatcher*** *Contopus cooperi*
Eastern wood peewee*** *Contopus virens*
Yellow-bellied flycatcher*** *Empidonax flaviventris*
Least flycatcher*** *Empidonax minimus*

Great crested flycatcher*** *Myiarchus crinitus*
Eastern phoebe*** *Sayornis phoebe*
Eastern kingbird*** *Tyrannus tyrannus*
Alder flycatcher** *Empidonax alnorum*
Willow flycatcher* *Empidonax traillii*
Acadian flycatcher* *Empidonax virescens*
Western kingbird* *Tyrannus verticalis*
Ash-throated flycatcher° *Myiarchus cinerascens*

Vireonidae
Warbling Vireo*** *Vireo gilvus*
Red-eyed Vireo*** *Vireo olivaceus*
Philadelphia Vireo** *Vireo philadelphicus*
Blue-headed Vireo** *Vireo solitarius*
Yellow-throated Vireo* *Vireo flavifrons*
White-eyed Vireo* *Vireo griseus*
Bell's Vireo° *Vireo bellii*

MAMMALS
Balaenidae
Northern right whale* *Eubalaena glacialis*

Balaenopteridae
Minke whale* *Balaenoptera acutorostrata*
Finback whale* *Balaenoptera physalus*
Humpback whale* *Megaptera novaeangliae*
Sei whale° *Balaenoptera borealis*
Blue whale ° *Balaenoptera musculus*

Bovidae
Bison° *Bison bison*

Canidae
Gray wolf*** *Canis lupus*
Dog*** *Canis lupus familaris*
Gray fox*** *Urocyon cinereoargenteus*
Red fox* *Vulpes vulpes*
Coyote° *Canis latrans*

Castoridae
Beaver*** *Castor canadensis*

Cervidae
White-tailed deer*** *Odocoileus virginianus*
Elk** *Cervus elaphus*
Moose* *Alces alces*

Delphinidae
Short-beaked common dolphin** *Delphinus delphis*
Long-finned pilot whale** *Globicephala melas*
Bottlenose dolphin** *Tursiops truncatus*
Atlantic white-sided dolphin* *Lagenorhynchus acutus*
Striped dolphin* *Stenella coeruleoalba*
Risso's dolphin° *Grampus griseus*
White-beaked dolphin° *Lagenorhynchus albirostris*
Killer whale° *Orcinus orca*
Pantropical spotted dolphin° *Stenella attenuata*

Didelphidae
Virginia opossum° *Didelphis virginiana*

Erethizontidae
Porcupine* *Erethizon dorsatum*

Felidae
Bobcat*** *Lynx rufus*
Mountain lion*** *Puma concolor*
Canada lynx° *Lynx canadensis*

Hominidae
Human*** *Homo sapiens*

Leporidae
Eastern cottontail*** *Sylvilagus floridanus*
New England cottontail** *Sylvilagus transitionalis*
Snowshoe hare* *Lepus americanus*

Mephitidae
Striped skunk*** *Mephitis mephitis*

Monodontidae
Beluga° *Delphinapterus leucas*

Muridae
Meadow vole*** *Microtus pennsylvanicus*
Muskrat*** *Ondatra zibethicus*
White-footed mouse*** *Peromyscus leucopus*
Deer mouse*** *Peromyscus maniculatus*
Southern red-backed vole** *Clethrionomys gapperi*
Pine vole** *Microtus pinetorum*
Woodland jumping mouse** *Napaeozapus insignis*
Meadow jumping mouse** *Zapus hudsonius*
Allegheny woodrat* *Neotoma magister*
Southern bog lemming* *Synaptomys cooperi*

Mustelidae
North American river otter*** *Lontra canadensis*
Mink*** *Neovison vison*
Fisher** *Martes pennanti*
Long-tailed weasel** *Mustela frenata*
Wolverine* *Gulo gulo*
Short-tailed weasel (Ermine)* *Mustela erminea*
Least weasel* *Mustela nivalis*
American marten° *Martes americana*

Phocidae
Harbor seal*** *Phoca vitulina*
Hooded seal** *Cystophora cristata*
Harp seal* *Pagophilus groenlandicus*
Gray seal° *Halichoerus grypus*
Ringed seal° *Phoca hispida*

Phocoenidae
Harbor porpoise*** *Phocoena phocoena*

Physeteridae
Sperm whale** *Physeter catodon*
Pygmy sperm whale* *Kogia breviceps*

Procyonidae
Raccoon*** *Procyon lotor*

Sciuridae
Southern flying squirrel*** *Glaucomys volans*
Eastern gray squirrel*** *Sciurus carolinensis*
Eastern chipmunk*** *Tamias striatus*
Woodchuck** *Marmota monax*
Red squirrel** *Tamiasciurus hudsonicus*
Fox squirrel* *Sciurus niger*
Northern flying squirrel° *Glaucomys sabrinus*

Soricidae
Northern short-tailed shrew*** *Blarina brevicauda*
Masked shrew*** *Sorex cinereus*
Least shrew** *Cryptotis parva*
Smoky shrew** *Sorex fumeus*

Talpidae
Eastern mole*** *Scalopus aquaticus*
Star-nosed mole** *Condylura cristata*
Brewer's mole** *Parascalops breweri*

Trichechidae
Florida manatee° *Trichechus manatus*

Ursidae
American black bear*** *Ursus americanus*

Vespertilionidae
Big brown bat*** *Eptesicus fuscus*
Silver-haired bat*** *Lasionycteris noctivagans*
Red bat*** *Lasiurus borealis*
Hoary bat*** *Lasiurus cinereus*
Little brown bat** *Myotis lucifugus*
Northern long-eared bat** *Myotis septentrionalis*
Eastern pipistrelle ** *Pipistrellus subflavus*
Eastern small-footed Myotis* *Myotis leibii*
Indiana bat* *Myotis sodalis*

Ziphiidae
Dense-beaked whale* *Mesoplodon densirostris*
Gervais's beaked whale* *Mesoplodon europaeus*
True's beaked whale* *Mesoplodon mirus*
Cuvier's beaked whale* *Ziphius cavirostris*

NOTES, SOURCES, AND ELABORATIONS

CHAPTER 1

There are a variety of different etymologies for the Lenape (Delaware) name *Mannahatta*, variously spelled "Manahata," "Manatans," "Manathus," "Manatus," "Manhates," "Manhattos," "Mannatens," and "Munnatous" in early documents (Grumet 1981). The term itself goes back to the earliest European records of the place, including those from Robert Juet, cited in the main text. Tooker (1901) translated the name as "a hilly island," and Ruttenber (1906) proposed "the island" or "the small island." William Morris, cited in Beauchamp (1907), suggested it might mean "cluster of islands with channels everywhere," from the Mohican word *Manahachtanicuk*. Heckewelder (1876), a Moravian missionary working with Delaware Indians in Pennsylvania and Ohio in the nineteenth century, recorded that the word *Manahachtanienk* meant "the island were we all became intoxicated," referring to an unconfirmed episode when Hudson gave the Lenape—pronounced "Le-NAH-pay" (Kraft 2001)—living on Manhattan alcohol. Heckewelder also suggested that it might have meant "place where timber is procured for bows and arrows." He reported that Delaware "traditions affirm that at the period of the discovery of America our nation resided on the island of New York . . . [and] at the lower end of the island was a grove of hickory trees of peculiar strength and toughness. Our fathers held this timber in high esteem, as material for constructing bows, water clubs, etc." Our ecological models (described in Chapter 6) confirm that the lower end of the island would have been suitable for hickory.

Although descriptions of Mannahatta's biodiversity may seem hyperbolic, they stand up surprisingly well against U.S. national parks of comparable latitude when comparing number of species per area. Though describing ecological communities is a subjective business, a standard source for Yellowstone National Park (Despain 1991) describes 66 vegetation types within the park's 2,219,789 acres; sometimes these are generalized to only 19 main types of forest, wetland, and grassland. In contrast, Mannahatta had 55 ecological communities in just 27,595 acres, including the adjacent marine communities within 1,000 yards of the modern shore (the Mannahatta study area). Mannahatta's ecological communities are based on standardized descriptions in Edinger et al. (2002); these communities are explained in Chapter 5 and listed in Appendix C. Botti (2002) lists 1,281 native plant species and subspecies for Yosemite National Park, over 761,266 acres. As described in Chapter 6, the potential ("possible") plant list for Mannahatta includes up to 1,194 terrestrial species on 13,021 acres of land and one other plant, eelgrass (*Zostera marina*), found in the marine waters surrounding Manhattan; see full list in Appendix C. Alsop III (1995) lists 240 species of birds observed in the Great Smoky Mountains National Park, including rare species, over 521,495 acres. Including the rare species, Mannahatta may have seen as many as 353 native bird species over the course of a year, sometimes in flocks of millions—migratory species, including the passenger pigeon and various shorebirds (including sandpipers, curlews, plovers, phalaropes, killdeers, godwits, willets, turnstones, and yellowlegs) were particularly abundant.

Lawrence (1889) provides a nineteenth-century account of passenger pigeons on Manhattan: "About the first of September, when there was a strong northwest wind, Passenger Pigeons (*Ectopistes migratorius*) were sure to appear in great numbers, flying more abundantly in morning, though there were occasional flocks all day. From our place [on Morningside Heights] north to Fort Washington Point, three miles distant, the view was unobstructed, and for the entire distance it was an almost unbroken forest. We could see the flocks make their appearance over the Point, consisting of twenty-five to over a hundred Pigeons. . . . These flights continued as long as I lived in Manhattanville [until 1850], and Pigeons were quite abundant, I was informed, for some years after, but at the present time a single one would be a rarity."

Jasper Danckaerts, visiting in 1679, recounted the fish: "It is not possible to describe how this bay [New York Harbor] swarms with fish, both large and small, whales, tunnies and porpoises, whole schools of innumerable other fish, which the eagles and other birds of prey swiftly seize in their talons when the fish come up to the surface, and hauling them out of the water, fly with them to the nearest woods or beach, as we saw" (James and Jameson 1913). Other descriptions of the wildlife of Mannahatta are provided in Chapters 2 and 6 and in the accompanying notes.

Chapter 4 describes the Lenape of Mannahatta in more detail. Modern Lenape (Delaware) people now live in Oklahoma, Wisconsin, Ontario, and New Jersey, as described in Pritchard (2002) and Weslager (1972); see afterword in notes to Chapter 4.

Not that it needs much proving, but the average resident of Manhattan has been pretty well-off, both by U.S. and international standards. According to the U.S. Bureau of Economic Analysis (2007), the total personal income earned in New York County (conterminous with Manhattan) in 2005 was $161,229,536,000, which worked out to an average per capita income of $100,768 for approximately 1.6 million people, or approximately $276 per day. Of course the distribution of income is not equal, as these calculations might imply; *The Wall Street Journal* reported an estimate of 61,000 millionaires living on Manhattan in 2007 (though to be fair, New York County didn't even rank within the top-ten most millionaire-populous counties in the United States; Los Angeles County, CA, was reported to have 268,136 millionaires that same year; Frank 2007). The assessed value of property on Manhattan in 2007 was $674,091,600,000 (i.e., $674 billion; City of New York Department of Finance 2007). The adopted city budget for fiscal year 2008 was $52,940,235,260 (i.e., nearly $53 billion; City of New York 2007). In contrast, in 2005 nearly 3 billion people worldwide lived on less than two dollars per day (Watkins 2006).

The City of New York's claims that the city is an ecologically efficient place to live rest mainly on statistics gathered as part of PlaNYC, a remarkably detailed plan for urban sustainability through 2030 (City of New York Office of Long-term Planning and Sustainability 2007). The plan is available online (www.nyc.gov/html/planyc2030/html/home/home.shtml). In addition, according to American Public Transportation Association (2007), in 2005, 3.4 billion trips were made using public transit (bus, subway, railway, ferry) in the New York–Newark area of New York, New Jersey, and Connecticut (out of approximately 9.8 billion trips nationally). New York–Newark passengers traveled 18.7 billion miles by public transit that year; in contrast, nationwide, Americans drove 3,009,218,000,000 (more than 3 trillion) miles in personal vehicles and trucks the same year (U.S. Department of Transportation Federal Highway Administration 2006). Recent new green buildings in New York include the Condé Nast Building, at 4 Times Square; the Bank of America Tower, at 1 Bryant Park; the Hearst Tower, at 300 West Fifty-seventh Street; and the Center for Global Conservation, in the Bronx; however, elements of green building design are also incorporated into some of the classics of New York architecture, as described in Chapter 7. Modern green buildings are assessed according to rating standards, like the Leadership in Energy and Environmental Design (LEED) Green Building Rating System, developed by the U.S. Green Building Council (www.usgbc.org).

Coming to New York

The Wildlife Conservation Society (www.wcs.org) was originally founded as the New York Zoological Society, in 1895. Its original mission was to support a zoological park in New York City and save animals in the wild. Today this mission is fulfilled through more than 300 field projects in over sixty countries, including a commitment to save thirty of the wildest landscapes on the planet forever, and four zoological parks and one aquarium in New York City. WCS field projects involve working with partners in government and local communities to save tigers, elephants, whales, sea turtles, gorillas, jaguars, and other global-priority species. This work is supported through grants from international aid agencies, private foundations and donors, and through contributions from visitors to the world's largest system of urban wildlife parks: the Bronx Zoo, the New York Aquarium, and the wildlife centers in Central Park, Prospect Park, and Flushing Meadows–Corona Park.

Several good books cover the history of the Dutch founding of New York, including Shorto (2004), Burrows (1999), and Kammen (1975). Shorto describes the influence of New Amsterdam's Dutch founders on modern American culture and provides an entertaining portrait of Adrian van der Donck, an important Dutch settler and chronicler of New Netherland, who is quoted several times in this book. Unfortunately Dutch tolerance did not extend far enough to stop a series of massacres of Lenape people in 1643–44, though several Dutch individuals, including Van der Donck, spoke out against the atrocities at the time and afterward. More about the sad history of Dutch–Native American relations can be found in the notes to Chapter 4.

The Bronx, where I ride my bike today, played a minor role in the campaign of 1776. After Washington was chased from Manhattan (as described in Chapter 2), the British landed first at Throgs Neck, where they were repulsed after a sharp skirmish at Westchester Creek and then at Rodman's Neck, in today's Pelham Bay Park, finally catching up to Washington in White Plains for an anticlimactic battle. Afterward the Bronx (known then as Westchester) was a no-man's-land of ambushes, reprisals, and general unhappiness for its residents. Delancey's Pine, a white pine in the Bronx Zoo, was once one of the most famous landmarks in the Bronx (McNamara 1989). It grew to be more than 122 feet tall and was estimated to be over 250 years old when it was declared a hazard and cut down in 1913 by the Parks Department. Legend has it that Rebel sharpshooters would hide in the pine waiting for an opportunity to shoot at Tories who manned a blockhouse at West Farms, just south of the zoo. Across Long Island Sound, Theodore Roosevelt spent summers in the nineteenth century playing with his kids at his family home at Sagamore Hill, now a national historic site, near Oyster Bay, New York. Roosevelt got his start as a naturalist by measuring a dead seal found lying on a Manhattan street (Grondahl 2004).

Reading a New Landscape

The accounts of Juet and Hudson in September 1609 are quoted from Jameson (1909) and Johnson (1993). Some authors place Hudson off of Greenwich Village on the eleventh, not the twelfth of 1609, as I have done; the difference of a day is remarkable only in light of later events. Hudson's early reference to "salmon" in the Hudson River has spawned much confusion over the years, including an attempt to reintroduce Atlantic salmon (*Salmo salar*) from Maine in the 1880s (Waldman 1999). Those attempts failed, and today most experts agree that the Hudson River is too far south for the salmon, which has its most southerly run in Connecticut. Waldman believes Hudson's salmon were likely weakfish or sea-run trout. With respect to the copper or silver mines, Juet may have been referring to the Palisades, though no copper or silver has ever been found embedded in those cliffs. Serpentine, a green metamorphic rock, was once found on Staten Island and in Manhattan in a small patch in today's West Fifties (Merrill et al. 1902), giving rise to a distinctive barrens community of grass and scrawny trees. The burned trees Juet describes may have been due to Native American burning; see the notes from Chapter 4. The quote "O this is Eden" is from the Dutch poet Jacob Steendam's "In Praise of New Netherland."

Though people have long been observers of nature, the science of ecology was slow in coming. Ernest Haeckel coined the term *ecology* in 1866, but it wasn't until the twentieth century that the field developed in the United States. New York and, in particular, scientists associated with the New York Botanical Garden were important to the rise of ecology in America during the early twentieth century (Kingsland 2005). Today most universities have departments in ecology and/or evolution and numerous standard textbooks (e.g., Krebs 2008; Begon 2006). Although ecologists have always been aware of the issues of scale and heterogeneity that landscape ecology attempts to understand, the subdiscipline arose only in the mid-1980s, enabled by technological advances; important early works include Forman and Godron (1986) and Turner (1989). Now it is one of the fastest-growing areas of ecology, with its own professional society (the International Association of Landscape Ecology; www.landscape-ecology.org), professional journal (*Landscape Ecology*) and textbooks (e.g., Turner 2001). A related discipline, conservation biology, seeks to understand how human activities can ensure the continuing existence of species and ecological processes. Further details can be found in Borgerhoff Mulder and Coppolillo (2005) and Groom (2006) and in the journal *Conservation Biology* and magazine *Conservation*, both published on behalf of the Society for Conservation Biology (www.conbio.org).

The Human Footprint

Collaborators on the Human Footprint project include Gillian Woolmer and Kent Redford of the WCS, and Marc Levy, Malanding Jaiteh, and Annette Wannebo of the Center for International Earth Science Information Network (CIESIN) at the Earth Institute of Columbia University. Further descriptions of the Human Footprint map, along with technical details, can be found in Sanderson et al. (2002) and Sanderson et al. (2006). Downloadable maps of the Human Footprint are available (www.wcs.org/sw-high_tech_tools/landscapeecology/humanfoot printatlas), and the geographic information system (GIS) data can be downloaded (www.ciesin.columbia.edu/wild_areas/).

For more about global urbanizing trends, see United Nations Population Division (2006), and for a focus on the developing world, see Montgomery (2008). Jackson (1995) provides population figures for Manhattan through time.

Recent instances of the cinematic destruction of Manhattan include *I am Legend* (2008), *Cloverfield* (2007), *King Kong* (2005), *The Day After Tomorrow* (2004), *Godzilla* (1998), *Independence Day* (1996), and the classic *Escape from New York* (1981).

CHAPTER 2

The quote by Ambrose Serle is cited in Diamant (2004). In 1609 Hudson's assigned task was to explore a "North East" passage to the Orient by traveling north of Norway and Russia. The Northwest Passage must have been on his mind though, because his contract with the Dutch United East India Company included a specific provision *not* to go there. Rather, his contract read that he was "to think of discovering no other route or passage, except the route around the north or northeast, above Nova Zembla. . . . If it could not be accomplished at that time, another route would be subject of consideration for another voyage" (as quoted in Johnson 1993). Instead, after trying and abandoning the northeastern route, Hudson sailed the *Half Moon* across the Atlantic Ocean, making landfall near Chesapeake Bay, then sailed carefully north up the coast, exploring Delaware Bay, and finally slipping into New York Harbor and sailing up the Hudson River. On Hudson's last voyage, in 1610, he finally had backing to search for a Northwest Passage, leading his ship the *Discovery* into what is now known as Hudson Bay. Unfortunately, after a long and difficult voyage, his crew mutinied, leaving Hudson and eight others, including his young son John, adrift in the icy waters, where they were never heard from again.

John Jacob Astor started his commercial life as a fur trader and ended his life as the richest man in America, based largely on his real estate investments on Manhattan. Shortly before he died, he said, "Could I begin life again, knowing what I now know, and had money to invest, I would buy every foot of land on the island of Manhattan" (as quoted in Weiss 1995). Robert Moses's ambitions are documented in the famous biography by Caro (1974); his influence on New York is assessed in Ballon and Jackson (2007). Michael Bloomberg's ambitions for the city of the future are declared in PlaNYC (City of New York Office of Long-term Planning and Sustainability 2007) and manifested in his two terms as mayor between 2001 and 2009.

Early descriptions of Manhattan Island from Dutch and English sources are quoted from Jameson (1909) and Stokes (1915–28). Denton's quotes are from Neuman (1902). Additional sources include Merwick (2006), Rink (1986), Shorto (2004), Van der Zee and Van der Zee (1978), and Van Gelder (1982). The New Netherland Project aims to translate original documents in New York archives about New Netherland (www.nnp.org). Shorto (2004) provides additional biographical detail about Adrian van der Donck. Peter Kalm was a student of Carolus Linnaeus, who came to North America in 1750 to find a mulberry that would grow in Europe so that Europeans could produce their own silk. He did not succeed, but he did leave a delightful account of his journeys; see Benson (1987).

Descriptions of early explorers to the New World often seem fantastic, due to the phenomenon of shifting baselines, as described in reference to the changing oceans by Jackson (2001) and Pauly (1995). The essential idea is that people form their concept of what is "natural" from their experiences as children. As the natural world has been progressively degraded over the last four hundred years, and especially over the last century—see accounts by Matthiessen (1959), Lawrence (1991), Whitney (1994), Mann (2005), and McNeill (2000)—one generation's baseline conception of nature has it less abundant and less diverse than the generation before; in other words, the baseline has "shifted." As a result, we have difficulty knowing what we have lost and setting goals for its restoration (Sanderson 2006; Tear et al. 2005). A related idea is that of the "nature impoverishment" of modern American children, who spend less time playing outdoors than previous generations, to their detriment; see Louv (2005).

Historical ecology is the field of reconstructing the nature of the past; it helps rectify the loss of an appropriate baseline. Egan and Howell's handbook (2001) provides an overview. Most restoration ecologists argue that the goal is not to fix an idealized time and restore back to it, but rather to understand the processes and patterns of historical landscapes as a way of guiding restoration efforts today (Aronson, Dhillon, and LeFloc'h 1995). Palynology is the study of pollen through time; studies in New York include Kleinstein (2003), Pederson (2002), Russell (1980), and Sirkin (1967). Dendrochronology is the study of tree rings through time; see works by Cook and Jacoby (1977, 1979) and Cook and Mayes (1987). Archaeological references are described in the notes for Chapter 4.

The Campaign of 1776

The history of New York during the American Revolution has been retold many times, including recently in McCullough (2005), Schecter (2002), and Gallagher (1995). Firsthand accounts are compiled in Scheer and Rankin (1957) and Burgoyne (1990). The history of the Murrays of Murray Hill is related by Monaghan (1998). The account of the *Turtle* is adapted from Diamant (2004); the *Turtle* made a second attack later in 1776, in the Hudson River, near Washington Heights. Again, luck was against the *Turtle*, which was damaged during the proceedings and abandoned shortly thereafter. Hibbert (1990) provides a useful popular description of the war from the British perspective.

The British Headquarters Map

The map itself is in the collections of the National Archives of the United Kingdom, under catalogue reference MR 1/463. An earlier, incomplete version of the map is listed under reference MR 1/590. The appellation *the British Headquarters Map* appears to have been first applied by B. F. Stevens in 1900. Stevens's memoir was edited by his friend G. Manville Fenn (1903). Interestingly, there are many small, unexplained differences between the National Archives manuscript map and Stevens's facsimile. Stevens may have been working from a different state of the map, now unknown, or he may have made alterations based on additional sources, also unknown. Further research is required.

A Remarkably Accurate Map

Geographic information systems are described in Tomlinson (2007) and Ormsby, Napoleon, and Burke (2004). For the Mannahatta Project, we used ArcView 3.2 and ArcGIS 9.x packages provided through the Environmental System Research Institute (ESRI; Redlands, CA) Conservation Program, with customized applications written in the Arc Macro Language, supplemented by scripts in the open-source programming language perl (www.perl.org). To georeference the British Headquarters Map we collected the modern-day geographic coordinates for more than two hundred features visible on the British Headquarters Map, including street corners (in Lower Manhattan), streams, hills, valleys, and wetlands, as described in sources like Haswell (1896), Janvier (1894), and Dunshee (1952); see the notes to Chapter 3 and features in Appendix A. The georeferencing process provides an estimate of the root mean square error, referred to as "spatial error" in the main text. The geographic coordinate system for all the Mannahatta data is Universal Transverse Mercator, zone 18. The GIS data are available online (www.TheMannahattaProject.org).

Why So Accurate?

Woodward (1974) and Gronim (2001) provide insight into current interests in historical cartography. Studies of the accuracy of eighteenth-century British county maps can be found in Laxton (1976) and Ravenhill and Gilig (1974). British military cartography during the Revolution is described in Guthorn (1972, 1974) and Harley (1978). Guides to major Revolutionary-era map collections include Penfold (1967–74), Brun (1959), and the American Memory Web site at the Library of Congress (lcweb2.loc.gov/ammem/gmdhtml/gmdhome.html).

Sir Henry Clinton's fascination with maps is described in Wilcox (1954, 1964). Clinton's bitter retrospective can be found in Wilcox (1954). The quote from Frederick the Great is from Luvass (1999). The interaction between Clinton and Cornwallis is recounted in Hibbert (1990).

Carleton Takes Over

New York burned on September 21, 1776, perhaps as a result of arson by the retreating American forces; nearly one-third of the city was destroyed, especially Trinity Church and adjoining areas on the western side of town. New York burned again on August 3, 1778, destroying sixty-four houses and a number of stores on the waterfront. The same day, lightning struck an ordnance sloop tied up at the foot of Wall Street, and the resulting explosion created more havoc—a bad day all around; see details in Wertenbaker (1948) and Schecter (2002). The winter of 1779–80 was remembered for years as the "Hard Winter," with its deep snows starting in November and lasting through March and severe cold temperatures, including several days with temperatures below 0°F. The harbor was ice-locked from December 20, 1779, to February 20, 1780. Following winters, though not quite as harsh, were still frigid by modern standards; see Thaler (2000). Washington's description of northern Manhattan is cited in Schecter (2002). Revolutionary-era maps, including excellent maps of Boston, Massachusetts, and Charleston, South Carolina, provide the basis for giving other cities the Mannahatta treatment, and analogous resources are also available for other cities (e.g., Washington, D.C., San Francisco, CA).

CHAPTER 3

Terms like *abiota* and *overburden* can be found in ecology and geology textbooks like Begon, Townsend, and Harper (2006) and Tarbuck, Lutgens, and Tasa (2002), respectively.

The Many Lives of Manhattan

The summary of New York's geological history is based on descriptions by Baskerville (1982), Brock and Brock (2001), Merguerian and Sanders (1988), Schuberth (1968), and Sirkin and Bokuniewicz (2006). Mittelbach and Crewdson (1997), Horenstein (2007), and Hanley and Graff (1976) provide accessible popular accounts of Manhattan's geology, with walking tours. For analytical purposes we adapted the maps of surficial and bedrock geology by Merrill et al. (1902), including the more recent interpretation by Baskerville (1994). Cozzens (1843) and Gratacap (1904) provide detailed historical accounts. Note that *gneiss* is pronounced like "nice," with a silent *g*, hence the pun about Roosevelt Island. There were once active marble quarries on Manhattan, especially in the Inwood neighborhood and on "Marble Hill," formerly the northernmost portion of Manhattan Island. Marble Hill is now geographically part of the Bronx, having been separated from Manhattan by the construction of the Harlem Ship Canal in the 1890s, but is still politically part of Manhattan.

How High Were the Hills?

Measuring elevations in a post-9/11 city is not without its complications. One student working on the project was questioned by officials for making a GPS measurement beside the African American Burial Ground site on Duane Street, which is now across from the Federal Building, whose construction led to the burial ground's discovery. Another student was chased from Marcus Garvey Park by people who didn't desire observers, topographical or otherwise. For comparison to our historical digital elevation model, we used the United States Geological

Survey digital elevation models downloaded from the Cornell University Geospatial Information Repository (cugir.mannlib.cornell.edu).

Cohen (1988), Cohen and Augustyn (1997), and Rose-Redwood (2003) provide lively accounts of John Randel, Jr., and his activities on Manhattan and elsewhere. Later in life, Randel proposed a system of overhead railways to solve mid-nineteenth-century transportation problems in the city. Tim Bean's unraveling of Randel's notebook observations is described in Bean (2004).

The Commissioners' Plan of 1811, which guided Randel's surveys, ran from 1st Street only to 155th Street (today the northernmost numbered street on Manhattan is West 220th Street). The commissioners' full explanation for stopping at 155th Street is quoted in Dean (2008): "To some it may be a matter of surprise, that the whole island has not been laid out as a City; to others, it may be a subject of merriment, that the Commissioners have provided space for a greater population than is collected at any spot on this side of China. . . . [I]t is improbable, that (for centuries to come) the grounds north of Harlem Flat will be covered with homes." Though the commissioners stopped there, Randel didn't; his notebooks indicate observations north of 155th Street. Although the New-York Historical Society has a significant collection, it appears from our summary that its collection of Randel's notebooks is incomplete, as streets he surely surveyed are not included. In addition to sources cited in the main text, we also compiled elevation information from Egbert Viele's water map, a locally famous nineteenth-century antecedent of the Mannahatta Project. Viele prepared a map of Manhattan's original topography and buried watercourses in 1865, but without the benefit of the British Headquarters Map. See additional details in Cohen and Augustyn (1997); the original is the holdings of the New York Public Library. We also used information from topographic maps of northern Manhattan prepared under Olmsted's supervision; these maps are also in the New York Public Library. Further details on the hills and valleys can be found in Appendix A.

The story of the competition for the design of Central Park and its construction has been told compellingly in Rosenzweig and Blackmar (1992) and Miller (2003). Miller found this 1874 description of the material moved during Central Park's creation in Park Department records: "The underground drainage tiles that snaked under the Park measured more than sixty miles. Ten million one-horse cartloads carried five million cubic yards of stone and earth to the site from Long Island and the New Jersey Meadowlands—a feat equal to a single-file procession of thirty thousand miles. The moving of materials alone was equal to changing the level of the Park roughly four feet. The construction of the Park, which occurred before the invention of dynamite, required the use of the more dangerous gunpowder to blast away the rock outcrops and cost several workers their lives." The model of a city with a park at its center has influenced cities worldwide, including locally, where the other four boroughs of New York City also have central parklands.

Sources of place-names on Manhattan fall into a couple of different categories. Nineteenth-century industrialization and development in Manhattan led to numerous nostalgic accounts documenting the names and locations of natural features that were rapidly disappearing. Prominent among these were Hill and Waring, Jr. (1897), Janvier (1894), and Haswell (1896) and geological accounts by Cozzens (1843) and Gratacap (1904). Also useful are place-based historical guides to the city, including Kelley (1909); the Federal Writers' Project (1939); von Pressentin Wright, Miller, and Seitz (2002); and of course Stokes (1915–28) and Jackson (1995). Sources detailing etymologies of street names include Feirstein (2001) and Moscow (1978). An eclectic but useful account is Dunshee (1952). Detailed sources for the names of hills, streams, springs, and other abiotic features are summarized in Appendix A.

How Deep Were the Waters?
The history of the other islands around Manhattan has been summarized by Seitz and Miller (1996). The waters of the estuary on the Hudson River side have been described by Boyle (1969); Stanne, Panetta, and Forist (1996); Levington and Waldman (2006); those in the harbor by Waldman (1999) and Steinberg et al. (2004); and those in Long Island Sound by Andersen

(2002). The story of the unsuccessful chevaux-de-frise is from Diamant (2004). Sources of historical bathymetric information include eighteenth-century charts from DesBarres's *Atlantic Neptune* series, viewable online (www.nmm.ac.uk/collections/explore/index.cfm/category/90437), and early nineteenth-century charts from the U.S. Coast Survey, available for download online (chartmaker.ncd.noaa.gov/csdl/ctp/abstract.htm). Also see a series of hydrographic surveys of the Hudson River from the mid-nineteenth century, by Edward Ewen, at the British Library.

Buttenweiser (1987) describes the early history of landfill in New York. In an effort to expand the area available for navigation, colonial officials once sold "water lots"; individuals would buy the land between low and high tide on condition that they filled it in, with permission to construct a new wharf on the edge of the land. Several rounds of public and private landfill expanded the eastern side of Manhattan from the original shoreline, roughly along the line of Pearl Street (named for Lenape shell middens), to Water Street and subsequently to State Street, as shown on the British Headquarters Map. Landfill on the western side of Manhattan was comparatively quiescent until the twentieth century.

The historian of Harlem James Riker describes the ferocity of Hellgate on certain tides: "Being a narrow passage, there runneth a violent stream both upon flood and ebb, and in the middle lieth some islands of rocks, which the current sets so violently upon that it threatens present shipwreck; and upon the flood is a large whirlpool, which continually sends forth a hideous roaring, enough to affright a stranger from passing further, and to await for some Charon to conduct him through" (Riker 1881).

Horenstein (2007) cites two other possible etymologies for *Spuyten Duyvil Creek*: the story of Anthony Corlear, a Dutch settler, swimming the creek on a stormy night "in spite of the Devil," as recounted in Irving (1880), and the voluminous spring and/or the vigorous tide in the creek as originally proposed by McNamara (1991).

The statistics on sediments exchanged in the harbor come from Geyer and Chant (2006); see also Bokuniewicz (2006) and Cochran, Hirschberg, and Feng (2006). By way of comparison to the rates of natural deposition, the Army Corps of Engineers removes approximately 3.1 million metric tons from the harbor each year. During the course of the major channel-deepening project currently under way, federal and state agencies project spending more than $2 billion on removing 60 million metric tons of materials to improve navigation for New York Harbor (Ascher 2005).

Rich in Dirt

Wendell Berry's quotes about the virtues of soil are from Berry (1987); I've also borrowed the Whitman quote from Berry. A detailed account of the importance of soil to civilizations past and present can be found in Montgomery (2007). A typical urban-soil description, from New York City Soil Survey staff (2005), reads as follows: "Laguardia-Ebbets-Pavement & buildings, wet substratum complex, 0 to 8 percent slopes: Nearly level to gently sloping areas filled with a mixture of natural soil materials and construction debris over swamp, tidal marsh, or water; a mixture of anthropogenic soils which vary in coarse fragment content, with 15 to 49 percent of the surface covered by impervious pavement and buildings." The Natural Resources Conservation Service has mapped more than twenty thousand soil types (called "series") nation-wide; official soil descriptions can be accessed online (soils.usda.gov/technical/classification/osd/index.html). Soil accumulation rates are provided for selected sites in Boul, Southard, and Graham (2008); the rate for Mannahatta is based on a standard rule of thumb for temperate latitudes. For those who wish to delve deeper into soil science, a typical textbook is Singer and Munns (1991). We would have liked to have found a place on Manhattan where we could excavate undisturbed soil to confirm our soil map, but we couldn't determine where that place would be.

Dutch complaints about the soil quality are cited in Fayden (1993). An Italian count traveling through New York in 1790 concurred with the protests, noting: "The soil of the island of N. York, as we already said elsewhere, cannot be compared in richness of the nearby countries. Thus the land is not cultivated except in the vicinity of the few houses that are to be found on the road, which are taverns for the most part. The farmers profit better by cultivating the opposite of the Jersey, where the soil is fertile. The land fit for cultivation would be of mediocre quality, if it were not full of big boulders rolled over there, most of which were probably transported from far away by the waters of the river, or by some great upheaval" (Marino and Tiro 2006).

The Brooks Above and Below
The early history of freshwater on Manhattan is usefully told by Koeppel (2000). Allan (1995) provides an overview of stream ecology. The accounts of monsters in and fishing regulations for the Collect Pond are from Stokes (1915–28). Other details are found in Barlow (1969), and selected waterways are described in Appendix A.

The Changing Climate
The climatological account of New York City is assembled from Baron (1992); Boose, Foster, and Fluet (1994); Hurrell (1995); Ludlum (1966); Mittelbach and Crewdson (1997); Jackson (1995); and Neumann, Jarvinen, and Pike (1987). For the consequences of a near-miss hurricane in New York City, see Graves (1945). Climate change predictions for the city are from Rosenzweig and Solecki (2001); also see Jacob, Gornitz, and Rosenzweig (2007). For climate modeling of historical conditions, we relied on the Central Park climate record available from the National Climatic Data Center (www.ncdc.noaa.gov/oa/ncdc.html).

CHAPTER 4
Most of the non-place-specific information about the Lenape in Chapter 4 comes from sum-maries by Kraft (1986, 2001), Grumet (1989), and Weslager (1972). On Manhattan specifically, Grumet (1981) provides a thorough review of Native American place-names in New York and attempts to sort the wheat from the chaff. In the mainly chaff category are Beauchamp (1907), Tooker (1901), and Schoolcraft (1845). The early twentieth century saw an explosion of interest in Native Americans on Manhattan, associated with new finds by amateur archaeologists in the Inwood section of Manhattan and on Staten Island. Key references from that period include Bolton (1909, 1920, 1924, 1934), Skinner (1909, 1919, 1947), Calver (1948), and Calver and Bolton (1950). Firsthand accounts of Lenape in Mannahatta in addition to those mentioned in the main text include Danckaerts, from 1679–80 (in James and Jameson 1913) and Jogues (1646); Cantwell and Wall (2001) provide a useful summary of both pre- and post-contact archaeology, then fol-low up in a second volume with walking tours of sites of archaeological activity in New York (Wall and Cantwell 2004).

The Manahate, Rechgawawank, and Wiechquaeseck
According to Kraft (2001), the three main Lenape phatries, or clan affiliations—turtle, turkey, and wolf—have sometimes been confused with the three dialects of the Lenape language—respectively, Munsee, spoken in the northern part of Lenapehoking and presumably on Mannahatta; Unalachtigo, spoken across the central part of today's New Jersey and into Pennsylvania; and Unami, spoken in today's southern New Jersey, Delaware, and southeast Pennsylvania. During the Lenape diaspora, some people settled in what later became the state of Indiana—Muncie, Indiana, is named after the Munsee Indians who lived nearby formerly; today many Munsee speakers live in Canada. Other Lenape today live in Oklahoma and Wisconsin (see afterword to the Chapter 4 notes). The subclan designations described in the main text are from Morgan (1877) as cited in Kraft (2001); it's unclear how far back in time these affiliations, which were first recorded in 1865, extended.

Ruttenber (1872) made a heroic attempt to sort out the names on Manhattan, much to everyone's confusion. My reconstruction of the tribal groups on Mannahatta largely follows Grumet (1981), leaning heavily on information in Dutch records unearthed by the New Netherland Project; see Gehring and Grumet (1987) and Gehring (1980).

Estimating the population of Mannahatta in 1609 with any degree of certainty is very difficult. Cook (1976) argues along several lines of evidence that the "Manhattans" had a population of about three to four hundred, though what Cook calls "Manhattans" Ruttenber (1872) would call "Reckgawawancs" and I would call "Wiechquaesecks." I'm not sure it matters at this point—they were all Lenape. Cook's estimate for the "Weckquaesgeeks," after they had retreated to the middle part of what is now Westchester County in the 1640s (roughly along the line of Interstate 287 from Dobbs Ferry, NY, to Norwalk, CT), was nine hundred. De Rasieres (1628) estimated a few years after the first Dutch settlements that "[Manhattan Island] is inhabited by the old Manhatans (Manhatesen); they are almost 200 to 300 strong, men and women." Brash (2007) estimates that the population for all of the New York City area was 2,250. Bragdon (1996) suggests that precontact population densities along the coast of southern New England might have been 190 to 250 people per hundred square kilometers, which would make Mannahatta's population in the range of 212 to 278. To estimate the area of habitation sites, we assumed that the Lenape lived in wigwams with a fifteen-foot diameter and in longhouses that were twenty by sixty feet, that the outdoor space was approximately five times the indoor space, and that the winter population (~300 people) was half the size of the summer population.

Our extrapolation of Lenape-habitation-site suitability on page 111 is based on archaeological evidence on Manhattan culled from the above-named sources and the New York State Historic Preservation Office (nysparks.state.ny.us/shpo/resources/index.htm), as summarized in Appendix B. The statistical algorithm to create the computer model is based on the maximum entropy algorithm described by Phillips, Anderson, and Schapire (2006) and distributed in the program MAXENT, available online (www.cs.princeton.edu/~schapire/maxent/). This kind of predictive spatial approach to archaeology has been advanced by Kvamme (2005) and Leusen and Kamermans (2005). We adapted the trail system from Bolton (1922), after finding it concurred remarkably well with the historic topography and archaeology.

The argument about Native American values related to property, in contrast with the European system soon to replace it, follows Cronon (1983).

A Visit to Shorakapok

The description of Shorakapok in northern Manhattan, along the line of modern-day Isham Street, between Isham Park and Inwood Hill Park, is based on a synthesis of the sources described above. Danckaerts gives a firsthand account of a longhouse in Brooklyn in 1679: "Their house was low and long, about sixty feet long and fourteen or fifteen feet wide. The bottom was earth, the sides and roof were made of reed and the bark of chestnut trees; the posts, or columns, were limbs of trees stuck in the ground, and all fastened together. The top, or ridge of the roof was open about half a foot wide, from one end to the other, in order to let the smoke escape, in place of a chimney. On the sides, or walls, of the house, the roof was so low that you could hardly stand under it. . . . They build their fire in the middle of the floor, according to the number of families which live in it, so that from one end to the other each of them boils its own pot, and eats when it likes" in James and Jameson (1913). An overview of the factors shaping hunter-and-gatherer cultures is provided in Shepard (1998) and Mithen (2003).

People as Landscape Species

Ceci's work on maize horticulture in coastal New York is described in Ceci (1977, 1979, 1982); Bridges (1994) followed up with a study of isotope ratios in Lenape bones from Manhattan. The health effects of shifting to an agricultural-based food supply are described by Diamond (1987). While some anthropologists and archaeologists point to evidence of the native use of fish as fertilizer (e.g., Dimmick 1994), others believe that fish fertilization showed up only after contact with colonialists (Ceci 1975; Cronon 1983). Sarna-Wojcicki (2005) describes the application of the Decision Support System for Agrotechnology Transfer (DSSAT3) computer model (www.icasa.net/dssat/) to the problem of bean fertilization as part of Lenape horticulture; he also describes the shifting horticultural model we built. Champlain's observations are cited in Quinn and Quinn (1983). We modeled horticultural fields for presumed Lenape sites at the Collect Pond, near Minetta Water, at Konnade Kongh, at the "Great Maize Land," near Shorakapok, and along the Muscoota (Harlem) River. For modern street locations, see Appendix B. Loeb (1998) describes evidence of Native American planting in the Bronx.

The Lenape as Ecosystem Managers

Much ink has been spilled over the question of the extent and frequency of Native American fire prior to European contact. Day (1953), Pyne (1997), Whitney (1994), and Williams (1989) all read the evidence as indicating that not only were local fires set for the purpose of clearing land for horticulture, but there was also much more widespread burning; Krech (1999), Parshall and Foster (2002), and Russell (1983) argue for a more nuanced approach, emphasizing cultural and ecological variation between areas. Everyone agrees there was burning near habitation sites; the question is, how far beyond those areas did intentionally set fires extend? Mannahatta might not be the best test case, however, because of the limited area of the island; effectively every fire would have been a "local fire near a habitation site," though, as described in the main text, fires were mainly limited by the water surrounding the island, not by any internal physical barrier or climatic events. Interestingly, the palynological data generally support a large increase in fire, as evidenced by charcoal deposits, *after* European colonization (Parshall and Foster 2002; Kleinstein 2003). Presumably this reflects the transition from low-intensity understory burns to whole-scale land clearance through fire.

Bean's computer simulations for the Harlem Plains are described in Bean and Sanderson (2008). The FARSITE model is described in Finney (1998) and is available online (www.farsite. firemodels.org); we applied fuel models from Scott and Burgan (2005), selecting the ones most appropriate for the Northeast. Fisher wrote a script that matches the Central Park climate record for a tree-ring-derived drought record of New York City, kindly provided by Ed Cook (pers. comm.), allowing us to model variability in weather conditions over time. Ignition points were assigned probabilistically, on the edges of the horticultural fields (2 percent per annum chance of fires escaping from fields), along the modified Bolton trail network (set to ignite a given trail segment not more than once every twenty years), and, for hunting purposes, on the Harlem Plain (burning at least once every ten years; per Bean and Sanderson 2008). Putz (2003) makes the argument that an alternative reason some fires are set is just for fun, to relieve boredom. The ecological effects of fire on eastern forest ecosystems have been described in Abrams (1992), Foster et al. (2002), and Yahner (1995).

"Spirits no less important . . ."

Sources summarizing and retelling Lenape folk tales and myths are Hitakonanu'laak (2005), Bierhorst (1995), Adams (1997), and Kraft (2001). Richard Adams described the Mesingholikan from Delaware living in Kansas in the nineteenth century (1997). The Tale of Corn Woman is adapted from Hitakonanu'laak (2005). Lenape folklore is deeply metaphoric and amply repays study; I've only scratched the surface here.

The Lenape After Hudson and Today (An Afterword)

The unpleasant history of Lenape-Dutch relations on Manhattan is described in Merwick (2006), as well as in any standard history of the city—Burrows and Wallace (1999) is representative. Relations soured quickly after some confused and unsatisfactory trading with Hudson, who then kidnapped two Lenape individuals before departing upriver to find China. Having not made it to the Far East, on Hudson's return, his ship was attacked by Lenape from Mannahatta in October 1609. After the Dutch came to permanently settle in 1625, a variety of agreements were made, but these led to further misunderstandings on both sides, including regarding the exact nature by which Peter Minuit, Dutch governor-general, "bought" Manhattan from the "Indians."

In 1638, a new Dutch governor-general, Willem van Kieft, arrived to replace the more accommodating Peter Minuit, who had at least paid *something*, and began demanding "contributions" to protect the Lenape from their neighbors. With a level of affront worthy of any New Yorker, one Tappan noted that Van Kieft "must be a very mean fellow. . . . To come to live in this country without being invited . . . , and now wish to compel them to give him their corn for nothing" (quoted in Burrows and Wallace 1999). Unfortunately, violence erupted on both sides, leading to Van Kieft's War of 1642–1645. On February 25, 1642, Dutch soldiers under the governor-general's orders massacred groups of Lenape at Pavonia, just across the Hudson River from Manhattan, and at Corlear's Hook, along the East River. David Pietersz de Vries wrote of how babies were "torn from their mothers' breasts, and hacked to pieces in the presence of their parents, and the pieces thrown into the fire, and other sucklings, being bound to small boards, were cut, stuck and pierced, and miserably massacred in a manner to move a heart of stone." As a result, nearly all the Lenape in the lower Hudson River region banded together to fight the Dutch, resulting in a number of sharp skirmishes and fierce reprisals on Manhattan, as well as in New Jersey, Westchester, and Long Island. Anne Hutchinson, an English exile from New England, was killed near the river (and parkway) that now bears her name in the Bronx in 1642. By the time the war concluded, some sixteen hundred Lenape and scores of Dutch settlers had been killed.

By the 1680s most of the Lenape had left Manhattan for the North or West. In coming decades they would lose all of their historical homeland in the East, emigrating to western Pennsylvania and then into the Ohio River valley, where they were known as the Delaware people. Through the eighteenth and early nineteenth centuries, relations were continuously tense between European-Americans and the Delaware, as the Delaware were steadily pushed west through a series of battles, treaties, and reservations—Weslager (1972) provides details of the long march west by a proud and angry people. Kazimiroff (1982) gives a fascinating but tragic account of perhaps the last Lenape person living according to traditional ways in the New York City region. Today the Lenape Nation is centered in Oklahoma, and there are also reservations in Wisconsin and Ontario, Canada (see www.delawarenation.com; www.delawaretribeofindians. nsn.us; for an online reference for the Lenape language, see www.talk-lenape.org).

CHAPTER 5
The modern human neighborhoods of the city are described in any good guidebook; see historically-oriented descriptions in Jackson (1995). The ecological communities of Mannahatta are based on a standard system developed for New York State by Edinger et al. (2002); some community descriptions are available online, along with supplemental information from the New York Natural Heritage Program (www.acris.nynhp.org/). Attribution of these communities to Mannahatta, with supporting evidence, is described in Sanderson and Brown (2007). Coral reefs and tropical forests have many more species in a comparable area than Mannahatta did, but community diversity, or beta-diversity, is generally lower (McKnight et al. 2007). This chapter, more than any other, is a treatise on landscape ecology, the study of the ecosystem mosaic, as defined in Chapter 1.

Destined for Wealth
The description of the ecological changes after the last glaciation follows the palynological research cited in Chapter 2, particularly Sirkin (1967). For an account of the mastodons of New York City, see Horenstein (2008). The city's location at a biogeographic crossroads for plants has been noted by Small (1935), and its importance on the Atlantic flyway by Fowle and Kerlinger (2001), among others. For the importance of New York City parks to hungry migrant birds, see Seewagen (2008) and Seewagen and Slayton (2008). A delightful account of animal adaptations for the cold in the Northeast is provided in Heinrich (2003).

The productivity of the lower Hudson River estuary is documented in Howarth et al. (2006), though computer models must be used to separate the underlying biological productivity caused by wastewater in the modern estuary from natural processes; see Miller and St. John (2006). Oceanographic and sedimentary processes in the estuary are described by Geyer and Chant (2006) and Bokuniewicz (2006), respectively.

The Neighborhoods of the Sea

Shoreline ecological communities are described in Perry (1985). Conrad (1935) noted the sudden decline of eelgrass during his studies in the early 1930s on Long Island; also see McRoy and Helfferich (1977). Marine communities of New York Harbor are described in Waldman (1999) and Dowhan et al. (1997). Whales in the charter of Trinity Church are cited in Stokes (1915–28). McGrath (2007) wrote about the sad fate of Sludgy in *The New Yorker*. More about the triumphs and trials of salt marshes is provided in Bertness (2006); more about Mannahatta's wetlands, including salt marshes, in Sanderson (2005).

The Neighborhoods of Freshwater

A textbook review of the varieties of wetlands is provided in Mitsch and Gosselink (1993); a regional twist in Jorgensen (1978). Peatlands in the Northeast are described in Johnson (1985). The possibility of canoeing across the island is suggested by Hill and Waring (1897); the account of ice-skating in Lower Manhattan is from Haswell (1896). This same relatively low area might flood in a major storm today, making the tip of Manhattan into an island; see model results online from NASA (www.nasa.gov/mission_pages/hurricanes/archives/2006/sealevel_nyc.html).

The life history of eels is adapted from Werner (2004); that of beavers from Müller-Schwarze and Sun (2003). For more on beaver effects on soil and water, see Johnston et al. (1995) and Johnston and Naiman (1990). Greenwich Village's being founded in an area of rich soils is from Stokes (1915–28).

The Neighborhoods of the Land

The account of Mannahatta's forests is based on Jorgensen (1978), Brash (2007), Greller (1972), Dunwiddie et al. (1996), White and White (1996), and Whitney (1994). Paillet (2002) gives a useful summary of the American chestnut and the blight that has brought it down; prospects for recovery are described in the *Journal of the American Chestnut Foundation* (www.acf.org/index.php). Whitney (1994) provides photographs and dimensions of Northeast old-growth trees. Kershner and Leverett (2004), a field guide to remaining ancient forests in the Northeast, lists four sites in New York City, including Inwood Hill Park in Manhattan. The derivation of the list of berries and nuts is explained in the notes to Chapter 6. Riker (1904) discusses the grasslands of Harlem; Harper (1911) and Cain, Nelson, and McLean (1937) describe the Hempstead Plains grassland, a native eastern prairie, before it was buried beneath the suburbs of south central Long Island.

Disaster! Calamity! And . . . Renewal!

A prominent early ecologist, Frederic Clements, argued for the importance of "climax" states of ecosystems (Clements 1916); Henry Gleason, from the New York Botanical Garden, countered with the "individualistic" hypothesis for plant distributions (Gleason 1926). The general importance of disturbance processes to natural landscapes is described in Lertzman and Fall (1998), Pickett et al. (1997), and Pickett and White (1985), and for the Northeast in particular in Lorimer (2001) and Foster and O'Keefe (2000). Selected specific disturbances and successional sequences relevant to Mannahatta are described in Abrams (1992; for fire); Barnes and Dibble (1986; for beavers); Boose, Chamberlin, and Foster (2001; for large storms); and Rooney and Waller (2003; for white-tailed deer).

Disturbing the Peace

References for computer ecological models of fire and horticultural disturbances are provided in the notes for Chapter 4; models of blowdown from storms in Boose, Foster, and Fluet (1994), and models of flooding in Jonkman et al. (2008). Similar models are used to describe the effects of natural disasters on cities; see the U.S. Federal Emergency Management Agency's U.S. Multi-Hazard Model (HAZUS; www.fema.gov/plan/prevent/hazus/index.shtm). Repeated runs of phenomena to generate probabilistic understanding are referred to as "Monte Carlo" simulations. Manly (2006) provides an overview of Monte Carlo techniques for understanding ecological phenomena.

The Old Collect

The death of the Collect Pond is recounted in Koeppel (2000), and the rise and fall of the Five Points neighborhood is described in Anbinder (2001) and Ashbury (1927). Riis's photographs of the slums lying over the Collect Pond can be seen in Riis (1902). On the oft-repeated television program *Law and Order*, the steps of the courthouse lie near the old Collect Pond's shore.

CHAPTER 6

Ascher (2005) provides a fascinating description on the infrastructure of the city; for a longer-term view, see PlaNYC (City of New York Office of Long-term Planning and Sustainability 2007). Weisman's (2007) chapter on New York reminds us how much we depend on the people who build and maintain the infrastructure of the city and how fast it might all come crashing down if those maintainers disappeared.

Naturalists in New York

Colden (1750) provided the first classification of New York flora using the then quite new Linnaean system of Latin binomials to name plants and animals; see his biography by Keys (1906). The work of Colden's daughter Jane, from the late eighteenth century, is described in Vail (1906), and that of John Torrey in Callery (1995), who wrote: "[Torrey] established the approach to field work that distinguished botanists in New York City in the nineteenth century." Much early botany was a closet activity, where botanists worked from herbarium specimens to describe species, as opposed to studying plants in the wild, which was the method Torrey preferred. Several of the papers consulted for the Mannahatta Project are from the *Journal of the Torrey Botanical Society*, which is still an active and important botanical journal. John James Audubon lived happily at 155th Street and Audubon Terrace during the last decade of his life; Sivard (1995) writes that in the 1840s the mayor granted him permission to shoot rats on the Battery at dawn to obtain specimens for the *Viviparous Quadrupeds of North America*, then in production.

Chapman was a famous ornithologist for the American Museum of Natural History who also wrote about the birds of New York—see Chapman (1904, 1906); the Brittons were critical to the founding of the New York Botanical Garden and to establishing a new style of American botany in the early twentieth century—see the history by Kingsland (2005) for an overview. Beebe was also an important ornithologist and explorer from the New York Zoological Society (Gould 2004) who wrote about New York City (Beebe 1953); Hornaday was the first president of the New York Zoological Society and wrote about the animals of Hudson's day for the 1909 tricentennial of Hudson's voyage (Hornaday 1909). Other important naturalists of New York City and beyond include Eugene Bicknell, Raymond Ditmars, Henry Fairfield Osborn, Roger Tory Peterson, and Ernst Mayr.

Natural history organizations active in the city today include the Linnaean Society of New York (linnaeannewyork.org), the Metropolitan Biodiversity Project at the American Museum of Natural History (cbc.amnh.org/center/programs/metro.html), the Metropolitan Flora Project at the Brooklyn Botanic Garden (www.bbg.org/sci/nymf/), the New York chapter of the New York City Audubon Society (www.nycaudubon.org/home/), and WildMetro (www.wildmetro.org/). A subgenre of books is dedicated to the "surprising" wildlife in the midst of New York City; Matthews (2001), Kinkead (1974), and Garber (1987) are representative examples. For a bibliography of the extensive scientific literature on New York City natural resources, see the list compiled by the Institute of Ecosystem Studies, which is available online (www.oasisnyc.net/resources/Bibliography/docs/InstEcosystemStudies.pdf). Numerous individuals who have helped me with the Mannahatta Project are listed in the acknowledgments.

The method of passing the various taxa lists through multiple filters, as described in the main text, is current in restoration ecology; see Temperton et al. (2004). Restoration ecology is the science of healing nature through human interventions (Van Andel and Aronson 2005; Falk, Palmer, and Zedler 2006).

The Plants and Animals of Mannahatta

The plant list was compiled from the following sources: Art (1976); Bicknell (1925); Buegler and Parisio (1981); Buell et al. (1966); Cain (1936); Cain and Penfound (1938); Cain, Nelson, and McLean (1937); Clemants and Moore 2003); Conrad (1935); Davidson and Buell (1967); DeCandido, Muir, and Gargiullo (2004); Dowhan et al. (1997); Frankel (1978, 1979); Gleason (1935); Gratacap and Woodward (1884); Greller (1975); Greller (1977, 1979, 1985, 1991); Hollick and Britton (1879, 1930); Honkala and McAninch (1980); LeConte (1812); Loeb (1986); Luttenberg, Lev, and Feller (1993); Lynn and Karlin (1985); McIntosh (1972); Poggenburg et al. (1888); Rawolle and Pilat (1857); Robinson, Yurlina, and Handel (1994); Small (1935); Stalter (1981); Stalter and Lamont (1987); Taylor (1915); Torrey, Eddy, and Knevels (1817); Tulig and Thiers (2004); and Weiss et al. (1995).

Nomenclature for the plants was standardized according to the Plants Database of the U.S. Department of Agriculture and the National Resources Conservation Service (USDA and NRCS 2002); some older names were assigned to modern designations through consultation with the International Plant Names Index, available online (www.ipni.org), and with Mitchell (1997) and Gleason (1991).

The fish list was compiled from the following sources: Briggs and Waldman (2002); Dowhan et al. (1997); Halliwell, Whittier, and Ringler (2001); Lake (2007); Nichols (1913); Rachlin, Pappantoniou, and Warkentine (2001); Schmidt (1986); Smith and Lake (1990); Van Holt, Murphy, and Chapman (2006); Weigmann and Nichols (1915); Whittier, Halliwell, and Daniels (1999); and Zeisel (1990). Fishbase, the online database (www.fishbase.org), was used as the nomenclatural reference.

The reptile and amphibian list was compiled from the following sources: American Museum of Natural History (2007), Bishop (1941), Davis (1884), Deckert (1914), Digiovanni (2008), Ditmars (1896, 1905, 1905), Engelhardt et al. (1915), Feinberg and Burke (2001), Fisher (1920), Gibbs et al. (2007), Lake (2007), Macauley (1829), Mathewson (1935), Murphy (1916), Myers (1929), Pehek (2007), Sherwood (1895, 1898), U.S. Fish and Wildlife Service (2007), and Yeaton (1972). Gibbs et al. (2007) was used as the nomenclatural reference.

The bird list was compiled from the following sources: Bull (1964, 1970); Cruickshank (1942); Davis (1991); Davis (1994); Delaney, Serrano, and Cox (2002); Fiore (1998); Fisher and Benzener (1998); Fowle and Kerlinger (2001); Freedman (1998); Hornaday (1909); Joost (2008); Koeppel (2000); Kreshkoff and Winn (undated); Lawrence (1889); Levine (1998); Sloan (2007); and Zeranski and Baptist (1990). The American Ornithological Union's checklist of North American birds, available online (www.aou.org/checklist/index.php3), was used as the nomenclatural reference.

The mammal list was compiled from the following sources: American Museum of Natural History (2007), Anonymous (1647), Beebe (1953), Coastal Research and Education Society of Long Island (2007), Connor (1971), De Laet (1640), De Rasieres (1628), De Vries (1655), DeKay (1842), Digiovanni (2008), Gompper (2002), Hornaday (1909), Koeppel (2000), Neuman (1902), Riker (1881), Roosevelt (1891), Rowley (1902), Sanderson (2006), Van der Donck (1650), Van Wassenaer (1624–30), Wilson (1892), and Zahler (2008). The nomenclatural reference was the Integrated Taxonomic Information System database, available online (www.itis.gov/info.html).

Other taxa received less complete treatment. For marine invertebrates, we consulted Bachand (1994), Crowder (1931), Pollock (1998), and Weiss et al. (1995); for terrestrial invertebrates, Beutenmuller (1893, 1902), Borror and White (1970), Boyd (1978), Glassberg (1993), Gochfeld and Burger (1997), Hoback and Riggins (2001), Johnson and Catley (2002), Lutz (1941), Matteson (2006), Tudor et al. (2001), Wagerik (1999), and Walter (2001); for freshwater invertebrates, Crocker (1957), Daniels (1998), Strayer and Jirka (1997), and Voshell (2002); for lichens, Brodo (1968) and Halsey (1823); for fungi, Fergus and Fergus (2003), Lincoff (2001–2), and Torrey, Eddy, and Knevels (1817); for mosses, Britton (1899), Cain, Nelson, and McLean (1937), Cain and Penfound (1938), Grout (1916), Leonardi (1987), and Leonardi and Thiers (1987); for marine algae, Conrad (1935), Hylander (1928), and Martindale (1889). We also consulted general natural history references that cover multiple taxa, including Dowhan et al. (1997), Kieran (1959), Mittelbach and Crewdson (1997), Waldman (1999), and Weiss et al. (1995).

New York's importance to migratory birds was observed by Beebe, who wrote of an evening's observations: "Still more realistic did migration become when I once spent a night in the head of the Statue of Liberty, and watched the tiny wrens and warblers shoot into the light, like golden bees, either to sheer outward and disappear into the safety of darkness, or to crash head-on against the glass and drift down, down—pitiful, disorder, lifeless fluffs of feathers" (1924). Unfortunately, the lights of New York continue to be a hazard to migratory birds in spring and fall—see Sloan (2007).

A summary of major introductions, including that of the starling, is provided by Crewdson (1996); for a primer on the ecological problems created by introductions of species from other places, see Lockwood, Hoopes, and Marchetti (2006). For an account of Hal, the coyote who discovered Central Park, see Barron (2006)—like Hudson, he came to an untimely end. Fener et al. (2005) describes the ongoing colonization of New York State by the coyote (*Canis latrans*). Peterson wrote about birds crossing the George Washington Bridge: "When I first came to New York City as an art student nearly seventy years ago, I had to take the 125th Street ferry across the Hudson if I wished to see cardinals or tufted titmice. They were common on the Palisades in New Jersey, but it was only after the big bridge was built that I saw my first cardinal and my first titmouse on the New York side of the river. . . . [T]hese relatively nonmigratory birds might have made the crossing strut by strut and span by span on the new bridge" (2007).

Connecting the Parts
Accessible, popular accounts of network science can be found in Buchanan (2002) and Barabási (2003). May (2006) and Proulx, Promislow, and Phillips (2005) provide recent reviews into the biological implications of network theory. This is a rapidly developing field of science that integrates insights in biology, mathematics, and computer science.

A Grammar of Habitat
To document the habitat relationships for "likely" species in the Mannahatta Muir web, we relied heavily on field guides and natural histories. For the plants we consulted Eastman (1992, 1995, 2003), Gleason and Cronquist (1991), Little (1980), Taylor (1915), Thieret, Niering, and Olmstead (2001), and Torrey, Eddy, and Knevels (1817); for the fishes, Froese and Pauly (2007), McClane (1978, 1978), and Werner (2004); for the amphibians and reptiles, Gibbs et al. (2007); for the birds, Bull and Farrand (1994), Cornell Lab of Ornithology (2007), Dunne (2006), and Eastman (1997, 1999, 2000); for the mammals, Palmer (1954) and Whitaker (1996); for insect groups, Borror and White (1970); and for multiple taxa, Bachand (1994), Benyus (1989), and Martin, Zim, and Nelson (1951). We consulted the general references on soil science, hydrology, and geology cited in the notes for Chapter 3 for abiotic factors.

Seeing the Invisible
Muir's insight vis-à-vis the connectivity of nature is from Muir (1911). The concept of the "Muir web" came about as part of the Mannahatta Project. The Muir webs were constructed in a relational database, Microsoft Access (Microsoft, Redmond, WA), and analyzed with a series of perl scripts and freeware network-analysis programs like Pajek (vlado.fmf.uni-lj.si/pub/networks/pajek/) and Network Workbench (nwb.slis.indiana.edu/index.html).

The Resiliency of Groups
Interestingly, the recent trend in food-web studies has been to compartmentalize, rather than expand, groups. By placing species with similar trophic positions together in one group, the logic goes, it is easier to see the network structure. Of course the pattern of grouping is a strong predictor of the network structure one sees. Recognizing groups as identified commonly in field guides and natural histories and expanding them bucks this trend, and also threatens to overwhelm the computing resources for visualization and analysis.

The Mannahatta Time Machine

Markley Boyer used the software package Visual Nature Studio 3 (3D Nature, LLC, Morrison, CO) to build the scenes of Mannahatta, using a combination of constructed tree models and photographs of living trees. Tree models were built using Xfrog 3 (Greenworks Organic Software, Berlin, Germany). Some reconstructions include vertical exaggeration to emphasize the typography. The resulting images represent scientifically reconstructed views, inclusive of all the factors discussed in the book: topography, soils, waters, disturbance processes, and species distributions (including people), interpolated into the geography of New York City. Nevertheless they are not the same as photographs. The human eye and brain evolved over millennia to recognize small anomalies in natural landscapes; we can detect when a tree is right and when it is wrong, the passage of an animal in the grass. Computers have not yet achieved the simple perfection of a lovely September afternoon in the woods.

CHAPTER 7

One pleasure of the early twenty-first century is the remarkable number of good, concrete ideas about how to make more cities livable and sustainable, many of which can be implemented with existing technology (e.g., Register 2002, Hiss 1990, Beatley 2000, Kahn 2006, Jacobs 1961, Breen and Rigby 2004). These ideas stem from a broad-based critique of late twentieth-century urban policy and suburban development in the United States, particularly from an environmental perspective (Duany, Plater-Zyberk, and Speck 2000; Gillham 2002; Gandy 2002; Burchell et al. 2005; Kunstler 1996; among others).

See notes from Chapter 1 about population figures for New York City. Statistics on commuters traveling into Manhattan are provided in Bram and McKay (2005); tourism numbers are from the city tourism agency NYC and Company (nycvisit.com). Urbanization trends are sourced in the notes from Chapter 1. Jervey (2006) is a resource for green living in New York City.

Food

For a history of garbage in New York, see Miller (2000); for the statistics behind the pile of fast-food waste, see Murphy (1998). The case for local foods has been made cogently by Pollan (2006), Nabhan (2002), and others. Linder and Zacharias's book (1999) fills in the largely forgotten history of farming in Brooklyn, underscoring the case with nineteenth-century agricultural statistics. The resurgence of specialty farms in the Hudson Valley is described by Greenberg (2003), and the list of fresh fruits and vegetables grown in the Garden State is available online (www.state.nj.us/jerseyfresh/index.html). The analysis of land use within a hundred miles of New York City is based on the National Land Cover Database (Multi-Resolution Land Characteristics Consortium [MRLC] 2001). The remarkable recovery of fish in New York Harbor is documented in Steinberg et al. (2004). The historical figures on the oyster catch are from Waldman (1999); also see Kurlansky (2006). The shad statistic is from MacKenzie (1992); the sturgeon number from Boyle (1969). The account of changing winter foods is from Whitman (1996).

Jasper Danckaerts (James and Jameson 1913) provides a wonderful description of a meal in Brooklyn in 1679:

> There had been already thrown upon it [the fire of oak and hickory], to be roasted, a pail-full of Gouanes [Gowanus] oysters, which are the best in the country. They are fully as good as those of England, and better than those we [eat] at Falmouth [in Massachusetts]. I had to try some of them raw. They are large and full, some of them not less than a foot long, and they sometimes grow ten, twelve and sixteen together, and are then like a piece of rock. Others are young and small. . . . We had for supper a roasted haunch of venison, which we had bought [off] the Indians for three guilders and half of *seewant* [wampum]. . . and which weighed thirty pounds. The meat was exceedingly tender and good, and also quite fat. It had a slight spicy flavor. We were also served with wild turkey, which was also fat and of a good flavor; and a wild

goose, but that was rather dry. Everything we had was [from] the natural production of the country. We saw here, lying in a heap, a whole hill of watermelons, which were as large as pumpkins.

Water

The history of the Collect Pond can be read in Koeppel (2000). The storage figure for the modern Catskills/Delaware Watersheds is from the New York City Department of Environmental Protection (www.nyc.gov/html/dep/html/drinking_water/history.shtml). The saga of clean water for New York City and its environmental benefits in terms of land protection are described by the U.S. Environmental Protection Agency (www.epa.gov/region02/water/nycshed/filtad.htm). Flow data for the Bronx and Cross rivers in June 2008 in the graph on page 220 are from the U.S. Geological Survey's National Water Information System (waterdata.usgs.gov/nwis/rt). The Staten Island bluebelt is detailed in Vokral et al. (2003); the successful application of water gardens and other green design features as an integrated whole, in Corbett and Corbett (2000); the ecological characteristics of green roofs, in Oberndorfer et al. (2007). Arnold (1996) describes the less desirable aspects of impervious surfaces. Statistics about New York's combined-sewer overflows can be found online (www.bronxriver.org/swimmableNYC.cfm); also see Plumb (2007). The history of the waterfront development is adapted from Buttenweiser (1987) and Bone (2004).

Shelter

Representative examples of sustainable building design and essays explaining its principles can be found in Gissen (2002), Buchanan (2005), and the Earth Pledge Foundation (2000). Alexander (1977) is a classic text, drenched with good ideas. Leadership in Energy and Environmental Design (LEED) standards from the U.S. Green Building Council cover many areas of energy-efficient and environmentally friendly design and are worthy of study (www.usgbc.org). The Flatiron Building's deflected winds led to the "23 skiddoo," when police officers would usher along the men loitering around Twenty-third Street in order to see women's ankles exposed by errant winds.

Energy and Transportation

Analysis of New York City's electricity requirements is from the New York City Energy Policy Task Force (2004). Sources of energy are provided by the New York State Energy Research and Development Authority (2007) and derived from analysis of the eGRID database, available online (www.epa.gov/cleanenergy/energy-resources/egrid/index.html). The average amount of electricity used per capita shown in the graph on page 228 for the United States as a whole and for New York City are from City of New York Office of Long-term Planning and Sustainability (2007) and, for Tanzania, from the United Nations Common Database (data.un.org). The Tanzanian data is meant as an example of the unequal distribution of resources and not as an ideal for future electricity use. With respect to the energy supply, New York City is not atypical of the nation as a whole in its very low dependence on renewable sources—which in 2008 was less than 1 percent in most states. Musial and Butterfield (2004) estimate that the potential offshore wind energy supply for the United States is in excess of a thousand gigawatts; Musial, Butterfield, and B. Ram (2006) provide an analysis of the costs and benefits of developing this resource. Approximately one half of the U.S. offshore wind potential is in New England and the mid-Atlantic waters. In their report, Rickerson et al. (2007) summarize increasing photovoltaic solar use in the city.

The statistics on New York City transit use are from the American Public Transportation Association (2007). In their report, Sanderson and Brown (2007) provide a historical analysis of Manhattan land use, comparing 1609, 1782, and 2004—from which the street and sidewalk usage calculation is drawn. Various authors have suggested ways of making the streets of New York more pedestrian-friendly; see, for example, Breines and Dean (1974). For a summary of the case for bicycles in the city, see New York City Department of City Planning (1997); also see information online from Transportation Alternatives (www.transalt.org). The New York City Department of Transportation estimates in its report (2008) that the number of bicycle commuters in New York increased 77 percent between 2001 and 2007, though cycling still accounts for less than 1 percent of commuter trips in the city. The modern case for streetcars has recently been made in Ohland and Poticha (2006). Bus rapid transit provides another public-transportation alternative to cars; see Levinson et al. (2003). For more photographs of the once ubiquitous Manhattan streetcar, see Meyers (2005). The state of U.S. streetcars in 1902 is summarized in Steuart (1905), from which the table on page 233 is derived. The idea for moving materials underground comes from Crawford (2002). The benefits of transit-oriented development are summarized in Dittmar and Ohland (2004).

Raising the Kids
The value of conservation in cities is described in Miller and Hobbs (2002) and Fuller et al. (2007). One of the ironies of Robert Moses's vision for New York is that although he is remembered for the destruction of communities from his roadwork, one of his primary motivations for building roads was to give urbanites access to parks in the surrounding rural areas (Caro 1974)—though his notion of parks emphasized structured exercise and socializing, rather than nature conservation; a slight tweak would have made a world of difference. The case for unstructured outdoor play for children is made by Louv (2005) and others. Estimates of the cost of saving nature at different levels of infrastructural development are made by Balmford et al. (2003). Also note, in Balmford and Whitten (2003), the interesting argument about who should bear the costs of nature conservation— estimated at *less than $300 billion* per year. For mountain lions in New York, see Van Wassenaer (1624–30); for brook trout, see Scott (1989); and for red-tail hawks in love, see Winn (1999).

Manhattan 2409
The estimate of the number of planet Earths we would need if everyone consumed like the average American is from Wilson (2002). To gauge your personal consumption, see ecological footprint calculators provided online at the Global Footprint Network (www.footprintnetwork.org) and similar sites. Plato's comments on the growth of the city-state are from *The Republic* (Cornford 1981); note that Plato conceived of some optimum size of a city, though the exact size is unclear ("it will not be very large, . . . but it will not be so very small either"). It would be enough, in any case, to secure harmony, happiness, and security for all citizens, not just a privileged few—see Cornford's commentary. The Empire State Building was begun on March 17, 1930, and completed on May 1, 1931. For a summary of changes in the harbor, see Steinberg et al. (2004). For an account of José the beaver, who recolonized the Bronx River after a two-hundred-year beaver-free period, see O'Connor (2007). The visualization of the future city from a satellite perspective on page 241 includes an analysis of sea level rise in the New York City region, using the figures in Chapter 3; assumes a housing density comparable to Manhattan's current density in the urban cores; and allows for enough space to house 12 million people in approximately 36 percent of the current area.

Abrams, M. 1992. Fire and the development of oak forests. *BioScience* 42:346–53.

Adams, R. C. 1997. *Legends of the Delaware Indians and picture writing.* Syracuse, NY: Syracuse University Press.

Alexander, C. 1977. *A pattern language: Towns, buildings, construction.* New York: Oxford University Press.

Allan, D. J. 1995. *Stream ecology: Structure and function of running water.* New York: Chapman & Hall.

Alsop III, F. J. 1995. *Birds of the Great Smoky Mountains, a checklist for the birds of Great Smoky Mountains National Park.* Gatlinburg, TN: Great Smoky Mountains Natural History Association, in cooperation with Great Smoky Mountains National Park.

American Museum of Natural History. 2007. Herpetological Collections Database. entheros.amnh.org/db/emuwebamnh/logon.php

———. 2007. Mammalian Collections Database. entheros.amnh.org/db/emuwebamnh/logon.php

American Public Transportation Association. 2007. Public transportation fact book. Washington, D.C. www.apta.com/research/stats/factbook/index.cfm

Anbinder, T. 2001. *Five Points: The 19th-century New York City neighborhood that invented tap dance, stole elections, and became the world's most notorious slum.* New York: Free Press.

Andersen, T. 2002. *This fine piece of water: An environmental history of Long Island Sound.* New Haven, CT: Yale University Press.

Anonymous. 1647. Journal of New Netherland. In *Narratives of New Netherland, 1609–1664*, edited by J. F. Jameson. New York: Barnes & Noble, Inc.

Arnold, C. L. 1996. Impervious surface coverage—the emergence of a key environmental factor. *Journal of the American Planning Association* 62 (2): 243–58.

Aronson, J., S. Dhillon, and E. LeFloc'h. 1995. On the need to select an ecosystem of reference, however imperfect: A reply to Pickett and Parker. *Restoration Ecology* 3 (1): 1–3.

Art, H. W. 1976. *Ecological studies of the Sunken Forest, Fire Island National Seashore, New York.* National Park Service Scientific Monograph Series, vol. 7. Washington, D.C.: National Park Service.

Ascher, K. 2005. *Anatomy of a city.* New York: Penguin Press.

Ashbury, H. 1927. *The gangs of New York: An informal history of the underworld.* New York: Alfred A. Knopf.

Bachand, R. G. 1994. *Coastal Atlantic sea creatures: A natural history.* Norwalk, CT: Sea Sports Publications.

Ballon, H., and K. T. Jackson, eds. 2007. *Robert Moses and the modern city: The transformation of New York.* New York: W. W. Norton.

Balmford, A., K. J. Gaston, S. Blyth, A. James, and V. Kapos. 2003. Global variation in terrestrial conservation costs, conservation benefits, and unmet conservation needs. *Proceedings of the National Academy of Sciences* 100 (3): 1046–50.

Balmford, A., and T. Whitten. 2003. Who should pay for tropical conservation, and how could the costs be met? *Oryx* 37 (2): 238–50.

Barabási, A.-L. 2003. *Linked: How everything is connected to everything else and what it means for business, science and everyday life.* New York: Plume.

Barlow, E. 1969. *The forests and wetlands of New York City.* Boston: Little, Brown and Company.

Barnes, W., and E. Dibble. 1986. The effects of beaver in riverbank forest succession. *Canadian Journal of Botany* 66:40–46.

Baron, W. 1992. Historical climate records from the northeastern United States, 1640 to 1900. In *Climate since A.D. 1500*, edited by R. Bradley and P. Jones. London: Routledge.

Barron, J. 2006. Hal coyote, 1, known for romp in Central Park, is dead. *The New York Times*, April 1, 2006.

Baskerville, C. 1982. The foundation geology of New York City. In *Geology under cities*, edited by R. Legget. Boulder, CO: Geological Society of America Reviews in Engineering Geology.

———. 1994. *Bedrock and engineering geologic maps of New York County and parts of Kings and Queens counties, New York, and parts of Bergen and Hudson counties, New Jersey.* New York: United States Geological Survey.

Bean, W. T. 2004. What made the Harlem Plains a grassland?: Computer modeling for historical ecology of an urban environment. Senior thesis, Department of Ecology, Evolution and Environmental Biology, Columbia University, New York.

Bean, W. T., and E. W. Sanderson. 2008. Using a spatially explicit ecological model to test scenarios of fire use by Native Americans: An example from the Harlem Plains, New York, NY. *Ecological Modelling* 211:301–8.

Beatley, T. 2000. *Green urbanism: Learning from European cities*. Washington, D.C.: Island Press.

Beauchamp, W. M. 1900. Aboriginal occupation of New York. *New York State Museum Bulletin* 32 (7).

———. 1907. Aboriginal place names of New York. *New York State Museum Bulletin* 108.

Beebe, W. 1924. *Galapagos, world's end*. New York: G. P. Putnam's Sons.

———. 1953. *Unseen life of New York as a naturalist sees it*. New York: Duell, Sloan and Pearce.

Begon, M., C. A. Townsend, and J. L. Harper. 2006. *Ecology: From individuals to ecosystems*. New York: Wiley-Blackwell.

Benson, A. B., ed. 1987. *Peter Kalm's travels in North America: The America of 1750*. New York: Dover.

Benson, E. 1849. Memoir, on names, read before the Society, December 13, 1816. *Collections of the New-York Historical Society*, 2nd ser. (2).

Benyus, J. M. 1989. *The field guide to wildlife habitats of the eastern United States*. New York: Fireside.

Berry, W. 1987. *Home economics*. San Francisco: North Point Press.

Bertness, M. D. 2006. *Atlantic shorelines: Natural history and ecology*. Princeton, NJ: Princeton University Press.

Beutenmuller, W. 1893. Descriptive catalogue of the butterflies found within fifty miles of New York City, together with a brief account of their life histories and habits. *Bulletin of the American Museum of Natural History* 5:241–310.

———. 1902. The butterflies of the vicinity of New York City. Supplement to *American Museum Journal* II (5): 1–52.

Bicknell, E. P. 1925. Flora of northern New York City (unpublished manuscript). New York: New York Botanical Garden.

Bierhorst, J. 1995. *Mythology of the Lenape: Guide and texts*. Tucson: University of Arizona Press.

Bishop, S. C. 1941. The salamanders of New York. *New York State Museum Bulletin* 324.

Bokuniewicz, H. 2006. Sedimentary processes in the Hudson River estuary. In *The Hudson River estuary*, edited by J. S. Levington and J. R. Waldman. New York: Cambridge University Press.

Bolton, R. 1881. *The history of several towns, manors, and patents of the county of Westchester, from its first settlement to the present time*. New York: C. F. Roper.

Bolton, R. P. 1905. The Amerindians of Manhattan Island. *Tenth annual report of the American Scenic and Historical Preservation Society*, Appendix C:153–74.

———. 1909. The Indians of Washington Heights. *Anthropological Papers of the American Museum of Natural History* 3:77–109.

———. 1920. *New York City in Indian possession*. New York: Museum of the American Indian, Heye Foundation.

———. 1922. *Indian paths of the great metropolis*. Miscellaneous Series 23. New York: Museum of the American Indian, Heye Foundation.

———. 1924. *Washington Heights, Manhattan, its eventful past*. New York: Dyckman Institute.

———. 1934. *Indian life of long ago in the city of New York*. New York: Bolton Books.

Bone, K., ed. 2004. *The New York waterfront: Evolution and building culture of the port and harbor*. New York: Monacelli Press.

Boose, E., D. Foster, and M. Fluet. 1994. Hurricane impacts to tropical and temperate forest landscapes. *Ecological Monographs* 64:369–400.

Boose, E. R., K. E. Chamberlin, and D. R. Foster. 2001. Landscape and regional impacts of hurricanes in New England. *Ecological Monographs* 71:27–48.

Borgerhoff Mulder, M., and P. Coppolillo. 2005. *Conservation: Linking ecology, economics and culture*. Princeton, NJ: Princeton University Press.

Borror, D. J., and R. E. White. 1970. *A field guide to the insects of America north of Mexico*. The Peterson Field Guide Series. Boston: Houghton Mifflin.

Botti, S. J. 2002. *An illustrated flora of Yosemite National Park*. El Portal, CA: Yosemite Association.

Boul, S. W., R. J. Southard, and R. C. Graham. 2008. *Soil genesis and classification*. New York: Wiley-Blackwell.

Boyd, H. P. 1978. The tiger beetles (Coleoptera: Cicindelidae) of New Jersey with special reference to their ecological relationships. *Transactions of the American Entomological Society* 104:191–242.

Boyle, R. H. 1969. *The Hudson River: A natural and unnatural history*. New York: W. W. Norton.

Bragdon, K. 1996. *Native peoples of southern New England*. Norman, OK: University of Oklahoma Press.

Bram, J., and A. McKay. 2005. The evolution of commuting patterns in the New York City metro area. *Federal Reserve Bank of New York: Current issues in economics and finance: Second District highlights* 11 (10): 1–7.

Brash, A. R. 2007. New York City's primeval forest: A review characterizing the "Type ecosystem." *Transactions of the Linnaean Society of New York* X:55–78.

Breen, A., and D. Rigby. 2004. *Intown living: A different American dream*. Washington, D.C.: Island Press.

Breines, S., and W. J. Dean. 1974. *The pedestrian revolution: Streets without cars*. New York: Random House.

Bridges, P. 1994. Prehistoric diet and health in a coastal New York skeletal sample. *Northeast Anthropology* 48:13–23.

Briggs, P. T., and J. R. Waldman. 2002. Annotated list of fishes reported from the marine waters of New York. *Northeastern Naturalist* 9:47–80.

Britton, E. G. 1899. Musci—mosses. In Lists of plants in the grounds, by N. L. Britton, 1898. *Bulletin of the New York Botanical Garden* 1:195.

Brock, P., and P. Brock. 2001. *Bedrock geology of New York City: More than 600 m.y. of geologic history*. New York: Queens College.

Brodo, I. M. 1968. *The lichens of Long Island, New York: A vegetational and floristic analysis*, *Bulletin of New York State Museum and Science Service*. Albany: University of the State of New York, Albany.

Brun, C. 1959. *Guide to the manuscript maps in the William L. Clements Library*. Ann Arbor: University of Michigan.

Buchanan, M. 2002. *Nexus: Small worlds and the groundbreaking theory of networks*. New York: W. W. Norton.

Buchanan, P. 2005. *Ten shades of green: Architecture and the natural world*. New York: The Architectural League of New York.

Buegler, R., and S. Parisio. 1981. A comparative flora of Staten Island 1879–1981. In A century of change in the Staten Island flora: Ecological correlates of species losses and gains, Robinson, G. R. and Handel, S. N. 1994. *Bulletin of the Torrey Botanical Club* 121 (2): 119–129.

Buell, M. F., A. N. Langford, D. W. Davidson, and L. F. Ohmann. 1966. The upland forest continuum in northern New Jersey. *Ecology* 47 (3): 416–32.

Bull, J. 1964. *Birds of the New York area*. New York: Harper & Row.

———. 1970. Supplements to *Birds of the New York area. Proceedings of the Linnaean Society of New York* 71:1–54.

Bull, J., and J. Farrand. 1994. *National Audubon Society field guide to North American birds: Eastern region*. New York: Alfred A. Knopf.

Burchell, R. W., A. Downs, B. McCann, and S. Mukherji. 2005. *Sprawl costs: Economic impacts of unchecked development*. Washington, D.C.: Island Press.

Burgoyne, B. E. 1990. *A Hessian diary of the American Revolution*. Norman, OK: University of Oklahoma Press.

Burrows, E. G., and M. Wallace. 1999. *Gotham: A history of New York City to 1898*. New York: Oxford University Press.

Buttenweiser, A. L. 1987. *Manhattan water-bound: Planning and developing Manhattan's waterfront from the seventeenth century to the present*. New York: New York University Press.

Cain, S. A. 1936. The composition and structure of an oak woods, Cold Spring Harbor, Long Island, with special attention to sampling methods. *American Midland Naturalist* 17 (4): 725–40.

Cain, S. A., M. Nelson, and W. McLean. 1937. *Andropogonetum hempsteadi*: A Long Island grassland vegetation type. *American Midland Naturalist* 18 (3): 334–50.

Cain, S. A., and W. T. Penfound. 1938. *Aceretum rubri*: The red maple swamp forest of central Long Island. *American Midland Naturalist* 19 (2): 390–416.

Callery, B. G. 1995. Botanical gardens. In *The encyclopedia of New York City*, edited by K. T. Jackson. New Haven, CT: Yale University Press.

Calver, W. L. 1948. Recollections of northern Manhattan. *New-York Historical Society Quarterly* 32:20–31.

Calver, W. L., and R. P. Bolton. 1950. *History written with pick and shovel*. New York: New-York Historical Society.

Cantwell, A.-M., and D. D. Wall. 2001. *Unearthing Gotham: The archaeology of New York City*. New Haven, CT: Yale University Press.

Caro, R. A. 1974. *The power broker*. New York: Vintage Books.

Ceci, L. 1975. Fish fertilizer: A native North American practice? *Science* 188:26–30.

———. 1977. The effect of European contact and trade on the settlement pattern of Indians in coastal New York, 1524–1665. Dissertation, Department of Anthropology, City University of New York, New York.

———. 1979. Maize cultivation in coastal New York: The archeological, agronomical and documentary evidence. *North American Archaeologist* 1:45–74.

———. 1982. Method and theory in coastal New York archaeology: Paradigms of settlement behavior. *North American Archaeologist* 3:5–36.

Chapman, F. M. 1904. Birds' nests and eggs, with an annotated list of the birds known to breed within fifty miles of New York City. Supplement to *American Museum Journal* IV (2): 1–31.

———. 1906. The birds of the vicinity of New York City. *Guide Leaflet to the Collection in the American Museum of Natural History, New York* 22:1–96.

City of New York. 2007. *Adopted budget fiscal year 2008 expense revenue contract*. New York.

City of New York Department of Finance. 2007. *Annual report of the NYC property tax, fiscal year 2007*. New York.

City of New York Office of Long-term Planning and Sustainability. 2007. *PlaNYC: A greener, greater New York*. New York.

Clemants, S., and G. Moore. 2003. Patterns of species richness in eight northeastern United States cities. *Urban Habitats* 1 (1): 3–89.

Clements, F. E. 1916. *Plant succession: An analysis of the development of vegetation*. Washington, D.C.: Carnegie Institution of Washington.

Coastal Research and Education Society of Long Island. 2007. Pinnipeds CRESLI seal research program. www.cresli.org/cresli/seals/sealpage.html

Cochran, J. K., D. J. Hirschberg, and H. Feng. 2006. Reconstructing sediment chronologies in the Hudson River estuary. In *The Hudson River estuary*, edited by J. S. Levington and J. R. Waldman. New York: Cambridge University Press.

Cohen, P. 1988. "Civic folly": The man who measured Manhattan. *AB Bookman's Weekly* 81 (24): 2511–15.

Cohen, P. E., and R. T. Augustyn. 1997. *Manhattan in maps 1527–1995*. New York: Rizzoli.

Colden, C. 1750. Plantae Coldenghamiae in Provincia Noveboracensi Americes sponte crescentes: Quas ad methodum Cl. Linnæi sexualem, anno 1742, &c. observavit & descripsit. Published in two parts by C. Linnæus, *Acta societatis regiae scientiarum Upsaliensis* 4 (1743): 81–136, and 5 (1744–50): 47–82.

Connor, P. F. 1971. The mammals of Long Island, New York. *New York State Museum Science Service Bulletin* 416:1–78.

Conrad, H. S. 1935. The plant associations of central Long Island. *American Midland Naturalist* 16 (4): 433–516.

Cook, E. R., and G. C. Jacoby. 1977. Tree-ring-drought relationships in the Hudson Valley, New York. *Science* 198:399–401.

———. 1979. Evidence for quasi-periodic July drought in the Hudson Valley, New York. *Nature* 282:390–92.

Cook, E. R., and P. Mayes. 1987. Decadal-scale patterns of climatic change over eastern North America inferred from tree rings. In *Abrupt climate change: Evidence and implications*, edited by W. Berger and L. Labeyrie. NATO Advanced Study Institutes' Series C.

Cook, S. F. 1976. *The Indian population of New England in the seventeenth century.* Berkeley: University of California Press.

Corbett, J., and M. Corbett. 2000. *Designing sustainable communities: Learning from village homes.* Washington, D.C.: Island Press.

Cornell Lab of Ornithology. 2007. All about birds. www.birds.cornell.edu/AllAboutBirds/ (accessed March–October 2007).

Cornford, F. M., ed. 1981. *"The Republic" of Plato.* London: Oxford University Press.

Cozzens, I. 1843. *A geological history of Manhattan or New York Island.* New York: W. E. Dean.

Crawford, J. H. 2002. *Carfree cities.* Utrecht: International Books.

Crewdson, M., and M. Dion. 1996. Alien invaders—they came from planet Earth. In *Concrete jungle*, edited by M. Dion and A. Rockman. New York: Juno Books.

Crocker, D. 1957. *The crayfishes of New York State.* Albany, NY: New York State Museum and Science Service.

Cronon, W. 1983. *Changes in the land: Indians, colonists and the ecology of New England.* New York: Hill and Wang.

Crowder, W. 1931. *Seashore life between the tides.* New York: Dover.

Cruickshank, A. D. 1942. *Birds around New York City: Where and when to find them.* The American Museum of Natural History Handbook Series, no. 13. New York: The American Museum of Natural History.

Daniels, R. A. 1998. Changes in the distribution of stream-dwelling crayfishes in the Schoharie Creek system, eastern New York State. *Northeastern Naturalist* 53 (2): 231–48.

Davidson, D. W., and M. F. Buell. 1967. Shrub and herb continua of upland forests of northern New Jersey. *American Midland Naturalist* 77 (2): 371–89.

Davis, R. 1991. *Wild birds of the New York Zoological Park.* Bronx, NY: New York Zoological Society.

Davis, T. R. 1994. *Birds of the Jamaica Bay Wildlife Refuge.* Queens, NY: U.S. National Park Service, Gateway National Recreation Area.

Davis, W. T. 1884. The reptiles and batrachians of Staten Island. *Proceedings of the Natural Science Association of Staten Island* 1:13.

Day, G. M. 1953. The Indian as an ecological factor in the northeastern forest. *Ecology* 34 (2): 329–46.

de Laet, J. 1640. New World. In *Narratives of New Netherland, 1609–1664*, edited by J. F. Jameson. New York: Barnes & Noble, Inc.

de Rasieres, I. [1628?]. Letter of Isaack de Raiseres to Samuel Blommaert. In *Narratives of New Netherland, 1609–1664*, edited by J. F. Jameson. New York: Barnes & Noble, Inc.

de Vries, D. P. 1655. Korte historiael ende journaels aenteyckeninge. In *Narratives of New Netherland, 1609–1664*, edited by J. F. Jameson. New York: Barnes & Noble, Inc.

Dean, W. J. 2008. Manhattan's straight streets. *New York Law Journal.* April 17.

DeCandido, R., A. Muir, and M. B. Gargiullo. 2004. A first approximation of the historical and extant vascular flora of New York City: Implications for native plant species conservation. *Journal of Torrey Botanical Society* 131 (3): 243–51.

Deckert, R. F. 1914. Salamanders collected in Westchester County, New York. *Copeia* 13:3–4.

DeKay, J. E. 1842. *Natural History of New York.* Part I, *Zoology.* Albany, NY: Thurlow Weed.

Delaney, J., J. Serrano, and K. Cox. 2002. (Pers. comm.) Spring birds along the Bronx River in the Bronx Zoo. New York.

Despain, D. G. 1991. *Yellowstone vegetation: Consequences of environment and history in a natural setting.* Lanham, MD: Roberts Rinehart Publishers.

Diamant, L. 2004. *Chaining the Hudson: The fight for the river in the American Revolution.* New York: Fordham University Press.

Diamond, J. 1987. The worst mistake in the history of the human race. *Discover Magazine,* May:64–66.

Dickens, C. 1842. *American notes, for general circulation.* London: Harper & Brothers.

Digiovanni, R. 2008. (Pers. comm.) Marine turtles and marine mammals of New York Harbor. Riverhead, NY.

Dimmick, F. 1994. Creative farmers of the Northeast: A new view of Indian maize horticulture. *North American Archaeologist* 15:235–52.

Ditmars, R. L. 1896. The snakes found within fifty miles of New York City. *Proceedings of the Linnaean Society of New York* 8:9–24.

———. 1905. The batrachians of the vicinity of New York City. *American Museum Journal* 5: 160–206.

———. 1905. The reptiles of the vicinity of New York City. *Journal of the American Museum of Natural History* 5:93–140.

Dittmar, H., and G. Ohland, eds. 2004. *The new transit town: Best practices in transit-oriented development.* Washington, D.C.: Island Press.

Dowhan, J., T. Halavik, A. Milliken, A. MacLachlan, M. Caplis, K. Lima, and A. Zimba. 1997. *Significant habitats and habitat complexes of the New York Bight Watershed.* Charlestown, RI: U.S. Fish and Wildlife Service, Southern New England–New York Bight Coastal Ecosystems Program.

Duany, A., E. Plater-Zyberk, and J. Speck. 2000. *Suburban nation: The rise of sprawl and the decline of the American dream.* New York: North Point Press.

Dunne, P. 2006. *Pete Dunne's essential field guide companion.* Boston: Houghton Mifflin.

Dunshee, K. H. 1952. *The firefighter's guide to old New York.* New York: Bibliographic Press.

Dunwiddie, P., D. Foster, D. Leopold, and R. T. Leverett. 1996. Old-growth forests of southern New England, New York and Pennsylvania. In *Eastern old-growth forests: Prospects for rediscovery and recovery,* edited by M. B. Davis. Washington, D.C.: Island Press.

Earth Pledge Foundation, ed. 2000. *Sustainable architecture.* Laval, Quebec: Quebecor Printing, Inc.

Eastman, J. 1992. *The book of forest and thicket.* Mechanicsburg, PA: Stackpole Books.

———. 1995. *The book of swamp and bog.* Mechanicsburg, PA: Stackpole Books.

———. 1997. *Birds of forest, yard and thicket.* Mechanicsburg, PA: Stackpole Books.

———. 1999. *Birds of lake, pond and marsh.* Mechanicsburg, PA: Stackpole Books.

———. 2000. *Birds of field and shore.* Mechanicsburg, PA: Stackpole Books.

———. 2003. *The book of field and roadside.* Mechanicsburg, PA: Stackpole Books.

Edinger, G. J., D. J. Evans, S. Gabauer, T. G. Howard, D. M. Hunt, and A. M. Olivero. 2002. *Ecological communities of New York State.* 2nd ed. A revised and expanded version of Carol Reschke's *Ecological communities of New York State* (draft for review). Albany, NY: New York Natural Heritage Program, New York State Department of Environmental Conservation.

Egan, D., and E. A. Howell. 2001. *The historical ecology handbook: A restorationist's guide to reference ecosystems.* Washington, D.C.: Island Press.

Engelhardt, G. P., J. T. Nichols, R. Latham, and R. C. Murphy. 1915. Long Island snakes. *Copeia* 17:1–4.

Falk, D. A., M. A. Palmer, and J. B. Zedler, eds. 2006. *Foundations of restoration ecology.* Washington, D.C.: Island Press.

Fayden, M. P. 1993. Indian corn and Dutch pots: 17th century foodways in New Amsterdam/ New York City. Dissertation, City University of New York, New York.

Feinberg, J. A., and R. L. Burke. 2001. *Amphibians and reptiles of Long Island, Staten Island and Manhattan.* people.hofstra.edu/faculty/russell_l_burke/HerpKey/.

Feirstein, S. 2001. *Naming New York: Manhattan places & how they got their names.* New York: New York University Press.

Fener, H. M., J. R. Ginsberg, E. W. Sanderson, and M. E. Gompper. 2005. Chronology of range expansion of the coyote, *Canis latrans,* in New York. *Canadian Field-Naturalist* 119 (1): 1–5.

Fenn, G. M., ed. 1903. *Memoir of Benjamin Franklin Stevens.* London: Chiswick Press.

Fergus, C. L., and C. Fergus. 2003. *Common edible & poisonous mushrooms of the Northeast.* Mechanicsburg, PA: Stackpole Books.

Finch, J. 1909. Aboriginal remains on Manhattan Island. *Anthropological Papers of the American Museum of Natural History* 3:65–73.

Finney, M. A. 1998. FARSITE: Fire Area Simulator—model development and evaluation. Ogden, UT: U.S. Department of Agriculture, Forest Service, Rocky Mountain Research Station.

Fiore, T. 1998. Birds through the year in Central Park. In *Red-tails in love: A wildlife drama in Central Park*, edited by M. Winn. New York: Vintage Departures.

Fisher, C. C., and A. Benzener. 1998. *Birds of New York City, western Long Island and northeastern New Jersey.* Renton, WA: Lone Pine Publishing.

Fisher, G. C. 1920. A spadefoot in summer. *Copeia* 85:76–78.

Fitzgerald, F. S. 1925. *The great Gatsby.* New York: Charles Schribner's Sons.

Forman, R. T. T., and M. Godron. 1986. *Landscape ecology.* New York: John Wiley & Sons.

Foster, D. R., S. Clayden, D. A. Orwig, B. Hall, and S. Barry. 2002. Oak, chestnut and fire: Climatic and cultural controls of long-term forest dynamics in New England. *Journal of Biogeography* 29:1359–79.

Foster, D. R., and J. F. O'Keefe. 2000. *New England forests through time: Insights from the Harvard Forests Dioramas.* Cambridge, MA: Harvard University Press.

Fowle, M. T., and P. Kerlinger. 2001. *The New York City Audubon Society guide to finding birds in the metropolitan area.* Ithaca, NY: Comstock Publishing Associates.

Frank, R. 2007. Where do all the millionaires live? *Wall Street Journal.com.* May 2, 2007. blogs.wsj.com/wealth/2007/05/02/where-do-all-the-millionaires-live/.

Frankel, E. 1978. A floristic survey of the vascular plants of the Bronx River Park in Westchester County, New York. *Bulletin of the Torrey Botanical Club* 105 (2): 147–55.

———. 1979. A floristic survey of the vascular plants of the Bronx River Park in Westchester County, New York. Supplement 1977–78. *Bulletin of the Torrey Botanical Club* 106 (1): 46–47.

Freedman, S. 1998. Migrating hawks over Central Park. In *Red-tails in love: A wildlife drama in Central Park*, edited by M. Winn. New York: Vintage Departures.

Froese, R., and D. Pauly. 2007. Fishbase (version 12/2007). www.fishbase.org (accessed July–December 2007).

Fuller, R. A., K. N. Irvine, P. Devine-Wright, P. H. Warren, and K. J. Gaston. 2007. Psychological benefits of greenspace increase with biodiversity. *Biology Letters* 3 (4): 390–94.

Gallagher, J. J. 1995. *The Battle of Brooklyn 1776.* Edison, NJ: Castle Books.

Gandy, M. 2002. *Concrete and clay: Reworking nature in New York City.* Cambridge, MA: The MIT Press.

Garber, S. D. 1987. *The urban naturalist.* Mineola, NY: Dover.

Gehring, C. T., ed. 1980. *New York historical manuscripts: Dutch.* Vols. gg, hh and ii, *Land papers.* Baltimore, MD: Genealogical Publishing Co., Inc.

Gehring, C. T., and R. S. Grumet. 1987. Observations of the Indians from Jasper Danckaerts's journal, 1679–1680. *William and Mary Quarterly* 44:104–20.

Geyer, W. R., and R. Chant. 2006. The physical oceanography processes in the Hudson River estuary. In *The Hudson River estuary*, edited by J. S. Levington and J. R. Waldman. New York: Cambridge University Press.

Gibbs, J. P., A. R. Breisch, P. K. Ducey, G. Johnson, J. L. Behler, and R. C. Bothner. 2007. *The amphibians and reptiles of New York State: Identification, natural history and conservation.* New York: Oxford University Press.

Gillham, O. 2002. *The limitless city: A primer on the urban sprawl debate.* Washington, D.C.: Island Press.

Gilmore, R. S. 1995. Fortifications. In *The encyclopedia of New York City*, edited by K. T. Jackson. New Haven, CT: Yale University Press.

Gissen, D. 2002. *Big & green: Toward sustainable architecture in the 21st century.* Princeton, NJ: Princeton Architectural Press.

Glassberg, J. 1993. *Butterflies through binoculars: A field and finding guide to butterflies in the Boston–New York–Washington region*. New York: Oxford University Press.

Gleason, H. A. 1926. The individualistic concept of the plant association. *Bulletin of the Torrey Botanical Club* 53 (1): 7–26.

Gleason, H. A. 1935. *Plants of the vicinity of New York*. Bronx, NY: New York Botanical Garden.

Gleason, H. A., and A. Cronquist. 1991. *Manual of vascular plants of northeastern United States and adjacent Canada*. Bronx, NY: New York Botanical Garden.

Gochfeld, M., and J. Burger. 1997. *Butterflies of New Jersey: A guide to their status, distribution, conservation and appreciation*. New Brunswick, NJ: Rutgers University Press.

Gompper, M. 2002. The Ecology of northeast coyotes: Current knowledge and priorities for future research. *Wildlife Conservation Society Working Paper* 17:1–52.

Gould, C. G. 2004. *The remarkable life of William Beebe: Explorer and naturalist*. Washington, D.C.: Shearwater Books.

Gratacap, L. P. 1904. *Geology of the city of New York*. New York: Henry Holt and Company.

Gratacap, L. P., and A. Woodward. 1884. *The fresh water flora and fauna of Central Park*. New York: Macgowan & Slipper.

Graves, A. H. 1945. Damage to trees in New York City in the hurricane of September 14, 1944. *Torreya* 44:66–73.

Greenberg, J. 2003. *Hudson Valley harvest*. Woodstock, VT: Countryman Press.

Greller, A. M. 1972. Observations on the forests of northern Queens County, Long Island, from colonial times to the present. *Bulletin of the Torrey Botanical Club* 99 (2): 202–6.

———. 1975. Persisting natural vegetation in northern Queens County, New York, with proposals for its conservation. *Environmental Conservation* 2 (1): 61–71.

———. 1977. A vascular flora of the forested portion of Cunningham Park, Queens County, New York, with notes on the vegetation. *Bulletin of the Torrey Botanical Club* 104 (2): 170–76.

———. 1979. A vascular flora of the forested portion of Cunningham Park, Queens County, New York: Corrections and additions. *Bulletin of the Torrey Botanical Club* 106 (1): 45.

———. 1985. A vascular flora of the forested portion of Cunningham Park, Queens County, New York: Corrections and additions—II. *Bulletin of the Torrey Botanical Club* 112 (3): 312.

———. 1991. A vascular flora of the forested portion of Cunningham Park, Queens County, New York: Corrections and additions—III. *Bulletin of the Torrey Botanical Club* 118 (3): 330–32.

Griswold, W. A. 2003. *The ground beneath her feet: The archeology of Liberty Island, Statue of Liberty National Monument, New York, New York*. Boston: U.S. Department of the Interior, National Park Service.

Grondahl, P. 2004. *I rose like a rocket: The political education of Theodore Roosevelt*. New York: Free Press.

Gronim, S. S. 2001. Geography and persuasion: Maps in British colonial New York. *William and Mary Quarterly* 58 (2): 373–402.

Groom, M. J., G. K. Meffe, and C. R. Carroll. 2006. *Principles of conservation biology*. Sunderland, MA: Sinauer Associates, Inc.

Grout, A. J. 1916. *The moss flora of New York City and vicinity*. New Dorp, Staten Island, NY: Published by author.

Grumet, R. 1989. *The Lenapes*. Edited by F. Porter, *Indians of North America*. New York: Chelsea House Publishers.

Grumet, R. S. 1981. *Native American place names in New York City*. New York: Museum of the City of New York.

Guthorn, P. J. 1972. *British maps of the American Revolution*. Monmouth Beach, NJ: Phillip Freneau Press.

———. 1974. *British maps of colonial America*. Edited by D. Woodward, for the Kenneth Nebenzahl, Jr., lectures in the history of cartography at the Newberry Library. Chicago: University of Chicago Press.

Halliwell, D. B., T. R. Whittier, and N. H. Ringler. 2001. Distributions of lake fishes of the northeast USA—III. Salmonidae and associated coldwater species. *Northeastern Naturalist* 8:189–206.

Halsey, A. 1823. Synoptical view of the lichens growing in the vicinity of the city of New York. *Annals of the Lyceum of Natural History of New York*. June 16.

Hanley, T., and M. M. Graff. 1976. *Rock trails of Central Park*. New York: Greensward Foundation, Inc.

Harley, J. B. 1978. *Mapping the American Revolutionary War*. Chicago: University of Chicago Press.

Harper, R. M. 1911. The Hempstead Plains: A natural prairie on Long Island. *Bulletin of American Geographical Society* 43:351–60.

Harrington, M. R. 1909. Ancient Indian shell heaps near New York City. *Anthropological Papers of the American Museum of Natural History* 3:169–82.

Haswell, C. H. 1896. *Reminiscences of New York by an octogenarian (1816 to 1860)*. New York: Harper & Brothers.

Heckewelder, J. 1876. *History, manners, and customs of the Indian nations who once inhabited Pennsylvania and neighboring states*. Philadelphia: The Historical Society of Pennsylvania.

Heinrich, B. 2003. *Winter world: The ingenuity of animal survival*. New York: Ecco.

Herbster, H., J. C. Garman, J. Schuldenrein, and D. Thieme. 1997. *Phase IB archaeological survey of the Governors Island National Historic Landmark District*. Pawtucket, RI: Public Archaeology Laboratory, Inc.

Hibbert, C. 1990. *Redcoats and Rebels: The American Revolution through British eyes*. New York: Avon Books.

Hill, G. E., and G. E. Waring, Jr. 1897. Old wells and water-courses on the isle of Manhattan, part I. In *Historic New York: Being the first series of the* Half Moon *papers*, edited by M. W. Goodwin, A. C. Royce, and R. Putnam. New York: G. P. Putnam's Sons.

———. 1897. Old wells and water-courses on the isle of Manhattan, part II. In *Historic New York: Being the first series of the* Half Moon *papers*, edited by M. W. Goodwin, A. C. Royce, and R. Putnam. New York: G. P. Putnam's Sons.

Hiss, T. 1990. *The experience of place*. New York: Vintage Books.

Hitakonanu'laak. 2005. *The grandfathers speak: Native American folk tales of the Lenapé people*. New York: Interlink Books.

Hoback, W. W., and J. J. Riggins, eds. 2001. *Tiger beetles of the United States*. Jamestown, ND: Northern Prairie Wildlife Research Center Online.

Hollick, C. A., and N. L. Britton. 1879. *The flora of Richmond County*. Staten Island, NY: Published by author.

———. 1930. Survey of the flora of Richmond County, New York (unpublished). Staten Island, NY.

Honkala, D. A., and J. B. McAninch. 1980. *The New York Botanical Garden forest project*. Bronx, NY: New York Botanical Garden.

Horenstein, S. 2007. Inwood Hill and Isham parks: Geology, geography and history. *Transactions of the Linnaean Society of New York* X: 1–54.

———. 2008. New York City mastodons: Big Apple tusks. *Evolution Education Outreach* 1:204–9.

Hornaday, W. T., ed. 1909. *The wild animals of Hudson's day and the zoological park of our day*. New York: Hudson-Fulton Commission, in cooperation with the New York Zoological Society.

Howarth, R. W., R. Marino, D. P. Swaney, and E. W. Boyer. 2006. Wastewater and watershed influences on primary productivity and oxygen dynamics in the lower Hudson River estuary. In *The Hudson River estuary*, edited by J. S. Levington and J. R. Waldman. New York: Cambridge University Press.

Hurrell, J. 1995. Decadal trends in the North Atlantic oscillation: Regional temperatures and precipitation. *Science* 269:676–79.

Hylander, C. J. 1928. *The algae of Connecticut (State Geological and Natural History Survey of Connecticut Bulletin 42)*. Hartford, CT: State Geological and Natural History Survey of Connecticut.

Irving, W. 1880. *A history of New York from the beginning of the world to the end of the Dutch dynasty*. New York: G. P. Putnam's Sons.

Jackson, J. B. C. 2001. What was natural in the coastal oceans? *Proceedings of the National Academy of Sciences* 98 (10): 5411–18.

Jackson, K. T., ed. 1995. *The encyclopedia of New York City*. New Haven, CT: Yale University Press.

Jacob, K., V. Gornitz, and C. Rosenzweig. 2007. Vulnerability of the New York City metropolitan area to coastal hazards, including sea-level rise: Inferences for urban coastal risk management and adaptation policies. In *Managing coastal vulnerability*, edited by L. McFadden, R. Nicholls, and E. Penning-Rowsell. Cambridge, MA: Elsevier Inc.

Jacobs, J. 1961. *The death and life of great American cities*. New York: Random House.

James, B. B., and J. F. Jameson, eds. 1913. *Journal of Jasper Danckaerts 1679–1680*. New York: Charles Schribner's Sons.

Jameson, J. F., ed. 1909. *Narratives of New Netherland, 1609–1664*. New York: Barnes & Noble, Inc.

Janvier, T. 1894. *In old New York: A classic history of New York City*. New York: St. Martin's Press.

Jenny, H. 1941. *Factors of soil formation*. New York: McGraw-Hill Book Company, Inc.

Jervey, B. 2006. *The big green apple: Your guide to eco-friendly living in New York City*. Guilford, CT: Insiders' Guide.

Jogues, I. 1646. Novum Belgium. In *Narratives of New Netherland, 1609–1664*, edited by J. F. Jameson. New York: Barnes & Noble, Inc.

Johnson, C. W. 1985. *Bogs of the Northeast*. Hanover, NH: University Press of New England.

Johnson, D. S. 1993. *Charting the sea of darkness: The four voyages of Henry Hudson*. New York: Kodansha America, Inc.

Johnson, E. A., and K. M. Catley. 2002. *Life in the leaf litter*. New York: American Museum of Natural History.

Johnston, C., G. Pinay, C. Arens, and R. Naiman. 1995. Influence of soil properties on the biogeochemistry of a beaver meadow hydrosequence. *Soil Science Society of America Bulletin* 59:1789–1799.

Johnston, C. A., and R. J. Naiman. 1990. Aquatic patch creation in relation to beaver population trends. *Ecology* 71:1617–21.

Jonkman, S. N., M. Bockarjova, M. Kok, and P. Bernardini. 2008. Integrated hydrodynamic and economic modelling of flood damage in the Netherlands. *Ecological Economics* 66 (1): 77–90.

Joost, P. 2008. (Pers. comm.) Comments on historical bird list for Manhattan. New York.

Jorgensen, N. 1978. *A Sierra Club naturalist's guide to southern New England*. San Francisco: Sierra Club Books.

Kahn, M. E. 2006. *Green cities: Urban growth and the environment*. Washington, D.C.: Brookings Institution Press.

Kammen, M. 1975. *Colonial New York: A history*. New York: Oxford University Press.

Kardas, S., and E. Larrabee. 1976. *Report of archeological resources probability and significants and recommendations for protection, ferry slip and approach channel, Ellis Island*. New York: U.S. National Park Service.

Kazimiroff, T. L. 1982. *The last Algonquin*. New York: Walker and Company.

Kelley, F. B., ed. 1909. *Historical guide to the city of New York*. New York: Frederick A. Stokes Company.

Kershner, B., and R. T. Leverett. 2004. *The Sierra Club guide to the ancient forests of the Northeast*. San Francisco: Sierra Club Books.

Keys, A. M. 1906. *Cadwallader Colden: A representative eighteenth-century official*. New York: Columbia University Press.

Kieran, J. 1959. *A natural history of New York City*. Boston: Houghton Mifflin.

Kingsland, S. E. 2005. *The evolution of American ecology, 1890–2000*. Baltimore, MD: The John Hopkins University Press.

Kinkead, E. 1974. *A concrete look at nature: Central Park (and other) glimpses*. New York: Quadrangle/The New York Times Book Co.

Kleinstein, D. S. 2003. Paleoecological change during the past millennium at Saw Mill Creek Salt Marsh, Staten Island, New York. Master's thesis, Center for Environmental Research and Conservation, Columbia University, New York.

Koeppel, G. T. 2000. *Water for Gotham: A history*. Princeton, NJ: Princeton University Press.

Kraft, H. C. 1986. *The Lenape: Archaeology, history and ethnography*. Newark , NJ: New Jersey Historical Society.

———. 2001. *The Lenape-Delaware Indian heritage: 10,000 B.C. to A.D. 2000*. Elizabeth, NJ: Lenape Books.

Krebs, C. J. 2008. *Ecology: The experimental analysis of distribution and abundance*. 6th ed. San Francisco: Benjamin Cummings.

Krech III, S. 1999. *The ecological Indian*. New York: W. W. Norton.

Kreshkoff, R., and M. Winn. N.d. *An annotated checklist: The birds of Central Park*. New York: Central Park Conservancy and the City of New York Department of Parks and Recreation.

Kunstler, J. H. 1996. *Home from nowhere*. New York: Touchstone.

Kurlansky, M. 2006. *The big oyster: History on a half shell*. New York: Ballantine Books.

Kvamme, K. L. 2005. Archaeological modeling with GIS at scales large and small. In *Reading the historical spatial information in the world: Studies for human cultures and civilizations based on geographic information systems*. Kyoto, Japan: International Research Center for Japanese Studies.

Lake, T. R. 2007. (Pers. comm.) Hudson River fish. New Paltz, NY.

———. 2007. (Pers. comm.) Sea turtle sightings in the Hudson River. New Palz, NY.

Lawrence, B. 1991. *The early American wilderness as the explorers saw it*. New York: Paragon House.

Lawrence, G. N. 1889. An account of the former abundance of some species of birds on New York Island, at the time of their migration to the south. *The Auk* VI (2): 201–3.

Laxton, P. 1976. The geodetic and topographical evaluation of English country maps, 1740–1840. *Cartographic Journal* 13:37–54.

LeConte, J. 1812. Catalogus plantarum quas sponte crescentes in insula Noveboraco, observait. *American Medical and Philosophical Register* 2:134–42.

Leonardi, L. 1987. The bryophytes of the New York Botanical Garden Forest. *Evansia* 4:8–11.

Leonardi, L., and B. Thiers. 1987. Bryophytes of the NYBG Forest: Yesterday and today. *Garden Magazine* 11:33–34.

Lertzman, K., and J. Fall. 1998. From forest stands to landscapes: Spatial scales and the roles of disturbance. In *Ecological scale: Theory and applications*, edited by D. L. Peterson and V. T. Parker. New York: Columbia University Press.

Levine, E., ed. 1998. *Bull's birds of New York State*. Ithaca, NY: Comstock Publishing Associates.

Levington, J. S., and J. R. Waldman, eds. 2006. *The Hudson River estuary*. New York: Cambridge University Press.

Levinson, H., S. Zimmerman, J. Clinger, S. Rutherford, R. L. Smith, J. Cracknell, and R. Soberman. 2003. *Bus rapid transit. Vol. 1, Case studies in bus rapid transit*. Washington, D.C.: Transportation Research Board.

Lincoff, G. 2001–2. Mushroom hunters of the grasslands. *Mushroom the Journal* 74 (20): 5–8.

Linder, M., and L. S. Zacharias. 1999. *Of cabbages and Kings County: Agriculture and the formation of modern Brooklyn*. Iowa City: University of Iowa Press.

Little, E. L. 1980. *National Audubon Society field guide to North American trees: Eastern region*. New York: Alfred A. Knopf.

Lockwood, J., M. Hoopes, and M. Marchetti. 2006. *Invasion ecology*. New York: Blackwell Publishing.

Loeb, R. E. 1986. Plant communities of Inwood Hill Park, New York County, New York. *Bulletin of the Torrey Botanical Club* 113 (1): 46–52.

———. 1998. Evidence of prehistoric corn (*Zea mays*) and hickory (*Carya* spp.) planting in New York City. *Journal of the Torrey Botanical Club* 125:74–86.

Lorimer, C. G. 2001. Historical and ecological roles of disturbance in eastern North American forests: 9,000 years of change. *Wildlife Society Bulletin* 29 (2): 425–39.

Louv, R. 2005. *Last child in the woods: Saving our children from nature-deficit disorder*. Chapel Hill, NC: Algonquin Books.

Ludlum, D. A. 1966. *Early American winters, 1604–1820*. Boston, MA: American Meteorological Society.

Luttenberg, D., D. Lev, and M. Feller. 1993. *Native species planting guide for New York City and vicinity*. New York: Natural Resources Group, Department of Parks and Recreation, City of New York.

Lutz, F. E. 1941. *A lot of insects: Entomology in a suburban garden*. New York: G. P. Putnam's Sons.

Luvass, J. 1999. *Frederick the Great on the art of war*. New York: De Capo Press.

Lynn, L. B., and E. F. Karlin. 1985. The vegetation of the low-shrub bogs of northern New Jersey and adjacent New York: Ecosystems at their southern limit. *Torreya* 112 (4): 436–44.

Macauley, J. 1829. Serpents of New York State. In *Natural, civil and statistical history of the state of New York*. Albany: State of New York.

MacKenzie, C. L. 1992. *The fisheries of Raritan Bay*. New Brunswick, NJ: Rutgers University Press.

Manly, B. F. J. 2006. *Randomization, bootstrap and Monte Carlo methods in biology*. 3rd ed. Boca Raton, FL: Chapman & Hall/CRC.

Mann, C. C. 2005. *1491: New relevations of the Americas before Columbus*. New York: Alfred A. Knopf.

Marino, C., and K. M. Tiro, eds. 2006. *Along the Hudson and Mohawk: The 1790 journey of Count Paolo Andreani*. Philadelphia: University of Pennsylvania Press.

Martin, A. C., H. S. Zim, and A. L. Nelson. 1951. *American wildlife & plants*. New York: Dover.

Martindale, I. C. 1889. *Marine algae of the New Jersey coast and adjacent waters of Staten Island*. Vol. I, no. 2, *Memoirs of the Torrey Botanical Club*. New York: Torrey Botanical Club.

Mathewson, R. F. 1935. Reptiles and amphibians of Staten Island. *Proceedings of the Staten Island Institute of Arts and Sciences* 17 (2): 28–50.

Matteson, K. C. 2006. *Final report on diversity and conservation of insects in community gardens and one park in New York City*. Bronx, NY: Fordham University.

Matthews, A. 2001. *Wild nights: Nature returns to the city*. New York: North Point Press.

Matthiessen, P. 1959. *Wildlife in America*. New York: Viking Press.

May, R. M. 2006. Network structure and the biology of populations. *Trends in Ecology and Evolution* 21 (7): 394–99.

McClane, A. J. 1978. *McClane's field guide to freshwater fishes of North America*. New York: Holt, Rinehart and Winston.

———. 1978. *McClane's field guide to saltwater fishes of North America*. New York: Holt, Rinehart and Winston.

McCullough, D. 2005. *1776*. New York: Simon & Schuster.

McDonough, W. 2002. *Cradle to cradle: Remaking the way we make things*. New York: North Point Press.

McGrath, B. 2007. Fixer-upper. *The New Yorker*, December 12.

McIntosh, R. P. 1972. Forests of the Catskill Mountains, New York. *Ecological Monographs* 42 (2): 143–62.

McKnight, M. W., P. S. White, R. I. McDonald, J. F. Lamoreaux, W. Sechrest, R. S. Ridgely, and S. N. Stuart. 2007. Putting beta-diversity on the map: Broad-scale congruence and coincidence in the extremes. *PLOS Biology* 5 (10): 2424–32.

McNamara, J. 1989. *McNamara's old Bronx*. Bronx, NY: Bronx Historical Society.

———. 1991. *History in asphalt: The origin of Bronx street and place names*. Bronx, NY: Bronx County Historical Society.

McNeill, J. R. 2000. *Something new under the sun: An environmental history of the twentieth-century world*. New York: W. W. Norton.

McRoy, C. P., and C. Helfferich. 1977. *Seagrass ecosystems: A scientific perspective*. New York: Marcel Dekker, Inc.

Merguerian, C., and J. Sanders. 1988. Geology of Manhattan and the Bronx. Westbury, NY: Duke Geological Laboratory.

Merrill, F. J. H., N. H. Darton, A. Hollick, R. D. Salisbury, R. E. Dodge, B. Willis, and H. A. Pressey. 1902. New York City folio of the *Geologic atlas of the United States*. Washington, D.C.: U.S. Geological Survey.

Merwick, D. 2006. *The shame and the sorrow: Dutch-Amerindian encounters in New Netherland.* Philadelphia: University of Pennsylvania Press.

Meyers, S. L. 2005. *Manhattan's lost streetcars.* Charleston, SC: Arcadia Publishing.

Miller, B. 2000. *Fat of the land: Garbage of New York: The last two hundred years.* New York: Four Walls Eight Windows.

Miller, J. R., and R. J. Hobbs. 2002. Conservation where people live and work. *Conservation Biology* 16:330–37.

Miller, R. L., and J. P. St. John. 2006. Modeling primary productivity in the lower Hudson River estuary. In *The Hudson River estuary*, edited by J. S. Levington and J. R. Waldman. New York: Cambridge University Press.

Miller, S. C. 2003. *Central Park, an American masterpiece.* New York: Harry N. Abrams, Inc.

Mitchell, R. S., and G. C. Tucker. 1997. Revised checklist of New York State plants. *New York State Museum Bulletin* 490.

Mithen, S. 2003. *After the ice: A global human history, 20,000–5,000 B.C.* Cambridge, MA: Harvard University Press.

Mitsch, W. J., and J. G. Gosselink. 1993. *Wetlands.* New York: Van Nostrand Reinhold.

Mittelbach, M., and M. Crewdson. 1997. *Wild New York: A guide to the wildlife, wild places, and natural phenomena of New York City.* New York: Three Rivers Press.

Monaghan, C. 1998. *The Murrays of Murray Hill.* Brooklyn, NY: Urban History Press.

Montgomery, D. R. 2007. *Dirt: The erosion of civilizations.* Berkeley: University of California Press.

Montgomery, M. R. 2008. The urban transformation of the developing world. *Science* 319 (8 February 2008): 761–64.

Morgan, L. H. 1877. *Ancient society, or researches in the lines of human progress from savagery through barbarism to civilization.* New York: Henry Holt.

Moscow, H. 1978. *The street book: An encyclopedia of Manhattan's street names and their origins.* New York: Fordham University Press.

Muir, J. 1911. *My first summer in the Sierra.* Boston: Houghton Mifflin.

Müller-Schwarze, D., and L. Sun. 2003. *The beaver: Natural history of a wetlands engineer.* Ithaca, NY: Comstock Publishing Associates.

Multi-Resolution Land Characteristics Consortium (MRLC). 2001. National Land Cover Database. www.mrlc.gov/.

Murphy, M. 1998. Best ways to recycle fast-food waste. www.helium.com/items/713398-best-ways-to-recycle-fast-food-waste.

Murphy, R. C. 1916. Long Island turtles. *Copeia* 33:56–60.

Musial, W., S. Butterfield, and B. Ram. 2006. Energy from offshore wind. Paper presented at Offshore Technology Conference, Houston, TX. Golden, CO: National Renewable Energy Laboratory. www.nrel.gov/wind/pubs_research.html

Musial, W. D., and C. P. Butterfield. 2004. Future for offshore wind energy in the United States. In *EnergyOcean proceedings, Palm Beach, FL.* Golden, CO: National Renewable Energy Laboratory. www.nrel.gov/wind/pubs_research.html

Myers, A. C., ed. 1970. *William Penn's own account of the Lenni Lenape or Delaware Indians.* Moorestown, NJ: Middle Atlantic Press.

Myers, G. S. 1929. Amphibians and reptiles observed in the Palisades Interstate Park, New York and New Jersey. *Copeia* 173:99–103.

Nabhan, G. P. 2002. *Coming home to eat: The pleasures and politics of local foods.* New York: W. W. Norton.

Neuman, F., ed. 1902. *A brief description of New York, formerly called New Netherlands,* by Daniel Denton. Cleveland, OH: The Burrows Brothers Company.

Neumann, C., B. Jarvinen, and A. Pike. 1987. *Tropical cyclones of the North Atlantic Ocean 1871–1986.* 3rd rev. Asheville, NC: NOAA-National Climatic Data Center.

New York City Department of City Planning. 1993. *A greenway plan for New York City.* www.nyc.gov/html/dcp/html/bike/gpreal.shtml#report. New York.

———. 1997. *New York City bicycling master plan.* www.nyc.gov/html/dcp/html/bike/mp.shtml. New York.

New York City Department of Transportation. 2008. *Sustainable streets: 2008 and beyond: Strategic plan for the New York City Department of Transportation.* New York.

New York City Energy Policy Task Force. 2004. *New York City energy policy: An electricity resource roadmap.* New York.

New York City Soil Survey Staff. 2005. *New York City reconnaissance soil survey.* Staten Island, NY: U.S. Department of Agriculture, Natural Resources Conservation Service.

New York Common Council, ed. 1842–70. *Manual of the corporation of the City of New York (Valentine's manuals).* New York: City of New York.

New York State Energy Research and Development Authority. 2007. *Patterns and Trends: New York State Energy Profiles: 1991–2005.* Albany, NY.

Nichols, J. T. 1913. A list of the fishes known to have occurred within fifty miles of New York City. *Proceedings of the Linnaean Society of New York* 23:90–108.

O'Connor, A. 2007. After 200 years, a beaver is back in New York City. *The New York Times.* February 23.

Oberndorfer, E., J. Lundholm, B. Bass, R. R. Coffman, H. Doshi, N. Dunnett, S. Gaffin, M. Kohler, K. K. Y. Liu, and B. Rowe. 2007. Green roofs as urban ecosystems: Ecological structures, functions and services. *BioScience* 57 (10): 823–33.

Ohland, G., and S. Poticha, eds. 2006. *Street smart: Streetcars and cities in the twenty-first century.* Oakland, CA: Reconnecting America.

Ormsby, T., E. Napoleon, and R. Burke. 2004. *Getting to know ArcGIS Desktop: The basics of ArcView, ArcEditor and ArcInfo, updated for ArcGIS 9.* Redlands, CA: ESRI Press.

Paillet, F. L. 2002. Chestnut: History and ecology of a transformed species. *Journal of Biogeography* 29 (10/11): 1517–30.

Palmer, R. S. 1954. *The mammal guide: Mammals of North America north of Mexico.* Garden City, NY: Doubleday.

Parker, A. C. 1920. The archeological history of New York. *New York State Museum Bulletin* 236:1–743.

Parshall, T., and D. R. Foster. 2002. Fire on the New England landscape: regional and temporal variation, cultural and environmental controls. *Journal of Biogeography* 29:1305–17.

Pauly, D. 1995. Anecdotes and the shifting baseline syndrome of fisheries. *Trends in Ecology and Evolution* 10 (10): 430.

Pederson, D. C. 2002. Ecological impacts of land use and climate change in Piermont Marsh, Hudson River valley, New York: The past 700 years. Master's thesis, Center for Environmental Research and Conservation, Columbia University, New York.

Pehek, E. 2007. Salamander diversity and distribution in New York City, 1880 to the present. *Transactions of the Linnaean Society of New York* X:157–82.

Penfold, P. A., ed. 1967–74. *Maps and plans in the Public Record Office.* London: Public Records Office.

Perry, B. 1985. *A Sierra Club naturalist's guide to the middle Atlantic coast.* San Francisco: Sierra Club Books.

Peterson, R. T. 2007. *All things reconsidered.* New York: HMCo Field Guides.

Phillips, S. J., R. P. Anderson, and R. E. Schapire. 2006. Maximum entropy modelling of species geographic distributions. *Ecological Modelling* 190:231–59.

Pickett, S. T. A., R. S. Ostfeld, M. Shachak, and G. E. Likens. 1997. *The ecological basis of conservation: Heterogeneity, ecosystems and biodiversity.* New York: International Thomson Publishing.

Pickett, S. T. A., and P. S. White. 1985. *The ecology of natural disturbance and patch dynamics.* San Diego, CA: Academic Press.

Plumb, M. 2007. *Sustainable raindrops: Cleaning New York Harbor by greening the urban landscape.* New York: Riverkeeper.

Poggenburg, J. F., N. L. Britton, E. R. Sterns, A. Brown, T. C. Porter, and A. Hollick. 1888. *Preliminary catalogue of Anthophyta and Pteridophyta reported growing spontaneously within one hundred miles of New York City.* New York: Torrey Botanical Club and Columbia College Herbarium.

Pollan, M. 2006. *The Omnivore's dilemma: A natural history of four meals*. New York: Penguin Press.

Pollock, L. W. 1998. *A practical guide to the marine animals of northeastern North America*. New Brunswick, NJ: Rutgers University Press.

Pousson, J. F. 1986. *An overview assessment of archeological resources on Ellis Island, Statue of Liberty National Monument, New York*. Rockville, MA: U.S. National Park Service.

Pritchard, E. 2002. *Native New Yorkers: The legacy of the Algonquin people of New York*. San Francisco: Council Oak Books.

Proulx, S. R., D. E. L. Promislow, and P. C. Phillips. 2005. Network thinking in ecology and evolution. *Trends in Ecology and Evolution* 20 (6): 345–53.

Putz, F. 2003. Are rednecks the unsung heroes of ecosystem management? *Wild Earth* 13:10–14.

Pyne, S. T. 1997. *Fire in America: A cultural history of wildland and rural fire*. Seattle: University of Washington Press.

Quinn, D. B., and A. M. Quinn, eds. 1983. *The English New England voyages 1602–1608*. London: The Hakluyt Society.

Rachlin, J. W., A. Pappantoniou, and B. E. Warkentine. 2001. *An illustrated field guide to the aquatic fauna of the Bronx River: A guide for students and teachers*. Bronx: Lehman College and State University of New York—Maritime College.

Randel, J. J. 1864. City of New York, north of Canal Street, in 1808 to 1821. In *Valentine's manual*, edited by D. M. Valentine. New York: Valentine's Manual, Inc.

Rawolle, C., and I. A. Pilat. 1857. *Catalogue of plants gathered in August and September 1857 in the ground of the Central Park*. Part I. New York: M. W. Siebert, Steam Job Printer.

Ravenhill, W., and A. Gilig. 1974. The accuracy of early maps? Towards a computer-aided method. *Cartographic Journal* 11:48–52.

Register, R. 2002. *Ecocities: Building cities in balance with nature*. Berkeley, CA: Berkeley Hills Books.

Rickerson, W., L. Ettenson, T. Marotta, and T. Case. 2007. Solar and the city. *Renewable Energy Focus* September/October 2007:56–58.

Riis, J. A. 1902. *How the other half lives: Studies among the tenements of New York*. New York: Charles Scribner's Sons.

Riker, J. 1881. *Harlem (city of New York): Its origin and early annals*. New York: Published by author.

———. 1904. *A revised history of Harlem*. New York: New Harlem Publishing Company.

Rink, O. A. 1986. *Holland on Hudson: An economic and social history of Dutch New York*. Ithaca, NY: Cornell University Press.

Robinson, G. R., M. E. Yurlina, and S. N. Handel. 1994. A century of change in the Staten Island flora: Ecological correlates of species losses and invasions. *Bulletin of the Torrey Botanical Club* 121 (2): 119–29.

Rooney, T. P., and D. M. Waller. 2003. Direct and indirect effects of white-tailed deer in forest ecosystems. *Forest Ecology and Management* 181:165–76.

Roosevelt, T. 1891. *Historic towns: New York*. New York: Longmans, Green and Co.

Rose-Redwood, R. S. 2003. Recreating historical topography in the Cartesian city. *Geographical Review* 93 (1): 124–32.

Rosenzweig, C., and W. Solecki, eds. 2001. *Climate change and a global city: The potential consequences of climate variability and change—Metro East Coast*. (Report for the U.S. Global Change Research Program, National Assessment of the Potential Consequences of Climate Variability and Change for the United States.) New York: Columbia Earth Institute, Columbia University.

Rosenzweig, R., and E. Blackmar. 1992. *The Park and the people: A history of Central Park*. Ithaca, NY: Cornell University Press.

Rowley, J. 1902. The mammals of Westchester County, New York. *Proceedings of the Linnaean Society of New York* 14:31–60.

Russell, E. 1980. Vegetational change in northern New Jersey from precolonization to the present: A palynological interpretation. *Bulletin of the Torrey Botanical Club* 107:432–36.

———. 1983. Indian-set fires in the forests of the northeastern United States. *Ecology* 64:78–88.

Ruttenber, E. M. 1872. *Indian tribes of Hudson's River*. Saugerties, NY: Hope Farm Press (reprinted in 1992).

Sanderson, E. W. 2005. Urban legend: Discovering Manhattan's wetlands. *National Wetlands Newsletter* 27 (1): 1 and 15–17.

———. 2006. How many animals do we want to save?: The many ways of setting population target levels for animals. *BioScience* 57:911–22.

———. 2006. (Pers. comm.) Mammals seen on Manhattan. Bronx, NY.

Sanderson, E. W., and M. Brown. 2007. Mannahatta: An ecological first look at the Manhattan landscape prior to Henry Hudson. *Northeastern Naturalist* 14 (4): 545–70.

Sanderson, E. W., M. Jaiteh, M. A. Levy, K. H. Redford, A. V. Wannebo, and G. Woolmer. 2002. The human footprint and the last of the wild. *BioScience* 52 (10): 891–904.

Sanderson, E. W., P. Robles Gil, C. G. Mittermeier, V. G. Martin, and C. F. Kormos, eds. 2006. *The human footprint: Challenges for wilderness and biodiversity*. Mexico: CEMEX—Agrupacion Sierra Madre—Wildlife Conservation Society.

Santone, L., and J. D. Irish. 1997. Buried in haste: Historic interments from Governors Island, New York. *North American Archaeologist* 18 (1): 19–39.

Sarna-Wojcicki, D. 2005. Horticulture in Lenape Native American diet and its impact on the "Manahatta" landscape ecology. Senior thesis, Department of Ecology, Evolution and Environmental Biology, Columbia University, New York.

Schecter, B. 2002. *The battle for New York City: The city at the heart of the American Revolution*. New York: Walker and Co.

Scheer, G. F., and H. F. Rankin. 1957. *Rebels & Redcoats: The American Revolution through the eyes of those who fought and lived it*. New York: De Capo Press.

Schmidt, R. E. 1986. Zoogeography of the northern Appalachians. In *The zoogeography of North American freshwater fishes*, edited by C. H. Hocutt and E. O. Wiley. New York: John Wiley & Sons.

Schoolcraft, H. R. 1845. *Report of the aboriginal names and geographical terminology of the state of New York*. Part I, *Valley of the Hudson*. New York: New-York Historical Society.

Schuberth, C. 1968. *The geology of New York City and environs*. Garden City, NY: Natural History Press.

Scott, G. 1989. *Fishing in American waters*. New York: Harper & Brothers.

Scott, J. H., and R. E. Burgan. 2005. *Standard fire behavior fuel models: A comprehensive set for use with Rothermel's surface fire spread model. General technical report RMRS-GTR-153*. Fort Collins, CO: Rocky Mountain Research Station, U.S. Forest Service.

Scott, K., and K. Stryker-Rodda, eds. 1974. *New York historical manuscripts: Dutch*. Vol. 1, *Register of the provincial secretary, 1638–1642*. Baltimore, MD: Genealogical Publishing Company.

Seewagen, C. L. 2008. Lipid content of nearctic-neotropical migratory passerines killed during stopovers in a New York City park. *Northeastern Naturalist* 15 (1): 87–96.

Seewagen, C. L., and E. J. Slayton. 2008. Mass changes of migratory landbirds during stopovers in a New York City park. *Wilson Journal of Ornithology* 120 (2): 296–303.

Seitz, S., and S. Miller. 1996. *The other islands of New York City*. Woodstock, VT: Countryman Press.

Shepard, P. 1998. *Coming home to the Pleistocene*. Washington, D.C.: Shearwater Books.

Sherwood, W. L. 1895. The salamanders found in the vicinity of New York City, with notes upon extra-limital or allied species. *Proceedings of the Linnaean Society of New York* 7:21–37.

———. 1898. The frogs and toads in the vicinity of New York City. *Proceedings of the Linnaean Society of New York* 10:9–24.

Shorto, R. 2004. *The island at the center of the world: The epic story of Dutch Manhattan and the forgotten colony that shaped America*. New York: Doubleday.

Singer, M. J., and D. N. Munns. 1991. *Soils: An introduction*. New York: Macmillan Publishing Company.

Sirkin, L. 1967. Late-Pleistocene pollen stratigraphy of western Long Island and eastern Staten Island, New York. In *Quaternary Paleoecology: 7th International Cong. Association Quaternary Research, 1965, Proceedings*, vol. 7, edited by E. Cushing and H. J. Wright. New Haven, CT: Yale University Press.

Sirkin, L., and H. Bokuniewicz. 2006. The Hudson River valley: Geological history, landforms, and resources. In *The Hudson River estuary*, edited by J. S. Levington and J. R. Waldman. New York: Cambridge University Press.

Sivard, S. M. 1995. Audubon, John J(ames). In *The encyclopedia of New York City*, edited by K. T. Jackson. New Haven, CT: Yale University Press.

Skinner, A. 1909. Archaeology of Manhattan Island. *Anthropological Papers of the American Museum of Natural History* 3:113–63.

———. 1919. Exploration of aboriginal sites at Throgs Neck and Clasons Point, New York City. *Contributions from the Museum of the American Indian, Heye Foundation* 5 (4).

———. 1947. *The Indians of Manhattan Island and vicinity*. New York: American Museum of Natural History.

Sloan, A. 2007. Migratory bird mortality at the World Trade Center and World Financial Center, 1997–2001: A deadly mix of lights and glass. *Transactions of the Linnaean Society of New York* X:183–204.

Small, J. K. 1935. *Ferns of the vicinity of New York*. New York: Dover.

Smith, C. L., and T. R. Lake. 1990. Documentation of the Hudson River fish fauna. *American Museum Novitates* 2891:1–17.

Smith, C. S. 1950. The archaeology of coastal New York. *Anthropological Papers of the American Museum of Natural History* 43 (2): 91–200.

Smith, J. R. 1938. *Springs and wells of Manhattan and the Bronx, New York City, at the end of the nineteenth century*. New York: New-York Historical Society.

Stalter, R. 1981. A thirty-nine-year history of the aborescent vegetation of Alley Park, Queens County, New York. *Bulletin of the Torrey Botanical Club* 108 (4): 485–87.

Stalter, R., and E. F. Lamont. 1987. Vegetation of the Hempstead Plains, Mitchell Field, Long Island New York. *Bulletin of the Torrey Botanical Club* 114 (3): 330–35.

Stanne, S. P., R. G. Panetta, and B. E. Forist. 1996. *The Hudson: An illustrated guide to the living river*. New Brunswick, NJ: Rutgers University Press.

Steinberg, N., D. J. Suszkowski, L. Clark, and J. Way. 2004. *Health of the harbor: The first comprehensive look at the state of the NY/NJ Harbor estuary*. New York: Hudson River Foundation.

Steuart, W. M., ed. 1905. *Street and electric railways, 1902*. Washington, D.C.: U.S. Bureau of the Census.

Stokes, I. N. P. 1915–28. *The iconography of Manhattan Island*. 6 vols. New York: Robert H. Dodd.

Strayer, D. L., and K. J. Jirka. 1997. *The pearly mussels of New York State*. Albany: The State University of New York.

Tarbuck, E. J., F. K. Lutgens, and D. Tasa. 2002. *Earth: An introduction to physical geology*. 8th ed. Prentice Hall: Upper Saddle River, NJ.

Taylor, N. 1915. *Flora of the vicinity of New York: A contribution to plant geography*. Vol. 5, *Memoirs of the New York Botanical Garden*. Bronx, NY: New York Botanical Garden.

Tear, T. H., P. Kareiva, P. L. Angermeier, P. Comer, B. Czech, R. Kautz, L. Landon, D. Mehlman, K. Murphy, M. Ruckelshaus, J. M. Scott, and G. Wilhere. 2005. How much is enough? The recurrent problem of setting measurable objectives in conservation. *BioScience* 55:835–49.

Temperton, V. M., R. J. Hobbs, T. Nuttle, and S. Halle, eds. 2004. *Assembly rules and restoration ecology: Bridging the gap between theory and practice*. Washington, D.C.: Island Press.

Thaler, J. S. 2000. *Weather history and climate guide to the lower Hudson Valley*. Ossining, NY: George Candreva Environmental Center.

The Federal Writers' Project. 1939. *The WPA guide to New York City*. New York: Random House.

Thieret, J. W., W. A. Niering, and N. C. Olmstead. 2001. *National Audubon Society field guide to North American wildlflowers: Eastern Region*. Rev. ed. New York: Alfred A. Knopf.

Tomlinson, R. 2007. *Thinking about GIS: Geographic information system planning for managers*. Redlands, CA: ESRI Press.

Tooker, W. W. 1901. *The Algonquian series, I. Indian names of Manhattan*. New York: F. P. Harper.

Torrey, J., C. W. Eddy, and D. J. V. Knevels. 1817. *Catalogue of plants, growing spontaneously within thirty miles of the city of New York*. New York: Lyceum of Natural History of New York.

Tudor, G., D. Riepe, D. Pollack, and S. Walter. 2001. *Moths of Jamaica Bay Wildlife Refuge.* www.hmana.org/jbwr/index.htm.

Tulig, M., and B. Thiers. 2004. (Pers. comm.) Summary of New York City plants in New York Botanical Garden Herbarium records. Bronx, NY.

Turner, M. G. 1989. Landscape ecology: The effect of pattern on process. *Annual Review of Ecology and Systematics* 20:171–97.

Turner, M. G., R. H. Gardner, and R. V. O'Neill. 2001. *Landscape ecology in theory and practice.* New York: Springer-Verlag.

U.S. Bureau of Economic Analysis. 2007. *Regional economic information system 1969–2005.* Washington, D.C. www.fhwa.dot.gov/policy/ohpi/hss/index.cfm

U.S. Department of Agriculture. 2007. The PLANTS Database, version 3.5 (National Plant Data Center. 2002.). www.plants.usda.gov.

U.S. Department of Transportation Federal Highway Administration. 2006. *Highway statistics 2005.* Washington, D.C. www.fhwa.dot.gov/policy/ohpi/hss/index.cfm

U.S. Fish and Wildlife Service. 2007. *List of species of special emphasis in the Hudson River–New York Bight Watershed.* training.fws.gov/library/pubs5/web_link/tables/append1a.htm.

United Nations Population Division. 2006. *World urbanization prospects: The 2005 revision.* New York: United Nations Population Division.

Vail, A. M. 1906. Jane Colden, an early New York botanist. *Contributions of the New York Botanical Garden* 88:21–34.

van Andel, J., and J. Aronson. 2005. *Restoration ecology: The new frontier.* New York: Wiley-Blackwell.

van der Donck, A. 1650. The representation of New Netherland. In *Narratives of New Netherland, 1609–1664,* edited by J. F. Jameson. New York: Barnes & Noble, Inc.

van der Zee, H., and B. van der Zee. 1978. *A sweet and alien land: The story of Dutch New York.* New York: Viking Press.

van Gelder, R. 1982. A richly blessed land where milk and honey flow: New Netherland seen by Dutch eyes. In *The birth of New York: Nieuw Amsterdam 1624–1664,* edited by R. van Gelder, translated from the Dutch by G. Schwartz. Amsterdam: Amsterdam Historical Museum.

van Holt, T., D. M. Murphy, and L. Chapman. 2006. Local and landscape predictors of fish-assemblage characteristics in the Great Swamp, New York. *Northeastern Naturalist* 13 (3): 353–74.

van Leusen, M., and H. Kamermans, eds. 2005. *Predictive modelling for archaeological heritage management: A research agenda (Nederlandse Archeologische Rapporten 29).* Amersfoort: ROB.

van Wassenaer, N. 1624–30. Historisch verhael. In *Narratives of New Netherland, 1609–1664,* edited by J. F. Jameson. New York: Barnes & Noble, Inc.

Viele, E. L. 1857. The plan. In *First annual report for improvement of the Central Park.* New York: C. W. Baker.

Vokral, J., D. Gumb, A. D. Cavallaro, S. Mehrotra, and E. Rosenberg. 2003. Wetlands at work. *Civil Engineering,* February:56–63.

von Pressentin Wright, C., S. Miller, and S. Seitz. 2002. *New York blue guide.* New York: W. W. Norton.

Voshell, J. R. 2002. *A guide to common freshwater invertebrates of North America.* Blacksburg, VA: McDonald & Woodward Publishing Company.

Wagerik, N. 1999. Damselflies and dragonflies of Central Park. In *Red-tails in love: A wildlife drama in Central Park,* edited by M. Winn. New York: Vintage Departures.

Waldman, J. 1999. *Heartbeats in the muck: A dramatic look at the history, sea life, and environment of New York Harbor.* New York: Lyons Press.

Wall, D. D., and A.-M. Cantwell. 2004. *Touring Gotham's archaeological past: 8 self-guided walking tours through New York City.* New Haven, CT: Yale University Press.

Walter, S. 2001. *Butterfly flight dates in southeast New York.* New York: North American Butterfly Association.

Watkins, K. 2006. Human development report 2006: Beyond scarcity: Power, poverty and the global water crisis. In *Human development report.* New York: United Nations Development Program.

Weigmann, W. H., and J. T. Nichols. 1915. Notes on fishes near New York. *Copeia* 23:43–45.

Weisman, A. 2007. *The world without us.* New York: Thomas Dunne Books.

Weiss, H. M., D. Glemboski, K. Philips, P. Roper, A. Rosso, T. Sweeney, A. Vitarelli, L. Wahle, and J. Weiss. 1995. *Plants and animals of Long Island Sound: A documented checklist, bibliography and computer database.* Groton, CT: Project Oceanology.

Weiss, M. A. 1995. Astor, John Jacob. In *The encyclopedia of New York City,* edited by K. T. Jackson. New Haven, CT: Yale University Press.

Werner, R. G. 2004. *Freshwater fishes of the northeastern United States: A field guide.* Syracuse, NY: Syracuse University Press.

Wertenbaker, T. 1948. *Father Knickerbocker rebels: New York City during the Revolution.* New York: Charles Scribner's Sons.

Weslager, C. A. 1972. *Delaware Indians: A history.* New Brunswick, NJ: Rutgers University Press.

Whitaker, J. O. 1996. *National Audubon Society field guide to North American mammals.* New York: Alfred A. Knopf.

White, P. S., and R. D. White. 1996. Old-growth oak and oak-hickory forests. In *Eastern old-growth forests: Prospects for rediscovery and recovery,* edited by M. B. Davis. Washington, D.C.: Island Press.

Whitman, S. 1996. *What's cooking: The history of American food.* Minneapolis, MN: Lerner Publishing Group.

Whitney, G. G. 1994. *From coastal wilderness to fruited plain: A history of environmental change in temperate North America from 1500 to the present.* Cambridge: Cambridge University Press.

Whittier, T. R., D. B. Halliwell, and R. A. Daniels. 1999. Distributions of lake fishes in the Northeast—I. Centrarchidae, Percidae, Esocidae and Moronidae. *Northeastern Naturalist* 6:283–304.

Wilcox, W. B. 1954. *The American Rebellion: Sir Henry Clinton's narrative of his campaigns, 1775–1782, with an appendix of original documents.* New Haven, CT: Yale University Press.

———. 1964. *Portrait of a general: Sir Henry Clinton in the War for Independence.* New York: Alfred A. Knopf.

Williams, M. 1989. *Americans & their forests.* Cambridge: Cambridge University Press.

Wilson, E. O. 2002. *The future of life.* New York: Alfred A. Knopf.

Wilson, J. G., ed. 1892. *The memorial history of the city of New York from its first settlement to the year 1892.* New York: New-York History Company.

Winn, M. 1999. *Red-tails in love: A wildlife drama in Central Park.* New York: Vintage Departures.

Woodward, D. 1974. The study of the history of cartography: A suggested framework. *American Cartographer* 1:101–15.

Wooley, C. 1968. A two years journal in New York [1701]. In *Historical chronicles of New Amsterdam, colonial New York, and early Long Island,* edited by J. Cornell. Port Washington, NY: Ira J. Friedman.

Yahner, R. H. 1995. *Eastern deciduous forests: Ecology and wildlife conservation.* Minneapolis: University of Minnesota Press.

Yeaton, S. 1972. *A natural history of Long Island.* East Hampton, NY: The Nature Conservancy.

Zahler, P. 2008. (Pers. comm.) Comments on mammals of Mannahatta. Bronx, NY.

Zeisel, W. N. 1990. Shark!!! And other sports fish once abundant in New York Harbor. *Seaport* Autumn 1990:36–39.

Zeranski, J. D., and T. R. Baptist. 1990. *Connecticut birds.* Hanover, NH: University Press of New England.

Endpapers: Courtesy of The National Archives, ref. MR1/463.

Page 2: (left) Copyright ©Markley Boyer/The Mannahatta Project/Wildlife Conservation Society; (right) Copyright ©Yann Arthus-Bertrand/CORBIS. Composite image by Markley Boyer.

Page 8: Copyright ©Markley Boyer/The Mannahatta Project/Wildlife Conservation Society.

Page 11: Copyright ©Stephen Amiaga (www.amiaga.com).

Page 12 (top): Copyright ©Stuart Franklin/Magnum Photos.

Page 12 (bottom): Copyright ©Markley Boyer/The Mannahatta Project/Wildlife Conservation Society.

Page 14 (top): Courtesy of the Wildlife Conservation Society Library. *Ursus americanus, American black bear. Male & female.* In *The viviparous quadrupeds of North America*, by John James Audubon and John Bachman (created 1845–48).

Page 14 (bottom): Courtesy of the Wildlife Conservation Society Library. *Mus leucopus, white-footed mouse. Natural size. Male, female and young.* In *The viviparous quadrupeds of North America*, by John James Audubon and John Bachman (created 1845–48).

Page 15: Courtesy of the Historical Society of Pennsylvania Collection, Atwater Kent Museum of Philadelphia. Gustavus Hesselius, *Tishcohan.* HSP.1834.1.

Page 18: Copyright ©Markley Boyer/The Mannahatta Project/Wildlife Conservation Society.

Page 19: Copyright ©Stephen Amiaga (www.amiaga.com).

Page 20: U.S. Fish and Wildlife Service, Digital Library System. Gary Cramer, National Conservation Training Center—Publications and Training Materials.

Page 22: Copyright ©Markley Boyer/The Mannahatta Project/Wildlife Conservation Society.

Page 23: Copyright ©Stephen Amiaga (www.amiaga.com).

Page 26: Courtesy of General Research Division, The New York Public Library, Astor, Lenox and Tilden Foundations. *Black-throated blue wood-warbler. 1. Male. 2. Female. (Canadian columbine.)* In *The birds of America, from drawings made in the United States and their territories*, by John James Audubon. 1840–44. Vol. 2., pl. 95, opp. p. 63. Digital Image ID: 108353.

Page 28: Copyright ©Markley Boyer/The Mannahatta Project/Wildlife Conservation Society.

Page 29: Copyright ©Stephen Amiaga (www.amiaga.com).

Page 30 (top): Copyright ©Wildlife Conservation Society.

Page 30 (bottom, left): Copyright ©Eric W. Sanderson.

Page 30 (bottom, right): Copyright ©Wildlife Conservation Society.

Page 34: Courtesy of The National Archives, ref. MR1/463.

Page 37 (top): Library of Congress, Geography and Map Division. *Novi Belgii Novæque Angliæ: nec non partis Virginiæ tabula multis in locis emendata/per Nicolaum Visscher nunc apud Petr. Schenk Iun.* Amsterdam[?], 1685. Call Number: G3715 169- .V5 TIL Vault.

Page 37 (bottom): Library of Congress, Geography and Map Division. Inset view of *Nieuw Amsterdam op t eylant Manhattans*, from *Novi Belgii Novæque Angliæ: nec non partis Virginiæ tabula multis in locis emendata/per Nicolaum Visscher nunc apud Petr. Schenk Iun.* Amsterdam[?], 1685. Call Number: G3715 169- .V5 TIL Vault.

Page 38 (details): Library of Congress, Geography and Map Division. *Novi Belgii Novæque Angliæ: nec non partis Virginiæ tabula multis in locis emendata/per Nicolaum Visscher nunc apud Petr. Schenk Iun.* Amsterdam[?], 1685. Call Number: G3715 169- .V5 TIL Vault.

Page 41 (top): Courtesy of I. N. Phelps Stokes Collection, Miriam and Ira D. Wallach Division of Art, Prints and Photographs, The New York Public Library, Astor, Lenox and Tilden Foundations. *A view of Fort George with the city of New York, from the SW.* [1731–36?] Hand-colored engraving by John Carwitham after William Burgis. Digital Image ID: 54695.

Page 41 (bottom): Library of Congress, Geography and Map Division. Detail view of *A plan of the city of New-York & its environs to Greenwich, on the North or Hudsons River, and to Crown Point, on the East or Sound River, shewing the several streets, publick buildings, docks, fort & battery, with the true form & course of the commanding grounds, with and without the town. Survey'd in the winter, 1775. P. Andrews, sculp.* Created by John Montrésor (dedicated to Major Gen. Thos. Gage). Published in London, 1775. Call Number: G3804.N4 1766 .M61 Am. 5-19.

Page 42: Library of Congress, Geography and Map Division. *A plan of New York Island, with part of Long Island, Staten Island & east New Jersey, with a particular description of the engagement on the woody heights of Long Island, between Flatbush and Brooklyn, on the 27th of August 1776 between His Majesty's forces commanded by General Howe and the Americans under Major General Putnam, shewing also the landing of the British Army on New-York Island, and the taking of the city of New-York &c. on the 15th of September following, with the subsequent disposition of both the armies. Engraved & publish'd by Wm. Faden.* London, 1776. Call Number: G3802.L6S3 1776 . F32 Vault.

Page 45 (top): Courtesy of Emmett Collection, Miriam and Ira D. Wallach Division of Art, Prints and Photographs, The New York Public Library, Astor, Lenox and Tilden Foundations. *The landing of British forces in the Jerseys on the 20th of November 1776 under the command of Rt. Honl. Lieut. Genl. Earl Cornwallis.* Watercolor by Thomas Davies. 1776. Digital Image ID: 54210.

Page 45 (bottom): Courtesy of I. N. Phelps Stokes Collection, Miriam and Ira D. Wallach Division of Art, Prints and Photographs, The New York Public Library, Astor, Lenox and Tilden Foundations. *A view of the attack against Fort Washington and rebel redouts near New York on the 16 of November 1776 by the British and Hessian brigades.* Watercolor by Thomas Davies. 1776. Digital Image ID: 54209.

Page 47: Courtesy of The Lionel Pincus and Princess Firyal Map Division, The New York Public Library, Astor, Lenox and Tilden Foundations. *A chart of New York Harbour: With the soundings, views of land marks and nautical directions for the use of pilotage/composed from surveys and observations of lieutenants John Knight, John Hunter of the Navy & others.* [May 1779?] Map by Joseph J. F. W. Des Barres. Digital Image ID: 434588.

Pages 50–51: Courtesy of The National Archives, ref. MR1/463.

Page 55: Courtesy of The National Archives, ref. MR1/463.

Page 57 (top): Library of Congress, Geography and Map Division. *A plan of the Narrows of Hells-gate in the East River, near which batteries of cannon and mortars were erected on Long Island with a view to take off the defences and make breaches in the rebel fort on the opposite shore to facilitate a landing of troops on New York Island. Drawn by Chals. Blaskowitz.* [1776.] Call Number: G3804.N4R4 1776 .B5 Vault.

Page 57 (bottom): Courtesy of The National Archives, ref. MR1/463.

Page 58: Base map courtesy of The National Archives, ref. MR1/463. Georeferenced by The Mannahatta Project/Wildlife Conservation Society. Street centerlines from the City of New York Department of Information Technology and Telecommunications.

Page 59: Base map courtesy of The National Archives, ref. MR1/463. Georeferenced by The Mannahatta Project/Wildlife Conservation Society. Street centerlines and building footprints from the City of New York Department of Information Technology and Telecommunications.

Page 88: Copyright ©Markley Boyer/The Mannahatta Project/Wildlife Conservation Society.

Page 89: Copyright ©Stephen Amiaga (www.amiaga.com).

Page 91 (top): Courtesy of New York City Soil Survey, United States Department of Agriculture—Natural Resources Conservation Service.

Page 91 (bottom): Courtesy of I. N. Phelps Stokes Collection, Miriam and Ira D. Wallach Division of Art, Prints and Photographs, The New York Public Library, Astor, Lenox and Tilden Foundations. *Martel's New York Central Park.* J. C. Geissler after Pierre Martel [?] 1864. Digital Image ID: 55031.

Page 93: Copyright ©The Mannahatta Project/Wildlife Conservation Society. Design by Markley Boyer and Christine Moog, Pentagram.

Page 97: Copyright ©The Mannahatta Project/Wildlife Conservation Society. Design by Markley Boyer and Christine Moog, Pentagram.

Page 100 (top): Copyright ©Eric W. Sanderson.

Page 100 (bottom): National Weather Service/National Oceanic and Atmospheric Administration/United States Department of Commerce.

Page 102: Spencer Research Library, University of Kansas Libraries, Kansas Collection, RH MS C36 V.7.

Page 105: Courtesy of the Historical Society of Pennsylvania Collection, Atwater Kent Museum of Philadelphia. Gustavus Hesselius, *Lapowinsa*. HSP.1834.3.

Page 107: Copyright ©The Mannahatta Project/Wildlife Conservation Society. Design by Markley Boyer and Christine Moog, Pentagram.

Page 111: Copyright ©The Mannahatta Project/Wildlife Conservation Society. Design by Markley Boyer and Christine Moog, Pentagram.

Page 114: Copyright ©Eric W. Sanderson.

Page 116: Courtesy of the Division of Anthropology, American Museum of Natural History. Shell (clam) string. Catalog No.: 50.1/1580*. Donor: Erastus T. Tefft. Accession No: 1910-41; Heron decoy. Catalog No.: 50.1/5828. Donor: Charles Bradford. Accession No: 1911-47.

Page 118 (top): Courtesy of the American Museum of Natural History Library. Image number 24449.

Page 118 (bottom): Courtesy of the American Museum of Natural History Library. Image number 338948.

Page 121 (bottom): Copyright ©Eric W. Sanderson.

Page 122: Copyright ©The Mannahatta Project/Wildlife Conservation Society. Design by Markley Boyer.

Page 124: Copyright ©Markley Boyer/The Mannahatta Project/Wildlife Conservation Society.

Page 125: Copyright ©Stephen Amiaga (www.amiaga.com).

Page 127: Copyright ©The Mannahatta Project/Wildlife Conservation Society. Design by Markley Boyer and Christine Moog, Pentagram.

Page 130: Courtesy of the Division of Anthropology, American Museum of Natural History. Catalog No.: 50.1/1604.

Page 134: Copyright ©Jim Rementer.

Page 136: Copyright ©Eric W. Sanderson.

Page 139: Copyright ©The Mannahatta Project/Wildlife Conservation Society. Design by Markley Boyer and Christine Moog, Pentagram.

Page 140 (left): Copyright ©The Mannahatta Project/Wildlife Conservation Society.

Page 140 (right): Copyright ©DigitalGlobe.

Pages 144–59: Copyright ©Eric W. Sanderson.

Page 161 (top): U.S. Fish and Wildlife Service, Digital Library System. Gary Kemp, Bombay Hook National Wildlife Refuge.

Page 161 (bottom): U.S. Fish and Wildlife Service, Digital Library System. U.S. Fish and Wildlife Service, Division of Public Affairs.

Pages 162–63: Copyright ©Markley Boyer/The Mannahatta Project/Wildlife Conservation Society.

Page 166 (top): Library of Congress, Prints and Photographs Division. Call Number: LOT 5030-16. Reproduction Number: LC-USZ62-73688.

Page 166 (bottom): Copyright ©Markley Boyer/The Mannahatta Project/Wildlife Boyer/ The Mannahatta Project/WildlifeConservation Society.

Page 170: Library of Congress, Prints and Photographs Division. Call Number: BIOG FILE - Muir, John, 1838–1914. Reproduction Number: LC-USZ62-52000.

Page 175: Courtesy of the University of Wisconsin–Madison Digital Collections Center, Digital Library for the Decorative Arts and Material Culture. *Urogallus minor, fuscus cervice, plumis Alas imitantibus donata; Meadia.* In *The natural history of Carolina, Florida and the Bahama Islands: Containing the figures of birds, beasts, fishes, serpents, insects, and plants,* by Mark Catesby. 1754.

Page 176 (top): Courtesy of the University of Wisconsin–Madison Digital Collections Center, Digital Library for the Decorative Arts and Material Culture. *Aquila capite albo: The bald eagle. The natural history of Carolina, Florida and the Bahama Islands: Containing the figures of birds, beasts, fishes, serpents, insects, and plants,* by Mark Catesby. 1754.

Page 176 (bottom): Courtesy of the University of Wisconsin–Madison Digital Collections Center, Digital Library for the Decorative Arts and Material Culture. *Palumbus migratorius: The pigeon of passage; Quercus Esculi divisura foliis amplioribus aculeatis: The red oak.* In *The natural history of Carolina, Florida and the Bahama Islands: Containing the figures of birds, beasts, fishes, serpents, insects, and plants,* by Mark Catesby. 1754.

Page 178: Courtesy of the University of Wisconsin–Madison Digital Collections Center, Digital Library for the Decorative Arts and Material Culture. *Coccothraustes rubra: The red bird; Nux Juglans alba Virginiensis: The Hickory Tree; Nux Juglans Carolinensis fructu minimo putamine levi: The pignut.* In *The natural history of Carolina, Florida and the Bahama Islands: Containing the figures of birds, beasts, fishes, serpents, insects, and plants,* by Mark Catesby. 1754.

Page 180: Courtesy of the University of Wisconsin–Madison Digital Collections Center, Digital Library for the Decorative Arts and Material Culture. *Bison americanus; Pseudo Acacia hispida floribus roseis.* In *The natural history of Carolina, Florida and the Bahama Islands: Containing the figures of birds, beasts, fishes, serpents, insects, and plants,* by Mark Catesby. 1754.

Page 185 (top): Copyright ©The Mannahatta Project/Wildlife Conservation Society. Design by Christine Moog, Pentagram.

Page 185 (bottom): Courtesy of the Wildlife Conservation Society Library. *Castor fiber americanus, American beaver. 3/4 natural size.* In *The viviparous quadrupeds of North America*, by John James Audubon and John Bachman (created 1845–48).

Page 187: Copyright ©The Mannahatta Project/Wildlife Conservation Society. Design by Christine Moog, Pentagram.

Page 189: Copyright ©The Mannahatta Project/Wildlife Conservation Society. Design by Christine Moog, Pentagram.

Page 191: Courtesy of the University of Wisconsin–Madison Digital Collections Center, Digital Library for the Decorative Arts and Material Culture. *Rana maxima Americana Aquatica: The bull frog; Helleborine: The lady's slipper of Pensilvania.* In *The natural history of Carolina, Florida and the Bahama Islands: Containing the figures of birds, beasts, fishes, serpents, insects, and plants,* by Mark Catesby. 1754.

Page 192: Copyright ©Chris Harrison/The Mannahatta Project/Wildlife Conservation Society.

Page 194: Copyright ©Chris Harrison/The Mannahatta Project/Wildlife Conservation Society.

Page 197: Copyright ©The Mannahatta Project/Wildlife Conservation Society. Design by Christine Moog, Pentagram.

Page 202: Copyright ©The Mannahatta Project/Wildlife Conservation Society. Design by Markley Boyer.

Page 203: Copyright ©The Mannahatta Project/Wildlife Conservation Society. Design by Markley Boyer and Christine Moog, Pentagram.

Page 205: Copyright ©Markley Boyer/The Mannahatta Project/Wildlife Conservation Society.

Page 206: Copyright ©Stephen Amiaga (www.amiaga.com).

Page 207: Copyright ©Markley Boyer/The Mannahatta Project/Wildlife Conservation Society.

Page 208: (left) Copyright ©MarkleyBoyer/The Mannahatta Project/Wildlife Conservation Society; (right) Copyright ©Yann Arthus-Bertrand/CORBIS. Composite image by Markley Boyer.

Page 211 (top): Copyright ©Stephen Amiaga (www.amiaga.com).

Page 211 (bottom): Copyright ©Julie Larsen Maher/Wildlife Conservation Society.

Page 214 (top): Copyright ©Eric W. Sanderson.

Page 214 (bottom): Library of Congress, Prints and Photographs Division, Farm Security Administration—Office of War Information Photograph Collection. Call Number: LC-USW3- 042669-C. Reproduction Number: LC-USZ62-130923 DLC.

Page 221 (top): Copyright ©Marni Horwitz (www.alivestructures.com).

Page 221 (bottom): Copyright ©Julie Larsen Maher/Wildlife Conservation Society.

Page 222: Copyright ©Allan Baxter/Getty Images.

Page 225 (top): Courtesy of The Skyscraper Museum. Image from Bankers Trust Collection, Archive ID: bt0068r.

Page 225 (bottom): Copyright ©Lynn Saville/Getty Images.

Page 229 (top): Library of Congress, Geography and Map Division. Detail from inset view of *Novi Belgii Novæque Angliæ: nec non partis Virginiæ tabula multis in locis emendata/per Nicolaum Visscher nunc apud Petr. Schenk Iun.* Amsterdam[?], 1685. Call Number: G3715 169- .V5 TIL Vault.

The Mannahatta Project would never have come to pass without the many people who believed in the idea of Mannahatta and its potential to change New York City, and through New York, the world. There are more people than I can possibly remember to thank, but let me try to thank those I can and beg the forgiveness of those I have missed.

I would like to thank the many scientists, scholars, and other professionals who provided their knowledge, advice, and, at times, healthy skepticism to the project, including George Amato, Robert Augustyn, Mark Becker, John Behler, Kathleen Benson, Eugene Boesch, Emery Boose, Alexander Brash, Charles Canham, Anne-Marie Cantwell, Steven Clemants, Paul Cohen, Ed Cook, Christina Coppolillo, Pete Coppolillo, William Cronon, Robert DeCandido, Catherine Delano-Smith, Karl Didier, Robert DiGiovanni, Brian Dunnigan, Francis Dunwell, Dave Dyson, Greg Edinger, David Foster, John Fraser, Ned Gardiner, Richard Goldberg, Andrew Greller, Sarah Gronim, Joel Grossman, Robert Grumet, Roy Halling, Sarah Henry, Francis Herbert, Sidney Horenstein, Alice Hudson, Frank Indiviglio, Klaus Jacob, Jerry Jenkins, Elizabeth Johnson, Peter Joost, Matt Knutzen, Fred Koontz, Steve Laise, Tom Lake, Upmanu Lall, Marit Larsen, Marc Levy, Don Melnick, Daniel Miller, Michael Miscione, Gerry Moore, Daniel Pagano, Michael Palmer, Dorothy Peteet, Francis "Jack" Putz, Hector Rivera, David Rosane, Reuben Rose-Redwood, Cynthia Rosenzweig, Nan Rothschild, John Rowden, Joe Scott, Chad Seewagen, Rich Shaw, Ralph Solecki, Sacha Spector, Steve Stanne, Eleanor Sterling, Samantha Strindberg, Martin Stute, Barbara Thiers, Melissa Tulig, Charles Vörösmarty, John Waldman, Bill Weber, Dan Wharton, and Peter Zahler. I would also like to acknowledge the ghosts of the Mannahatta Project; without their foundational work and love of the New York landscape, this effort would not have been possible. Here's to the spirits of Jane Jacobs; Frederick Law Olmsted; John Randel, Jr.; Isaac Newton Phelps Stokes; John Torrey; Adrian van der Donck; Egbert Ludovicus Viele; George Waring; Walt Whitman; the cartographers of the British Headquarters Map; and the unnamed but not forgotten Lenape ancestors.

For helping me understand how New York City works today and how it will continue to evolve in the future, I would like to thank Rohit Aggarwala, Paula Berry, Jessica Blaustein, Jim Breheny, John Calvelli, Betty Chen, Sue Chen, Brad Cloepfil, Linda Cox, Teresa Crimmins, Bram Gunther, John Gwynne, Fritz Haeg, Jamie Hand, Ernie Hutton, Peter Kohlman, Maya Lin, Paul Mankiewicz, Alex Marshall, Tom Naiman, Robert Pirani, Steven Romalewski, Clifford Ross, Anne-Marie Runfola, Janette Sadik-Kahn, Adi Shamir, William Solecki, Bill Tai, Frank Tuerkheimer, and Alexandros Washburn.

Much of the actual work has been done by students, volunteers, and, more recently, colleagues, whose enthusiasm for the project has been a continual source of strength, and without whom it might have taken another four hundred years to finish! I would like to thank Hunter Allen, Stephen Amiaga, Christina Baranetsky, Kyle Beucke, Marianne Brown, Malgorzata Bryja, Natalie Cash, John Delaney, Sarah Dziedzic, Steve Fairchild, Jessica Forrest, Dan Greenwald, Chris Harrison, Jennifer Ma, Michael Misner, Heidi Neilson, Robert Olley, Leticia Orti, Phillip Pond, Erika Reuter, Robert Rose, Stephen Sautner, Yemi Tessema, Leilani Veila, Gillian Woolmer, Eric Wright, Charles Yackulic, the WCS (Wildlife Conservation Society) Public Affairs Department, and the spring 2008 Mannahatta Landscape Ecology class at the Center for Environmental Research and Conservation at Columbia University. In particular I would like to thank Tim Bean for helping decipher Randel's notes and developing our approach to modeling fire; Jeremy Feinberg for helping compile the species lists; Lisa Liquori Fine for her grant-writing prowess and remarkable enthusiasm; Kim Fisher for creating a retroactive perspective on the climate, extending the fire model, exploring approaches to visualizing the Muir web, and much more; Amanda Huron for employing her skilled hand at GIS and her imaginative flair for geographic education; Danielle LaBruna for keeping me sane through data and deadlines; Valerie Navab for spending many hours in libraries, dusty academic halls, and at powwows, pursuing first

Mannahatta's topography and later its original human inhabitants; and Daniel Sarna-Wojcicki for helping model the horticultural habits of the Lenape of four hundred years ago.

This book and this project would have faltered long ago except for the extraordinary skill, commitment, and sense of humor of my friend and colleague Markley Boyer. Mark turned the roiling mass of data into the bracing, clear images that illustrate this book literally cover to cover and that, more than a thousand words could ever do, bring Mannahatta back to life.

The management at the Wildlife Conservation Society has been generous in supporting a project that on one level has nothing to do with zoological parks and international conservation and on another is exactly why urban zoos and conservation efforts are necessary. I would like to thank my mentors over the years: William Conway, Joshua Ginsberg, Kent Redford, John Robinson, Steven Sanderson, and Amy Vedder. Thanks are also due to members of the WCS Board of Trustees, particularly Frederick Beinecke, Edith McBean, David Schiff, and Ward Woods for their support. I would also like to thank Toby Adams, Ellen McCarthy, and the rest of the staff and volunteers at the New York Botanical Garden's Ruth Rea Howell Family Garden for letting me experiment with Lenape gardening and wigwam construction on their turf.

Journalists have enriched the project by asking excellent questions and showing me how to put the answers into words. My thanks go to Patrick Di Justo, Marguerite Holloway, Peter Miller, Nick Paumgarten, Mike Peed, Alan Weisman, and many others.

This book would not have been possible without the remarkable support from the staff at Harry N. Abrams, Inc., and in particular Deborah Aaronson, my stern but fair and occasionally hilarious editor; Julia Coblenz; Ashley Gillespie; Carrie Hornbeck; Caitlin Kenney; Anet Sirna-Bruder; and Katrina Weidknecht. My thanks also extend to Abbott Miller, Christine Moog, Susan Brzozowski, and Megan Chaney of Pentagram Design for their brilliant book design, and to my agents, Martha Kaplan and Renee Zuckerbrot, who, much earlier than I did, saw the book that this would eventually become.

The Mannahatta Project has been supported through funding from the Center for Environmental Research and Conservation at Columbia University; Furthermore Grants in Publishing, a program of the J. M. Kaplan Fund; the Hudson River Foundation; the New England Interstate Water Pollution Control Commission; the New York State Department of Environmental Conservation's Hudson River Estuary Program; the New York State Environmental Protection Fund Coastal Access Program; Nurture New York's Nature; the Prospect Hill Foundation; SESI Consulting Engineers; the Seed Fund for Urban Projects; the Van Alen Institute and Social Science Research Council; the WCS-NOAA (National Oceanic and Atmospheric Administration) Lower Bronx River Partnership; the Wildlife Conservation Society; and numerous anonymous donors. The ESRI (Environmental Systems Research Institute) Conservation Program provided GIS software donations.

Finally, I would like to thank my wife, Han-Yu Hung, and my son, Everett Sanderson, for their companionship on field trips, their willingness to listen as I rattled on, and their patience while I worked away. I would also like to acknowledge and thank my mother and father, to whom this book is dedicated, for instilling in me the mania to follow such impossible dreams.

Page numbers in *italics* refer to illustrations.

C R E E K

R L E M

B. O

PLAN Nº 2

New York. Hudson's River &c.

Continuation of Number One

Scale 800 feet to an Inch.

a Fort George   Works
b Lower Battery   and im
                              Sir Guy
c Batteries upon the Nor
   and improved in the Sp
d Star Redoubts construc
e Bunkers Hill Redoubt ere
f A Circular Redoubt ma
   the Town.
g Citizens Redoubt so call
h A Line begun in the S
   and was far advanced
   put a stop to it.
i Additions made on the